by Robin D. Laws

Credits

"FENG SHUI"

AN ATLAS GAMES PRODUCTION OF A ROBIN D. LAWS GAME

DESIGNED BY ROBIN D. LAWS   PUBLISHED BY JOHN NEPHEW

PRODUCTION COORDINATOR AND LAYOUT MONKEY JEFF TIDBALL

EDITORIAL ASSISTANCE JOHN NEPHEW AND MICHELLE BROWN   COVER ART LEE MOYER

INTERIOR ART TOREN ATKINSON, RALPH HORSLEY, HEATHER HUDSON, THOMAS MANNING, JEFF MIRACOLA, ROGER RAUPP, GREY THORNBERRY, BRIAN SNODDY, AND MARK TEDIN

HONORARY BATTLECHIMPS BOB BRYNILDSON AND JERRY CORRICK

THE DAEDALUS EDITION OF FENG SHUI WAS PRODUCED BY JOSE GARCIA AND MARIA GARCIA. THEY WERE ASSISTED BY MARIA CABARDO, DANIEL GELON, ROB HEINSOO, JOHN TYNES, SCOT YONAN, AND A HORDE OF PLAYTESTERS TOO NUMEROUS TO MENTION. WE THANK THEM FOR BLAZING THE TRAIL.

Feng Shui is ©1996, 1999 Robin D. Laws, published under license by Trident Inc., d/b/a Atlas Games. Feng Shui is a trademark of Robin D. Laws, used under license. All rights reserved. Feng Shui's game mechanics derive from the roleplaying game Nexus: The Infinite City by Jose Garcia, © Daedalus Entertainment, Inc., and are used with permission. Reproduction of this work by any means without written permission from the publisher, except short excerpts for the purpose of reviews, is expressly prohibited. Respecting the intellectual property rights of this game's creators and publishers will allow them to bring you more fantastic games.

ATLAS GAMES
PO BOX 131233
ROSEVILLE, MN 55113
651-638-0077
INFO@ATLAS-GAMES.COM

VISIT US ON THE WORLD WIDE WEB AT
WWW.ATLAS-GAMES.COM

ISBN 1-887801-76-6

Table of Contents

Welcome!

1: Kiii-Yaaahhh!	an introduction to *Feng Shui*	4

Player Info

2: Characters	the stars of the show	12
3: Skills	the tools of the trade	46
4: Guns	the way of the killer	60
5: Fu Powers	the way of the warrior	75
6: Magic	the way of the sorcerer	88
7: Creature Abilities	the way of the beast	100
8: Transformed Animals	the way of the ascended	108
9: Arcanowave Gear	the way of the future	116

GM Info

10: Fights	fast and furious	126
11: GM Tips	style and substance	143
12: Getting Even Tougher	power and glory	160
13: Feng Shui Sites	wind and water	162
14: Monsters	foul and forbidden	169

World Info

15: Groups	the secret war	172
16: Time War	the unseen world	190
17: Netherworld	the inner kingdom	200
18: Hong Kong	the battle ground	210

Appendixes

A: Baptism of Fire	your first *Feng Shui* episode	228
B: Hong Kong Action Movies	your guide to the greats	243
C: Reference Section	photocopiable rules references	249

Helpful Stuff

Index	you've seen these before	254
Blank Character Sheet	keep track of your hero	256

Chapter 1

January 11

My last job, I promised myself. I had to go along with Fast Eddie Lo—or pretend to, anyway. He had Steve stashed away somewhere in Kowloon. I owed Steve. Ever since he saved my life at the orphanage, when we were eight. I could not let my blood brother down when he needed me, even if it meant serving Fast Eddie one last time. And Fast Eddie wanted me to take out his rival, Big Brother Tsien. He'd tried it twice before, and now he was desperate. Desperate enough to want the best in the business: me. I wasn't happy about having to kill again. But if I had to pick someone the world wouldn't miss much, Big Brother Tsien would have been pretty near the top of the list anyway.

I was in the parking garage, wearing the uniform of a janitor. Must have been over a hundred times I'd pulled this trick, and it worked just like always. I had the C-4 planted in a garbage barrel right near the ramp to street level. Big Brother was on the alert for another hit attempt; chances of getting something planted in his car, or getting past his bodyguards, were too low even for me. But planting something here in the garage was a snap. All I had to do was wait for the big man's Mercedes to pass the garbage can on its way out, hit the button, and me and Steve would be home free.

At least, that was how it was supposed to work. Can you blame me for not predicting that when Big Trousers' car came along, it'd come roaring out with a chick in a mask planted to the hood? Someone else was trying to wax him: someone with a serious weird act! She was in silver spandex from head to toe, and I was almost laughing 'til I saw her punch her way through the windshield. Maybe I should have hit the button when I had the chance and blown them all to bits, but I didn't. Maybe that's a mistake I'm still paying for. Anyway, I hesitated.

She pulled Big Brother—who can't weigh less than a hundred and fifty kilograms—out of the speeding car and through the windshield with one arm! Then they both bounced off the hood and rolled across the concrete. I decided this was enough nonsense and pulled out my 9 mm. They were rolling around on the concrete something fierce, and no ordinary marksman could hope to tag Tsien without hitting the babe in the mask. But I'm not an ordinary marksman.

I was about to empty the clip into him when I noticed that Tsien's mooks had stopped the car and gotten out. There were six of them, about to open up with SMGs—on me, of course. I was using a nine-round mag with hollowpoints. I squeezed off one shot on my way behind a pillar. BANG: One down, five to go. Must have been a thousand rounds hit the other side of that pillar. Good thing it was concrete. I could get the positions of the five remaining mooks from the reflection in the mirrored windows of a nearby Saab. I took a chance, turned, and broke for a spot behind a panel van. On the way: BANG BANG BANG. Three went down, but one of them popped up again. Okay, so I was having an off day. The remaining autofire was raining on the side of the panel van now, turning the windows to dust.

That was when the white-haired guy in the old-fashioned costume showed up. He came backwards down the ramp, executing this series of funny back flips. It was like he was in slow motion, but he was hard to watch somehow. I had to refocus my eyes to even look at him. The mooks looked just stunned for a moment; they turned their guns towards him, ready to pull the triggers. BANG BANG BANG. I'm not the kind of person you want to turn your back on in a gunfight. End of the mook situation.

I didn't know what the old guy was going to do, and I didn't much care. Tsien was my target. When I glanced back at him, he'd changed a bit. Grown about four feet. Sprouted horns. And scales. And there was this strange energy crackling around him.

BANG BANG. Two right between his bulbous red eyes.

The scumbag didn't even flinch. Instead he grinned, exposing these nasty shark-type teeth. He had the masked chick by the throat, and with his other hand he was daring me to come for him.

And that was just the start of the whole mess.

CHAPTER 1

Kiii-Yaaahhh!

AN INTRODUCTION TO FENG SHUI

Feng Shui is a roleplaying game of rocket-paced action and adventure. You play the heroes in a titanic struggle in which the fate of humankind depends on your exotic kung fu powers, your ancient magics, your pirated supertech, or your plain old-fashioned trigger finger. You might be a maverick cop, a cranky kung fu fighting master, an everyman hero, a masked avenger, or a bioengineered monster out for revenge on your creators. Against you is arrayed a legion of fearsome foes. This battle rages throughout time, pitting you against sinister eunuch magicians of the past, secretive power groups of the present, and the twisted scientists who control the future.

This secret war is fought by those who know a simple, elemental truth of existence: the power of the Earth. Certain sites which harness and intensify **chi**, the life force that animates man and nature, are scattered across the planet. Those who control these sites benefit from the increased flow of chi, and gain great fortune in matters both mundane and mystical. Since ancient times, the Chinese have honed their knowledge of Earth magic—or **geomancy**—into the discipline known as **feng shui**.

History belongs to those who are **attuned** to Feng Shui sites—those who have formed a mystical bond with the chi energy of those sites and gain power thereby. The scramble to possess the world's feng shui sites has now begun in earnest; when the war ends, we will live the way the victors want us to because the flow of chi controls the flow of time and the course of history. Only you and your fellow heroes can prevent these powerful sites from falling into the hands of maniacal tyrants. In order to travel through time, you move through a mysterious realm known as the **Netherworld** or **Inner Kingdom**. Those who participate in the struggle are therefore known as **Innerwalkers** or **Secret Warriors**.

Fortunately, this is a world that rewards heroism. If your heart is strong, you can dodge machine-gun bullets. You can take eighteen slugs in your chest and still come back for one final blazing attack against the bad guy. If your kung fu is mighty, you can run sideways up a tree, bounce off a branch, and clash swords with your opponent who has just done the same thing from the opposite direction. The world of *Feng Shui* is a world where it is not a dumb idea at all to cling to the bottom of the bad guy's Maserati as it screeches down the

Say What?
There are zillions of different ways to pronounce *feng shui*, depending on what dialect of Chinese you want to pick. We've developed the habit of saying *feng schwee*; if you want to pick the most appropriate dialect for the Hong Kong setting presented later in this book, go with the Cantonese pronunciation and say *fung soy*.

If the melodramatics and fast pace of *Feng Shui* sound familiar to you, there's a good reason. *Feng Shui* is an action-movie roleplaying game because it is inspired by the vast number of action movies that most of us have grown up with.

If you think about it, no matter what the story or setting of an action movie is there are some things that don't change. The characters are always catchy archetypes: the assassin with a heart of gold, the rogue cop out for justice, the noble kung fu master. The stories are as familiar to us as tales of Beowulf or Coyote the Trickster were to our ancestors: innocents in jeopardy, double-crossing drug deals, a master villain's plot to destroy the world. The style and structure of action movies is what *Feng Shui* is all about.

Chapter 1

midnight streets of Hong Kong. It is a world where, armed only with a toothpick, you can face down a ten-foot hybrid of supernatural monster and futuristic machine and still have a chance of winning.

The world of *Feng Shui* is a world of high melodrama. You might seem to be a ruthless, icy-cool assassin, but in your heart you know that you're doing just one last job to pay for your mother's lung transplant. The villain you've been tracking down for years might turn out to be the best friend who betrayed you in a moment you remember just like yesterday. The new masked ally who just saved your bacon with some well-placed throwing stars could well be the mysterious lover you met last night in the club. The master who raised you from a shivering orphan may be the leader of a sect of evil. In *Feng Shui*, there's no such thing as a hoary plotline. Here we proudly admit that we tell the same stories over and over again because those are the best stories.

THE GAME

Feng Shui is a roleplaying game for two or more players. In a roleplaying game, you direct the actions of a fictional character of your own devising through a series of adventures run by a player who takes on the role of **Game Moderator,** or **GM**. The game sessions you participate in are like episodes in a series of action movie sequels or an adventure TV show. Your GM starts each session with an idea of the plot line he wants to follow, but the actions taken by your character and those of your fellow players will no doubt lead to surprises for everyone.

When in doubt as to what happens during the game, the GM and players roll dice and consult the rules given in this book. For example, if your character unleashes a spinning kick at her opponent, you roll dice to see if she succeeded in hitting him and if so, how well. These rules help create a feeling of challenge and unpredictability that will keep you on the edge of your seats. Is this the last bullet your Armani-clad avenger can take without collapsing, or can he fight on? Is your master of kung fu able to leap onto the top of the escaping hovercar? Roll the dice and find out, with the help of your Game Moderator and the rules.

As you read this book you will learn more about the game, and will learn enough about it to decide what kind of character you want to play. The characters run by you and other players are called, not surprisingly, **Player Characters** (**PCs** for short). Your character will interact with a supporting cast of other characters controlled by the Game Moderator: villains, their henchmen, bit characters and innocent bystanders. These are called **Game Moderator Characters**, abbreviated as **GMCs**.

We start by presenting background information on the world in which *Feng Shui* adventures are set. On the surface, it looks much like our own contemporary world. But underneath, it seethes with mystical and conspiratorial secrets, secrets which you and your fellow players will uncover to a soundtrack of crunching fists, blazing machine guns, and swooshing swords. The only limit to the fun is your own imaginations: Remember, in your head you have an unlimited special effects budget. If you blow up half of Hong Kong in the story you make up together, you don't have to pick up the insurance tab, or pay the set technicians to work overtime.

> There's nothing clumsier than reading a lot of sentences with the words "he or she" and "his or her" stuck in them time after time. In this book, when we need a singular pronoun of indeterminate gender we're going to switch back and forth. Sometimes the GM or a hypothetical player will be referred to as "he," sometimes as "she." One of the cool things about the Hong Kong films that this game is inspired by is that they depict equal opportunity butt-kicking. Both men and women can be ultra-competent warriors. Both can be either amazingly heroic or despicably evil. We want both women and men to play and enjoy this game.
>
> When we use second person narration, sometimes we're referring to you as players, sometimes to your characters. This will make sense in context.

After the basics of the setting, we present rules for creating your characters, and for resolving actions between characters. Following the rules section is special information for the Game Moderator. If you're just going to be playing *Feng Shui*, you'll have more fun if you skip this section, leaving yourself some surprises for the actual game sessions.

We conclude the book with a roundup of our favorite Hong Kong action movies, the source material that inspired *Feng Shui*. You don't need to have seen any of these exciting flicks to play or understand this game, but they're certainly a ton of fun if you can track them down. We predict that a growing number of fans will find and enjoy the thrilling work of John Woo, Jackie Chan, Chow Yun Fat, Tsui Hark, Jet Li, and countless others during the next few years. Be the first on your block to get hip to the films of Hong Kong, where they still make 'em like they used to!

HEY RPG FANS!

On first inspection, this game appears to fly in the face of most roleplayers' assumptions about what a good roleplaying game consists of. *Feng Shui* emphasizes combat as a major story element, does not provide rules for detailed character generation, encourages players and GMs to make use of cliché-ridden character concepts and background elements, glorifies violence and death as a form of entertainment, and generally appears to say that the last several years' worth of advancement in roleplaying rules and storytelling are a bunch of hooey.

Well, no. Not really.

This game is all about action movies. The characters are based on action-movie archetypes. The plots are told with action-movie pacing and structure. The setting is a melange of many action-movie ideas. Action movies work in part because almost nothing stands between the movie and the audience. As soon as Arnold Schwarzenegger appears on the screen, you've got a decent idea of what his character is going to be like. When the bad guy sets the bomb in the schoolyard, you can bet the hero will clip the red wire and save the day. Even though this stuff is all somewhat cliché, action movies are still incredibly exciting and entertaining. Even though your *Feng Shui* characters start off as off-the-shelf movie heroes, they'll become more and more real as you play. Even though *Feng Shui* adventures are a series of action combat scenes with a plot wrapped around them, they get more and more involved and gain added depth during the session. That's what we're after in *Feng Shui*.

THE SETTING

Feng Shui is designed so that players can sit down, look at the various player character archetypes, choose one and then start playing within an hour or less. The GM will need to have read this book carefully, but the rest of you can hit the ground running. (That doesn't mean that you can't read the rest of the book if you're a player, but you don't have to; on the other hand, the less you know about the setting, the more cool surprises you'll have in store during play!) Before this section, we briefly covered the highlights of the game setting. (The next section, "The Rules," covers the highlights of the game system.) Roleplaying games take time to play; many players prefer sessions of three to four hours, though some players go much longer.

Your character may or may not know any of the following stuff when the first session starts. In order to find out how much your character knows, consult briefly with your GM before you start playing. She'll be able to tell you how much of the background your player is aware of. If you know more than your player character does, you'll be expected to play your character without using that information. If you do use information your character doesn't have, your GM may rule that you can't make whatever action you're proposing based on that information.

For example, if you're playing a modern-day hitman who has never encountered any supernatural or futuristic weirdness, you know lots about being in a gang but nothing about secret warriors or the Netherworld. If your response to a problem is "Let's look for an entrance to the Netherworld," your GM can respond, "Oh, no you don't!" and stop you from doing it because your character doesn't know about the Netherworld yet.

> ## Hey Shadowfist Fans!
> The setting of *Feng Shui* is shared by a trading card game called *Shadowfist*. Maybe you've heard of it. If you've always wanted to know more about the mysteries behind the *Shadowfist* cards, this is the place to look. If you haven't checked out roleplaying games before then this is a simple, straightforward place to start. You do not need to be familiar with *Shadowfist* in order to play *Feng Shui*. Everything you need to get started on your whirlwind of action is right here in this book.
>
> *Feng Shui* and *Shadowfist* share the same world, the same characters, and the same storylines. But they aren't the same game, and you shouldn't expect game elements you recognize from *Shadowfist*—such as Toughness or Fighting scores—to work the same way in *Feng Shui*. You'll recognize characters from *Shadowfist* in this book and others, but their powers in *Feng Shui* may not resemble their powers in the card game because the way each game works is very different and the characters are statted up according to very different rules and very different play needs. Battlechimp Potempkin is still the Battlechimp you know and love, but he may kick butt in a totally different way from game to game. Characters that really kick butt in *Shadowfist* might not be as tough—or they might be tougher—in *Feng Shui*. Keep in mind that *Feng Shui* is not an adaptation of *Shadowfist*; rather, they're both adaptations of the same source material. Got it?
>
> For those of you keeping score at home, Atlas Games isn't and won't be the publisher of *Shadowfist*. Sorry to let you down. Not only that, we don't know whether anyone else will ever bring *Shadowfist* back to market. We hope someone does, but we don't know anything about it. Trust us—you'll know when we know.

Chapter 1

THE RULES

We'll handle the rules in detail in a chapter of their own later in the book. But there are some basics you should have a feel for before you get started on choosing a character to play, and here they are.

TASK CHECKS

Whenever you tell the group that your character is trying to do something, your GM has to decide whether he is successful. If he is successful, your GM will need to decide just how successful he is. If he fails, the GM needs to know what the consequences of the failure might be. (This process is called a task check.)

The rules help the GM do this. But the rules are only an aid in creating the story, not the whole point of the exercise. *Feng Shui* has simple rules but even these should be ignored if it makes for a better story.

The Dice

Whenever you are called upon to roll dice in a *Feng Shui* game, you will be rolling **two standard six-sided dice**. Each should be a **different color**. One die represents a **positive** value; the other, a **negative**. At the beginning of each session, tell your GM which color is which and stick to this choice. No fair deciding which is positive after you've seen the roll results!

Whenever you roll the dice, subtract the negative die roll from the positive. The result may be a negative number.

Example: Mary designates her green die as positive and her red die as negative. She rolls and gets a 3 on the green die and a 1 on the red. She subtracts the result for

The Netherworld

The Netherworld, also known as the Inner Kingdom, is a mysterious realm connected to our own world. It can be reached by various magical doorways called portals. These are usually hidden in out-of-the-way places, and can often only be seen by those with strong chi.

The Netherworld is mostly a series of dimly lit tunnels. Although there is no visible source of lighting in the Netherworld, it is always possible to see. Most of the tunnels are gray and indistinct; it's hard to tell what they're made of. Some of the residents of the Netherworld can reshape its physical nature as they wish, so some tunnels have been changed and are now made of brick, dripping limestone, gleaming metal, or other recognizable materials. The air in the Netherworld is dusty and moist at the same time. Little tendrils of fog hang about its floor levels. Any shaft of light has lots of slow-moving dust particles to bounce off of.

The Netherworld is the permanent home of thousands of people—not all of them human. These people come from any number of different times and places. Many of them are time travelers who have been stranded here; others are losers in the secret war who have been erased from history and who stay in the Netherworld because it's the only place they know anymore. Some of these residents are dangerous, and are plotting to return to power and take vengeance on their enemies. Others will help you—if only to further their own ends.

From the Netherworld, you can find other gates that take you to other places in your own time. Or you can find exits that lead to other times, either in the past or in the future. Each time period that is accessible from the Netherworld is called a *juncture*. Only a few time periods can be reached from the Inner Kingdom at any given moment. For the last few years, there have been only four accessible junctures: 69 AD, 1850, our own time, and 2056. Junctures move forward with the passage of time, though, so they'll go to 70 AD, 1851, and so forth a year from now.

The various organizations that struggle for power in the secret war use the Netherworld as a means of traveling from juncture to juncture, where they attack one another's feng shui sites and generally wreak havoc. There are a number of groups which any right-thinking action hero will want to thwart, as well as one group the PCs might be interested in joining.

The Eaters of the Lotus

The Eaters of the Lotus is a secret society that controls the government of China in 69 AD. They are eunuch attendants to the Emperor who covertly practice sorcery. They summon various supernatural creatures to do their bidding. Although until recently they were concerned only with maintaining their own power in China, they have now discovered the Netherworld and the secret war. They have been trying to seize feng shui sites in the other three junctures in hopes of expanding their empire across the time stream.

The Ascended

The Ascended are members of a nearly one thousand year-old conspiracy; its members control the most feng shui sites in both the 1850 juncture and in the present day. Therefore, they secretly control the world. They recruit ambitious conspirators through a series of service organizations. The really promising ones are asked to join a secret group known as the Pledged, but they report in turn to a higher echelon called the Lodge (only the higher-ups of the Pledged are likely to know about the Lodge). Members of the Ascended rely heavily on supernatural powers based on chi. They have a serious aversion to magic, which is a controlled, directed form of natural chi energy. But mostly they rely on their vast resources and political clout: they secretly control police forces, armies, major corporations, the media...you name an area of influence, and the Ascended are there. Their origins and goals are obscure, and some claim that the Ascended's leaders aren't even human. But one thing is clear: They aim to keep the power they have already gathered for themselves.

The Guiding Hand

This is a group founded in 19th century China, with roots in the 1850 and contemporary junctures. Fierce Chinese patriots and traditionalists, they are afraid that their world is collapsing into decadence and decay. They want to capture feng shui sites from the Ascended in order to institute a regime of obedience and discipline based on their interpretation of the teachings of Confucius. Although there are Guiding Hand members in both the 1850 and contemporary junctures, the leadership is made up of Shaolin monks in the 1850s. Guiding Hand operatives rely on chi powers, and are often masters of kung

(8)

the red die from the green die: 3 - 1 = 2. Her die result is 2.

Closed and Open Rolls

Sometimes your GM will ask you to make a **Closed Roll**. This is a normal roll of the two dice, as given above.

Most of the time, you will be asked to make **Open Rolls**. In an open roll, you reroll any die that comes up 6, adding to that die's total. This gives a wider range of results, which simulates the wild and chancy actions typically undertaken by *Feng Shui* characters.

Example: Mary makes an open roll, and gets a 6 on her green die and a 5 on her red die. She rerolls the green die, getting a result of 4. She adds the results of the two green die rolls: 6 + 4 = 10. She then subtracts the negative result, 5: 10 - 5 = 5. Her final result is 5.

If, on an Open Roll, both dice come up sixes (**boxcars**), the GM should decide that something unusual happens. You reroll both dice, ignoring each instance of boxcars (but not a single 6) in your final total. The unusual happening may be good or bad, depending on the overall result of the roll.

Determining Success or Failure

Usually when you make a roll, you will then add the result to another number—that number is usually one representing one of your character's abilities, and is called an **Action Value** (abbreviated as **AV**). When you choose your character type, you will want to make sure that she has high Action Values in the abilities you want her to be especially good at. On page 10 is a chart that gives you an idea of the level of ability that various Action Values correspond to.

fu. They will employ guns if absolutely necessary, but regard them as morally suspect. They regard all sorcerers and supernatural creatures as irredeemably corrupt. Although it is possible to sympathize with many of their aims, the average player character is unlikely to want to live in the strict world of obedience and discipline they wish to create.

Architects of the Flesh

The Architects of the Flesh are the scientific masterminds and political tyrants of 2056. They have managed, by capturing the feng shui sites of their era, to turn the United Nations from an ineffectual meeting place for diplomats into an authoritarian world government. The world is now one massive police state, a drab and dreary place where the everyday movements of citizens are monitored and tightly controlled. Along with their stranglehold on the juncture's feng shui, the Architect leaders keep a tight rein on their people through the use of arcanowave technology. This is a nasty way of manipulating magical wave energy through technological means. It has allowed the Architects to create the Abominations, supernatural creatures who have been cybernetically altered to turn them into obedient and terrifying super-soldiers. The Architects regularly send monster hunters back to the 69 juncture to capture supernatural creatures for this purpose. They also want to conquer past junctures, starting with our contemporary world.

The Jammers

The Jammers are a group of rebels from the future who want to overthrow the Architects. Most of them are misfit humans, although their leadership prominently includes some early cybernetic experiments carried out by the Architects. As the well-policed world of 2056 is too tough an environment even for the most hardened revolutionary, the Jammers have retreated to the Netherworld, from which they launch ferocious guerrilla raids on feng shui sites in all four junctures. Unlike most other groups—who seek to harness the power of feng shui sites to their own ends—the Jammers want to entirely eliminate the hold of chi over human destiny. They are radically opposed not only to magic but to all exotic chi powers as well. If they were to succeed, they would collapse the Netherworld, end the secret war—and possibly destroy humanity. Many who would sympathize with their rebel aims are afraid that their anti-chi program could lead to the elimination of the human soul.

The Four Monarchs

The Four Monarchs are a minor force in the secret war, but are important powers in the Netherworld. These four siblings are Ming I, Queen of the Darkness Pagoda; Huan Ken, King of the Thunder Pagoda; Li Ting, King of the Fire Pagoda; and Pi Tui, Queen of the Ice Pagoda. Each is a powerful sorcerer. They used to rule the Earth, back when the history of the world was vastly different. For centuries—up through 1988, in fact!—they controlled a world where magic was commonplace and the Industrial Revolution had never happened. But they were too occupied with internal bickering to pay enough attention to the secret war, and were erased from history when the Ascended captured critical feng shui sites in a previous juncture. Now exiled to the Inner Kingdom, they plot their revenge and return to power—and also continue to plot against one another. Some of them have formed alliances with the more important power groups. Others could be patrons for your characters.

The Dragons

And speaking of your characters...the Dragons have recently lost a titanic battle played out through the Inner Kingdom and all four junctures. They were a group founded in our juncture to preserve the freedom and dignity of ordinary people from the various villains, tyrants, and destroyers of the secret war. Although heroic in intention, they made too many enemies too fast, and were themselves crushed. Simultaneous assaults on their feng shui sites by the Jammers, Architects, and Lotus severely weakened them, allowing their enemies to finish them off. Now most of the warriors of this group are dead, maimed, or lost in time. A few of their gurus and support people remain alive, but are in hiding. Are your characters brave enough to pick up the mantle of this broken force—and smart enough to survive where previous heroes have failed?

Chapter 1

When you add the final roll to an Action Value, you get a number we call the **Action Result**. When your character tries to do something, that Action Result is compared to a number decided upon by the GM which represents the difficulty of the task your character is attempting. This number is called—surprise, surprise—the **Difficulty**. If the Action Result equals or exceeds the Difficulty, your character succeeds at the task. How well she does depends on the difference between the Difficulty and the Action Result. The difference is called the **Outcome**. If the Action Result is lower than the Difficulty, the attempt fails. Again, the difference between the two numbers can determine the degree of the failure if necessary.

Sample Action Values

Action Value	Description
0	Totally incompetent
3	Worse than most normal people
5	As good as the average person
7	Slightly above average
9	Competent, of professional caliber
11	Highly qualified
13	Top notch
15	Totally kick-ass
17	World Class
19	Frigging Astounding!
20	Beyond frigging astounding!

There may be times when the GM decides to ignore the results of the dice, or even to not roll the dice in the first place, because the outcome shouldn't be determined randomly. For example: if a PC sacrifices her life in a battle to allow the other characters to escape, the GM might not bother rolling to see if any bad guys can get around the PC or fire a parting shot at the rest of the group. Because the sacrifice was dramatic and very true to the action-movie style, the player is rewarded by making her sacrifice fully successful. Moments of drama and crisis can, if the GM wishes, be arbitrated without using the dice. The GM always has the last say.

Example: Chin's character, Jimmy Kwan, is attempting to break a board with his head at a kung fu tournament. His Action Value for Martial Arts is 6. The GM decides that the Difficulty of breaking the board without injury is 6. Chin rolls 2 on his positive die and 4 on his negative roll, for a total of -2. He adds this to his Action Value: -2 + 6 = 4. This is below the Difficulty, so Jimmy Kwan fails. The GM decides how to describe the failure. Since the difference between the Action Result and the Difficulty is only 2, the GM decides that Jimmy half-succeeds—he breaks the board but stuns himself in the process, embarrassing himself in front of the large audience. Had the difference been 4 or more, the GM might rule that not only did Jimmy fail to break the board, but he also injured himself.

Way-Awful Failure

Even outrageously skillful heroes have their off moments. Bad luck can strike at any time, bringing with it humiliation, agony, humiliation, slapstick embarrassment, or humiliation. A task check that results in this sort of way-awful failure is called a **fumble.**

Fumbles occur in one of two ways:

- You get a negative Action Result.
- You roll double sixes (boxcars) and then fail to meet the Difficulty of the check.

Most of the time, your GM will think up excruciatingly appropriate fates for your character to meet when you fumble. Standard fumble results are provided for some common task checks. Gun-wielding characters who suffer fumbles usually have their guns malfunction on them. Sorcerers suffer something nasty called **backlash**. But that's detail, and we'll get to the details later on.

Sample Difficulties

Okay, the last thing you'll really need to know before you flip that page and get on with character design is what kind of Difficulty numbers you'll be coming up against. That will allow you to gauge how effective your character will be as you decide which abilities to invest in. Note that your GM might not have you roll for some actions that appear on this chart if he thinks your character is good enough at the action that it isn't worth rolling for, or if the action isn't all that critical. It's easy to hide in broad daylight, for example, if there's no one around to be hiding from anyway!

Sample Difficulties

Difficulty Number	Description	Examples
0	too easy to bother rolling for	walking, breathing, watching TV
3	simple	personal grooming, cleaning a gun, making cookies
5	a little tricky	ducking a falling object, sneaking up on average person, punching alert average person
7	tricky	picking basic lock, repairing a computer, trailing wary individual
10	tough	picking sophisticated lock, sneaking up on trained guard, outrunning attack dog
15	real tough	hiding in brightly-lit area, safely leaping from speeding car, intimidating undead monster
20	forget it	deflecting bullets with a sword, leaping fifteen feet straight up, defusing missile while riding it
25	two words: im possible!	walking along trail of bullets to foe, punching right through one foe to hit another, leaping Grand Canyon

Chapter 2

March 9

I was guarding the circle of stones along with the gadget guy from the future and the young kung fu chick from the past. At that point I was really wondering what was in it for me. All of the talk about chi and feng shui sites and changing history had gone right over my head. The Queen of the Ice Pagoda had told me that the only way to see my blood brother cured of the Poison Needles was to reform my own soul. Soul? That was a word I never had much use for. I told the Queen I'd hang up my guns and never shoot another person again for as long as I lived if it meant saving Steve—but she said that wasn't the point. I could reform my own soul and still blast as many people as I'd ever blasted before. In fact, she said maybe I might have to blast even more people now: The trick was to blast the right people. Heal the world's pain, protect the chi. Every time I tried to understand what the heck she was talking about, my head began to swim. I asked her to explain it to me like a set of orders I could follow. She looked peeved, then told me to find the circle of stones and make sure that it stayed in one piece. She also said that finding my soul was obviously going to be a long-term project.

I asked the future guy what he knew about the whole business. I didn't know him very well. Last time I'd seen him was that firefight with The Thing That Used To Be Big Brother Tsien in that freaky place where the Queen lived. The Netherworld or something like that? Man, there was so much to take in. Anyhow, the last time I saw this guy, we were on different sides, and he nearly tagged me with that heinously large piece of artillery he had slung over his shoulder. Now we were on the same side, and I didn't know why. So I asked him why he was here and what the whole thing meant to him. Was he trying to reform his soul too?

"Reform my soul? I'm trying to keep my soul! It's those crazy Jammers. They want to solve all the problems of history by destroying all of our souls. They think we'll be better off without 'em. I'm not religious, HK boy, but I figure if I'm going to lose my soul I want to get something good out of the deal, you suss? Sure, I'd like to get rid of the Bobos as much as the next anarchistically inclined phreakazoid, but that price is a little steep."

That was the first time I heard the word "Jammer." I asked him what it meant.

"Look, I shouldn't have said anything, HK. I used to be a Jammer, and Ba–uh, somebody, somebody installed some hardware in me so if I spilled the wrong coffee, it's instant cerebral hemorrhage time. You grep me? Maybe someday somebody else will point you towards the clue dispenser."

Great. Now I was up a notch on the Confused Meter. I was about to turn to the girl to ask her what she knew when something came over the horizon, with this awful buzzing noise.

I don't know about you, but the movie Wizard of Oz always scared the crap outta me when I was a kid. The flying monkeys, man, I can remember hiding behind my mom's nyloned legs when those freaking things came on.

Well, here was a bunch of flying monkeys coming at us. Their heads were like chimps and gorillas and orangutans. Their bodies were bigger than mine, gleaming metal. Covered with rockets and whirring blades and knives. They had little helicopter blades on their backs, holding them aloft. Something inside me just curdled, man. Flying monkeys, for real!

Then I opened fire, and suddenly I felt a whole lot better.

CHAPTER 2

Characters

THE STARS OF THE SHOW

Creating a character in *Feng Shui* is easy. Grab a character sheet (you can photocopy the one from the back of this book) or a blank piece of paper and go to it. Here's all you have to do.

PICK A TYPE

Characters in action movies generally conform to a number of basic types: the maverick cop, the stalwart young kung fu student, the crusty old kung fu master, and on and on. So do characters in a *Feng Shui* game. Hey, this isn't Dostoevsky, this is action-adventure! Each of these is presented as a **type**, which provides you with a numerical starting point for your character as well as ideas that will help you portray your character in play. Starting on p. 20, we present the various types available as player characters. Pick the one you think is coolest. Each type has advantages and drawbacks that correspond to the sort of role this type of character is supposed to play in the series. You may want to consult with the other players so that you have a variety of types that complement each other, rather than having an entire cast of Karate Cops or whatever. Your GM may also place some restrictions on the types available. He may want to run a strictly contemporary series at first, and restrict you to modern types. He may be running his own version of the setting in which certain types do not exist. He should let you know about any restrictions before you create your character.

PERSONALIZE YOUR CHARACTER

Once you've picked a type, then you should think of all of the things that makes your character unique. Pick a name for her. Figure out what her past history is. Decide on her basic personality traits—is she humble, boastful, obnoxious, witty, bitter? Pick a couple of catch phrases she uses in conversation. In general, think of yourself as one of a team of authors creating an adventure series. Your job on the team is to come up with just one really interesting, entertaining character. Be creative, and keep it simple. A few really strong ideas are always more memorable than dozens of weak ideas. As you play, you'll find that you're adding new stuff to your character all the time; that's where the meat of the character will come from so don't sweat it too much for now.

Each *Feng Shui* character must have a **melodramatic hook**. (Some samples are on the next page.) This is a fact about your character that the GM can use to create storylines. It should be a classic staple of adventure fiction, one that motivates or haunts the character. Whenever this hook comes up in the story, your character should have a strong emotional reaction to it.

CHECK OUT THE NUMBERS

Each type gives you numbers that help you define how good your character is at doing things in the game world. The numbers you'll be looking at are **attributes** and **skills**.

Melodramatic Hook Examples
- Has sworn vengeance against the person who killed his father (or lover, or mother, or child, or best friend, or other loved one).
- Is the son (or other loved one) of notorious bad guy.
- Has sworn to clear the name of his late father (or other loved one).
- Is searching for kidnapped spouse (or other loved one).
- Is torn by remorse after seeming to betray his best friend (or other loved one).
- Is torn by remorse, responsible for the accidental injury or death of an innocent victim.
- Has been poisoned by bad guy and is trying to get the antidote before slowly dying.
- Has terminal disease.
- Has sworn to bring bad guy, who is also a close relative, to justice.
- Is trying to raise money for a life-saving operation for best friend (or other loved one).
- Is being pursued by a dangerous enemy.
- Is not human, or is only partially human, and is all torn up about it.
- Is in love with someone whose position forbids their union. For example: cop in love with criminal or vice versa; human in love with non-human; in love with member of enemy organization.

You get the idea. Seen it in a movie? Great—use it!

ATTRIBUTE NUMBERS

Attributes are numbers that measure the character's innate physical, mental and spiritual abilities. These are all natural talents or aptitudes rather than learned capabilities. There are four **primary attributes**; each of these can, if you want, be broken down into three or four **secondary attributes**. This allows you to refine your notion of what your character is talented at. A character's score in all secondary attributes is the same as the relevant primary attribute unless otherwise specified. So if your character has a Body of 5, the three secondary attributes are also 5. Some types allow you to increase a secondary attribute on its own. Other types already provide secondary attributes that have different numbers than their primary attributes because it's appropriate for that type.

The four primary attributes are described below.

Body

(Abbreviated as **Bod**.) This measures your character's overall physique and health. A feeble or elderly person has a Bod of 2; the average person has a Bod of 5; an extraordinary athlete has a Bod of 8. Anything beyond Bod 10 is beyond normal human capabilities in the real world, though not in the world of the action movies and therefore not in *Feng Shui*. The secondary attributes for Bod are **Move** (abbreviated as **Mov**), **Strength** (abbreviated as **Str**), **Constitution** (abbreviated as **Con**), and **Toughness** (abbreviated as **Tgh**.)

Move measures how fast a character can run. The most important unit of time in *Feng Shui* is measured in three-second **sequences**, which are explained in full in the Fights chapter, which starts on p. 126. During a sequence, you can cover a distance equal to three times your Move rating in meters while doing other things, like engaging in combat. If all you're doing is running, you can travel up to four times your Move rating in meters.

Strength measures the character's ability to exert force on objects and things: lift stuff, hit people really hard, and have really buff muscles.

Constitution is the ability to resist pain and shock; it also measures how robust the character's immune system is in fighting off disease and neutralizing poisons.

Toughness measures how much injury the character can sustain before keeling over or dying.

Chi

(No abbreviation required.) This measures your character's general level of attunement with the mystical life force that flows from the Earth. The average person in the modern world is not particularly attuned to mystic forces and has a Chi rating of 0. A particularly lucky, successful, or spiritual person might have a Chi of 2. The average sorcerer or mystic would have a Chi of 5. A powerful secret warrior might have a Chi of 7 or more.

The secondary attributes for Chi are **Fortune** (abbreviated as **For**), **Kung Fu** (abbreviated as **Fu**), and **Magic** (abbreviated as **Mag**).

Fortune shows how lucky a character is, and how much chi energy "likes her" and arranges events to flow in her favor. Each session, each character may spend a number of **Fortune Dice** equal to her

Fortune score. Each expended Fortune Die allows the player to roll an additional positive die when making a task check. Only one Fortune Die may be spent per task check. Sometimes the GM will decide to have good things happen to you because you have the highest Fortune rating in the group. However, if your Fortune rating is the lowest in the group, you might find that fate is always giving you the nasty end of the stick. If you've spent Fortune Dice in the current session, your Fortune rating is reduced by the number of dice you've spent until the session ends.

Kung Fu does not refer simply to a martial art technique. It means the amount of inner power one has to fuel mystical **fu schticks**. Someone who is good at using fu schticks, which are detailed in Chapter 5, is said to have "powerful kung fu." Having a Kung Fu score does not mean that the character knows any fu schticks, just that she has the potential to use them.

Magic measures the character's potential to perform magical spells. It does not mean that she starts the game knowing how to do so. It also measures the character's ability to resist the effects of magic spells. Magic is detailed in Chapter 6.

Mind

(Abbreviated as **Mnd**.) This measures the character's mental and interpersonal abilities. The human average score is 5; 7 is notably above average, and 8 or more reflects genius level. Its secondary attributes are **Charisma** (abbreviated as **Cha**), **Intelligence** (abbreviated as **Int**), **Perception** (abbreviated as **Per**) and **Will** (abbreviated as **Wil**).

Charisma is personal magnetism: someone with a high Charisma rating can evoke strong first impressions in others. As desired, these might be love, admiration, or fear. Characters with unusually low Charisma ratings actively evoke contempt, ridicule, and revulsion in others.

Intelligence is the ability to think clearly and systematically. Characters with high Intelligence ratings are good at solving puzzles, remembering things, and meaningfully expressing abstract ideas.

Perception measures general alertness and powers of observation. A Perceptive character is good at deduction, and at reading the emotions and motivations of others.

Will measures emotional resilience, self-confidence, and determination. It is useful in resisting the persuasions of Charismatic characters, and in overcoming magical effects that target the mind.

Reflexes

(Abbreviated as **Ref**.) This measures the character's coordination and dexterity. An infant has a Ref of 2; a clumsy person has a Ref of 3. The human average Ref is 5; a superb athlete might have a Ref of 8, and anything beyond 10 is superhuman. Secondary attributes are **Agility** (abbreviated as **Agl**), **Manual Dexterity** (abbreviated as **Dex**), and **Speed** (abbreviated as **Spd**).

Agility measures aptitude for gross motor skills, those that involve the entire body. These include dancing, acrobatics, and hand-to-hand combat.

Manual Dexterity measures fine motor skills and hand to eye coordination. Useful for playing video games, firing guns, and stunt driving, among other things.

Speed measures reaction time to external stimuli. It governs who gets the first move in a fight, and how fast you are in combat.

SKILL NUMBERS

Skills are things that your character has learned to do. They are measured by **Skill Bonuses**, which reflect the level of training that your character has invested in a skill. The Action Value for each skill is based on a secondary attribute (such as Fortune or Perception), which is called the **Base Attribute** for that skill. To get your Action Value for a given skill, you add the Skill Bonus to the Base Attribute. Once you've done this, you don't have to mess with Skill Bonuses again until you improve a skill or add a new one. In the type listings, Skill Bonuses are shown as a positive number such as +3 or +5 or some other number. One Skill Bonus equals +1.

Some types will have a '=' sign placed before the Action Value. This means that the skill in question can't be raised during character generation. You can increase these Skill Bonuses during the course of play; the limitation imposed by the presence of the '=' sign only applies when you're first creating your character. For information on improving your skills, see Chapter 12.

CHANGE THE NUMBERS

Now that you know what attributes and skills are, it's time to change the numbers given on your type in order to personalize your chosen type and make it your own. You might want to flip to the example of character creation that appears on p. 19 as you look through this section. As you'll notice later on, we haven't set up a big chunk of rules giving point costs and guidelines for changing these numbers; instead, we've broken out those rules so that the relevant information appears within each type instead on a case-by-case basis. This makes things a lot simpler, since the info you need to know is already included in the type you're looking at.

Remember, if an attribute or skill appears after an '=' sign, you can't increase that number at all during character creation. These are usually the character's defining abilities. They're fixed to focus the types on their most important abilities and prevent them from stealing the limelight from other characters with sideline talents. Some types, like the Karate Cop and Magic Cop, have a mix of abilities; instead of being better than everyone else in one area, they're okay at a couple of things. They trade pure power for versatility.

CHANGING ATTRIBUTES

After the type's starting attributes, you are given some changes you can make to attributes that don't appear after an '=' sign. Some attributes also give you a Maximum Action Value, abbreviated as Max. You may not increase an attribute beyond its max during character creation.

Example: The Big Bruiser type's starting attributes are: Bod =11 (Tgh =12), Chi 0, Mnd 5, Ref 5. This type allows you to "Add 2 to one primary attribute." You could therefore increase Chi to 2, Mnd to 7, or Ref to 7.

CHANGING SKILLS

Once you're finished adding to attributes, go on to the list of skills. For each skill, you are given a Skill Bonus and an Action Value.

Changes you make in your character's attributes affect the character's skills, also. Before you start changing your skills around, note which skills have increased because the secondary attribute on which they are based has increased. If you added a point to Chi, for example, any skill based on a secondary attribute of Chi (such as Fortune) will go up by a point, also—unless that skill's Action Value is preceded by a '=' in which case the number *won't* change.

Below the skill listing for each type, you are given a number of skill bonuses you can use to customize your character. You can add these to the existing skills, or use them to start new skills. Adding a new skill doesn't cost you any extra. You just spend one of the skill bonuses you have available, and you get that skill at +1. You can add more than one to a new skill, of course, unless the type description says otherwise; so you could spend two skill bonuses and gain a new skill at +2 instead.

Skills may have Maximum Action Values, in which case you can't raise them above that number. (Recall that a skill's Action Value is equal to the skill's Base Attribute added to the Skill Bonus.) If you add a skill that does not appear on your type, it automatically has a Max of 12.

Some skills cannot be added to your type during character creation. These are typically the combat-oriented skills that define characters in this shoot 'em up, punch 'em innaface game. Again, this is done to make sure that your character isn't outclassed in its defining ability by some other character that has taken it only as a sideline. Those skills are noted in the summary of skills in the next section.

Skill Summary

Here's a quick summary of the skills available in the game. Later we devote a whole chapter to explaining what each skill does in detail. But this should serve as a quick guide to hunt down what you might want to add to your character. You can make up your own skills, but we don't recommend this if you're a beginning player, or if the GM is itching to get the story rolling.

The Base Attribute of each skill (which is always a Secondary Attribute) appears in parentheses after its name. Skills that can't be added to your type during character creation appear in *italics*.

Arcanowave Device (Magic): the operation of Architect gear that combines magic and technology. Only available to starting characters from the 2056 juncture.

Creature Powers (Magic): the use of innate magical powers of supernatural creature Types, including Abominations and Ghosts.

Deceit (Charisma): fooling others.

Detective (Perception): professional training as a private detective.

Driving (Manual Dexterity): vehicle operation.

Fix-It (Perception): repairing stuff, whipping up inventions.

Gambling (Fortune): winning bets.

Guns (Manual Dexterity): firing guns and other ranged weapons.

Info (Intelligence): not a single skill, but a category of knowledge skills. You pick an area of knowledge for each Info skill you take: history, geography, bee keeping, photography, or whatever. If a type provides you with a specific area of knowledge and you'd like to swap it for a different area to better fit your character, ask your GM for approval to do so. Your GM shouldn't deny reasonable requests. Customizing a type to come from a particular juncture (such as Everyman Hero) is a common reason for changing Info areas of knowledge. All characters automatically know general information about their home junctures; don't bother taking a skill to reflect this.

Intimidation (Charisma): bullying others.

Intrusion (Agility): going where you're not allowed and not getting caught.

Journalism (Intelligence): professional training as a reporter.

Leadership (Charisma): giving orders that others will follow.

Martial Arts (Agility): hand-to-hand combat and throwing weapons.

Medicine (Intelligence): healing. If you're from the 69 juncture, use Magic as the Base Attribute.

Police (Perception): police investigative techniques. Can't be learned in the course of play, so if you want it, take it now.

Sabotage (Manual Dexterity): wrecking stuff.

Seduction (Charisma): making yourself an object of desire.

Sorcery (Magic): casting spells.

REDUCING ATTRIBUTES AND SKILLS

Although we don't recommend that you do so until you're familiar with the game, you can decrease any attribute or skill rating given in a type if it suits your vision of your character. For example, you may want to play an apprentice who will grow into the role of a master martial artist, killer, sorcerer, or whatever. Or you might want to play your Big Bruiser as having below normal intelligence.

You gain no compensating advantages for reducing attributes and skills; you're doing it because you want to play the character this way, not to ratchet up some other ability. Even ratings that appear after an '=' sign can be reduced if you want. It's your character, after all, and if you think it'd be entertaining for your Gambler to have a lousy Fortune score (he can be the unluckiest gambler alive!) then go right ahead.

> ### If At First You Don't Succeed
> If, after your first session, you decide that you want to make different choices in the creation of your character, feel free to do so. It's better to jump into things quickly and fiddle later than to agonize over your decisions while everyone else taps their feet waiting for the action to start. So if you find that you aren't happy with the way you changed your attributes or skills, or with the schticks you picked, or whatever, you can go back and do it all over again, changing as much or as little as you like. It's your character, and you should be happy with her. Getting stuck with a bad choice due to inexperience is no fun, and *Feng Shui* has been designed from the ground up to be as fun as possible. After all, why should you be penalized for inexperience?

PICK YOUR SCHTICKS

Most characters come with **schticks**—particular nifty things associated with their character types. For example, many martial artist types can perform a number of Fu schticks, described in detail in Chapter 5.

Characters who fight mainly with weapons get to pick their preferred implements of destruction, which are described in Chapter 4. When choosing a weapon, characters must pick weapons from their character's home juncture. This does not preclude the character from picking up new weapons in the course of play.

Characters also might have the option of acquiring some gun schticks, which are particularly crunchy abilities that their characters have learned from years of experience.

Supernatural creatures may choose between a number of Creature Powers (Chapter 7). Sorcerers pick spells, as detailed in Magic, Chapter 6. Some other types get to pick Arcanowave Devices, as per Chapter 9.

Some characters are given Unique Schticks that apply only to their types. You can decide not to take a Unique Schtick if it doesn't fit your character conception, but you can't trade it for something else.

In game terms, schticks operate differently from type to type. Some schticks use skills as a base number, while other schticks use an attribute, such as Kung Fu or Chi. Still other schticks don't have a base skill or attribute. For some types, such as a Martial Artist, you might use your Kung Fu or Chi rating at times while using your Martial Arts skill at other times when you use a Fu Schtick. Look over the descriptions of each ability, and you'll be able to tell soon just how that schtick works.

For each type, we provide a number of **quick schtick picks**. These are good choices if you're in a hurry to create a character and want to get started right away. You're not obligated to take them, though, so if you have the time, feel free to look over the relevant chapters and pick the schticks you like best. If you don't have time and the GM wants to get started quickly, take the schticks given for your first session. Like attributes and skills, you can always choose different ones before the next session if you don't like the ones you've chosen. This applies whether you went for the quick schtick picks or not.

So You Want to Break the Rules

What if you want to have your character from 69 AD be fully proficient with a Buro Godhammer handgun from 2056 that some time-hopping Buro agent showed you how to use when you were a kid? Or say you want your 2056 Monster Hunter to be an expert on 19th-Century Chinese government (and have a relevant Info skill)? If you're confident in the conception of your character, you can go ahead and do anything you like—but *only* with your GM's permission, and *only* if it's not going to make everyone else wait while you hash out your situation. Your GM may have very good reasons not to let you do what you want to do; perhaps your GM has tweaked the 1850 juncture in her campaign so it's not what you expect and she doesn't want to give this away just yet, or perhaps she has some important plotline in mind that would fall apart if you have the special exemption you're after. You're welcome to tweak anything you want to about your type during character creation, especially if you're an experienced roleplayer and are prepared to do some funky customizations. But your GM always has the final say, and if she won't go for it then don't get upset. Go with the chi flow and move on, because the GM always has control of the best feng shui sites, y'know...

POSSESSIONS

Don't worry about jotting down a big list of possessions other than schtick-related items. In the course of play, you may decide that your character ought to have a particular item, whether it be a notebook computer, a jade ring, or an electric drill. If you can convincingly explain to your GM that your character would logically own this item, she will rule in your favor; alternately, your GM might let you make an Attribute Check (perhaps using Fortune or Intelligence) to see if you own the item or have it on you at that moment. Otherwise, forget it.

Many types allow the character to start the game with particular weapons. If you want weapons you can't choose for your character during creation, your PC will have to acquire them in the course of play; characters from 69 AD won't be running around with Buro Godhammers from 2056. Characters who are given weapon choices are given suggestions under the Quick Schtick Picks section to speed things up. If you decide after your first session that you want to make different choices, do it.

Wealth Level

Each character type comes with a **wealth level**. Feng Shui characters have better things to do than balance their check books and keep track of each individual dime in their savings account. Wealth levels are a shortcut that allows your GM to decide what financial resources a character has. Wealth does not necessarily translate from juncture to juncture; currency in 69 is not useful in 1850, the present day, or 2056, and so on. Of course, gems and gold speak the same language no matter what the calendar date.

If you can convince your GM that your version of a type clearly requires a wealth level different from the one given, you can have it. It should be easier to convince your GM to move the wealth level down than up.

Rich characters can buy any piece of gear they want, including vehicles. They have access to any type of luxury item, and can temporarily hire people to perform basic services for them. They don't have to spend much time maintaining their fortunes. In general, GMs will worry about a rich character's personal expenses only when the character seems to be abusing the privilege. Then the GM will hit the character with "cash flow problems" when he tries to do something unreasonable.

Working Stiff characters are on a salary and take home a pay check. When rent and food and basic needs are taken care of, they have a hard time buying expensive items. If they quit their jobs, they'll need to come up with some other means of support, like a patron in the secret wars who will clothe, house and feed them.

Poor characters have nothing but their starting gear and the clothes on their backs. Many of them are wanderers or outcasts. They'll need to make arrangements for housing and food and so forth in the course of play.

Note that the limitations and opportunities created by your type's wealth level are meant to serve dramatic purposes, not realistic ones. If you're poor, you don't have to justify where every single meal comes from; but when you need to buy a shotgun on short notice, the GM is within her rights to make you sweat over how to make this happen.

EXAMPLE OF CHARACTER CREATION

Maribel is creating a Big Bruiser character, Archie "Two Fists" Jackson. She pictures him as a brawling giant whose snarling demeanor disguises a heart of gold. His melodramatic hook is that he's looking for the girl he took under his wing during his childhood on the streets. Maribel wants him to be a contemporary character.

The Big Bruiser's starting attributes are: Bod =11 (Tgh =12), Chi 0, Mnd 5, Ref 5. This type allows you to "Add 2 to one primary attribute."

Maribel can therefore increase Two Fists' Chi to 2, his Mnd to 7, or his Ref to 7. Maribel wants Two Fists to be lucky, so she gives him a Chi of 2. She could have just as easily decided to make him smarter or more coordinated. The one thing she can't do is increase his Bod rating or any of its secondary attributes: they're already jacked up big time, being the defining ability of the Big Bruiser.

His final attributes are: Bod=11 (Tgh=12), Chi 2, Mnd 5, Ref 5.

Now Maribel moves on to skills. The Big Bruiser gets Guns +3 (8) [Max 10], Info / your choice +2 (7), Intimidation +4 (9), Martial Arts +7 (=12), and may "Add a total of +6 in skill bonuses."

First she checks to see if her attribute changes alter the skill ratings. Since none of the skills here are based on Chi, they don't. Otherwise she'd make these changes to the skill ratings before going on to add her optional skill bonuses.

Maribel decides to leave the Guns rating as is; she sees Two Fists as more of a hands-on roughneck than a shooter. She decides to use 4 of her free skill bonuses to crank up Two Fists's Intimidation rating to an impressive 13. She decides that Two Fists spent his early days after the orphanage in a life of petty crime, and spends 1 skill bonus each on Gambling and Sabotage. (Maribel figures that Two Fists has worked for mobsters as muscle, which includes incidents of vandalism and arson.) The Base Attribute of Gambling is Fortune, which Two Fists has at 2. With the +1 bonus, he has an Action Value of 3 in Gambling. The base attribute of Sabotage is Manual Dexterity, which Two Fists has at 5. A +1 bonus gives him an Action Value of 6 in this skill. Finally, Maribel decides which Info skill Two Fists has. She decides he was a math whiz during his orphanage days, and defines the Info skill as Mathematics.

So Two Fists' skills end up as follows: Gambling 3, Guns 8, Info/Mathematics 7, Intimidation 13, Martial Arts 12, Sabotage 6.

Big Bruisers get a Unique Schtick that gives them a higher Death Check threshold; Maribel notes this on her character sheet. She also gets to pick three weapons. In accordance with how she imagines Two Fists she picks a club, a set of brass knuckles, and a .50 caliber Desert Eagle. She figures he'll use this really big gun mostly to augment his Intimidation attempts.

WHAT ARE YOU WAITING FOR?

That's all you have to do. Get started checking out the different types and their schticks, and then get ready to kick some butt.

Type Format
The format for the types should be self-explanatory, but just in case you're wondering...

Each type begins with the name of the type, like Masked Avenger or whatever. Then there's a quote; this is the kind of thing that this kind of character might say. Your character doesn't ever have to say this or talk like this, though; it's up to you. This is followed by a text description of the character type, which you can use as a starting point in personalizing your character. These are just meant to get you thinking; use only the ideas you like.

Juncture tells you which of the available junctures your character can hail from; if the character could live in the Netherworld, that is indicated as well.

Attributes lists your starting attributes, and then tells you how much you can fiddle with them.

Skills lists the skills your character starts with, including Skill Bonuses. Then it lets you know what you can add.

Schticks tells you how many schticks you can pick, and from which categories you may pick them. Not all types have schticks.

Weapons tells you what weapons the character can choose from. Some archetypes don't have a Weapons listing; that's because they have other nifty schticks that serve them well.

Quick Schtick Pick is an easy way of getting your character into the action in no time. You can choose these popular schticks for your character or you can choose other schticks if it suits you.

Wealth Level tells you the character's Wealth Level.

Abomination

"I may be a... monster... but I am no more... monstrous... than those who... made me..."

You are a former Supernatural Creature who was captured from its original juncture of 69 by Architect Monster Hunters; you were then altered using cybernetic and Arcanowave technology, converting you into a futuristic super soldier. Although Abominations are programmed in such a way as to suppress their intellects and self-preservation instincts in favor of blind loyalty to the Architects and their Buro associates, a rare few of them break free from this domination. Some of them commit suicide; others join the resistance and fight to destroy their former masters. You are among this small group of rebel Abominations. The Buro goes to enormous lengths to track down and destroy Abominations who get away from them; chances are you stumbled into the Netherworld in order to escape them. There, you learned about the secret war, and how the Architects came to control the world by seizing feng shui sites. You live in constant pain, having been twisted into a perverse mockery of your former self. However, this agony is not all for naught, as much as you want it to stop. With your pain has come a sense of moral awareness, one that would have completely eluded you in your former demonic form. If the Architects could change you, you must therefore be able to change yourself. You will redeem yourself for the actions you took, first as a demon and then as a monstrous super-commando. You have sworn vengeance against your former Architect masters. Using the information you have gathered in the Netherworld, you now intend to join the secret war. You want to do nothing less than erase the Architects and their dread regime from the time stream.

Juncture: 2056

Attributes: Bod 5
Chi =0 (Mag =8)
Mnd 3 (Cha 1)
Ref 5

Add 5 to one primary attribute. Add 1 to one other primary attribute.

Skills: Arcanowave Device +5 (=13)
Creature Powers +5 (=13)
Guns +5 (10) [Max 13]
Martial Arts +5 (10) [Max 13]

Add 1 skill not listed above at a +3 Skill Bonus. Add +2 to the bonus of any single skill, including the new one. Info skills are generally inappropriate for Abominations; make sure you can justify any you choose to your GM.

Schticks: 3 Arcanowave schticks
2 Creature Powers

Quick Schtick Pick: Feedback Enhancer
Helix Rethreader
Wave Suppresser
Armor
Transformation

Limitation: You can't be healed by characters using the Medicine skill, unless they learned the Medicine skill in 2056.

Wealth Level: poor

Illustration by Jeff Miracola

Big Bruiser

"Was that supposed to hurt or something?"

You fight well because you are very big and very strong. You are not particularly fast, and don't hit your opponent every time you swing. But when you do connect—look out. You can also take much more punishment than the average opponent. You can take most fighters' best shots and remain standing. You can often head off a fight simply by standing and raising yourself to your full height. You've had lots of practice being intimidating. Most people assume that you're stupid simply because you're big, a mistake that you've learned to play to your advantage. Sometimes you play dumb, causing others to underestimate you. You find it easy to get jobs that require physical strength: You may have worked as a manual laborer, or as a guard of some kind. You might have been a security guard, a bouncer, or a bodyguard to someone rich and/or famous. You might be a quiet, gentle giant or a bullying loudmouth. You are definitely a mountain of determination and endurance.

Juncture: any

Attributes: Bod =11 (Tgh =12)
Chi 0
Mnd 5
Ref 5

Add 2 to any one primary attribute.

Skills: Guns +3 (8) [Max 10]
Info/your choice +2 (7)
Intimidation +4 (9)
Martial Arts +7 (=12)

Add a total of +6 in Skill Bonuses to these skills and/or to additional skills of your choice.

Weapons: 3 weapons of appropriate juncture

Unique Schtick: You make Death Checks (see p. 135) only when you reach 50 Wound Points; -1 Impairment at 40 Wound Points, and -2 Impairment at 45 Wound Points.

Quick Schtick Pick:
69: really big sword, club, bow
1850: really big sword, club, rifle
Cntp.: baseball bat, Colt King Cobra, Bernadelli shotgun
2056: club, Buro Beat Patroller, Buro Crimestopper

Wealth Level: poor

Illustration by Jeff Miracola

Cyborg

*"For an obsolete model I can poke a pretty big hole in your head—
so I'd drop that attitude a couple of notches, Consumer."*

You are a failed early experiment by the Architects of the Flesh. Before they hit upon the bright idea of kidnapping Supernatural Creatures from the past and altering them cybernetically, they spent some time working on cybernetic alterations of humans and even other primates. The idea was that super soldiers could be created through cybernetics; the dictatorial Buro wanted combatants who could strike fear into entire enemy units. What they didn't tell their recruits was that they were only able to master cybernetic technology by combining it with Arcanowave theory; the devices operated on magical as well as scientific principles. The program was an enormous failure; for every individual who survived the multi-million dollar process, there were a dozen who either croaked on the operating table or who mutated into hideous creatures beyond the control of their Buro masters. You were one of the lucky ones—if luck is what you can call it. After a few abortive missions (in which you were exposed to battlefield horrors that haunt you to this day) you were unceremoniously discharged from the armed forces. After a few laughable counseling sessions, you were sent back to the life of drudgery that most workers in 2056 face. You were expected to act like any other consumer, as if nothing had happened. You may have managed to grab yourself some restricted military hardware before being kicked off the base but you haven't used it much, if at all. You've heard that those who use the devices can come down with all manner of weird symptoms. And you heard other things, too: That there was a network of rebels who wanted to bring the Buro down. They were to be found in this weird magical realm called the Netherworld. Despite the unblinking eye of the security state, you risked your life to track down the people who knew how to find this place. You found the Netherworld and learned about the secret war. You are more than ready to put your unnatural abilities to good use—probably against the very government that rebuilt you and then tossed you away like yesterday's processing chip.

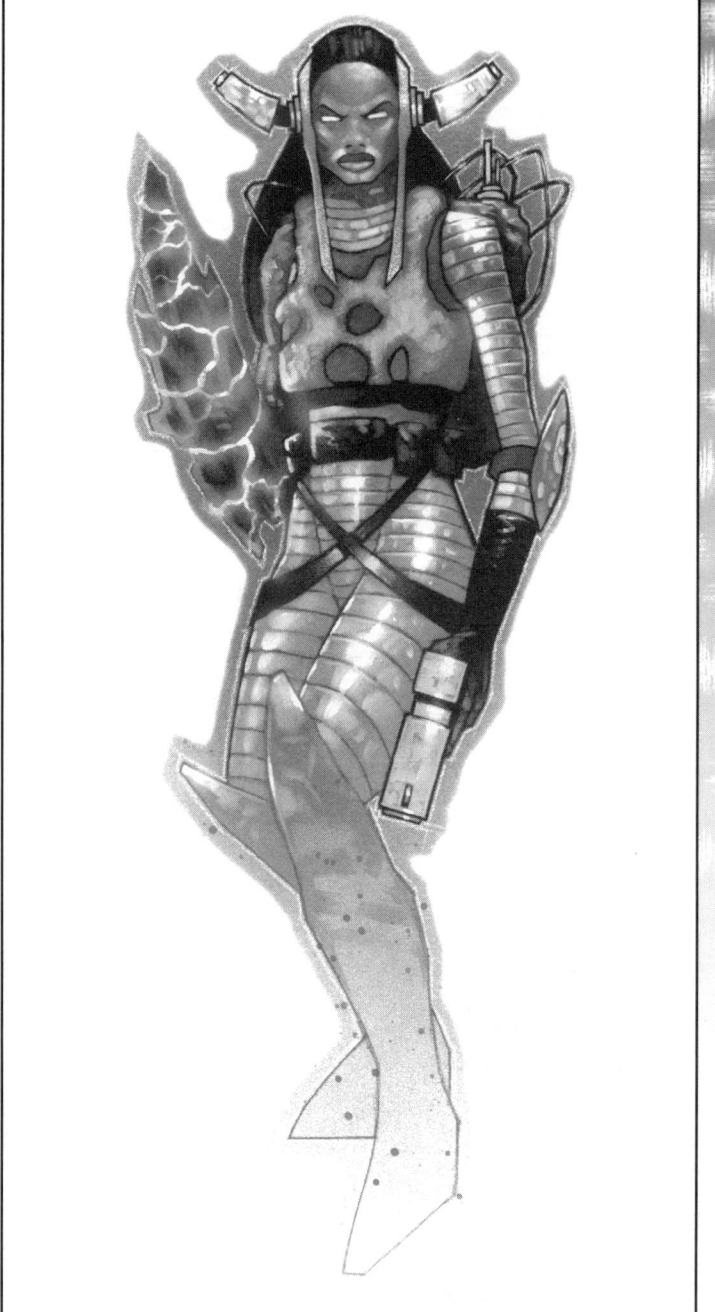

Juncture: 2056

Attributes: Bod 5
Chi 0
Mnd 5
Ref 5

Add 3 to any single primary attribute. Add 1 to any other primary attribute. Add 2 to any secondary attribute.

Skills: Arcanowave Device +7 (7) [Max 11]
Guns +8 (=13)
Martial Arts +6 (=11)
Sabotage +2 (7) [Max 13]

Add 6 skill bonuses. Swap the Skill Bonuses and Action Values of Guns and Martial Arts if desired.

Schticks: 4 Arcanowave Devices, 1 gun schtick

Weapons: Two guns from the 2056 juncture

Quick Schtick Pick:
  Arcanowave Devices: Neural Stimulator, Robot Arm, Slap Patch, Spirit Shield Generator
  Gun Schtick: Carnival of Carnage
  Weapons: Buro9A, Buro Blue Flag

Wealth Level: working stiff

Illustration by Jeff Miracola

Everyman Hero

"Hey, I may not have the faintest clue what's going on here, but I'm an American, dammit! And that means I got two strong American fists, and a big American heart—and a big American gun!"

The Everyman Hero is just a regular person who works for a living, probably in a blue collar job. Maybe you're a factory worker, a truck driver, a plumber, or a sailor. In past junctures, you might be a good-hearted and brave—but dim—peasant or serf. You may be on vacation when the action begins, or find yourself in a crossfire as the result of a job-related errand. Aside from taking care of your melodramatic hook, all you really want to do is sit down with a can of beer and watch some sports at the local bar. But somehow trouble always comes looking for you. That's because of your basic, essential decency and/or stupidity. And also your peculiar luck. On one hand, your luck gets you through situations that even you don't believe you could survive. But on the other hand, your luck tends to get you into weird and frightening situations to begin with because the good guys need your help. Whenever you go on vacation, you find yourself mixed up with gangsters, weird cultists, or mysterious creatures. Whenever you go into a bar, there's always some blowhard spoiling for a fight. If you're among a crowd of thousands at a sports stadium, and a kid running away from kidnappers is going to break from her captors and run pell-mell into somebody screaming for help, it's you she'll run into. You always promise yourself that the next time trouble starts, you're just going to turn your back and walk away. But when it comes right down to it, when you see somebody being bullied, or bad guys running rampant, you can't resist diving into the fray in order to set things right. You're a simple person who believes in simple, old-fashioned values. Values that suddenly seem to be an endangered species in this increasingly crazy world. You may not be the smartest, or the strongest, or the most skilled person in the world. But you're a good guy, and "Good guys always finish—ugh! Hey, wha'd you shoot me for? Oh, man, now I'm bleeding... howzabout a knuckle sandwich?"

Juncture: any

Attributes: Bod 5
Chi 0 (For =10)
Mnd 5 (Wil 6)
Ref 5

Divide 4 points among your primary attributes. Add 1 to a single secondary attribute.

Skills: Driving +4 (9) [Max 14]
Guns +1 (6) [Max 13]
Info/Beer +8 (13)
Info/Classic Cars +5 (10)
Info/Sports Fan +8 (13)
Info/Stadium Rock +7 (12)
Martial Arts +5 (10) [Max 13]

Add 5 Skill Bonuses. If you want new areas of knowledge for your Info skills, be prepared for the GM to veto anything which isn't sufficiently lowbrow. You should change your Info skills to more appropriate areas if you're from 69, 1850, or 2056.

Unique Schtick: 1) Fortune Dice you've spent do not reduce your Fortune rating for the purposes of making Fortune checks. 2) You get +1 AV for any creative attack you make with an improvised weapon. Pool cues, barbells, frozen chicken dinners, weathervanes, beer bottles, and so on can all be weapons. If the same improvised weapon is used excessively, no bonus is recieved—it is no longer considered an improvised weapon.

Weapons: None. You'll just have to find one somewhere. However, if the campaign starts in the middle of a fight then you might want to consult with your GM to see if you've already snagged one.

Wealth Level: working stiff

Illustration by Jeff Miracola

Ex-Special Forces

"So after the charges go off and blow up the oil tank, I'll come in on the chopper hanging from the rope ladder and take care of the dozen-or-so guards on the terrace. Once they're outta the picture, drop me onto the roof and I'll break into the secret lab and stop the mad scientist."

You are a veteran of extensive military training. A former member of an elite force trained in counter-terrorism, hostage rescue, and sabotage missions, you had a hard-bitten military mindset drilled into you along with your extensive list of deadly skills. It is possible that you were dishonorably discharged from your beloved unit, fairly or otherwise; this might be your melodramatic hook. You've probably had some trouble adjusting to civilian life. People keep expecting you to relax, to kick back, to get along, just like everybody else. But you can't. Your nerves are still on edge. Whenever you get into a fender bender, or a confrontation on the street, it takes all of your determination not to leap on the guy harassing you and beat him to a pulp. In another age, you would have been a great warrior, renowned throughout history for your achievements. You would have solved your problems with your strong arm and your sword, and would have been justly celebrated for it. But in this world, you're just another underemployed citizen with abilities you can't put to proper use. You long for a new cause to believe in, one you can feel as much fervor for as your old corps. You want glory again. Most of all, you want the pure rush you get from combat. It's not the kind of thing you're supposed to admit to anybody, but combat was like a drug to you. There's nothing you'd like more than to feel the taste of blood and fear in your mouth on another battlefield. If that battlefield involves a fight for justice and freedom against tyrants from across the timestream, so much the better. Perhaps you will get the fame and glory you seek after all, fighting alongside the ancient warriors you have admired since you were a child.

Juncture: any

Attributes: Bod 5
Chi 0 (Fu =4)
Mnd 5
Ref 5

Add 6 points to your primary attributes. No more than 5 points can be spent on any single attribute.

Skills: Driving +7 (=12)
Guns +9 (=14)
Info/Anti-Terrorism +5 (10)
Martial Arts +5 (=10)
Sabotage +4 (9)

Add 3 Skill Bonuses. Swap the Skill Bonuses and Action Values of Guns and Martial Arts if desired.

Schticks: Your choice of the following:
5 gun schticks
3 fu schticks
4 gun schticks and 1 fu schtick

Weapons: 5 weapons of the appropriate juncture

Quick Schtick Pick:
Gun Schticks: Carnival of Carnage: 2, Eagle Eye: 2, Lightning Reload
Weapons: 69: dagger, throwing stars, sword, bow, nunchakus; 1850: dagger, throwing stars, sword, cap and ball pistol, cap and ball rifle; Cntp.: dagger, Glock 17, Heckler & Koch P7, Heckler & Koch MP5, M16; 2056: dagger, Buro 9A, Buro Godhammer, Buro Blade of Truth, Buro Blue Spear

Wealth Level: poor

Illustration by Jeff Miracola

Gambler

"The odds of my having that card are 145,987 to one. But then again, I am feeling lucky today. And you know that things go my way when I feel lucky. So do you want me to look at your card, or do you just want to give me the money now?"

In any time period, the Gambler is a constant. You're a devil-may-care hang-glider on the winds of fate, one who turns natural luck and a flair for getting yourself out of scrapes and into a profitable career. You've learned to handle yourself in a fight—not all losers are good sports, after all. But mostly you rely on your drop-dead smile and your airtight instincts to keep yourself out of trouble. With these two weapons at your disposal, you've carved out a life of luxury for yourself—no pleasure is too flashy or shallow for your tastes. After all, what's the fun of winning all the time if you can't flaunt it? You came from humble beginnings and made your fortune using only your brains and your need for victory. The latest clothes, the shiniest gadgets: these are things you've dreamed of since childhood. But the real prize is the sheer joy of beating the odds, of triumphing over your opponents when logic decrees that you should be down for the count. And although you count many criminals among your opponents, you've never slipped over the line from shadiness to outright criminality. But now a melodramatic hook has pulled you into the secret war, a situation where all of the odds you've memorized are turned upside down. Still, you face this new adventure with a grin and your characteristic self-confidence. You know it won't take you long to figure the angles.

Juncture: any

Attributes: Bod 5
Chi 0 (For =7)
Mnd 6 (Cha 7)
Ref 5

Add 3 points to one primary attribute, 2 points to a second primary attribute, and 1 point to a third. Add 2 to one secondary attribute; it may not exceed 11.

Skills: Gambling +8 (=15)
Guns +8 (=13)
Martial Arts +2 [Max 11]
Seduction +6 (=13)

Add 6 Skill Bonuses.

Schticks: 1 gun schtick

Weapons: 1 weapon from appropriate juncture

Unique Schtick: You're an expert at calculating odds. You can make a Fortune check with a Difficulty of 4 at any time; if you succeed, the GM must tell you the Difficulty of an upcoming check. You must be able to observe the situation you're figuring the odds for.

Quick Schtick Pick:
Gun Schtick:
Fast Draw
Weapons:
69: sling
1850: ball and cap pistol
Cntp.: Beretta Model 21 Bobcat
2056: Buro Backup Arm

Wealth Level: rich

Illustration by Brian Snoddy

Ghost

"Although the gulf of life and death separates us, can I still not love you?"

The 69 juncture, with its high level of magic, is rife with ghosts—spirits of the dead who refuse to leave the trappings of mortal life behind. The Netherworld is also home to many ghosts, former secret warriors whose life forces were too strong to depart the Inner Kingdom when their physical bodies died. You are a spirit who hails from one of these locations. Some ghosts are evil spirits who prey on the living, motivated either by jealousy of the living or by the same malign intentions they harbored in life. But you are tied to the Earth for some other reason. Your soul cannot rest, for in life you swore a solemn oath to complete some great undertaking. And you're not going to let a little thing like death stand in your way. This crucial unfinished business is probably your melodramatic hook. You may have sworn to protect someone, to wreak vengeance on an enemy, or to recover some lost treasure or artifact. Ghosts have a bad habit of falling in love with mortals, and can often be stunningly beautiful and attractive to the opposite sex. Although you know such loves are forbidden, you may already find yourself in a romantic entanglement that crosses the sacred barrier between the living and the dead. If you are not in such a doomed relationship, you are sufficiently prone to such temptations that you might end up in one before the series is out. Whether you willingly participate in the secret war, or whether the vow that keeps you tied to this plane forces you to do so, you are about to learn that dying was only the beginning of your troubles.

Juncture: 69, Netherworld

Attributes Bod 5
Chi 0 (Mag =7)
Mnd 5 (Cha =8)
Ref 5

Divide 6 points among primary attributes, spending no more than 4 on any one attribute.

Skills: Creature Powers +7 (=14)
Info/Musicianship +4 (9)
Seduction +5 (13) [Max 15]
Sorcery +6 (=13)

Add 4 Skill Bonuses. Feel free to change the Info skill to some other pleasant hobby or diversion that you loved to pursue when you were still alive.

Schticks: 2 Sorcery schticks
Creature Power: Flight
Creature Power: Insubstantial
1 other Creature Power

Unique Limitation: You can't be healed by characters using the Medicine skill, unless they learned the Medicine skill in AD 69.

Quick Schtick Pick: Blast
Influence
Flight
Insubstantial
Damage Immunity (bullets)

Wealth Level: poor

Illustration by Jeff Miracola

Journalist

"Yeah, yeah, I know I'm past deadline, but see, there's this demon chewin' on my leg and you know, somethin' like that tends to interfere with the old prose stylings, if you know what I mean. [BLAM!] Never mind, got the sucker. But look, there's this matter of my expense account..."

You're a journalist, possibly even a well-known one, but you are not exactly a beacon for professional standards and objectivity. In fact, you have a reputation for becoming the story instead of just reporting it. Maybe it's your passionate nature. Or your insatiable appetite for adventure. Or maybe your predilection for knocking it back in the press gallery bar. You just always find yourself getting into impossible situations, ones where the role of observer just won't do. Why, that time back in Afghanistan when the strange creatures poured out of the mountain pass down into the mujaheddin camp you were staying at: There was nothing to do but to pick up an AK-47 and start blasting at the things, was there? And that time in Stockholm: You couldn't let them get away with that hostage just because you're a reporter, could you? And that story about you chasing ex-President Carter with a nine iron has been totally blown out of proportion over the years. Chances are that you're not a newspaper reporter working a daily beat. You used to be, but after being fired from your tenth or twelfth major paper, you realized that the regular grind was not for you. Instead, you write magazine articles or even books about your exploits. Maybe you even disguise your weirder adventures as fiction, changing the names and turning them into pulp, horror or sci-fi paperbacks. Even so, you're in a constant battle with your editors, a fight waged via telephone, fax and e-mail: when you sniff another adventure full of fear and loathing, you're not going to let a measly thing like a deadline stand in your way.

Juncture: 1850, contemporary

Attributes: Bod 5
Chi 0 (For =5)
Mnd 6
Ref 5

Divide 5 points between primary attributes.

Skills: Detective + 3 (9) [Max 13]
Guns +8 (=13)
Info/Intoxicants +5 (11)
Info/World Politics +3 (9)
Info/your choice +3 (9)
Journalism +5 (11)
Martial Arts +6 (=11)

Add 4 Skill Bonuses. Swap Guns and Martial Arts skill ratings if desired.

Unique Schtick: When you encounter a contact made through your Journalism skill, you may spend a Fortune point to guarantee that the contact doesn't hate your guts.

Weapons: 1 gun from appropriate juncture

Quick Schtick Pick:
1850: pistol
Cntp.: Makarov

Wealth Level: working stiff, but your expense account abuse allows you to operate as if you're rich

Illustration by Brian Snoddy

Karate Cop

"You have the right to remain silent. [WHACK!] You have the right to an attorney. [WHACK!] Anything you say can and will [THUMP!] be used against you in a court of [WHACK!]"

You are a loyal, team-playing officer of the law who happens to be about as adept in the martial arts as you are with your service revolver. In modern or futuristic terms, you may be a plainclothes detective or a uniformed beat walker. But every era has its honest and efficient law enforcement officials, and the Karate Cop is found throughout the time stream. Your study of the ancient fighting arts of China has taught your a sense of calm and serenity that may elude your fellow police officers. You believe in doing things by the book, but when it comes to a crunch, you will bend the law to serve higher justice. Unlike the Maverick Cop, your transgressions against procedure stem from impulsiveness rather than a cynical disregard for the justice system. You're the officer that the lieutenant wouldn't mind his kid marrying. Your modest home is full of awards and citations for bravery. You strongly believe in being a good role model for kids, and probably help out as a volunteer in your spare time, helping underprivileged kids to learn the martial arts. You really think that it's still possible for honest people to get ahead in the world, and that good will always triumph in the end. The one thing that makes you lose your cool is genuine evil. You may have a positive view of life, but that doesn't make you naïve—or less determined to make sure that righteousness prevails.

Juncture: any

Attributes: Bod 5
 Chi 0
 Mnd 5
 Ref 5

Add 3 to one primary attribute and 2 to another. Add 2 to one secondary attribute and 1 to another. Max 10 on all primary and secondary attributes.

Skills: Driving +6 (11)
 Guns +8 (=13)
 Martial Arts +9 (=14)
 Police +4 (9)

Add 6 Skill Bonuses.

Unique Schticks: 1) You can deliver a stirring speech that will convince any basically righteous and law-abiding GMC of your honesty and integrity. People you impress in this way will want to help you out, although they won't wreck their own lives to do it. If you spend a Fortune die, you can likewise win over a shady or disreputable person. This ability doesn't work on GMCs that the GM considers to be the main antagonists in the current storyline or who would otherwise derail the plot. 2) You gain a +2 Action Value bonus when using your Martial Arts skill to execute acrobatic maneuvers that aren't direct attacks on opponents in combat.

Weapons: 2 weapons of appropriate juncture

Quick Schtick Pick:
 69: sword, staff
 1850: club, pistol
 Cntp: Colt Detective Special, Remington 870
 2056: Buro Beat Patroller, Buro Crimestopper

Wealth Level: working stiff

Illustration by Jeff Miracola

Killer

"Forty of them, one of me. Looks like the odds are about even."

You used to be employed as a professional assassin. Maybe you worked for an intelligence agency. More likely you whacked people for the mob. You prided yourself on cool, calculated efficiency and the ability to get the job done without getting involved. Sometimes you managed to take out your targets with minimal risk. But now and then things went wrong and you had to shoot your way out. You still have the news clippings of the more spectacular incidents of this type. You created miniature war zones in the heart of the city, and you were target number one. You know everything there is to know about the acquisition, handling and employment of firearms. You have used those firearms on numerous occasions, on human targets. You've been perforated by bullets more times than you can count, but you figure there hasn't been a bullet made that will take you down permanently. You and bullets have a relationship, see? Or so you've convinced yourself. Your victims meant little to you; they were just figures in your bank account. You were more interested in executing the perfect kill than in the identity of those you were called upon to wipe out. But now something has changed. Possibly through your melodramatic hook, you have become involved in the secret war. Now you have the power to change history with your trigger finger, instead of just wiping out unsuspecting victims. And maybe, just maybe, you have the chance to redeem yourself...

Juncture: 69, 1850, contemporary

Attributes: Bod 5
Chi 0
Mnd 5
Ref 5

Add 3 to one primary attribute. Add 2 to a different primary attribute. Add 1 to a secondary attribute.

Skills: Deceit +2 (7) [Max 12]
Driving +3 (8) [Max 13]
Guns +10 (=15)
Info/Gangland Politics +2 (7)

Add 6 Skill Bonuses.

Schticks: 5 gun schticks

Weapons: 5 weapons of appropriate juncture

Quick Schtick Pick:
Gun Schticks: Carnival of Carnage: 2, Both Guns Blazing: 2, Lightning Reload
Weapons:
69: sword, bow, throwing stars, dagger, blowgun
1850: sword, pistol, rifle, dagger, throwing stars
Cntp: Browning Hi-Power, Glock 17, HK MP5, Beretta 1201 Riot shotgun, AK-47

Wealth Level: rich

Illustration by Jeff Miracola

Magic Cop

"There are some things that man was meant not to know. It's my job to hunt down those things and kill them."

Even in junctures where magic is rare and difficult to perform, there are still supernatural occurrences. Many large police jurisdictions secretly maintain small units of officers trained in the mystic arts. These cops are able to take on the occasional renegade sorcerer or shaman who might pop up, and can dispatch demons and ghosts without freaking out. You are one of these cops. You're probably a loner; the system is set up so you have little contact with regular law enforcement officials. Other officers think you're nuts, if they know who you are at all. Alternately, you might be a crusading priest or exorcist who fights supernatural forces in the name of your religion. Depending on the religion, you might act as part of a formal church hierarchy, taking orders from your clerical superiors. Or, in the case of religions without an organized structure, you might be a self-appointed crusader against magical forces. Whether you are police officer or clerical crusader, whether you take orders or follow your own private mission, you have built up tough mental defenses against the creatures of the night. To normal folks, you come off as grim or aloof. You might think of yourself as a holy warrior, implacably gunning down anything that smacks of the occult. Or maybe you wish you could build a bridge between the world of the supernatural and the world of everyday humanity. Magic cops are often drawn into the secret war as they hunt down agents of the Lotus or Architects, discovering that there is much of the unseen world that even they know nothing about.

Juncture: any

Attributes:
- Bod 5
- Chi =2 (Mag =8)
- Mnd 5
- Ref 5

Add 6 to primary attributes, spending no more than 3 points on any one attribute.

Skills:
- Guns +7 (=12)
- Info/Occult +7 (12)*
- Police +3 (8)*
- Sorcery +5 (=13)

* For crusading priests, replace with Info/[Your Specific Religion] +6 (11)

Add 8 Skill Bonuses. Swap Guns and Sorcery if desired.

Schticks: 2 gun schticks

Sorcery Abilities: Summoning, plus your choice of Divination, Fertility, or Heal

Weapons: 2 of appropriate juncture

Unique Schticks: 1) You get an extra effect within the Summoning schtick: True Form: You can cause a magically-altered being, such as a transformed animal or a supernatural creature using the Transformation Creature Power, to revert to its true form. The Difficulty is the subject's highest Action Value rating. In the case of transformed animals, you may attempt to use this spell on any given individual once only, and it costs you a Magic point to try. This cost is permanent. If you fail, you automatically suffer a serious Backlash, suffering 5 Wound Points for each point of difference between your Action Result and the Difficulty. These Wound Points are not reduced by Toughness or Armor. 2) You suffer no juncture penalties, if any, when using Sorcery in your home juncture.

Quick Schtick Pick:
Sorcery: Summoning, Divination
Gun Schticks: Eagle Eye, Hair-Trigger Neck Hairs
Weapons: 69: staff, sword; 1850: staff, sword; Cntp.: Colt Detective Special, Remington 870; 2056: Buro Beat Patroller, Buro Crimestopper

Wealth Level: working stiff

(30)

Illustration by Brian Snoddy

Martial Artist

"Your kung fu is strong. You shall be a worthy opponent."

You are an accomplished young student of one or more schools of hand-to-hand combat. You are as effective with your bare hands as with a variety of hand-to-hand weapons. You have also begun to learn a number of exotic chi powers. You have learned that the martial arts are more than just a series of combat moves. They represent an ancient and learned philosophy, one that preaches restraint, discipline, and humility. You work hard to live up to that philosophy. You choose your fights carefully, and work to uphold the values you have learned, such as reverence for elders, respect for the traditions of the past, and self-sacrifice for the greater good. You probably work at a humble job, caring little for material goods. The only goal you consider worthy of pursuing is the physical and spiritual perfection attained by the great masters of the past. You spend most of your time working out or studying the ancient texts. Your extreme dedication leaves you somewhat isolated from most people. Some think of you as naïve, others as insufferably self-righteous. You strive to shrug off the taunts and jealousies of the average person, but sometimes it's hard. The extreme self-discipline you must exercise is sometimes wearying. But still you fervently believe that the goal is worth the sacrifice. When you encounter the outlines of the secret war, your dedication to honor and self-perfection leads you into the battle against evil without a second thought.

Juncture: any

Attributes: Bod 5
Chi 0 (Fu =8)
Mnd 5
Ref 5

Add a total of 6 points among your primary attributes. Max for all attributes is 10.

Skills: Info/Eastern Philosophy +6 (11)
Leadership +2 (7)
Martial Arts +10 (=15)

Add 3 Skill Bonuses.

Schticks: Any three fu schticks

Weapons: One hand-to-hand weapon

Quick Schtick Pick:
Fu Schticks: Hands Without Shadow, Dim Mak, Lightning Fist
Weapons: nunchakus

Wealth Level: poor

Illustration by Jeff Miracola

Medic

"I don't see plugging a maniac like you as a violation of the Hippocratic Oath at all. Basically, I look on it as preventative medicine."

You are a trained medical practitioner used to life in a combat zone. Maybe you've spent some time as an army doctor. Maybe you've been a trauma team member in an inner-city combat zone. Or maybe you've done a stint as an aid worker, helping the afflicted in trouble spots around the world. The one thing you've learned is that people willing to maim and kill their fellow human beings are like microbes—they're everywhere. You used to be a pacifist, until one day you started thinking of the world's killers and criminals as a disease that needed to be wiped out. That's when you added a 9mm autopistol—or a sword, or your fists—to your standard list of medical equipment. You realized that taking out a murderous drug dealer early in his career would save the lives of many innocents. You've been used to holding the power of life and death in your hands, and your program of pre-emptive euthanasia came surprisingly easy to you. But still, you were troubled. Something feels wrong about what you've been doing. It's not guilt exactly—more a sense that you need to change things on a broader scale. You're ripe to discover the secret war, and how the battle for feng shui sites can bring about a better world. You're ready to tend to fallen comrades—and to fell a few of the enemy along the way.

Juncture: any

Attributes: Bod 4
Chi 0
Mnd 7
Ref 4

Add 6 points to primary attributes, devoting no more than 3 points to a single attribute. Add 5 points, divided as you wish, among secondary attributes (if you're taking fu schticks, bumping up the Chi or Kung Fu attribute is a good idea). No secondary attribute may exceed 10.

Skills: Detective +3 (10) [Max 12]
Driving +2 (6) [Max 12]
Guns +9 (=13) or Martial Arts +9 (=13)
Info/your choice +4 (11)
Info/your choice +2 (9)
Medicine +8 (=15)

Add 4 Skill Bonuses.

Schticks: 2 gun or fu schticks

Weapons: 1 weapon of appropriate juncture

Quick Schtick Pick:
　Gun Schticks: Lightning Reload, Signature Weapon
　Fu Schticks: Flow Restoration, Corners of the Mouth
　Weapon:
　　69: katana
　　1850: musket
　　Cntp.: Sig Sauer P-220
　　2056: Buro Beat Patroller

Wealth Level: rich

Illustration by Brian Snoddy

Masked Avenger

"Tremble in fear, evildoers! Your time of reckoning is at hand!"

For many years, you have watched as your society has slowly sunk into corruption. Crime is rampant on the streets. Justice is unattainable for the common man. Criminals are rewarded; victims are forgotten. The police and judiciary are hopelessly tainted or just plain unable to deal with the rising tide of evil in the world. The time for brooding is over. Seeking to strike fear into the hearts of evildoers, you have donned a distinctive costume and identity-concealing mask to take the law into your own hands. You use your own uncompromising moral compass to find wrongdoers and beat the crap out of them. The Masked Avenger is typically at odds with law enforcement, and may even be an active revolutionary against a corrupt regime, such as that of the Lotus or Architects. Strangely enough—given their fierce populist agenda—Masked Avengers are often aristocrats, members of the ruling elite, or independently wealthy individuals. You look back towards a golden age—possibly a mythical one—when everything was right in the world. With your fierce fists and barking automatic pistols, you aim to turn back the clock and return to an age of justice. Although your abilities are formidable, you do not expect to transform society all on your own. You want others to act as you do. Only when people stand up for themselves and take back their own streets will the criminals of the world truly quake in fear—they are a superstitious and cowardly lot. Your mission may not be entirely altruistic: The Masked Avenger's melodramatic hook usually involves sworn vengeance of some sort. Chances are there was some terrible event that pushed you over the edge from thinking about vigilantism to stalking the streets in funny clothes looking for villains to punish. Okay, so maybe you're a little crazy—but the really crazy ones are the bad guys who stand in your way.

Junctures: any

Attributes: Bod 5 [Max 10]
Chi 0 [Max 2]
Mnd 5 [Max 10]
Ref 5 [Max 10]

Add 6 points among your primary attributes. Add 2 points to one secondary attribute and 1 point to another secondary attribute. Maxes for primary attributes also apply to their secondary attributes.

Skills: Detective +10 (=15)
Guns +8 (=13)
Fix-It +2 (7) [Max 12]
Info/Science +2 (7)
Info/your choice +2 (7)
Info/your choice +2 (7)
Intimidation +3 (8) [Max 12]
Martial Arts +7 (=12)

Add 8 Skill Bonuses. Swap the Skill Bonuses and Action Values of Guns and Martial Arts if desired.

Schticks: 2 gun schticks

Weapons: 2 weapons of appropriate juncture

Unique Schtick: You are an expert on the criminal mind. Intimidation attempts on unnamed hoodlum characters get a +5 Action Value bonus.

Quick Schtick Pick:
Weapons: 69: sword, throwing stars; 1850: sword, pistol; Cntp,: twin Colt 1911s; 2056: Buro Beat Patroller, Buro Crimestopper
Gun Schticks: Carnival of Carnage, Signature Weapon

Wealth Level: rich

Illustration by Jeff Miracola

(33)

Maverick Cop

"Freeze, scumbag!"

The Maverick Cop is a plainclothes detective assigned to a major crime unit of a big city. You may work undercover, you may be in an anti-mob unit, or you may be a homicide detective. Good-looking but slovenly, you may have a drinking problem and definitely have a personal life in a state of serious disorder. Despite the fact that you are an authority figure yourself, you've always had a big problem with authority figures. You see yourself as a loner, but this may date back only as far as your last partner getting killed, which might relate to your melodramatic hook. You are always on the verge of being fired and are often on suspension. You keep your job only because your gruff superior officer has a secret soft spot for you, and because you get results. Although you always get the job done in the end, things always seem to conspire to make you look bad. People connected to your investigations have a bad habit of getting killed. Witnesses get snuffed. Bystanders fall like tenpins whenever you get into a gunfight. You may even have had a string of partners who have died in the line of duty. Most of all, you never seem to be able to just apprehend a crook. It's not like you deliberately set out to empty the contents of your high-caliber revolver into each and every scumbag you're supposed to arrest. They always force you to do it. You warn them even, tell them they shouldn't be feeling lucky, shouldn't ever get you riled. But they keep crossing you. And you keep bringing them down. Punks just never learn.

Juncture: 69, 1850, contemporary, 2056

Attributes: Bod 5
Chi 0
Mnd 5
Ref 5

Add 3 points to one primary attribute. Add 2 points to another primary attribute. Add 2 points to one secondary attribute.

Skills: Driving +10 (=15)
Guns +9 (=14)
Martial Arts +3 (8) [Max 10]
Police +2 (7)

Add 4 Skill Bonuses.

Schticks: 4 gun schticks

Weapons: 3 weapons of appropriate juncture

Quick Schtick Pick:
Gun Schticks: Carnival of Carnage
Fast Draw
Lightning Reload
Signature Weapon
Weapons: 69: sword, polearm, bow
1850: club, rifle, pistol
Cntp.: Desert Eagle .357, Magnum, Colt Detective Special, Remington 870
2056: Buro 9, Buro Godhammer, Buro Blade of Truth

Wealth Level: working stiff

Illustration by Jeff Miracola

Monster Hunter

"Sure, I worked for the Architects. It was better than a life as a vat worker, Consumer."

You are a former low-level operative of the Architects, one trained to go back in time through the Netherworld and capture Supernatural Creatures to be transformed into Abominations. This curious specialty requires both a general fighting ability and the ability to wield Arcanowave weapons technology. When you signed up for duty in a SERU, or Supernatural Entity Retrieval Unit, you didn't really know what you were getting into. You probably came from a modest working-class background, one of the billions of gray and downtrodden citizens under the tight control of the Buro. Without people to pull strings for you, you knew from a young age that the only way to get ahead was to be smart and determined. You excelled in school, and passed the tough exams to qualify for elite police work. You didn't want to be one of the hated PubOrd officers, though, and thought you'd lucked out when you were posted to a SERU. You didn't know much about SERU duties—ordinary folks aren't supposed to know stuff like that—but you knew it was dangerous and comparatively well paid. In other words, glamor city. Well, the glamor began to wear off when you encountered the disturbing weirdness of the Netherworld. It got even thinner when you found yourself face to face with gnarled attuners, brain eaters, and other horrific demons. You were trained to be fearless and unflappable in the face of weird danger, and maybe you were. But you saw a lot of your fellow SERU members chewed up by monsters they weren't prepared to handle, mostly due to the incompetent and impossible orders you were issued by out-of-touch superiors. Then you started to realize that—even though the things you were fighting were demons—what they were being turned into was something even worse. Although most SERU officers remained loyal (if cynical) servants of the Buro, your exposure to other junctures and the nature of the secret war changed your perspective. You began to realize that the bleak world you grew up in was not the only possible world. If you could use what the Buro taught you against them, you could change the course of history. Then you'd have a shot at taking out the real monsters.

Juncture: 2056

Attributes: Bod 5
Chi 5
Mnd 5
Ref 5

Divide 5 points among your primary attributes.

Skills: Arcanowave Device +10 (=15)
Guns +7 (=12)
Info/Ancient China +4 (9)
Martial Arts +4 (9) [Max 10]

Add 4 Skill Bonuses.

Schticks: 1 gun schtick, 2 Arcanowave Devices

Weapons: 1 gun

Quick Schtick Pick:
Weapon: Buro 9A pistol
Gun Schtick: Eagle Eye
Arcanowave Devices: Agony Grenade, Helix Rethreader

Wealth Level: poor

Illustration by Jeff Miracola

Ninja

"If I wished to kill you, you would be dead already. You would not have seen me coming."

If you hail from the 1850 juncture, you may be an actual member of the legendary Japanese secret society of assassins. But in *Feng Shui,* the term "Ninja" is also used generically to describe any operative who specializes in stealth and penetration missions. Although capable of holding your own during a fight, you prefer deception and surprise over the frontal assault. Ninjas maintain a mystique around themselves, often pretending to have secret mystical powers. Although the Ninja does have a passing acquaintance with exotic chi abilities, the mystery surrounding you is mostly due to your own wit and presence. It is not fame that you crave so much as cultivating that mystique. You wish your deeds to be famous, but your identity a secret. You want to be feared. You want to be whispered about. Nothing amuses you more than to stand among people who have no clue just how quick and deadly you are. You are also in love with the idea of the perfect intrusion. The less of a trace of yourself you can leave behind after an operation, the better you feel. Your sense of pride in your work is the thing that keeps you going. But lately, you have begun to feel a sense of emptiness. Maybe you have suffered a loss in love, or some other personal blow that has made you feel less invincible than usual. Perhaps you've begun to question your amoral existence. When you discover the secret war, you are pulled in either by your melodramatic hook, or by the awakening of a desire to do something—to leave a mark on the world, even if no one will ever know your name.

Juncture: any

Attributes: Bod 5
Chi 0 (Fu =7)
Mnd 5
Ref 5

Add 3 to one primary attribute. Add 1 each to two other primary attributes. Add 1 to one secondary attribute.

Skills: Deceit +4 (9) [Max 12]
Guns +2 (7) [Max 11]
Info/your choice +2 (7)
Intrusion +9 (=14)
Fix-It +3 (8) [Max 12]
Martial Arts +9 (=14)

Add 6 Skill Bonuses.

Schticks: 1 fu schtick

Weapons: 6 weapons of appropriate juncture

Quick Schtick Pick:
Fu Schtick: Friend of Darkness
Weapons:
69: sword, staff, throwing stars, dagger
1850: sling, bow
Cntp.: Glock 17, Uzi
2056: Buro 9A, Buro Blade of Truth

Wealth Level: working stiff

Illustration by Jeff Miracola

Old Master

"You think I am old and feeble, do you? Well, face my Flying Windmill Kick, asshole!"

You are an elderly expert who long ago conquered the most difficult principles of martial arts and chi powers. You have spent many long years tutoring others in the secrets of your art, and are used to being treated with utmost respect. You can therefore be a bit of a hothead when challenged by others who do not know enough to bow before your superior experience. You are a harsh disciplinarian; no matter what juncture you hail from, you grumpily pine for the good old days when proper respect was paid to elders and the heavens were in harmony with the Earth. Although you no longer possess the physical strength and endurance you had as a young student, your skill and Fu powers still make you a formidable opponent. You want to retire from active participation in the world of martial arts, leaving the field to the young men and women you have trained to follow in your footsteps. When you were young, you cared about proving your martial arts supremacy to all challengers. In your old age, you recognize that impulse as foolish pride. Now you want to rest, and to study the arts and ancient poems. But the tide of evil in the world seems to be growing again. Perhaps your students have been slaughtered by villains. Perhaps your juncture is ruled by unjust leaders who must have wisdom bludgeoned into them. At any rate, there will always be young heroes in need of your leadership. You cannot rest now, not when so much is at stake. You must show them how to become masters themselves, as your masters taught you. Your skill and experience give you an immense responsibility to the world, one you mean to fulfill. Such is the lot of the superior man.

Juncture: any

Attributes: Bod =4
Chi =10 (For =0)
Mnd 5
Ref 5

Divide 4 points among your primary attributes.

Skills: Info/Calligraphy +5 (10)
Info/Chinese Painting +4 (9)
Info/Chinese Poetry +4 (9)
Info/Eastern Philosophy +7 (12)
Info/Noodle Making +5 (10)
Leadership +2 (7)
Martial Arts +11 (=16)

Schticks: 5 fu schticks

Unique Schtick: You are an expert in perceiving chi flow through people's bodies, and can use that knowledge to strike at your opponent's most vulnerable spot in combat. Base damage with a punch or kick is Strength +6.

Quick Schtick Pick: Abundant Leap
King on the Water
Prodigious Leap
Willow Step
Walk of a Thousand Steps

Wealth Level: poor

Private Investigator

"All my life, I've been waiting for someone dressed like you to waltz into this office and give me a spiel like that. Not that I believe it for a second, but it's still cool to see your daydreams realized."

You are an experienced investigator with contacts throughout society: from well-heeled clients who can afford to hire you, to the enforcers of the law you must occasionally skirt, to the seediest elements of the underworld. You most often work for lawyers, digging up information for use in court cases. When one corporation sues another one, you find yourself poring over corporate ledgers and sifting for obscure references in old business publications. You've worked for insurance companies, keeping plaintiffs under surveillance to see if they're as injured as they claim to be. And then of course there are divorce cases: You've seen more marriages unravel than the most dedicated of soap opera fans. Sometimes you are hired by the defense in criminal cases to look for other possible suspects and otherwise find evidence that pokes holes in the prosecution's pet theories. Although you may have gotten into your line of work because you fell in love with the film noir world of Philip Marlowe and Sam Spade, you've spent more time hunched over a microfiche machine in a library than you have slugging it out with gangsters and crooked cops. Maybe that's why, when you sniff out the first clues that point you to the existence of the secret war, you're ready to chuck the real-life world of the private detective in favor of the fantastic adventure you've always dreamed of.

Juncture: any

Attributes: Bod 5
Chi 0 (For 2)
Mnd 5
Ref 5

Add 3 to one primary attribute. Add 2 to a different primary attribute. Add 1 to a third primary attribute. Add 2 to one secondary attribute.

Skills: Detective +10 (=15)
Guns +5 (10) [Max 13]
Info/Business +3 (8)
Info/Civil Law +3 (8)
Martial Arts +3 (8) [Max 13]
Intrusion +3 (8) [Max 11]

Add 8 Skill Bonuses.

Weapons: 1 weapon of appropriate juncture

Unique Schtick: You are an expert at applying logic to real-world situations. When you and the other PCs are speculating as to the best course of action, or as to the motivations of a given character, you can spend a Fortune point to have the GM tell straight out you whether your speculation is correct or incorrect.

Quick Schtick Pick:
69: staff
1850: cap and ball pistol
Cntp.: Walther P-5 compact
2056: Buro 9A

Wealth Level: working stiff

Illustration by Brian Snoddy

Scrappy Kid

"Hey, when do we get to stop the evil scientists from taking over the world? Huh, huh? When do we? Can I play with that gun? Ah, c'mon, I won't wreck it or nothin'. That sword is really cool. Can we stop the evil scientists now, can we, can we, huh, huh? Are we there yet?"

Life is simple. You're a kid. You like to have fun. But there are these bad guys who want to wreck everybody's fun. They think they're better than everyone else. They want to be the boss of you. So even though those boring old grown-ups want to keep you safely tucked away somewhere boring, you're gonna do something about it. After all, why should they get all the fun of shooting guns off and watching explosions and meeting cool monsters and all that stuff? Sure, you're not exactly a killing machine, like you plan to be when you grow up. But you're not bad for someone whose age isn't in the double digits yet. You're the best kung fu kid in your class, and you've learned some tricks you weren't supposed to learn yet. And you're fast, you know how to duck, and bad guys underestimate you. Secret war—hey, what could be cooler?

A Note: You don't have to play the Scrappy Kid as comic relief. (And shouldn't, if your GM and the rest of the group want to maintain a consistently dark and gritty tone in your *Feng Shui* series.) Maybe you're a grim little warrior, forced by tragedy to fight back in a grownup world. Just because you haven't hit puberty yet doesn't mean that you don't have a threatening squint worthy of Clint Eastwood.

Juncture: any

Attributes: Bod =4
Chi =7
Mnd 6
Ref 8

Add 2 to one primary attribute, 1 to another.

Skills: Deceit +2 (8)
Info/Comic Books +5 (11)*
Info/Computers +4 (10)*
Info/Skateboards +4 (10)*
Info/Pop Music +3 (9)*
Info/[your choice] +2 (8)
Martial Arts +5 (=13) or Sorcery +6 (=13)
Intrusion +2 (=10)

Only Scrappy Kids from 69 AD can take Sorcery. They lose the Info skills with asterisks. Swap Info skill specialties with other kid-like pursuits of the appropriate juncture, if desired.

Schticks: 2 sorcery schticks or 2 fu schticks

Unique Schticks: 1) You can decide to attack to distract an opponent—rather than injure him—by throwing things at him, pulling his shirt over his head, squirting him with whipped cream, and so on. Your opponent suffers 3 points of Impairment (see p. 135) for a number of shots equal to your Outcome. This Impairment can't be increased by further distraction attacks. 2) You may not do much damage, but you're hard to hit. Your Dodge Action Value is always 2 more than your Martial Arts or Sorcery Action Value.

Quick Schtick Pick:
Sorcery: Blast, Influence
or, *Fu Schticks:* Fox's Retreat, Eyes of the Fox

Wealth Level: poor

Illustration by Jeff Miracola

Sorcerer

"You do not want to taste the wrath of the Abysmal Fountain, poltroon! So step aside!"

You are a master of the occult arts, capable of focusing and directing chi forces so that it powers your dread incantations. You can melt sabers by uttering a few words of power, set enemies aflame, and reduce speeding vehicles to so much primordial goop. Although there are many ways to do harm to an opponent, none has quite the awe-inspiring effect of a lightning bolt cast from a magician's hand. You have some trouble activating your great powers in later junctures, such as our own and 1850, where the chi flow has been suppressed. But in other junctures, your power is terrifyingly great. However, in most places the sorcerer is synonymous with cruelty and sinister doings. You wish that it were otherwise, but the sad fact is that most who follow the ways of the occult end up doing great harm to the people. They have been corrupted by exposure to the Underworld, the home of demons and evil spirits. Or perhaps they have been seduced by their own lust for power. Given the bad reputation of sorcerers, you have learned to keep your mystic abilities hidden. You feel a special responsibility to prevent your corrupted brethren from having their foul way with the world. Your natural enemies are the Ascended, who wish to suppress magic throughout the time stream, and the Architects, who wish to twist it and make it a servant of their technology. You may be involved in the secret war in order to fight these foes, or to pursue your own melodramatic hook.

Juncture: 69

Attributes: Bod 5
Chi 0 (Mag =8)
Mnd 5
Ref 5

Add 2 points each to three different primary attributes. Add 2 points to one secondary attribute.

Skills: Info/History +4 (9)
Info/[your choice] +4 (9)
Info/[your choice] +2 (7)
Sorcery +7 (=15)

Schticks: 5 sorcery schticks

Quick Schtick Pick: Blast
Divination
Fertility
Heal
Movement

Wealth Level: rich

Illustration by Jeff Miracola

Spy

"They never tell you this in training school, but really the best thing to do in a situation like this is get yourself captured so you can figure out what the enemy is up to."

You used to work for an intelligence agency—but not anymore. There are any number of reasons why you might have left the agency. Maybe you were squeezed out by the machinations of new superiors. (This would make a great melodramatic hook.) Maybe you left under a cloud, after making a tragic mistake that led to the deaths of those under you. Or maybe you just got bored with the cloak-and-dagger world after the end of the Cold War. At any rate, now you're looking for a new way to get the blood pumping, to bring back the excitement of the chase and put your years of training in shadow operations to good use. Maybe you're now a security consultant, or even an industrial spy. But what you're really looking for is a good fight to fight again. When you stumble across the secret war, you realize that you've found a motherlode of mysteries to plumb and dangers to defy. It's time to press your tuxedo, polish up your ballroom dancing skills, and strap on your Walther PPK.

(Although the above assumes modern times, there have been spies for as long as there have been rival governments. In 69, you might have worked in the court of a general or even as an operative for the Emperor, before the corrupt eunuchs took over. In 1850, you could be a world traveler and former agent of China or one of the world powers currently putting the squeeze on it. If you hail from 2056, you used to spy on the activities of private citizens; you probably got sick of serving the Buro and would like to make amends for your past.)

Juncture: any

Attributes: Bod 5
Chi 0 (For =6)
Mnd 5
Ref 5

Add a total of 8 points to primary attributes, adding no more than 3 points to any one attribute.

Skills: Deceit +10 (=15)
Fix-It +2 (7) [Max 13]
Guns +5 (10) [Max 13]
Info/Fashion +6 (11)
Info/Food and Drink +6 (11)
Info/Politics +4 (9)
Intrusion +4 (9) [Max 12]
Martial Arts +5 (10) [Max 13]
Seduction +5 (10) [Max 13]

Add 4 Skill Bonuses.

Schticks: 1 gun schtick

Weapons: 1 weapon of appropriate juncture

Unique Schtick: People can't resist telling you things. You may spend a Fortune point to get a reluctant or hostile GMC to tell you something they shouldn't. Best used when you're captured, to induce gloating in villains.

Quick Schtick Pick:
Weapons: 69: sling; 1850: pistol;
Cntp.: Walther PPK; 2056: Buro 9A
Gun Schtick: Fast Draw

Wealth Level: rich

Illustration by Jeff Miracola

Supernatural Creature

"Arrrhhhhh!"

You are a being from the Underworld, a mystic realm haunted by demons and the spirits of the dead. You are yourself a being that humans would describe as a monster or evil spirit. But you are not evil, for even the spawn of the Underworld are capable of exercising free will and doing right instead of wrong. You realize, however, that almost none of your kindred bother to make this effort. They live to terrorize and to inflict pain. You did, too, until you were summoned and dominated by the cruel eunuch sorcerers of the Eaters of the Lotus. At first, you followed their orders—you had no choice, shackled by mystic bonds. But eventually you were able, through intense mental effort, to break free of their influence. You saw around you people who lived in fear, people whose lives were seen as mere playthings by your Lotus masters. And although most demons would never even think such thoughts, you decided that you would atone for the wrongs you had done, and destroy those who had forced you to do them. Or maybe you just want to find a permanent escape from your former tormentors. Supernatural Creatures vary widely in appearance, but all are horrific. Some appear as decomposed human corpses, others as grotesque ogres. Others bear no resemblance to the humanoid form. Although you may now fight for the forces of good, your alarming features prevent you from ever passing as a normal member of society. Perhaps this is your greatest dream. You hide in isolation, or maybe walk among men using the power of transformation to resemble them. If so, your greatest fear is that you will one day be unable to hold back the bestial instincts that still swirl mightily in your soul—that you will in some furious manner or another reveal the monster that lurks within you.

Juncture: 69

Attributes: Bod 5
Chi 0 (Mag =8)
Mnd 3
Ref 5

Add 5 to any one primary attribute. Add 3 to another primary attribute. Add 1 to a third primary attribute.

Skills: Creature Powers +7 (=15)
Martial Arts +4 (9) [Max 12]

Add 3 Skill Bonuses. The GM should reject any skills that don't make sense for a Supernatural Creature.

Schticks: 5 Creature Powers

Quick Schtick Pick:
 Blast
 Damage Immunity (unarmed attacks)
 Flight
 Foul Spew (Glutinous Goo)
 Transformation

Limitation: You can't be healed by doctors (characters using the Medicine skill), except by those trained in 69 AD.

Wealth Level: poor

Illustration by Jeff Miracola

Techie

"Fortunately, I whipped up a little something in my workshop this morning in preparation for this eventuality..."

You're an inventor type whose primary weapon is your specially-designed gear. Sure, you know guns inside and out—you've been assembling and disassembling them since you were a toddler—but that's just the beginning of your talents. Whether it's surveillance or espionage gear, ingeniously-disguised weapons, or more exotic equipment rigged up for a special occasion, you have a beeping, whirring or pinging device for any occasion. You are always covered in grease. Your idea of a thrilling evening is to sit in a chair, eat junk food, and memorize a technical manual. The last time you fell in love, it was with a classic car. This whole business of the secret war seems awfully confusing to you. You've never understood why tyrants struggle for power; the evening news has always gone right over your head. As far as you're concerned, why everybody doesn't just want to sit in their workshops and make stuff is life's biggest mystery. But you know that the first thing bad guys want to control in any situation is technology. You know how to make stuff, and to the power groups of the secret war that makes you dangerous. If you don't want to be captured and locked up in a lab for the rest of your life making weapons and other boring items, you're going to have to get up off your overall-wearing butt and do something to make the world a safer place. Maybe after you're done that, you can finally get back to perfecting that phase capacitor you've been tinkering with for years.

Juncture: contemporary, 2056

Attributes: Bod 5
 Chi 0 (For 1)
 Mnd 5
 Ref 5

Add 3 to one primary attribute, 2 to another, and 1 to a third primary attribute.

Skills: Driving +10 (=15)
 Fix-It +10 (=15)
 Guns +6 (11) [Max 13]
 Info/Science +4 (9)

Add 3 Skill Bonuses.

Weapons: 1 gun of appropriate juncture

Unique Schtick: You always happen to have the right item on hand. When you want to pull any tool or gadget item out of your handy toolkit, spend a Fortune point and—bingo—you got it!

Quick Schtick Pick:
 Cntp.: Rossi Model 851
 2056: Buro Beat Patroller

Wealth Level: working stiff

Illustration by Jeff Miracola

Thief

"You know, I was thinking of myself as retired. But then the head of that museum came on TV and said that their defenses were foolproof, that no one could get to the Guildenstern Diamond. And then I got all tempted."

You are a master thief. Although you make your living taking things from their legal owners, you don't do so primarily for the money. Sure, you live in luxury from the proceeds of your past misdeeds. But it's the challenge that keeps your senses keen and your ambitions sharp. As long as there have been valuables, there have been security experts who have claimed to be able to keep thieves away from them. You have made a career out of proving them wrong. You operate through careful research, by assembling every available scrap of information about your target. When you go in, you have every angle planned out to the millisecond. You also plan for something to go wrong. That's when the adrenaline kicks in, when you have to think fast and get it right the first time. When the alarms are screaming and the footfalls of heavily-armed guards are rushing your way, when the distance to your getaway vehicle seems to be impossible to cross in the moments you have left to you—that's the moment you live for. The money is just gravy. Still, there's a thought nagging at the back of your skull that maybe all of this thrill-seeking is just a little bit meaningless—maybe even adolescent. After all, you already have more dough than you'll ever need. And maybe it was a bad thing to blow away all of those guards; after all, they were just working stiffs doing their jobs. Maybe "they shouldn't have got in my way" isn't just a great excuse after all. You don't feel bad about the pretty objects you've taken from rich guys, but that trail of blood is starting to haunt you at night. Lately you've been thinking about leaving a positive mark on the world. Robbing from the rich and giving to the poor, or something like that. Is there a way to use your skills for the greater good, you wonder?

Juncture: any

Attributes: Bod 5
Chi 0 (For 3)
Mnd 5
Ref 5

Add 3 points to one primary attribute, 2 points to a second, and 1 point to a third. Add 2 points to one secondary attribute.

Skills: Deceit +4 (9) [Max 13]
Detective +2 (7) [Max 13
Guns +6 (11) [Max 13]
Info/Arts and Antiques +6 (11)
Info/Gems and Jewels +6 (11)
Intrusion +11 (=16)
Martial Arts +5 (10) [Max 12]

Add 8 Skill Bonuses.

Weapons: 1 weapon of appropriate juncture

Quick Schtick Pick:
69: bow
1850: rifle
Cntp.: Bernadelli combat shotgun
2056: Buro Blue Flag

Wealth Level: rich

Illustration by Brian Snoddy

Transformed Animal

"Humanity is not a matter of lineage. It is a matter of soul."

In the 69 AD juncture, transformed animals are beings who have assumed human form through years of meditation and spiritual practice. Once they were intelligent snakes, foxes, tortoises, spiders or other creatures. But they have defied natural law to become human in all outward aspects. They have taken a short cut on the ladder of reincarnation because they envy the life of humans. You are one of these beings. You live in constant apprehension of attacks by sorcerers, some of whom seek to restore the natural order by casting transformed animals back into their original forms. This is terrifying to you because, once changed back to your original animal form, you will not be able to become human again. You are not like a werewolf or other creature that can change back and forth between human and animal forms at will. (Use the supernatural creature archetype if you want to play a werecreature.) You want only to live in peace among humans, but have somehow been drawn into the secret war. Maybe you're protecting the humans you love from harm. Perhaps you're simply trying to protect yourself from exposure.

In the 1850 or contemporary junctures, a transformed animal is actually the descendant of one of the above beings. You were born in human form, as were generations upon generations of your ancestors. But you are still vulnerable to the effects of magic; exposure to it can permanently revert you into the form of your ancestor animal. Most transformed animals are members of the Ascended. You, however, are either unaware of your true heritage or have turned your back on Ascended membership for some reason. It is likely that the Ascended know of your existence. You think that you've managed to cover your trail, and that they don't know your current identity. But you know that they have eyes and ears everywhere, and you find yourself looking over your shoulder, wondering whether that person behind you is a spy for the Lodge.

Reclusive by nature, only atypical transformed animals are sufficiently interested in matters of power or politics to become involved with the secret war for its own sake. But you are an emotional entity, easily drawn into conflict through ties of love, family, or sacred vow. In other words, if you take this kind of character then make sure your melodramatic hook gives you a good reason to get involved in the action.

Juncture: 69, 1850, contemporary

Attributes: Bod 5
Chi 7 (For 2)
Mnd 5
Ref 5

Attributes are changed depending on which transformed animal package you choose. See Chapter 8: Transformed Animals on p. 108.

Skills: Guns +2 (7) [Max 13]
Info/History +3 (8)
Info/your choice +3 (8)
Martial Arts +6 (11) [Max 13]

Add 8 Skill Bonuses.

Schticks: 5 schticks in 1 transformed animal package

Quick Schtick Pick: spider

Special Limitation: Cannot learn Sorcery; if returned to animal form through exposure to magic, your character is retired from the game. Transformed Animals from 69 are somewhat better at resisting reversion than those from other junctures.

Wealth Level: working stiff

Illustration by Jeff Miracola

Chapter 3

April 11

I was surprised to find myself begging to live. In my mind, I'd imagined myself getting whacked lots of times, always going down in slow motion, with a grim smile on my face, the sun glinting off my sunglasses and my clothes looking fine. Maybe the problem was that I wasn't going to go down in a fight. I was being dragged out back of a factory loading dock to get executed like some cheap mobster. Two guys in paramilitary gear. I was well and truly hog-tied. One of them had a steel grip on each of my arms, and my legs were shackled.

I was arguing with them, cajoling, bantering, anything to try to even get a response out of them. Looking back on it I want to pretend to myself that I was just looking for an opening, a distraction, an angle, anything. But the truth of it was that I was pleading for my life like a whining idiot. I was giving the same loser speech I'd heard a dozen times on the other side of the trigger, back before I started trying to give a damn about things. As they shoved me down to the pavement behind a bunch of oil drums, I wondered whether I'd done enough to save my soul. I had a feeling the answer was gonna be "not yet, sucker." The paramilitaries stepped back in unison. The crunch of their boot soles on the pavement sounded loud, as loud as the gates of Hell clanging open to welcome me. The pumping of their shotguns sounded even louder.

The next sound was, surprisingly, not the sound of my skull being blown to mush. It was the satisfying thud of flesh hitting flesh. I rolled over to see a guy moving like a whirlwind, subjecting one of the paramilitaries to an eye-twisting barrage of blows. Where he'd come from, I had no clue. Still don't. The other paramilitary was down already, and it didn't take long for his buddy to join them. My savior was young, with a wide-open face still swaddled in baby fat. He was barefoot, wearing a linen peasant outfit. My relief went south when he pulled out the hugest sword I've ever seen and hefted it over his head, ready for a ferocious downward stroke. I am proud to say that my drawers remained unsullied as he used this monstrous hunk of metal to break the chain between my leg shackles.

"I owe you one, pal," I said. "The Prof send you?"

"You do owe me a debt, assassin." His voice was a lot older than his face. "And no, I do not serve your master. It serves the purposes of my teachers that you should live to fulfill a destiny."

"Uh, sure, friend, whatever you say." I held out my hand so he could help pull me to my feet. He didn't take it. Just stood there staring at me like I was a plate full of rotting meat.

"I am not your friend. I abhor everything you stand for. It is you and your kind who are driving this world to disaster. You are blind and foolish—beyond teaching. One day, we shall see to it that you are never born. Your erasure from history shall be a great victory for the world. The fact that you serve a temporary purpose does not alter my contempt for you."

Then he took my hand and pulled me to my feet—and reached into a small knapsack, drawing out a brand new, shiny MAC-10. He held it like it was a snake about to twist back and bite him, and then tossed it to me. Snake or not, I was glad to see it.

"I believe this is your preferred instrument of destruction. You will find it fully loaded."

He turned his head, pointing out the platoon's worth of paramilitaries running in our direction. I took the new hardware for a test drive, scattering them across the parking lot. They had a fair distance to run to the nearest cover, and they went down like bowling pins. I parked myself behind the oil drums, looking for the nearest avenue of escape. The water looked like the best bet, and sure enough, there was a grimy motorboat less than a hundred meters behind me. I could easily get to it while holding off these mooks. And I could just tell that it had the keys waiting for me in the ignition. See, my luck had turned around, and when my luck turns, it turns big time.

CHAPTER 3

Skills

THE TOOLS OF THE TRADE

This section details the various skills available to *Feng Shui* characters. Skills are learned abilities that characters have acquired through study and practice. All skills have an Action Value. This number is the sum of the Secondary Attribute that the skill is based on plus the Skill Bonus value representing the degree of training that the character has devoted to it. To resolve the use of a skill, make a task check using that Action Value and an appropriate Difficulty as determined by the GM. The most common skill attempts have standard Difficulties applied to them.

INTERPRETING SKILLS

Feng Shui plots are meant to move quickly. Its stories feature extremely competent lead characters who should never spend more than a scene or two dithering about in a state of confusion or uncertainty. One of the primary tools that PCs have to move the story forward is their list of skills. They can use skills to figure out where to go next and whose butts to kick. Searching for clues and solving puzzles are only minor elements of an enjoyable action-adventure yarn. Mystery can be fun but extended confusion and frustration is not.

GMs should therefore interpret skills as broadly as possible. The skill descriptions below are meant as basic lists of abilities associated with a skill; they are not exclusive! As long as the application of a given skill to a particular situation doesn't completely defy credibility, allow it. When the PCs seem to be stretching the definitions of their skills, it's better to jack up the Difficulty for an attempt than to rule it out altogether. The forward momentum of a plot should never depend on a single task check being successful. If the GM depends on a PC's skill use to get the story to the next scene, she should allow the attempt to succeed automatically. However, it is important when doing so to still require the player to make the check; dice rolling is not only an excellent source of suspense in roleplaying games, but will serve to mask the importance of the skill check to your storyline.

SKILL COMPONENTS

Many skills confer a number of capabilities in a single package. These can include:

Physical Ability

This refers to the ability to actively do something, like fire a gun or hit an opponent in combat. The skill description describes what this action is, when applicable, and what the standard Difficulty for such attempts is, if any. This is the standard manner of using many skills, and therefore is not referred to by any special term.

Knowledge

The character also knows a lot of background information related to the physical ability. A character familiar with Guns also knows a great deal of technical information about them. A martial artist is familiar with the history of martial arts in general and of his own school in particular. The skill description gives parameters of the character's knowledge, if applicable. Using a skill in this manner is referred to as making a **knowledge check**.

Difficulties for attempts to use the knowledge associated with the skill should be determined by the GM, based on the obscurity of the knowledge. Basic information which anyone remotely familiar with the skill would know should be granted automatically. Information of an intermediate grade has a Difficulty of 5. Information known only to advanced students would have a Difficulty of 10, while exceedingly obscure information known only to a few top practitioners in the field would have a Difficulty of 15. (GMs are not bound to multiples of 5 when deciding upon the Difficulties of knowledge attempts. These are just examples.) If the character's Action Result exceeds the Difficulty, the character happens to know the fact in question; the GM gives the player the desired information.

Example: Lao Baixing is an Everyday Hero from the boondocks of modern China. He knows real Martial Arts, though. Embroiled in an argument with one of his buddies, he finds himself needing to know the name of the ancient hero who pioneered the use of the fu power Claw of the Tiger. Lao's player, Lisa, tells her GM that she's making a knowledge roll against her Martial Arts skill, which has an Action Value of 13. The GM rules that the fact in question is known to any advanced student of the field, and therefore has a Difficulty of 10. Lisa rolls a 0, for an Action Result of 13, a success.

The GM says to Lisa: "Of course, Lao Baixing knows very well that the originator of the Claw of the Tiger was the great Chen Feng, also known as Green Monk Number One."

If the check had failed, the GM would say something like: "Unfortunately, you have no idea who the originator of the Claw of the Tiger was."

When characters get a particularly high Outcome, GMs may choose to provide additional information on the general topic. This is of course assuming that they have extra information in their notes or are prepared to make something up on the spot.

Contacts

Characters trained in a particular area know others who move in the same world, and know how to get in touch with them. This does not necessarily mean that these GMCs will be positively disposed towards them or automatically prepared to offer aid of whatever sort. Using a skill in this manner is known as a **contacts check**.

When a PC wishes to bring a new contact into the storyline, his player makes a task check with the relevant skill. The Difficulty of such attempts is determined by the GM. Although the GM may wish to include other factors, the two most important things to consider are the current **location** of the PC, and the **degree of specialization** of the desired contact.

If the PC is in a place which is crawling with contacts of the desired type, there is a -5 Difficulty modifier. If the PC is in a place with a normal distribution of contacts of the desired sort, the Difficulty modifier is 5. If the PC is in a place where such individuals are rare, the Difficulty modifier is 10. The GM can rule that you just can't find contacts of a given type in certain locations: for example, she may have decided that in her series, there are no Magic Cops in the Netherworld. Note that in some cases international communications make location modifiers irrelevant: if you can phone a university in Switzerland or cruise the Internet to find the contact you need, you can ignore those constraints.

Example: If Lao were looking for other martial artists, the Difficulty of the Martial Arts check would in part refer to his location. If he were looking for martial artists at a martial arts tournament, the Difficulty would be -5. If he were looking in a big city in Asia, the Difficulty would be 5. If he were looking in a small town in Kentucky, the Difficulty would be 10.

The degree of specialization refers to what sort of contact the player wants the character to have. If just any other practitioner of the same skill will do, the Difficulty modifier is 0. If you want someone with a certain subskill or set of credentials, the Difficulty modifier is 5. If that person is particularly prominent, or the desired credentials or subskills are rare, the Difficulty modifier is 10. Extremely rare types carry a modifier of 15. If you want a particular person, the Difficulty modifier is also 10; it is 15 in the case of particularly prominent or reclusive individuals.

In either case, before making a contacts task check, the player must come up with a likely reason for her character to know the desired person, or a person of the desired sort. If the GM doesn't buy the reason, the check is not even made.

Example: Lao Baixing's sturdy band of heroes has discovered evidence of Lotus activity deep within modern China. They need to find a sympathetic high official in the Communist party so that he can bring in the army and clean out a nest of Gnarled Horrors. Lao Baixing is from this neck of the woods, so his player, Lisa, decides to make a contact check against his Martial Arts skill to see if he happens to know a Communist party

Skills

Illustration by Heather Hudson

official who is also an aficionado of the martial arts. The GM buys her explanation of why this might be credible and allows her to make the check. He rules that China is crawling with Communist party officials (-5 modifier) but that an official who is both highly influential and a martial arts fan is going to be extremely rare, for a modifier of 15. That makes the total Difficulty 10. Lao makes a check against Martial Arts, for an Action Result of 12.

The GM says: "You just happen to know an aide to Colonel Chen, commander of the local army regiment; the aide is a student of the martial arts who you've competed against at competitions."

Note that, as in this example, the contact you actually know may simply be able to provide an introduction to the one you really want.

SUBSKILLS

A broadly defined skill doesn't always make sense in every situation. Some skills have subskills listed in their skill descriptions when basic plausibility demands it. For example, we've collapsed all hand-to-hand fighting into the Martial Arts skill for reasons of simplicity. But that doesn't mean that everyone who can throw a punch is a student of a formalized fighting school; that's why we describe a Brawling subskill in the skill description for Martial Arts. In this case, a subskill reflects a narrowed range of abilities.

Subskills can also reflect a greater degree of ability in a specialized area. For example, only highly-skilled practitioners of Medicine can use the Surgery subskill. These additional abilities may require a higher skill bonus.

Not every skill has a subskill; we've only used them where absolutely necessary.

Subskills have the same skill bonus as the main skill, and are not improved or worsened independently. They just refine what you can or cannot do with your skill during play.

SKILLS AND ATTRIBUTES

After the name of each skill, we list a Base Attribute that the skill is based on. Use this not just for figuring the Action Value for standard task checks, but for knowledge and contact checks as well. If you wanted to be really picky, you could argue that these ought to be figured based on Intelligence and Charisma instead, but we don't want to be picky, do we?

SKILLS AND JUNCTURE

Most of the skill descriptions below assume a character from the contemporary juncture. If we were to list all of the picky little distinctions for the three other junctures, this section would begin to rival War and Peace in the length sweepstakes.

GMs should apply common sense in deciding whether a particular type of contact or body of knowledge makes sense for a character from a given juncture. For example, a character with the Sabotage skill who hails from the 69 juncture is not going to know anything about modern demolition techniques or have a network of shady arms dealers in his nonexistent Rolodex. When attempting to use benefits of a skill that seem questionable due to the character's background, players should suggest believable equivalents that do reflect the PC's juncture of origin.

SKILLS NOT COVERED

We haven't bothered to come up with a list of every ability and occupation known to human history. Instead, we present the central skills that *Feng Shui* characters will be using most often in the course of play. These are either skills of general use, or skills that certain types should be using often in order to play the roles assigned to them by generations of action-adventure movies.

If you want your character to have a skill not listed here, by all means make it up. Consult with your GM to find out which Secondary Attribute the skill is based on. Explain to your GM what you think the skill covers; if she agrees, you're all set. If she thinks your skill is too broad or is a way to circumvent existing rules, she'll send you back to the drawing broad.

Example: Edmund wants his Karate Cop character to have the skill "Psychoanalysis," which is not explicitly described in this section. He looks at the other skills that are listed, and tries to come up with a description that best matches them. He decides that it is a Perception-based skill. He defines it as the ability to diagnose and treat mental illness through interviews with patients. Like most skills, it should include a range of contacts: someone with Psychoanalysis should logically know other psychoanalysts and possibly some patients. Edmund reads his description out to his GM, who approves it.

However, Roger wants to create a skill for his character called "Crushing Ninja Kick." He defines this as a mystic ability for ninjas only, based on Willpower, and doing twice the normal value of a standard Martial

Arts attack. His GM correctly identifies this as an attempt to hose the normal combat and fu power rules, and does not allow him to give this skill to his PC.

INCREASING SKILL BONUSES

During the course of play, your character gains experience points which you can use to improve your character. You can increase a bonus in a skill you already know by spending experience points equal to the new Action Value you will have once you have learned the skill. Nothing is required of the character in the game world; he just gets better without making a big deal of it. You can only raise a skill by 1 bonus at a time.

Example: Johnny Tso's player wants to increase his Guns skill bonus. He currently has a rating of 8 in the base attribute of the skill, Manual Dexterity, and a Guns skill bonus of +6. His Guns Action Value is therefore 14. Johnny's player spends 15 experience points, immediately increasing the Guns skill bonus to +7, for a new Guns Action Value of 15.

LEARNING NEW SKILLS

Characters can learn new skills in the course of play by spending (8 + x) experience points; x = your rating in the base attribute of the skill. They can then use the skill with no bonus; the skill check is equal to their rating in the skill's base attribute. The character must then undergo a **training montage**; you describe to the GM and other players a series of short clips from the character's learning process that collapses several weeks or months into a few sentences. (Think of the "wax on, wax off" sequence from *The Karate Kid.*) Your character must have the free time to learn a new skill. If other characters want to do other things, or if you are attacked by enemies in the course of the training montage, you can't learn the skill. This means that your character will have to clear the decks, as it were, and take care of any potential enemies before taking time off to train. Note that action heroes rarely have large blocks of free time for the learning of new skills; you'll be lucky to get more than two training montages in your character's career.

GMs should impose logical restraints on new skill acquisition; they should decide whether a skill can be learned through a few weeks of

Quick Skill List

Agility
Intrusion (pg. 56)
Martial Arts (pg. 57)

Charisma
Deceit (pg. 53)
Intimidation (pg. 56)
Leadership (pg. 57)
Seduction (pg. 59)

Fortune
Gambling (pg. 55)

Intelligence
Info (pg. 56)
Journalism (pg. 57)
Medicine (pg. 58)

Magic
Arcanowave Device (pg. 53)
Creature Powers (pg. 53)
Medicine (pg. 58)
Sorcery (pg. 59)

Manual Dexterity
Driving (pg. 54)
Guns (pg. 55)
Sabotage (pg. 58)

Perception
Detective (pg. 53)
Fix-It (pg. 54)
Police (pg. 58)

intensive training or whether more time is required. For example, Guns and Driving take a few weeks, while acquiring the Detective skill could take years. Learning the Sorcery skill has special rules, covered on p. 92 of the Magic chapter. Characters wishing to learn new skills must also find someone willing and able to teach them. Clever GMs who know that PCs want to learn certain new skills will make the finding and winning over of a famed teacher the objective of a story line.

USING SKILLS YOU DON'T HAVE

Sometimes a character, finding herself in a pinch, will want to make a task check with a skill she doesn't have. (Do you clip the red wire to stop the bomb, or the green one?) This is often possible; the Action Value for the attempt is usually the character's rating in the skill's base attribute minus 3.

Example: Lao Biaxing has no Driving skill. Unfortunately, he's the only one left conscious in a sports car blasting down the German autobahn after an enemy agent tosses a knockout gas grenade into the front seat. Lao Biaxing grabs the wheel and hopes he's paid close enough attention to his buddies' driving habits to steer the car to the side of the roadway without wiping out. The GM decides that this is just a little tricky, and assigns it a Difficulty of 5. Lao's Action Value for the check is 5. That's his rating of 8 in Manual Dexterity (the base attribute for Driving) minus 3. Lao's char-

...acter rolls a -1, for an Action Result of 4. Uh-oh, not quite good enough. The GM declares that Lao has caused the car to swerve sideways into oncoming traffic!

Now, some skills are harder to use with no training than others. It's up to the GM to make sure that the (Base Attribute - 3) Action Value is appropriate in a given situation. Conducting successful brain surgery without medical training should carry a greater penalty to the base attribute than -3. Telling your mom that you were at the library studying for exam instead of blasting evil sorcerers should be easier, like a -1, even if you don't have the Deceit skill.

JUNCTURE ADJUSTMENTS

You will sometimes wonder how good a character who learned a skill in one juncture is at performing that skill in another. Is a crack shot with a bow and arrow able to pick up an M16 and start blasting away with aplomb? Can an expert seducer familiar with the customs of first century China attract a partner in a modern singles bar?

In most cases, the answer is yes. Time-travelling characters in action-adventure movies usually experience a short period of comic unfamiliarity with the trappings of a new period, but fit right in after a scene or two.

When a character makes a skill attempt in an unfamiliar juncture, it's up to the GM to decide whether the difference in junctures matters. For example, a character using the Fix-It skill in 1850 isn't going to be hampered in his attempts to repair a laptop computer if he brought his entire toolkit with him from the contemporary juncture. If the difference does matter, apply a +4 Difficulty Modifier to the first attempt to use the skill in the particular manner at hand. The next time the character tries to repeat the same action, apply a +2 Modifier. The third time, apply a +1 Modifier. The time elapsed between

> ### Summary of Modifiers & Difficulties
> **Knowledge Check Difficulty Examples** (see p. 48)
> Basic Information — Automatic
> Intermetidate Information — 5
> Advanced Information — 10
> Exceedingly Obscure Information — 15
>
> **Contacts Check Difficulty Modifiers** (see p. 48)
> *Current Location*
> Saturated with appropriate types — -5
> Average distribution of appropriate types — +5
> Appropriate types are rare — +10
> *Degree of Specialization Required*
> Any — 0
> Certain subskill or credentials — +5
> Rate credentails or subskills, or particular person — +10
> Extremely rare credentials or subskills, or particular and reclusive person — +15
>
> **New Juncture Adustments** (see p. 52)
> First Try — +4
> Second Try — +2
> Third Try — +1

attempts makes no difference to the Modifiers; they apply whether the skill checks are made in quick succession, or over a period of game years.

Example: Fa Xian, famed Imperial Investigator of the 1850 juncture, is trying to figure out who murdered a security guard in contemporary Hong Kong. One of his maverick cop buddies has given him a fingerprinting kit, but has been called away by his superior officer to be threatened with suspension. This leaves Fa Xian to attempt to use his Detective skill with unfamiliar equipment. The first print he tries to take will be at a +4 Modifier. If he tries to take another, it will be at a +2 Modifier. If he waits for another situation to take his second set of fingerprints, it will still be at a +2 Modifier. The reduction of the modifiers applies only to fingerprinting; the first time he tries to figure out a DNA test result he'll again have a +4 Modifier.

SKILL LIST

Arcanowave Device — Base Attribute: Magic

Only characters native to the 2056 juncture may start the game with this skill.

Physical Ability: You can operate arcanowave devices—items created by the Architects of the Flesh through a blend of magic and biotechnology. Unlike conventional technology, the efficiency of these devices depends on your ability to magically manipulate your inner chi energy and relate it to the outer chi energy of the world. The performance of the devices can vary widely depending on how masterfully you manipulate chi. You may do so instinctively (as in the case of abominations) or through extensive training in standardized methods of concentrating chi energy developed by the Architects. Difficulties for Arcanowave Device checks depend on the device being used; see individual descriptions on pp. 120-124.

Knowledge: Unless you are an abomination, you know the basics of arcanowave theory. This means that you are familiar with the scientific principles behind the control of magical wave energy as formulated by the Architects. You can identify other arcanowave devices; you know what they do and why. You can participate in abstruse discussions on arcanowave theory with other experts. You can make minor field repairs on damaged arcanowave devices and A/IO ports (see p. 117 for a description of these).

If you have a skill bonus of 6 or more, you also have the subskill Arcanowave Technician. This allows you to install A/IO ports (assuming you also have the Surgery subskill of medicine), perform repairs on extensively-damaged arcanowave devices, and develop new arcanowave devices given sufficient lab time and access to proper equipment.

Contacts: You know others from the world of 2056 skilled in the use of arcanowave devices. If you are a techie, you know other Arcanowave Technicians: people who design and repair these devices for the Buro. If you are an abomination, you know and once fought alongside other abominations. If you are a cyborg, you remember being taught by Arcanowave Technicians; you know other cyborgs. Whichever type you belong to, it is unlikely that contacts still loyal to the Buro will be well-disposed towards you if you are a known opponent of the regime.

Creature Powers — Base Attribute: Magic

Only abominations, ghosts, and supernatural creatures may learn this skill.

Physical Ability: You can trigger and control your innate magical powers.

Knowledge: You are familiar with the reputations and careers of famous monsters. Similarly, you are aware of legends and rumors surrounding notorious magic cops and monster hunters. You know about other creature powers. You are familiar with fu powers that hose creature powers. You know the locations of haunted places and other locations amenable to supernatural creatures.

Contacts: You know a number of sorcerers, some of whom you hate bitterly for summoning and controlling you. You know other supernatural creatures and ghosts of various types.

Deceit — Base Attribute: Charisma

Physical Ability: You are adept at fooling others. You can lie convincingly. You can disguise your appearance, either to hide your identity or look like a specific individual. You can mimic voices. You can forge credentials and feign familiarity with skills you don't really have.

Knowledge: You are familiar with the tricks of the con man's trade, including knowledge of specific scams and grifts. You know the various legal penalties for various forms of fraud and deception. You know by reputation the law officers responsible for enforcing such laws in your usual area of operation. You know many colorful anecdotes of notorious deceivers of the past and present.

Contacts: You know other con men. You know shady lawyers and bail bondsmen. You may know, but are not likely to be friendly with, beat cops, fraud squad officers, and prison guards. You may know low-level gangsters and their associates.

Detective — Base Attribute: Perception

This skill is very similar to the Police skill, given below; it reflects a civilian with detective training. Characters with the Police skill will find it largely redundant.

Physical Ability: You can make shrewd deductions based on physical evidence and your familiarity with human nature. You can tell when people are lying or have something to hide. You are a good judge of character. You can pick locks, and are good at searching areas without leaving any trace of your own presence.

Difficulties for most Detective checks based on character assessment equal the Charisma rating of the person being assessed. When interpreting clues, the GM assigns a Difficulty to the situation based on its obscurity. If you make your Detective check, you are given a hint, or outright told what the clues mean, depending on the GM's needs in moving the story along. Easy clues to pick up should be Difficulty 5; an example of such would be obvious fingerprints in the area being investigated, or dropped objects in plain sight. Difficulty 10 clues might include latent fingerprints or carefully-hidden items.

Knowledge: You are familiar with police procedure and the law. You are familiar with many case histories of famous crimes. You know by reputation the famed cops, detectives, and criminals of your day. You are acquainted with the latest forensic techniques of your juncture.

Contacts: You know police officers, with whom you may have a tense relationship. You may have a range of low-level underground contacts from whom you can get useful tips, either through bribery or intimidation. If you have worked as a professional rather than amateur detective, you likely have contacts among well-respected citizens and business people for whom you've done work in the past.

Driving   **Base Attribute: Manual Dexterity**

Physical Ability: You can drive vehicles like there's no tomorrow. Vehicle stunts are second nature to you. You may drive any vehicle, but must choose a single type with which you are most familiar. This must be a vehicle you could have logically been exposed to in your home juncture. Given adequate time and equipment, you can repair and care for any vehicle you are familiar with. Note that the horse counts as a vehicle; if you specify horses as a vehicle of familiarity, you know the basics of the care and feeding of these animals. You can pick up new familiarities in the course of play by paying an experience point for each vehicle; you must have been exposed to these new vehicles as part of the storyline. Each vehicle type can be considered a subskill. Making emergency or stunt-oriented maneuvers with vehicles you are not familiar with carries a +1 Difficulty Modifier. This is in addition to any Modifiers for juncture adjustment; piloting a Buro hovercraft in 2056 when your main vehicle is a horse in 1850 would give you a +5 Difficulty Modifier (+1 for not being familiar with it, and +4 for the juncture difference on your first try).

Even without this skill, all characters can manage basic, non-emergency, non-stunt driving of a vehicle common to their juncture. This means horses for 69 and 1850, or automobiles for the contemporary and 2056 junctures.

Knowledge: You know about the history of the vehicle type you are familiar with. You know the quirks of various specific models of your favored vehicle. You can quote statistics about their technical specifications, if applicable. You know where to go to purchase vehicles, and how to negotiate good prices from sales staff. You are familiar with anecdotes about vehicles and famous drivers and pilots.

Contacts: Your contacts relate only to your designated vehicle(s). You know mechanics, other expert drivers, and vehicle sales people. (In the case of horses, you know riders, livery stable employees, breeders and owners.) You know people involved in racing, if applicable for your vehicle: these might include fans, sports writers, touts, and groupies of either sex.

Fix-It   **Base Attribute: Perception**

Physical Ability: You can repair almost any object, given enough time and the right equipment. If you are familiar with the object, the Difficulty is based on the complexity of the repair and the severity of the damage it has sustained. The Difficulty does not necessarily correspond to the technological advancement of the item: for example, many pieces of electronic gear can be repaired by simply popping out a fried component and sticking in a new one. If you are not familiar with the type of object, however, the GM should factor in the complexity as well. If you are used to fixing ox carts and pounding out punctures in plate armor, the control panel of a SCUD missile launcher is going to take you a while to puzzle out.

You can also jury-rig from scrounged parts devices whose basic design is familiar to you. The VCR you build from leftovers in a junk shop may not look as nice as a factory model, but it will work.

You can also design and build new inventions, as long as you can convince the GM that such a device is possible. Note that you can't create devices which are better in every way than equivalent objects described in this book: no ultra-concealable .22 handguns with the damage rating of a .45, for example.

In the case of either repairs or jury-rigged items, the GM decides how long the task takes.

If you find yourself in the middle of a tight spot and want a particular piece of equipment, make a Fix-It check to see if you just happen to have such a thing on your person. This is called the "Hey, I just happen to have one of those!" effect. Items that can be scrounged up via this method might be anything from a basic tool or utility item—a screwdriver, strapping tape, vinyl rope—to an exotic or juryrigged device such as a geiger counter, acetylene torch, or grappling hook. The GM chooses the Difficulty of the check, deciding how likely it is that you'd have been expecting to need the object you're asking for. Techies have a unique schtick that lets them do this automatically, as long as they spend a Fortune point. (Of course, Techies can make a Fix-It check instead like everyone else.) Other characters should face higher Difficulty numbers if the items in question don't match their archetypes: Ninjas have an easy time coming up with jury-rigged smoke grenades and the like, but have a lousy chance of having high-tech devices on hand. If it's a jury-rigged item appearing in the storyline for the first time, the GM will require an additional check to see if the thing actually works when you try to use it.

Knowledge: You know all about the standard technology of your day, from a practical point of view. You don't necessarily know about the science behind electricity, but you can fix a fried toaster oven. You know what tools to use for what task. You have a helpful hint for any home or industrial situation. You know how to get nasty stains of any sort out of almost any material. (You laugh now, but wait until all of the other PCs come to you wanting all of those nasty bloodstains out of their Armani jackets!)

Contacts: You know junk dealers, other fix-it artists, and people from your neighborhood who come to you to get things fixed.

Gambling   Base Attribute: Fortune

Physical Ability: You have a knack for gambling. When you enter games of chance, you win more often than the statistical odds should allow. Games of chance include stock speculation as well as more traditional casino games. You can sniff out opportunities to gamble even in completely unfamiliar environments, whether they be dice games in a Zen monastery or poker in a pit of demons. You can read faces and body language and sense whether people are bluffing or not. You can convince criminal gamblers and others on the shady side of the law that you're one of them, someone they can trust not to bug out on a wager or squeal to the cops. You can perform outrageous tricks: cock a die you are throwing in order to get a desired result, employ sleight of hand when playing cards, and so on. Gambling does not cover any risky activity, such as attempting to jump off a cliff and survive. Unless, that is, there is a wager riding on the result. You may not contrive to turn otherwise dangerous situations into wagers by placing bets with other PCs; to qualify, these situations must involve what the GM considers to be a genuine high-stakes bet with a GMC.

Knowledge: You know the rules, odds, and statistics of any popular game of chance like the back of your hand. You know where the best casinos are. You know their policies. You know how to dress impeccably for any gambling situation. You know gambler's etiquette as if it were taught to you at your mother's knee. (Heck, maybe it was.)

Contacts: You know gamblers, bookies, casino workers, casino owners, vice cops, hangers-on, and gambling groupies of either sex.

Guns   Base Attribute: Manual Dexterity

(There is an entire section devoted to the use of guns, appearing on pp. 60-74.)

Although this skill is called "Guns," it actually refers to all kinds of ranged weapons. The only exception is ranged arcanowave weapons; they operate according to magical principles rather than basic physics, and are covered under the Arcanowave Device skill described earlier.

When you first take the Guns skill, specify whether it covers either all firearms or all ancient ranged weapons, such as bows, crossbows, and slings. The first three times you use weapons from the set you're not familiar with, you face juncture adjustment modifiers as described earlier.

If you use ancient ranged weapons instead of firearms, read your weapons of choice into the description given below.

Physical Ability: You can fire guns at targets with a high degree of accuracy. You can repair guns, and you can diagnose problems with faulty or damaged guns. You can identify a quality gun when you see one.

Knowledge: You know the history of guns. You know the technical specifications of guns inside out, and can rattle off statistics about guns and ammo until the cows come home. You know the legal regulations concerning guns as enforced by various jurisdictions in your juncture. You know all about the companies that manufacture, import, and sell guns. You know by reputation the famed shooters of your juncture. You know stories about the great shooters of the past.

Contacts: You know gun dealers, legal and otherwise. You know gunsmiths. You know individuals involved with competitive shooting: fans, officials, and hangers-on. In the modern era, you know journalists who specialize in writing for gun publications.

Info   **Base Attribute: Intelligence**

Info is not a single skill, but a broad category. It means you are familiar with a particular body of knowledge. You make Info task checks to see if you know the answer to a particular question concerning the body of knowledge. That body of knowledge might be cooking, Taoist philosophy, the history of warfare, the Noh theatre of Japan, or whatever else you want. Come up with a term to describe the desired area of expertise, and indicate the skill on your character as Info/[Area]. So your skill might be Info/Cooking, Info/Taoist Philosophy, or whatever else.

An Info skill can be as broad or narrow as you want. The broader the skill, the higher the Difficulty ratings your GM will impose when you seek the answers to specialized questions. On the other hand, taking a broad skill allows you to at least take a shot at a wider range of possible questions.

Example: Laurel "Hacksaw" Chambers is looking at a painting in the traditional Chinese style; it was the only item in a heavily guarded storehouse belonging to the Order of the Wheel, and she figures it's an important clue. She wants to know who painted it. If her Info skill were Info/Art, the GM would impose a high Difficulty, say 12, because Laurel's player has defined her Info skill very broadly. If the Info skill were more specialized, like Info/Paintings, the Difficulty might be reduced to 10. If it were extremely specialized and on target, like Info/Chinese Painting, she would have a low Difficulty, like 5. But if she had specialized in something that excludes the object she's examining, like Info/Chinese Sculpture, she'd be completely out of luck.

Physical Ability: Info skills have no physical component.

Knowledge: In addition to being able to answer questions about your field, you know where libraries and other reference sources are. You know how to do research. You may know how to write academic papers on your subject, if it is of scholarly interest.

Contacts: You know other experts in your field. You know people involved with your field.

Example: If your skill is Info/Taoist Philosophy, you know not only other experts and academics, but also many Taoists, from priests to humble practitioners.

Intimidation   **Base Attribute: Charisma**

Physical Ability: You make others feel frightened, uncomfortable, self-conscious, or inadequate. You may do this by displaying impressive size, great skill, profound intellect, or just an indefinable quality of superiority. The Difficulty for Intimidation task checks is the Willpower of the subject you are attempting to intimidate. If you are attempting to intimidate a group of people at once, use the highest Willpower rating in the crowd. Targets of this skill may substitute their own Intimidation ratings for Willpower if desired. The GM may assess Difficulty modifiers to Intimidation checks based on circumstances. If you have the upper hand in a situation, or have done something threatening or inspiring, the Difficulty modifier is negative. If you are in a tight spot or have just done something embarrassing or awkward, the Difficulty modifier is positive.

Once you have successfully intimidated someone, he is more likely to go along with your suggestions. This does not mean that he will automatically adhere to any request you make, but he will give it much more weight than he otherwise would have.

Knowledge: Not applicable.
Contacts: Not applicable.

Intrusion   **Base Attribute: Agility**

Physical Ability: You are good at getting into places you're not supposed to be. You can rappel up or down vertical surfaces with the help of a rope and grappling hook. You can quickly examine secure areas and determine the best means of illicit entry. You can move quietly, hide in small places, and generally avoid being noticed under scrutiny. You can pick locks, crack safes, and circumvent electronic or magical security measures. You can install such measures to stop others like you from entering an area. The GM assigns Difficulties to such attempts based on the sophistication of the security measures, locks, and so on, or on the quality of the scrutiny.

Knowledge: You know about the latest security measures. You know what equipment you need, and how to find quality gear. You know about the great heists of history, and the techniques of the great intruders of the past. You know by reputation the best in your business today; the very best are known only by nicknames or by famous jobs they have pulled.

Contacts: You know criminals willing to fence stolen gear, middlemen who hire freelance spies for private or public clients, and, if you've been unlucky or careless, representatives of the justice system such as cops, lawyers, judges, and jailers.

Journalism   Base Attribute: Intelligence

Physical Ability: You can gather information and distill it into news stories for print or electronic media. You can rank ideas in order of importance and condense them into short and pithy reports. Your prose may not win you any literary prizes, but you know how to get a main idea across to even the thickest reader. You are good at remembering things people tell you, and at taking notes. You are good at research and legwork. You are especially good at following mundane details such as financial and travel records and using them to reconstruct the activities of your subject. You are an expert in interview techniques. You can make people feel comfortable, so they treat you as a confidant. You can cajole people who have trouble keeping secrets into spilling them. You can employ barbed questions to get people to blow their cool and become unwisely frank with you. Most importantly, you can judge who to needle and who to coddle. You can sense when people you're talking to have something to hide. You know how to use a still camera and can develop the film you shoot. You have an emergency knowledge of TV technique, including the operation of video cameras, editing consoles, and audio recording equipment.

Knowledge: You know who's who in the news industry, from serious business information to the juiciest gossip. An expert traveler, you know the best hotels, restaurants, and (especially) bars in any city in the world. You know a little about every topic under the sun. However, experts in any field you cover invariably hate the way you oversimplify complex issues and gloss over details in the reports you file. You know how to sound good on TV, though not necessarily how to look good.

Contacts: You know other reporters as well as editors, columnists, photographers, and technical people. From the stories you've covered, you have contacts in every walk of life. You've met everyone from heads of state to street corner scumbags. Unfortunately, although this skill provides a wider range of possible contacts than any other, the people whose stories you've told are highly likely to despise your intestines. Only if your Journalism contacts task check has an Outcome of 7 or more will a contact you've covered in the past be favorably disposed towards you. Note that contacts who'd like to see you squashed like a bug may, if they have some way to cause you grief, pretend to still like you. In these cases, the check you make may be just a ruse to cover the valid, secret check made by the GM on your behalf.

Leadership   Base Attribute: Charisma

Physical Ability: You exude an air of authority. Those who recognize you as their legitimate superior will follow your orders to the best of their ability. Those who do not may follow you instinctively in a pinch, just because you seem to expect it. Unwilling subjects make a Willpower or Intimidation check at the same time as your Leadership check; if their Action Result exceeds yours, your attempt fails. It is not possible to use this skill on an unwilling subject who also has the Leadership skill.

Knowledge: You know a particular theory of leadership and discipline, whether it be the code of obedience of Ancient China, or the bureaucratic management manuals of the Buro. If it has a written component, you can quote it to the last punctuation mark.

Contacts: You know others in the leadership hierarchy you belong to or once belonged to. Depending on your current circumstances, your superiors may still support you or want you dead. Your former underlings will still revere you, even if they've been ordered to smoke you on sight.

Martial Arts   Base Attribute: Agility

Physical Ability: You can strike opponents in hand-to-hand combat, either unarmed or with close-up weapons such as swords, clubs, bicycle chains, nunchakus, telephones, lawn mowers, and so on. You can dodge and parry in hand-to-hand combat. You can fight with thrown weapons, from shurikens to daggers to grenades. You can throw other objects accurately. For more on hand-to-hand combat, see the Fights chapter.

Note that the term "martial arts" is used as a catch-all to denote all hand-to-hand fighting ability. Your character may not have been formally trained at all, much less in a specific oriental fighting art. If your character is a karate cop, martial artist, masked avenger, ninja, old master, scrappy kid or ex-special forces type, you have been formally trained. If your character belongs to another type, you may spend an additional skill bonus to indicate formal training in a technique; otherwise you're an effective brawler with little style. If that's the case, then you have a limited subskill called Brawling instead, which does not include the knowledge and contacts elements of the full Martial Arts skill.

Knowledge: You know the history of your school, and of its great masters of the past and present. You have a less-extensive but still-acceptable knowledge of the histories of rival schools. You know the philosophy of your school, both as it pertains to fighting and to life in general. If it has an oral or written code of conduct, you have memorized some or all of it. You know by reputation the great martial artists of your juncture.

Contacts: You know other practitioners and teachers of your school. You will know members of rival schools, who may be your enemies. You know people involved in martial arts competitions, from judges to fans to patrons.

Medicine   Base Attribute: Intelligence (or Magic)

Characters from the 1850 juncture are limited to a skill bonus of +3 in this skill until they can undergo a training sequence in a modern or futuristic hospital setting. Characters from the 69 juncture are actually practicing a basic form of magic when they heal patients; they use Magic as the base attribute for the skill.

Physical Ability: You can heal the sick and wounded. You can diagnose injuries and illnesses. You can look at wounds and deduce what might have caused them.

If you are from the 69 juncture, you can act as an apothecary and concoct various medicines. Otherwise, you simply prescribe drugs for your patients. For rules on healing wounded characters with this skill, see p. 137 of the Fighting chapter.

If your skill bonus ranges from 0-2, you know a smattering of first aid. In modern terms, you are qualified to be a paramedic, military medic, or nurse. You can save lives, but complicated procedures and long-term care are not your specialty.

If your skill bonus is 3 or more, you are most likely a certified medical doctor. If not, you are qualified to be one but lack the certification for some reason.

If your skill bonus is 5 or more, you can not only act as a general practitioner but may pick a specialty of medicine as a subskill. The subskill Surgery allows you to operate on patients, for example; it is the most useful specialty in an action/adventure context. Forensic Pathology allows you to conduct autopsies and otherwise gather clues. If you want to pick something less practical in order to establish your character's background, other specialties include Internal Medicine; Eyes, Ears, Nose & Throat; or those focusing on particular diseases such as cancer, arthritis, or diabetes.

Knowledge: You know human anatomy. You are familiar with chemistry, particularly biochemistry. You know the latest medical advances of your juncture. You know the famous doctors in your field by reputation. You know the best hospitals in your area for the treatment of particular conditions.

Contacts: You know other doctors, nurses, and/or medics. You know patients from all walks of life. Unless you are from the 69 juncture, you know hospital staffers and administrators, academic researchers and lab technicians.

Police   Base Attribute: Perception

This skill can not be learned in the course of play.

Physical Ability: You are a current or former police officer. You are a good judge of character and can sense when people are lying; use the Charisma of the person you are judging as the Difficulty of such attempts.

You can employ a wide range of interrogation techniques, from friendly trickery to relentless browbeating, to get witnesses or possible suspects to tell you the truth. Use the subject's Willpower as Difficulty for such attempts.

You can assemble disparate clues into a mental recreation of a crime or other past event; in game terms, the GM assigns a Difficulty to the situation based on its obscurity. See the listing for the Detective skill, above, for examples. If you make your Police check, you are given a hint, or outright told what the clues mean, depending on the GM's needs in moving the story along.

Knowledge: You are familiar with the criminal law of your jurisdiction. You know police procedure. You know the basics of forensic science in your era. You know about famous crimes, criminals, and cases, as well as the careers of the top cops of your juncture.

Contacts: You know other cops, superiors in the police hierarchy, prosecutors, civilian staffers, and (depending on your era) journalists. You know many petty criminals, including stool pigeons, as well as ordinary citizens just trying to get along.

Sabotage   Base Attribute: Manual Dexterity

Physical Ability: You wreck stuff real good. "Stuff" includes vehicles, machines, electronic equipment, buildings, and other architectural structures such as bridges. Difficulties for these attempts hinge on the ruggedness of the thing you are sabotaging, the amount of time you have to do it in, the equipment available to you, and how obvious you want its destruction to be. It is more difficult to wreck something so that it does not appear at first glance to have been disabled than it is to just blow the crap out of your target. Unless you are from the 69 juncture, this ability includes working knowledge of demolitions and explosives of all sorts. This includes defusing as well as assembling explosive and incendiary devices.

Knowledge: You know the chemical properties of explosives and the physics of explosions. You know enough about electronics and computer hardware to dismantle them. You know enough about architecture to know what structural supports to take out when you want to collapse a building or other structure. You know the tools of the trade.

Contacts: The world of the saboteur is a shadowy one; who you know depends on how you learned this skill.

If you were trained by the military, you know other army personnel, including drill sergeants, trainers and lecturers, superiors, and supply officers. If you want, you know which of them are shady or owe you enough of a debt to "accidentally misplace" highly-dangerous explosives and send them your way.

If you were trained by a government intelligence organization, you know military personnel, as above, plus civilian intelligence officers.

If you learned your trade in the underworld of industrial espionage or terrorism, you know illegal dealers willing to sell you all the explosives and other illegal gear you need. You have contacts who used to hire you for jobs, although they may be difficult to reach and may have kept their real identities a secret from you.

Seduction   **Base Attribute: Charisma**

Physical Ability: You can manipulate others into feeling a powerful sexual attraction for you. Once you have done this, you can persuade them to abandon their usual inhibitions and commitments in order to please you. The base Difficulty of such attempts is the Willpower rating of the subject. The GM may add Difficulty modifiers based on the subject's situation: If he has just been burned by a tortured relationship, there may be a positive modifier. If he is desperately lonely, there may be a negative modifier. This skill never succeeds against a subject who is not attracted to persons of the seducer's gender; supernatural creatures may have this same problem with subjects who aren't up for sex with a zombie or whatever no matter how skillfully you come on to them.

Knowledge: You know a lot about human nature, at least as it relates to matters of the heart and/or mating rituals. You are especially expert on the social expectations placed by your home juncture on the sex you usually target.

Contacts: You have a little black book full of past conquests. Some of them still pine for you, and, in spite of their better judgment, would still do almost anything for you. Others have been deliberately putting money in a savings account; they plan to use this money to hire an assassin to kill you as soon as they get a clue as to your whereabouts. Although you think you are an expert on romance, you have no idea which contact fits into which category until you get in touch with them again. There are maybe one or two contacts in your little black book who fall between these two extremes.

Sorcery   **Base Attribute: Magic**

Only characters from the 69 juncture can start play with this skill.

Physical Ability: You can twist the chi energy of your environment to your will, creating magical effects through the use of ritual movements and chanting. An entire chapter devoted to the use of this skill begins on p. 88. You can conduct magical research; given the time and the right equipment you can divine the purpose and other characteristics of magical devices. The Difficulty of doing so is the Sorcery skill of the original creator of the device; if there was more than one creator, it is the sum of all of their Sorcery skills. Arcanowave devices are beyond the understanding of the pure sorcerer.

Knowledge: You know all sorts of abstruse occult theory, either learned orally or memorized from dozens of dusty and obscure manuscripts. You are familiar with the principles of geomancy, chi energy, and occult ritual. This allows you to engage in lengthy discourse with other sorcerers, and to figure out what methods other sorcerers have used to create their effects. You know legends of the great sorcerers of the past. You know by reputation the famous sorcerers of your day—but note that many powerful sorcerers take pains not to be identified as such. You have read or heard about various artifacts of magical power and know tales of their creation and history. You also know how to destroy such items. Arcanowave devices are beyond your knowledge, however.

Contacts: You know other sorcerers. You know merchants who specialize in the sale of magical ingredients.

Chapter 4

August 13

Lemming got wind that a certain Colombian cartel honcho was getting cosy with a Lotus-controlled New York family. The last thing we needed—considering how distracted we were trying to jimmy the Ascended-Hand war to our benefit—was for the Eaters to widen their resource base in the Americas while we were looking the other way. So Prof cut me loose from the Banshee operation and told me to pack my bags for Miami. If Lemming's scoop was chocolate, the NY capo and our Colombian would be meeting in two days at a certain swank hotel eatery.

Jetting in meant that I'd have to acquire a toolkit on site. I rang up my favorite Southeast dealer: Sunny Pak, the Pakman. I offered him a generous bonus to meet me in Miami a day after my arrival. By the time his fabled hockey bag full of guns was spread out before me on my hotel bed, I'd already scoped the restaurant.

"Lots of fine merchandise for you today," he said. "Hot special on righteous firepower." Sunny was grinning, wearing his customary Hawaiian shirt and flashing the diamond in his front tooth. He offered me an AMT Automag V, a .50.

"C'mon, Sunny. I'm not out to impress a bunch of Texas gun weenies, I'm gonna kill a man. Show a little taste."

"I take it then you're looking to be reunited with an old friend?" He was holding out a .40 S&W Browning Hi-Power, matte model, just the way I like it.

"It's a pistol job, all right, but it's gonna have to be a jacket pocket carry. Weather forecast says over a hundred degrees tomorrow, so anything thicker than a dinner jacket is gonna freak the bodyguards. Mr. Browning's 36 ounces would be a little much."

He dug into the bag, shaking his head. "Well, I know what you're going to say, but there's only one piece of ordnance for the job then." He pulled out a Glock 17. I frowned. I knew he was right, but I still needed to be argued into it.

"Don't give me the look now. 24 ounces and a 17 + 1 capacity. I mean, if we're talking a bodyguard scenario, capacity is everything. And don't tell me you can't make this puppy roll over and shake hands. You're talking to the Pakman here."

"Yeah, yeah, when you're right you're right. It's just embarrassing, it's like admitting you dig Schwarznagger over Chow Yun-Fat. Okay, sold. Now for an ankle bracelet..."

He held up a Beretta Bobcat, the .25ACP. I nodded. "You got holsters for all this stuff, right?"

"I'm humiliated that you would even feel the need to ask."

"Now...I want to stash something persuasive in a garment bag in the lobby to cover my retreat. I'm thinking shotgun."

"Benelli?"

"No, gotta have that pump. Much more demoralizing than the semi-auto."

"Bernadelli?"

"Looks too friggin' weird."

"Mossberg 590?"

"Done. And a little something for the car."

"Looka this baby," he said, hauling out an unfamiliar steel and fiberglass SMG. "Ruger M-9. A sweet little Uzi variant, 32 round capacity. Just under 6 pounds of compact, user-friendly death on wheels."

"Intriguing, but you know I don't take anything out on a first date before I've fired a few thousand rounds through it at the test range. Tell you what, why don't you ship a couple to the Hong Kong address and give me that MP5 there?"

"I had a feeling you might say that."

"You're a consummate salesman, Sunny."

"Pleasure doing business with the real deal. Let me tell you, a distinct shockwave went through the dealership community when word got out that you'd retired."

"That's heartwarming," I said, strapping on the ankle holster for the Bobcat.

"I mean, there's the financial element. You have a spin-off effect, my friend. Say for example you decide you like the Ruger and use it on a job. It's like Boris Becker endorsing a tennis racket. Sales will go through the roof. But also there's the sentimental attachment. True professionalism, it's a vanishing art."

"Well to tell you the truth, Sunny, I am kind of retired. I know it doesn't look like it—" I was grabbing a couple of extra mags for the Glock "—but things are different now."

He put a fatherly hand on my shoulder. "Look, I heard about Steve—"

"These days I ain't exactly a professional. These days—"

I pumped the Mossberg for punctuation.

"These days, I'm goin' for a little redemption action."

CHAPTER 4

Guns

THE WAY OF THE KILLER

This section is only important to you if you're playing a character with the Guns skill, or if you're a GM. It starts out with some special rules concerning guns, and then provides a list of guns you can use to blow away scumbags by the dozen.

BUT BEFORE WE START

If you are a gun enthusiast or otherwise have experience with the way guns really work in the real world, you're going to have a fair bit of forgetting to do to get into the *Feng Shui* spirit. Always remember: *this game simulates action movies, not real life!* We have deliberately made guns less deadly than they are in real life, both in absolute terms and in comparison to the punches and kicks so essential to true fu action. We ignore a lot of the fine details that gun users consider important, lumping effects together into broad categories.

If you do have a lot of gun knowledge and you're playing a gun-toting character, feel free to use that knowledge when coming up with dialogue for her. Your character knows all the fine details inside and out, and may talk about them obsessively. Gun lingo is second nature to her. But don't try to get your GM to bow to your superior knowledge and make things more "realistic." In this game, guns are as much a fantasy element as magic, supernatural creatures, or exotic fu powers.

Just in case somebody's mom is reading this, the author does not endorse the use of guns in the real world. That also goes for swords and fists and all those other things you could put an eye out with.

GUN SCHTICKS

On the next page you'll find the various schticks available to characters with the Guns skill. Gun schticks allow characters to do particularly tricky or wantonly-destructive things with their guns. Some characters start the game with a number of these schticks. You may spend multiple schticks on certain abilities in order to get cumulative benefits.

Example: Characters based on the Killer archetype start with 5 gun schticks. Ray is creating such a character. He buys one schtick in Signature Weapon, two schticks in Eagle Eye, one schtick in Fast Draw, and one schtick in Carnival of Carnage. That's a total of 5 schticks spent.

Characters can gain additional gun schticks in the course of play by spending experience points. See p. 160 for complete information on getting and spending experience points. A new gun schtick costs (8 + x) points per schtick; x equals the number of gun schticks you will have once you acquire the new one. Characters who have a current Action Value of 11 or less in their Guns skill can't acquire Guns schticks in the course of play until their Guns skill reaches 12.

Chapter 4

Gun Schticks List

Both Guns Blazing

You can hurt a single opponent really badly by shooting him simultaneously with a gun held in each hand. Needless to say, you need to be employing two guns that can be fired with one hand each: handguns fit the bill, and so do other firearms that are described as having a pistol grip or as capable of being fired one-handed.

When you successfully hit an opponent with the Both Guns Blazing schtick, the Wound Points suffered by the opponent are figured as follows: Total Damage Rating of Both Guns - (Opponent's Toughness x 2) + Outcome = Wound Points Suffered.

Your GM will tell you the Toughness of an opponent as you make a Both Guns Blazing attack. (If this bothers any GMs, remember that shooting somebody in the chest with a couple of .45s is actually a pretty good way of finding out how much punishment he can handle.) You have to do the figuring involved and give the GM the final result.

If you buy only one schtick's worth of Both Guns Blazing, any two-gun attacks you make with it are at a -2 Action Value penalty. If you buy two schticks in it, the penalty is -1. If you buy three schticks, the penalty is 0. For each additional schtick you purchase, you gain a +1 Action Value bonus when using Both Guns Blazing.

Carnival of Carnage

This is great for mowing down gobs of unnamed mooks. If you have one schtick in Carnival of Carnage, you can subtract 1 from the shot cost of any attack on an unnamed character or characters. If you have two schticks in Carnival of Carnage, you can subtract 2 from the shot cost of any attack on an unnamed character or characters. (Shot costs cannot be reduced to 0 or to a negative number.) If you have three schticks in Carnival of Carnage, you also put down unnamed characters on an Outcome of 4 or more. If you have four schticks in Carnival of Carnage, you take out unnamed characters on an Outcome of 3 or more. You can't spent more than four schticks in this ability.

Eagle Eye

You're particularly adept at firing at armored opponents and hitting the teeny-tiny bits of them that aren't armored. If you have Eagle Eye, you can ignore any personal armor worn by your target. (For rules on Armor, see p. 138.) Eagle Eye cannot be used to reduce an opponent's Toughness. Each shtick in Eagle Eye also lets you ignore 2 pts. worth of difficulty modifiers due to cover or range.

Fast Draw

For each schtick spent on Fast Draw, you may add 1 to your Initiative result at the beginning of each sequence. If you add to your Initiative result in this manner, you must attack with a gun as your first action of that sequence.

Hair-Trigger Neck Hairs

Even when you seem to be paying complete attention to something else, your senses are working overtime looking out for trouble. Hidden dangers such as enemy ambushes, falling rocks, lurking poisonous snakes and ticking bombs hidden underneath chairs rarely surprise you. When the GM makes a check on your behalf to see if you spot such things, you get a +2 bonus to your Perception Action Value for each Hair-Trigger Neck Hairs schtick you've purchased.

If you succeed in a Perception check and can usefully respond to the situation by firing a gun or dodging, the Outcome of your perception check is applied to that first Guns or Active Dodge task check.

Lightning Reload

Many action movie heroes seem to be able to fire their guns constantly without ever seeming to reload or keep track of rounds fired. Actually, they're reloading so fast that you can't see them, having bought the Lightning Reload schtick. For each schtick you buy in Lightning Reload, subtract 1 from the shot cost of reloading any gun. Shot costs can be reduced to 0 in this manner, but not to a negative number. If you have 3 or more schticks in Lightning Reload, you never run out of bullets, no matter what the situation, no matter how improbable.

Signature Weapon

For each schtick spent in this ability, you can select one specific gun as a signature weapon. Your character might have his lucky Glock, the combat shotgun his grandmother gave to him as a coming of age present, his collector's edition ankle holster .32, and so on. A character using a signature weapon gets a +3 damage rating bonus with that particular weapon. Note that this applies to a single, actual weapon, not to all identical weapons; your lucky Glock gives you a +3, but any other Glock of the same model doesn't do anything special for you. Signature weapons are described in more detail on p. 141 in the Fights chapter.

AUTOMATIC WEAPONS

In real life, fully-automatic weapons that can fire hellacious bursts of bullets are among mankind's deadliest inventions. In action flicks, automatic weapons are cool special effects that send bullets pinging everywhere in a gunfight without doing much more damage than other guns. In *Feng Shui*, a gun capable of firing automatic bursts gives the shooter a +1 damage bonus for every three-bullet burst fired. You can fire as many three-bullet bursts as you have ammo, but you have to announce how many you're firing before you make your Guns check to see if you hit or not.

Holding onto a gun while it's spitting out a steady stream of bullets is no easy task. For every three bursts you fire, you suffer a -1 Action Value penalty. There is no penalty for firing one or two bursts.

PACKING HEAT

There is a limit to the number of guns or clips you can reasonably carry on your person, especially if you want to walk around looking like something other than a walking arsenal. Assume that the average character can carry a maximum of 10 guns or clips on his body. Bigger people can carry more, subject to the GM's adjudication. Of course, there are situations where you can just haul a gym bag full of guns to the *Feng Shui* site you're attacking or defending, rendering this issue moot.

CONCEALMENT

There are times when you don't want others to know that you're carrying enough weaponry to single-handedly recreate the storming of the beaches at Normandy. So, each gun has a **Concealment** rating.

Ammo clips and magazines also have Concealment ratings. Clips for autoloading pistols have a Concealment rating of 1; clips for machine pistols and magazines for rifles and machine guns have a Concealment rating of 2.

When you add together the Concealment ratings of all guns, clips and magazines that a character is carrying, you get a bonus which is applied to the Action Values of Perception checks made by others observing the carrying character. This reflects the chance that even a casual observer will note all sorts of funny bulges in your clothing. The standard Difficulty for a casual observer to spot concealed weapons is 10; the Difficulty for a character specifically looking for same is 6. Casual observers get only one chance to detect concealed weapons, but if for some reason they later decide to specifically look, they get another check at the lower Difficulty.

When player characters see other characters who happen to be wearing concealed weapons, the GM secretly makes casual checks for them, only informing them if they do spot the telltale bulges. If they actively look for concealed weapons, the GM makes another series of checks. Because the GM is making the checks, the players will not be able to tell whether the information they're getting is correct, or whether their characters simply failed their rolls.

It is important to wear enough clothes to cover all of your hardware; an overcoat of some kind is an essential fashion statement in these situations. The GM may choose to jack up your Concealment rating

Illustration by Mark Tedin

Damage Values Chart - Guns

Description	Damage Value
arrow, crossbow bolt	7
small handgun (.22)	8
medium handgun (.38)	9
big handgun (9 mm/.45)	10
really big handgun (.357/.44)	11
BFG (.50)	12
hunting shotgun	10
combat shotgun	13 *
medium rifle (5.56 mm)	13 **
heavy rifle (7.62 mm)	13 †

* Damage value is 14 for pump action shotguns if you spend a shot to dramatically go "KA-CHINK!"
** Unnamed characters hit by this weapon go down on an Outcome of 4 or more.
† Unnamed characters hit by this weapon go down on an Outcome of 3 or more.

Concealment Rating Chart

Concealment: 1
- any pistol or revolver under 12 cm barrel length and 680 g weight
- any clip for an autoloading pistol

Concealment: 2
- any pistol or revolver under 15 cm barrel length and 1.1 kg weight
- any clip for a machine pistol
- any magazine for a rifle or machine gun

Concealment: 3
- any gun under 38 cm overall length (stock folded) and 3 kg weight

Concealment: 5
- any other rifle, shotgun, submachine gun you can carry

if you are wearing light clothing, or only one layer. For example, even an eminently concealable pistol like a Glock 17 will poke through if all you're sporting is a T-shirt and a pair of track pants.

Example: Johnny Tso is attempting to get on a luxury cruise liner long enough to blow away the gnarled marauder he knows to be lurking in its cargo hold. He is carrying a Walther PPK (Concealment 2) in a shoulder holster and a Colt .45 1911A (Concealment 2) holstered at the small of his back. Also in his shoulder holster is a pair of clips for each pistol (each of them Concealment 1: 4 total). His total Concealment rating is 8. As he walks up the ramp to the ship, the purser happens to glance at him. The purser is not looking specifically for weapons, so the Perception check is made at Difficulty 10. His Perception attribute is 4; it is added to Johnny's total Concealment rating of 8 for an Action Value of 12. The GM rolls for the purser, getting an Action Result of 9. The purser does not suspect Johnny of carrying an arsenal on board his vessel.

MALFUNCTIONS

Guns fail more often in the course of a *Feng Shui* fight than they do in real life. This gives you a reason to carry lots of guns. **Malfunctions** happen when you fumble a Guns attack check, usually by rolling boxcars and failing the check.

When you get a malfunction, make a Fortune check to see how bad the problem is. Make a task check based on your current Fortune rating. The Difficulty of the task check is 4.

If you match or exceed that Difficulty, your gun has **jammed**: it is malfunctioning but can be quickly fixed. It takes you 8 shots to clear the jam, after which you can continue to use the gun with no problems. If you don't have enough shots in the current sequence to do so, subtract the remaining shots from your initiative check for the subsequent sequence.

If you fail the Fortune check, the gun is **damaged** and cannot be used again until repaired by a gunsmith. The repair job should take at least several hours of concentrated labor in a well-equipped workshop, uninterrupted by hostile gunfire.

Example: It's shot seven in the third sequence of a fight. Johnny Tso is firing his Walther PPK at the gnarled marauder. He rolls boxcars, informing the GM that he has done so. This means that if he now fails to hit, there's a chance that his pistol will malfunction. Sure enough, his final Action Value is less than that of the vampire's Dodge rating, so he fumbles. Johnny must now make a Fortune check to see how bad the problem is. His Fortune rating is 3, but he has already used a Fortune die this session, so he only gets to add 2 to his roll. He rolls a 5, getting a result greater than the standard Difficulty of 4 for malfunction checks. That means that his gun has simply jammed; it is not permanently damaged. Johnny can try to clear the jam, but it will take him 8 shots to do so. That will tie him up for the rest of this sequence, and subtract one from his first shot next sequence. Wanting to get back into the action as quickly as possible, he simply drops the Walther, spending 1 shot to draw his backup pistol, a Colt .45. There's a reason your typical assassin doesn't leave the house without a bunch of guns!

RELOADING

Each type of gun has a ***capacity***; this is the number of bullets it can fire before you have to reload. You need to know your gun's capacity, and keep track of the number of bullets you have fired during a fight. When your bullets run out then you need to reload, which will cost you time.

The shot cost for reloading depends on the type of gun. Revolvers and shotguns take 5 shots to reload. Rifles, SMGs, and machine guns take 3 shots to reload. Automatic pistols take 1 shot to reload. 1850s-era black powder guns take 9 shots to reload.

This, of course, assumes that you have ammo on hand to reload with. Automatic pistols are reloaded with ***clips***. A clip is a metal sheath that holds a number of bullets; when slammed into the grip of the gun the bullets are ready to be fed into the barrel. Rifles, machine guns, and submachine guns have detachable ***magazines*** which similarly feed bullets into the gun. Revolvers and shotguns have to be opened up and the ammo manually inserted.

TYPES OF AMMO

Different types of bullets—hollowpoints, armor-piercing rounds and so forth—have no actual effect on the game mechanics. Characters in the game will still talk about them, use them, and believe that they matter. But they don't.

LOSING GUNS

Guns which are not signature weapons will often become lost or damaged, or get abandoned in the course of a session. In fact, any seriously gun-oriented character should be going through expensive firearms like facial tissue. It should never be a hassle—or even much of an issue—for a character to find replacement weaponry to bring her back up to her usual number of guns after she loses some in the field. Between one fight and another, the gun character simply acquires more guns from somewhere. GMs should never make a character with a gun schtick go out and find a connection for her rare or restricted firearms of choice, or scrounge for the money to pay for them. Don't even bother to play out scenes of firearms acquisition; just do what most movie screenplays do and assume that this happens between scenes. (Note, though, that this is not true of weapons from junctures other than the PC's main one. You don't just find Buro firearms laying around contemporary Hong Kong, after all.) Sometimes playing out a gun buy furthers the overall plotline in some way—for example, the black market gun dealer might be a contact who also has some important clues—but generally the detailed portrayal of any shopping expedition is a major snooze. Players and GMs who wish to make a big deal of this are advised to watch a home shopping channel instead.

OKAY, NOW FOR THE GUNS

The rest of this chapter is devoted to brief descriptions of common guns (and other ranged weapons) which characters may choose from. For our purposes, there isn't much difference between weapons of the same general type—one autoloading .45 pistol is the same as another. However, your gun character probably thinks there's a big difference, will knowledgeably swear by her weapon of choice, and repeats its model name like a mantra. The only relevant game numbers are Damage (which is tied to the type and caliber of the weapon), Concealment rating (which is keyed to its weight and size), and Capacity (which depends on the make of gun). After the name of each weapon are three numbers separated by slashes. These are, respectively, Damage, Concealment, and Capacity. Silhouettes of many weapons are also included for your enjoyment—cool profile means cool gun.

Finally, note that a Capacity number followed by "+1" means that when the gun is initially loaded, you can put a round in the chamber. Fast reloads with clips do not permit this extra round to be inserted.

Some basic gun terms are used frequently below. An ***autoloader*** pistol prepares another round to be fired each time it fires; they have a slide along the top which characters in action movies sometimes pop back for dramatic effect. ***Revolvers*** contain bullets in a cylinder in the middle of the gun frame and take longer to reload; adherence to movie iconography dictates that cops should be particularly fond of them. ***Fully automatic*** weapons are capable

Chapter 4

of autofire; see p. 62 for rules on firing in three-shot bursts.

Guns are divided by juncture. Characters may only choose weapons from their home juncture or an earlier one.

Since our game system doesn't sweat the fine details, most guns of the same basic type are the same as far as we're concerned. Therefore, we haven't listed every firearm ever manufactured. If you want your character to wield one of the dozens of variations that we haven't covered, pick up a gun buyer's guide and use the statistics provided there to come up with Damage, Concealment and Capacity for whatever gun you choose. This is, of course, more complicated than just picking one of the above-listed guns, but your desire to do so indicates to us that you want things to be more complicated. You have to show your GM your reference materials to get her approval for the numbers you assign to your carefully-selected hardware. For the first two numbers, you'll need the charts on this page and the next for reference.

69

Bow and Arrow 7/5/1
Your basic pre-gunpowder ranged weapon.

1850

Gun-toting characters from the 1850s will want to ditch their black powder weapons as soon as they get access to modern firearms. GMs should let them do so with minimal hassle. They can figure out the differences between muskets and AK-47s between scenes. These antiquated weapons are good for fighting duels, though.

Black Powder Pistol 7/3/1
Takes 9 shots to reload.

Crossbow 7/4/1
Already obsolete in 1850, by several centuries. Takes 9 shots to reload.

Musket 8/5/1
Your basic black powder rifle. Takes 9 shots to reload.

MODERN

The bulk of this chapter is given over to modern weaponry, which is the stuff people know best and therefore will want the most detail on.

Autoloader Handguns

Unless otherwise indicated, these all take 1 shot to reload.

American Derringer Mini Cop 11/1/4
Very small .357 Magnum which takes 5 shots to reload.

AMT Automag IV 11/3/7 + 1
Sometimes you want a great big stainless-steel gun to scare people with.

AMT Automag V 12/3/5 +1
This .50 cal stainless-steel phallic symbol is not for the subtle.

Auto-Ordnance Pit Bull 10/1/7 + 1
More concealable version of the Colt 1911 (described later), and with a cool name to boot. Guns with cool names are very important to action heroes.

Beretta 92 Centurion 10/2/15 + 1
Another common 9mm autoloader.

Beretta Model 21 Bobcat 8/1/8 + 1
Autoloader pistol small enough to go in your ankle holster.

Beretta Model 950BS Jet Fire 8/1/8 + 1
Even lighter than the above. Hey, these Beretta guys have the cool name thing down pat, don't they?

Browning BDM 10/2/15 + 1
Yet another common 9mm autoloader.

Browning Hi-Power 10/2/13 + 1
And another. I told you already, most of these are pretty much the same for our purposes.

Colt Delta Elite MKIV Series 80 11/2/8 + 1
10mm autoloader. Ex-military types may be irresistibly drawn to the word "Delta."

Colt 380 Gov't Pocketlite 8/1/7 + 1
Your basic diet .30 autoloader.

Guns

Autoloader Handguns

Chapter 4

Colt 1911A   10/2/7 + 1
The classic workhorse of 9mm autoloaders. Like the number says, it's based on a 1911 design. Most other models of autoloader listed here are minor modifications of this one. Until very recently this was the basic sidearm of the US military; it's still the basic pistol of action-movie heroes on screens worldwide.

Desert Eagle .357 Magnum   11/3/10 + 1
Wins the brand-name recognition contest in the really-big-handgun category. Finish comes in your choice of black oxide, nickel or chrome. Hey, if you're going to wave something this big around, you might as well go for the chrome.

Desert Eagle .50 Magnum   12/3/9 +1
As above, but substitute "BFG" for "really big handgun."

E.T. "Series One Laseraim"   10/3/8 + 1
Funky 10mm autoloader with high-tech looking scallops along the top of the barrel—sure to appeal to yuppie heroes and pretentious bad guys. Comes with laser targeting sight, which, in the cinematic world of *Feng Shui*, has no game effect but looks cool and is intimidating to be targeted by. Made by new-wave gun gods Emerging Technologies.

Glock 17   10/1/17 + 1
Very popular autoloader pistol with a polymer frame; it's light and small for a 9mm. Sneered at by many gun enthusiasts; killer types may consider it useful but unhip. But then again, US soldiers bought lots of them with their own money in preparation for the Gulf War. The default pistol of contemporary mooks.

Glock 18   10/1/17 +1; 10/2/33 + 1
Fully-automatic version of above. Stick with the 17 shot clip and stay highly concealable, or go nuts with the 33 shot clip—which is about twice the length of the gun's grip.

Grendel P-12   9/1/12 + 1
Small polymer/metal .38 autoloader pistol with a relatively high capacity. Cheap enough that your gun-toting PC probably puts them in all her friends' Christmas stockings.

Grendel P-30   8/1/30 + 1
This .22 autoloader looks like something out of the 1930s Flash Gordon serials and has a downright wacky capacity. Your character may be taunted for being seen in public with this oddity, but then again, it is named after the monster that Beowulf fought, and that oughtta count for something.

Heckler & Koch P7   10/2/8 + 1
Another 9mm autoloading pistol with name-brand credibility. If your character prefers one of these, she probably uses the phrase "fine German craftsmanship" a lot.

Kahr K9   10/1/7 + 1
A new, small 9mm hot off the presses. If we were strict realists, this would be 28g too heavy to qualify for its Concealment rating. Happily, we're not.

Intratec Tec-9   10/3/32 + 1
9mm handgun that looks like a baby SMG housed in high-impact plastic. Formerly perceived as a gun for weenies only (and hence ideal mook ordnance), it became much hipper in the US in the wake of the assault weapons ban. It has a magazine instead of a clip, so it takes 3 shots to reload.

Intratec Tec-22   8/2/30 +1
This .22 looks like a luger with a big curving high-capacity magazine stuck on it. High-impact plastic housing.

Llama Large Frame   10/2/7 +1
Some gunmen may prefer their 9mm Colt 1911A variant to be named after a fuzzy South American mammal.

Makarov   10/2/8 + 1
A common autoloading pistol in the former USSR and its former satellite and client states.

Norinco Type M1911   10/3/7 + 1
If they're regularly blowing up things in the Pacific Rim, the PCs will often be encountering this Chinese version of the Colt 1911A. That's a 9mm autoloader pistol if you haven't been reading in alphabetical order.

Norinco Tokarev   10/2/8 + 1
This version of the classic Soviet 9mm autoloader pistol will also be frequently encountered in Pacific Rim firefights.

Ruger K89   10/2/15 + 1
High-capacity 9mm autoloading pistol for action heroes who insist on ordnance manufactured in the good old US of A.

Guns

Colt Detective Special

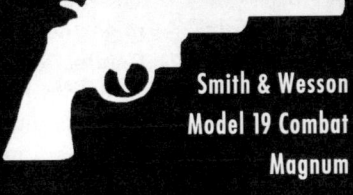
Smith & Wesson Model 19 Combat Magnum

Revolvers

Sig-Sauer P-220   10/2/9 + 1
Monster hunters and magic cops will want this .45 German-made autoloading pistol on the grounds that Mulder uses one on The X-Files. (Scully fans will stock up on the Sig-Sauer P230: 9/1/7 +1.)

Smith & Wesson 2213 Sportsman   8/1/8 + 1
Rugged little .22 autoloader pistol.

Smith & Wesson 3566   11/3/15 + 1
.356 autoloader pistol. If you're going to go for an easily-spotted, high-power weapon, you might as well pick one that you don't have to reload every sequence. Real-world shooters would be scared off by the unusual ammo, but that's not a problem for PCs with gun schticks.

Smith & Wesson Sigma   10/1/14 + 1
S&W's polymer-cased 9mm autoloader pistol.

Walther P-5 Compact   10/1/8 + 1
Another 9mm autoloader pistol with name cachet. You could go for the regular P-5, with a Concealment rating of 2, but it has the same Damage and Capacity ratings as this one, so why bother?

Walther PPK   9/1/6 + 1
James Bond carried this .38 autoloader pistol. He had to be ordered into it, though.

Revolvers

These take 5 shots to reload. There are fewer revolvers than autoloaders listed because we assume most gun-toting characters will be going for the latter.

Colt Detective Special   9/1/6
Hard to tell, but this might be what Danny Lee is pointing at Chow Yun-Fat's head on the video box for *The Killer*. If the name alone isn't a dead give-away, it's a .38 revolver.

Other names with the same game statistics: Rossi 88 'S' Series, Smith & Wesson Combat Masterpiece (modesty is not a virtue in gun sales, is it?), S&W Chiefs Special or Chiefs Special Airweight, S&W Bodyguard or Bodyguard Airweight, and Taurus Model 85.

Colt King Cobra   11/3/6
Matte stainless steel .357 revolver. Or, if you're looking for a slightly different snake name, the Colt Python and Colt Anaconda both have the same game stats and, if size matters to you, can come with an additional 5cm of barrel. The marketing guys at Colt are obviously devoted Freudians.

If you don't want a gun named after a reptile, the following makes are also 11/3/6 revolvers: European American Bounty Hunter, Rossi Model 971, Ruger GP100, Ruger Redhawk, and Smith and Wesson Model 29.

Rossi Model 515   8/2/9
The kind of gun that the old professor with the vital clue who is being attacked by the bad guys tries to grab out of his desk drawer but they're too fast for him and he never gets a chance to shoot it so the PCs have to rescue him. Different name, same stats: Taurus Model 94.

Rossi Model 851   9/2/6
Your basic .38 revolver. If you want a more bullish name, pick a Taurus Model 80.

S&W Model 19 Combat Magnum   11/2/6
As concealable as a .357 Magnum revolver is going to get. The S&W Model 13 Military and Police Heavy Barrel has the same game stats, as does another gun called the European American Armory Tactical.

Sub Machine Guns

SMGs, as they are abbreviated, are described below. Unless otherwise indicated, these take 3 shots to reload; the user slaps a magazine in the relevant slot and blasts away again. All of these are capable of fully automatic fire. Unless otherwise noted, these are all 9mm weapons.

Chapter 4

Colt M6351   10/5/32

Looks like a stubby assault rifle, but not small enough to be concealable. Guards at top secret installations run by the Ascended or other groups might tote these, as will SWAT teams, paramilitaries, and the like. This is the model for the mook in the know.

Heckler & Koch MP510   11/5/30

This less-common cousin of the ubiquitous MP5 (immediately below) takes a 10mm round, and may interest characters who crave that extra Damage point.

Hechler & Koch MP5   10/5/30

One of the most common SMGs around, this 9mm honey is used by police and military forces worldwide. The bad guys in the movie *Die Hard* used these, too.

Heckler & Koch MP5 K   10/3/30

Today's SMG of choice among special forces and well-equipped assassins. At just over 36 cm in length, this can be concealed beneath a heavy jacket, making it ideal on offensive missions. Its pistol grip allows characters to carry one in each hand and blaze away—see the Both Guns Blazing schtick, earlier in this section.

Heckler & Koch MP5 Police   11/3/30

Cop characters can take this 10mm version of the above if desired; it's produced in low quantities for law-enforcement clients.

MP40   10/5/32

This German WWII vintage SMG might be used by mooks and militias in third world countries.

M3   10/5/30

The vintage .45 "grease gun" used by the US military will likewise still be in use in various gun-laden back corners of the world.

Mini UZI   10/3/25

This concealable version of the famous Israeli SMG is particularly popular among low-level crooks and gangbangers, to whom the UZI name means prestige.

Ruger MP9   10/3/32

New gun going after the MP5's "lotsa death in a small package" niche market. Just a hair longer than its rival.

Thompson M1A1   10/5/30

The fabled tommy gun is long obsolete, but you might need the stats if a) a bad guy has an Al Capone fetish or b) there's a hit at a costume party with a Prohibition-era theme. Some Netherworld rabble stranded from a now-closed 1930s juncture might also have one of these gats around.

UZI   10/4/40

Like Xerox and Kleenex, this gun is so ingrained in the popular consciousness that its brand name is becoming a synonym for its type. Hey, it's made by Israelis, and they're tough as nails, right? This is the model for the status-conscious mook who wants to look good for movie casting agents.

Shotguns

Shotguns are very important weapons because they have that great pump thing going for them, where the hero or bad guy goes KA-CHINK in preparation for blasting the dickens out of somebody. Sometimes, for effect, they'll pump it two or even three times before even firing. In *Feng Shui* you can squeeze an extra point of Damage rating out of a pump action shotgun by taking an extra shot to mime out the pumping while making a loud "KA-CHINK" noise—yes, the player has to actually mime this action and make the "KA-CHINK!" sound. There's no further bonus for multiple pumps, though.

But they're only good up close. Double any Difficulty modifiers for range—see p. 141 for the range chart. Shotguns also take 6 shots to reload.

Benelli 121   13/5/7

Italian semi-auto with a classic look. Useful for secret warriors wishing to pass themselves off as ordinary hunters.

Benelli 90 M3   13/5/7

Both a semi-auto and a pump, for the best of both worlds. Has a pistol grip, which looks cool, and that's all that matters.

Beretta 1201 Riot   13/5/6

Sleek and streamlined classy semi-auto with that all-important brand name. Ideal for black tie and other formal events.

Bernadelli   13/5/10

This metallic pump-action 12 gauge with pistol grip looks more like a machine gun or assault rifle than a shotgun. A manstopper for the emo-

Guns

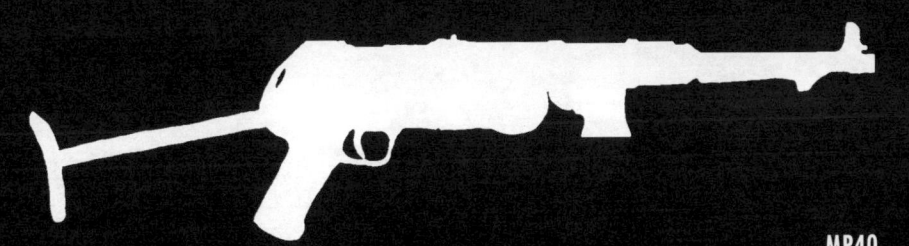

MP40

Thompson M1A1

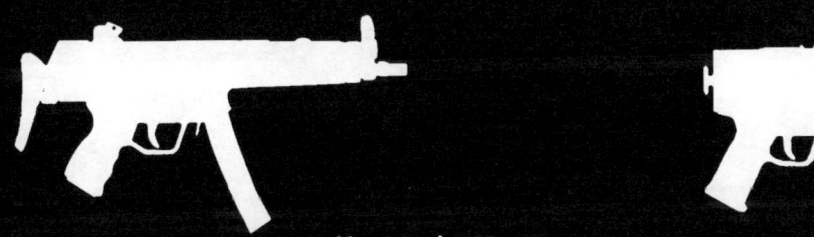

Heckler & Koch MP5   Heckler & Koch MP5 K

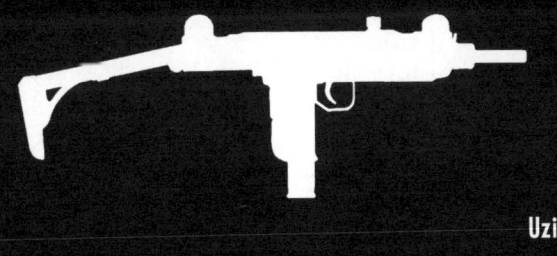

Uzi   Mini Uzi

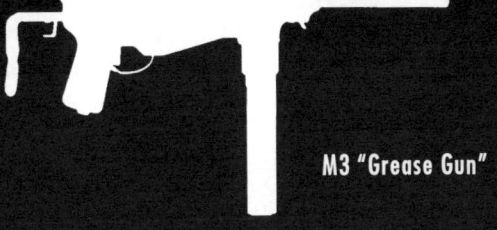

M3 "Grease Gun"

Submachine Guns

Chapter 4

Benelli 90 M3

Beretta 1201 Riot

Franchi SPAS-12

Mossberg Special Purpose

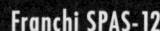

Remington 870 Police

Winchester Model 1300 Marine

Shotguns

tionally secure nonconformist. Or the gunman who prefers capacity over aesthetic classicism.

Franchi SPAS-12   13/5/7
An ergonomic pump, a pistol grip and a high-tech look distinguish this pump/semi-auto combo. This is a gun with a chip on its shoulder.

Mossberg Special Purpose   13/5/9
And just what might that special purpose be, hmmm...? Might it be: blowing people away? Pump action constructed to fulfill military specifications.

Remington 870 Police   13/5/7
A brand name that conjures up images of the old West. Pump action with classic stock design. Whenever a "not-as-dumb-as-his-cracker-act-would-suggest" Southern sheriff points a shotgun at your character's head, it's this one he's pointing.

Ruger Red Label   10/5/2
This is your basic hunting over/under shotgun (one barrel is over the other); use the same stats for any of the other zillion hunting guns on the market. I picked this one because it was used by Senator Bob Kerrey of Nebraska in a memorable TV ad in the 1994 mid-term elections. This is what irascible old coots will be firing at you when you trespass on their land looking for the *Feng Shui* site where the coot keeps his moonshine still.

Winchester Model 1300 Marine   13/5/8
Another historic brand name in a stainless steel pump action no-nonsense design.

Rifles

Sometimes the guerrilla war across time becomes a bona fide battlefield-type war, and that's when

Guns

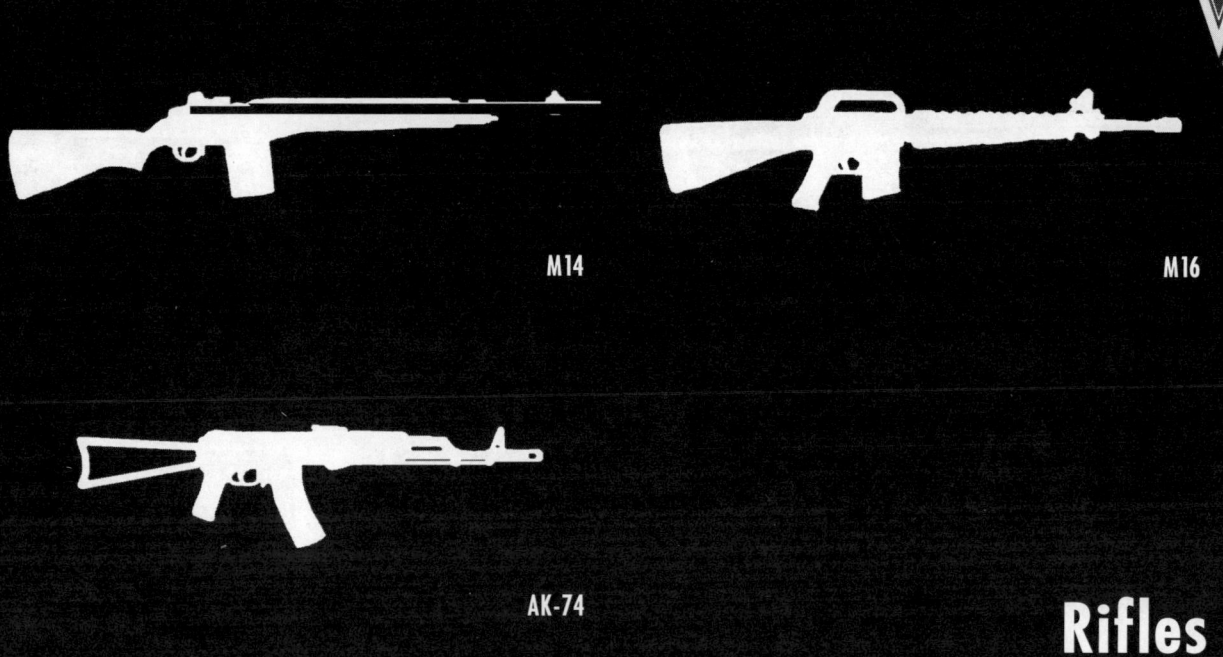

Rifles

assault rifles come in handy. These all take 3 shots to reload and are capable of fully automatic fire.

Weapons with a single asterisk (*) after the Damage rating take out unnamed characters with an Outcome of 4 or more. Weapons with a double asterisk (**) put 'em down on a 3 or more.

AK-47 13**/5/30
The classic Soviet assault rifle. There are a zillion of these around the world. You're especially likely to get shot at with them in nations that used to be Soviet clients or satellites.

AK-74 13*/5/30
The 47's younger brother. See above.

K2 13*/4/30
An almost-concealable 5.56 caliber rifle from South Korea.

M16 13*/5/30
The basic rifle of the US army, among many other militaries, including several on the *Planet of the Apes*. Since these weapons aren't manufactured for the consumer market, the flash and marketing glitz isn't a factor here. There are lots of variations on this one, none of which have cool names so let's just call them all M16s and be done with it.

M14 13**/5/20
A bigger-caliber buddy of the M16.

2056

Just as guns designed in the early part of the 20th century are still used today, basic gun design has not changed much by 2056. In fact, since everyone with a license to manufacture is a crony of the repressive Buro government, the quality craftsmanship that wins out in a competitive situation isn't present. Buro guns take 10 shots to unjam after a malfunction. Many secret warriors from 2056 prefer to grab contemporary weaponry as soon as possible; if you have a 2056 character with a gun schtick but the action of the game begins in the contemporary setting, you can pick contemporary guns instead of, or as well as, these ones. All guns in 2056 are manufactured to Buro specifications, and tend to be pretty much alike. Design is functional and groovy in a blocky sort of way. The names of the weapons are colorfully propagandistic.

The one advantage Buro guns have over contemporary ones is their weight; they are made of gonvex, a rugged polymer with most of the properties of steel. They don't beat contemporary guns in firepower, but win out in the concealability sweepstakes.

As there is little model variation in Buro guns, only one version of each type is listed.

Many of the guns listed here aren't issued to any but the most trusted special operations personnel. If you have a 2056 character and pick any of these, you have to come up with a credible reason why the character would have such weapons.

Chapter 4

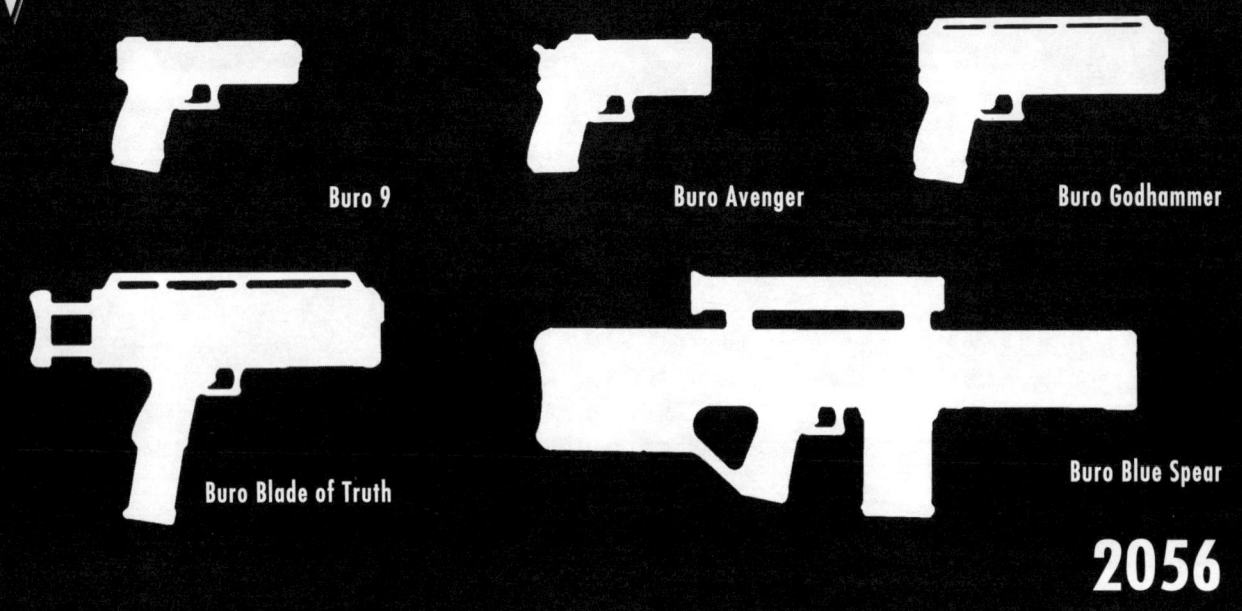

2056

Buro Backup Arm   8/1/5 + 1
Simple little .22 autoloading pistol.

Buro Beat Patroller   9/1/7 + 1
A .38 autoloading pistol.

Buro 9   10/1/17 + 1
A slightly-modified version of the contemporary Glock 17. Also available as the 9A, a fully automatic model.

Buro Avenger   11/2/6
A .357 magnum revolver with none of the sleek look but all of the punch of contemporary models. Issued only to special forces and elite military units such as the monster hunters.

Buro Godhammer   12/4/5
This .50 autoloading pistol isn't built to be concealable. It's supposed to be big and intimidating. As the Buro's Arcanoelite troops like to say, "God is dead and we have his hammer." Ontology aside, this hand cannon is capable of full autofire, though firing in bursts will shoot its wad right quick. Like the Avenger, its distribution is highly restricted.

Buro Crimestopper   13/5/7
Pump-action combat shotgun. One of the few Buro weapons with a chrome finish. Beat cops get these in the backs of their cruisers.

Buro Blade of Truth   10/3/30
Very concealable 9mm SMG, capable of full autofire. Restricted to special-ops types.

Buro Blue Flag   13*/4/30
Almost-concealable 5.56 caliber assault rifle. Full auto fire. Restricted.

Buro 16   13*/5/32
Slight variation on the M16. Full autofire.

Buro Blue Spear   13**/6/30
7.62 autofire rifle.

Buro Hellharrower   14**/8/20
A mammoth assault rifle that fires 9.76mm rounds on full auto. Mostly issued to abominations, since it requires a Strength rating of 11 to use.

The Buro has other nasty weapons, but these are all Arcanowave Devices; you can't get them without an AI/O port, the Arcanowave Device skill, and appropriate schticks.

Fu Powers

June 2

The CandCo deal turned into a slaughterhouse, and we were the beef. Chen was down, the Bronze Mask was down, West Willow was down, McCroun was down. Any or all of them were dead for all I knew. Jimmy was definitely dead, cut nearly in two. I was the last one standing. I was up on a catwalk, down to one mag. On a catwalk across the way there was the White Ninja, the Shattering Hand, C. C. Wang, and all three Lee brothers. Not to mention about two dozen mooks. I had them pinned down for the moment with some suppressing fire, but that wasn't going to last long. I'd seen these people operate. I could handle maybe one of them, plus all the mooks. All in all, the situation looked distinctly like the end of the line.

I tried to use the cross-time cell phone Prof had given me to call for reinforcements, but I was getting nothing but static. Signal interference. Shoulda figured. This whole deal had stunk bad from the start. We knew Tsien's forces were going to try to take this factory. But we didn't know enough about why. We didn't have time to research CandCo and figure it out. The geomancer had just told us the place had powerful chi, and that was enough for Prof to decide we didn't want Tsien plopping his fat mutant butt down on it. I argued against getting involved with so few facts in the briefing book, but I lost the debate. And now, unlike Prof, I was about to pay for it with my skin.

It was the White Ninja who decided to go for me. She did a triple midair somersault and landed herself on the stream of bullets I was laying down, running along the bullets like they were an escalator. Man, fu powers really get up my butt. I tried to raise the stream and wax her, but she skipped along it like she was John Travolta in a white suit and the bullets were a lit-up dance floor. Before I knew it, she was in my face with a handful of razor-tipped fingernails. I stumbled backwards over Jimmy's corpse, the nails missing me by millimeters. I grabbed Jimmy's sword and used it to feebly parry her next lunge. Close-up fighting was not my scene. I opened up the Uzi at close range right into her solar plexus, but she wove this pattern in the air with her steel fingertips and deflected every last round.

Suddenly there was this big clanging sound from behind us. The White Ninja looked back to see what it was, and I clocked her with my now-empty gun. I ran backwards along the catwalk, still holding onto Jimmy's sword, as if it would do me any good. The roof of the factory had opened up, and there was a team of combat-suited mercs rappelling down on ropes, blasting C.C., the Shattering Hand, and the rest back into the corners like rats. Not that I had plans to hang around to watch the score get evened. It was time to bug out. I backed off from the catwalk into an office area.

That's when I felt the dart on my neck. Everything went swirly, like a cheesy video effect, and then I was out of it.

I woke up in an oak-paneled room. Big budget all the way. I was seated in a very nice antique wooden chair, Victorian period. Hey, I know my style, and whoever put together this interrogation chamber had it to spare. The mirror all along the wall was a dead giveaway. I was going to get the third degree, that was for sure. It wasn't Tsien, because he's not a prisoner-taking kind of guy. My guess was it was whoever sent in the cavalry. That merc team wasn't our guys, that was for sure.

The door opened, and in waltzes a red-nosed Scot with a face like a steam shovel. Inspector MacAllister. This was getting weirder and weirder. Because this sure wasn't no police station.

"Now, son, you're gonna answer a few questions. And the folks behind that one-way mirror there are gonna listen to them, and very carefully decide whether to let you leave here breathing. Got my meaning, son?"

CHAPTER 5

Fu Powers

THE WAY OF THE WARRIOR

Fu powers are exotic martial arts abilities which require the user to expend chi energy. Some characters start the game with fu powers; most other character types can learn fu powers in the course of play.

USING FU POWERS

Characters with positive Chi or Kung Fu ratings may use fu powers. Each fu power has a **Chi Cost**. This is the number of Kung Fu or Chi points that it requires to use. (The rest of this chapter usually refers to Chi; characters may always use Kung Fu instead if it is higher.) You have a total number of chi points to spend on fu powers; this number equals your Chi rating. You can spend this number every sequence. You can't carry over chi points from sequence to sequence. Spending chi points does not change your overall Chi rating.

Each power also has a **Shot Cost**. This is the amount of time the action takes, including any checks (unless otherwise noted). Very brief actions have a cost of 1; the standard complex action undertaken in combat has a cost of 3. Unless otherwise noted, a fu power lasts only for those shots. Shots are fully explained in the section on initiative on p. 129. The use of some fu powers is a defensive action; defensive actions are also explained on p. 130.

SELECTING FU POWERS

Some character types start the game with fu powers. They may choose any given in this chapter, with one proviso. Fu powers are arranged along **paths** of learning; the first fu power on a given path will usually be the weakest power on that path. Each subsequent fu power in a path requires that you know one or more preceding fu powers in that path; these requirements are known as **prerequisites**. When starting the game, you may be able to select a number of fu powers. You can't select a power without also selecting its prerequisites. If a power has more than one prerequisite listed, you must already know all of the listed powers before selecting the one in question.

Example: Valerie is creating an Old Master. She wants to take the fu power Flying Windmill Kick, which has the prerequisite of Prodigious Leap. She can only take Flying Windmill Kick if she takes Prodigious Leap as well.

Note that some powers have special requirements; Aberrant Leap, for example, requires that you drink a bunch of booze before you can use the power. Other powers that have Aberrant Leap as a prerequisite don't need Aberrant Leap's same requirements to function, just the ones they specify (if any).

Typically, a character using fu powers will focus on just a couple of paths so that she can learn the most powerful fu powers that appear at the ends of the paths. However, you can jump around from path to path as you like.

LEARNING FU POWERS

Any character with a Chi or Kung Fu rating above zero can learn a new fu power. To do so you need a willing teacher who knows the power, or have access to ancient texts or some other source that tells you how to use it. The experience point cost of a new fu power is 3 + x, with x being the number of fu powers you will have when you gain the new one. Since it's boring for the other characters to wait around while you go off and train, the learning of new fu powers is something that should happen in the background of the story.

In fact, it's perfectly okay if you use the conceit that your character has known the power all along but just hasn't chosen to use it so far. Action heroes pull this one all the time.

Illustration by Thomas Manning

Chapter 5

POWER LIST

Each entry gives the name of the power, its chi cost, and its shot cost on the first line. The body of text explains how the power works in play. Prerequisites tells you which powers you need before you can acquire the one in question. Path indicates fu powers for which the power in question is a prerequisite. If there is no Path listing, no other power has the power in question as a prerequisite. Throughout this section, diagrams show the relationships between the powers in each path. In these diagrams, the powers in italics have more than one prerequisite.

Path of the Shadow's Companion

Friend of Darkness   Chi: 1 / Shots: 1
You can act normally in partial or complete darkness with no Action Value penalties; effect lasts until end of sequence. *Prerequisite: none, Path: Dark's Soft Whisper*

Dark's Soft Whisper   Chi: 4 / Shots: 3
An otherwise normal Martial Arts attack you make is completely silent; no one can hear any sounds you or your opponent(s) make during the shot that it occurs. *Prerequisite: Friend of Darkness, Path: Blade of Darkness*

Blade of Darkness   Chi: 1 / Shots: 3
You can mold chi energy and darkness together into a spontaneously created six-inch, razor-sharp blade. The blade lasts for a number of hours equal to your Outcome. It has a Damage rating equal to your Strength +3. Intimidation checks you make while brandishing this weapon have a +3 Action Value bonus. This ability is also highly useful when you're unable to smuggle a physical weapon into a secure area. *Prerequisite: Dark's Soft Whisper, Path: Gathering the Darkness*

Gathering the Darkness   Chi: X / Shots: 3
Draw the darkness and shadows in the area towards you like a protective cloak. Perception checks to detect your presence suffer a -X Difficulty Modifier for X minutes after you activate this fu power. *Prerequisite: Blade of Darkness, Path: Strike from Darkness*

Strike from Darkness   Chi: 4 / Shots: 3
Make a Martial Arts attack on an opponent who is unaware of your presence. If you are successful, damage you do is not reduced by opponent's Toughness. *Prerequisite: Gathering the Darkness, Path: Shelter of Darkness*

Shelter of Darkness   Chi: 7 / Shots: 0
When you successfully hit an opponent with a Martial Arts check, you may elect not to do damage to him. Instead, an area with the opponent as its center is plunged into absolute darkness until the end of the sequence. The area has a radius in meters equal to your Outcome. All combatants who are not somehow immune to the effects of darkness suffer a -4 Action Value penalty on any attack check made within, from, or into that area of darkness. At the GM's discretion, other actions that require sight also suffer the same penalty. The shot cost of Shelter of Darkness does not include the shot cost of the attack itself. *Prerequisite: Strike from Darkness*

Path of the Sharpened Scales

Bite of the Dragon   Chi: 2 / Shots: 3
Make a Martial Arts attack with a +2 bonus to your Damage. *Prerequisite: none, Path: Breath of the Dragon*

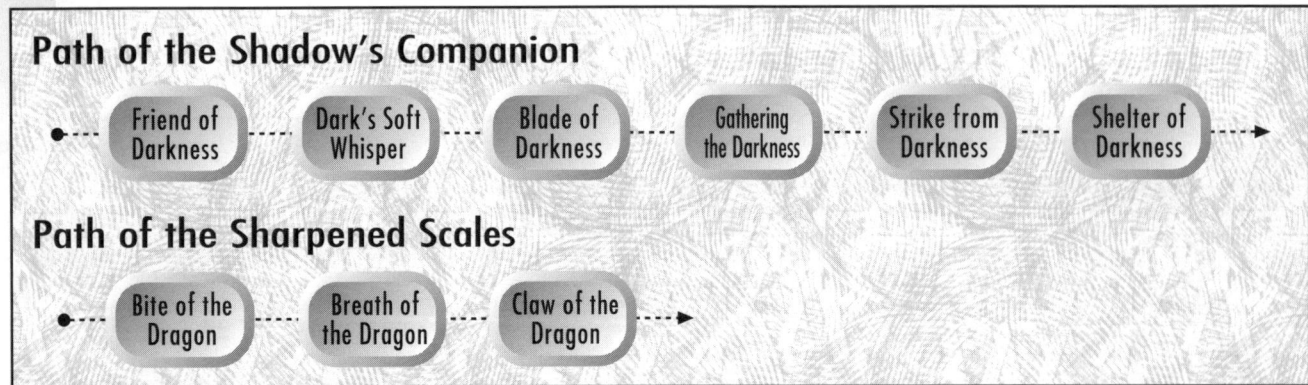

(78)

Fu Powers

Breath of the Dragon Chi: 3 / Shots: 3
Make a Martial Arts attack with a +3 bonus to your Action Value. *Prerequisite: Bite of the Dragon, Path: Claw of the Dragon*

Claw of the Dragon Chi: 5 / Shots: 0
Add 4 to the Outcome of an already successful Martial Arts attack you have just made. *Prerequisite: Breath of the Dragon*

Path of the Passive Wings

Crane Stance Chi: 1 / Shots: 1
If the opponent attempting to hit you has a Perception rating lower than your Agility rating, your Dodge increases by 5. Using Crane Stance is a defensive action. *Prerequisite: none, Path: Wing of the Crane*

Wing of the Crane Chi: 2 / Shots: 1
Until the end of turn, you may substitute your usual Chi rating (not your number of unspent Chi points in the current sequence) for your Strength rating when making any tests that require it, including Damage determinations. *Prerequisite: Crane Stance, Path: Beak of the Crane*

Beak of the Crane Chi: 1 / Shots: 3
On a successful Martial Arts task check, you may place an opponent in a hold that renders him immobile. Every 3 shots, the immobilized opponent may make a Strength task check with your Martial Arts Action Value as the Difficulty; if he succeeds, he breaks free from the hold. If you do anything other than passively dodge, he also breaks free of the hold. *Prerequisite: Wing of the Crane, Path: Talon of the Crane*

Talon of the Crane Chi: 3 / Shots: 3
On a successful Martial Arts task check, you may place an opponent in a hold that renders him immobile. Every 3 shots, the immobilized opponent may make a Strength task check with your Martial Arts Action Value as the Difficulty; if he succeeds, he breaks free from the hold. If you do anything other than passively dodge, he also breaks free of the hold. Every time the opponent makes the Strength check, he suffers 3 wound points. *Prerequisite: Beak of the Crane*

Path of the Hands of Light

Hands Without Shadow Chi: 1 / Shots: 3
Make a Martial Arts attack against which your opponent can't actively Dodge. *Prerequisite: None, Path: Dim Mak*

Dim Mak Chi: 2 / Shots: 3
Strike an opponent barehanded; if you succeed at a Martial Arts task check, your attack ignores any armor the opponent may have. *Prerequisite: Hands Without Shadow, Path: Lightning Fist*

Lightning Fist Chi: 6 / Shots: 3
Strike an opponent bare-handed; if you succeed with your Martial Arts task check, your opponent may not use Toughness to reduce damage from your strike. *Prerequisite: Dim Mak*

Path of the Clever Eye

The Fox's Retreat Chi: 1 / Shots: 1
Add +5 to your Dodge value. Counts as a defensive action. *Prerequisite: None, Path: Eyes of the Fox*

Eyes of the Fox Chi: 1 / Shots: 1
Study an opponent in combat; the GM must tell you the numerical value of one of the opponent's attributes, skills, or current point totals. You choose which one. *Prerequisite: The Fox's Retreat, Path: Laughter of the Fox*

Laughter of the Fox Chi: 1 / Shots: 3
Make a Martial Arts check; if successful, you grab a weapon from the hands of an opponent. Difficulty is opponent's Dodge value. Until end of sequence, all attacks made by you with this weapon against this opponent gain a +3 Action Value bonus. Add 5 to the Difficulty of your check if the weapon you're grab-

Path of the Passive Wings

Crane Stance → Wing of the Crane → Beak of the Crane → Talon of the Crane

Path of the Hands of Light

Hands Without Shadow → Dim Mak → Lightning Fist

bing at is someone else's signature weapon. *Prerequisite: Eyes of the Fox, Path: Vengeance of the Fox*

Vengeance of the Fox   Chi: 2 / Shots: 0
When you are hit by an opponent in hand-to-hand combat, you may make a Martial Arts attack check. If successful, the opponent is thrown a number of meters equal to the Outcome of the attack in the direction of your choice. Opponent suffers Damage equal to his Strength + the Outcome. *Prerequisite: Laughter of the Fox, Path: Luck of the Fox*

Luck of the Fox   Chi: 1 / Shots: 3
Execute a maneuver that draws chi energy from the world around you. You may spend Chi points as Fortune points until the end of the sequence, suffering 5 Wound Points each time you do so. *Prerequisite: Vengeance of the Fox, Path: Contract of the Fox*

Contract of the Fox   Chi: 8 / Shots: 0
Use immediately after Initiative is rolled. You have a first shot equal to the highest first shot rolled. *Prerequisite: Luck of the Fox*

Path of the Tightening Coils

Eyes of the Snake   Chi: 2 / Shots: 1
Execute a series of distracting tai chi moves; the shot costs of all attacks made against you are increased by 1 until end of sequence. *Prerequisite: none, Path: Slither of the Snake*

Slither of the Snake   Chi: X / Shots: 1
X unnamed characters, if they have a choice of targets, can't select you as their target until after the end of the sequence when all is normal again. If all characters on one side of a fight are using Slither of the Snake, the power is neutralized for all of them. *Prerequisite: Eyes of the Snake, Path: Strike of the Snake*

Strike of the Snake   Chi: 3 / Shots: 0
Reduce any 3 shot action which requires a Martial Arts task check to a 1 shot action. *Prerequisite: Slither of the Snake, Path: Coil of the Snake*

Coil of the Snake   Chi: X / Shots: 0
You may execute a Martial Arts attack on the current shot even if it isn't a shot you can attack on. X = the difference between the current shot number and your next shot number. This does not affect when your next shot number occurs; it's strictly a bonus attack, not an alteration to initiative. It also does not change any costs of the Martial Arts attack you make. *Prerequisite: Strike of the Snake, Path: Lunge of the Snake*

Lunge of the Snake   Chi: 3 / Shots: 0
Add 3 to the result of an Initiative Roll. *Prerequisite: Coil of the Snake*

Path of the Brilliant Flame

Fire Strike   Chi: 1 / Shots: 3
Strike an opponent barehanded with Martial Arts; add 2 to the final Damage if the strike hits. If your opponent is wearing flammable clothing, that clothing ignites and the opponent must take 3 shots to slap the fire out or suffer 1 Wound Point every 3 shots until something is done about the fire. Total damage from the fire effect cannot exceed your Chi rating. *Prerequisite: none, Path: Fire Stance*

Fire Stance   Chi: 6 / Shots: 1
Until end of sequence, any opponent striking you barehanded suffers 1 Wound Point per strike. These Wound Points are not reduced by Toughness. *Prerequisite: Fire Strike, Path: Fire Fist*

Fire Fist   Chi: 3 / Shots: 3
Strike an opponent barehanded with your fist wreathed in a flaming nimbus of chi energy. Damage rating of attack is 10. Even opponents somehow immune to Martial Arts attacks and/or fu powers

---

Path of the Clever Eye

The Fox's Retreat → Eyes of the Fox → Laughter of the Fox → Vengeance of the Fox → Luck of the Fox → Contract of the Fox

Path of the Tightening Coils

Eyes of the Snake → Slither of the Snake → Strike of the Snake → Coil of the Snake → Lunge of the Snake

Fu Powers

take full Damage from attack, unless they are also immune to the fire effect of the Sorcery's Blast schtick. *Prerequisite: Fire Stance, Path: Eyes of Fire*

Eyes of Fire Chi: 3 + X / Shots: 3
As per Fire Fist, but you can now damage opponents without touching them: a blast of flame emanates from your eyes. X = number of meters between you and opponent. *Prerequisite: Fire Fist, Path: Gathering the Fire*

Gathering the Fire Chi: 3 / Shots: X
You can stand in the middle of a raging blaze without suffering damage for any number of shots in a single sequence. For each shot spent enveloped in flames, you gain a temporary Chi point. (The total number of shots you spend in this manner is where the X shot cost comes from.) You may choose to spend these at any time to pay the chi cost for any fu power(s); once spent, they are gone forever. They do not change your Chi rating for checks; they only give you more points to spend on fu powers. If spent on powers in this path, those powers are at half cost. *Prerequisite: Eyes of Fire*

Path of the Selective Master

Signature Weapon Chi: 0 / Shots: 0
When you acquire this fu power, specify a single hand-to-hand weapon as your signature weapon—see p. 141 for general rules on signature weapons. This refers to a single, particular item, not all weapons of its type. When you use this weapon, your Damage increases by 3. *Prerequisite: None*

Path of the Immutable Clay

Creative Thunder Chi: 1 / Shots: 3
Strike a character wielding an arcanowave device barehanded. If your Martial Arts task check succeeds, add the current Difficulty for the character's next mutation check to the Outcome. *Prerequisite: None, Path: The Wandering Cow*

The Wandering Cow Chi: X / Shots: 1
When you suffer an arcanowave effect that would force you to make a mutation check at the end of the session, spend Chi equal to the Difficulty of that check if it were held immediately. You may then apply an equal number as an Action Value bonus to the next action you take. The mutation check still occurs normally at the end of the session. *Prerequisite: Creative Thunder, Path: No Medicine*

No Medicine Chi: 3 / Shots: 8
Lay hands on an individual (including yourself) who will have to make a mutation check at the end of the session due to arcanowave exposure. Make a Martial Arts check with the Difficulty being that of the mutation check were it held immediately. If you succeed in the check, the current Difficulty of the victim's mutation check restarts at 0. If you fail in the check, you must make a mutation check at the end of the session, with the victim's current Difficulty added to your own, if any. The victim's Difficulty is not changed in this case. *Prerequisite: The Wandering Cow, Path: Unexpected Harvest*

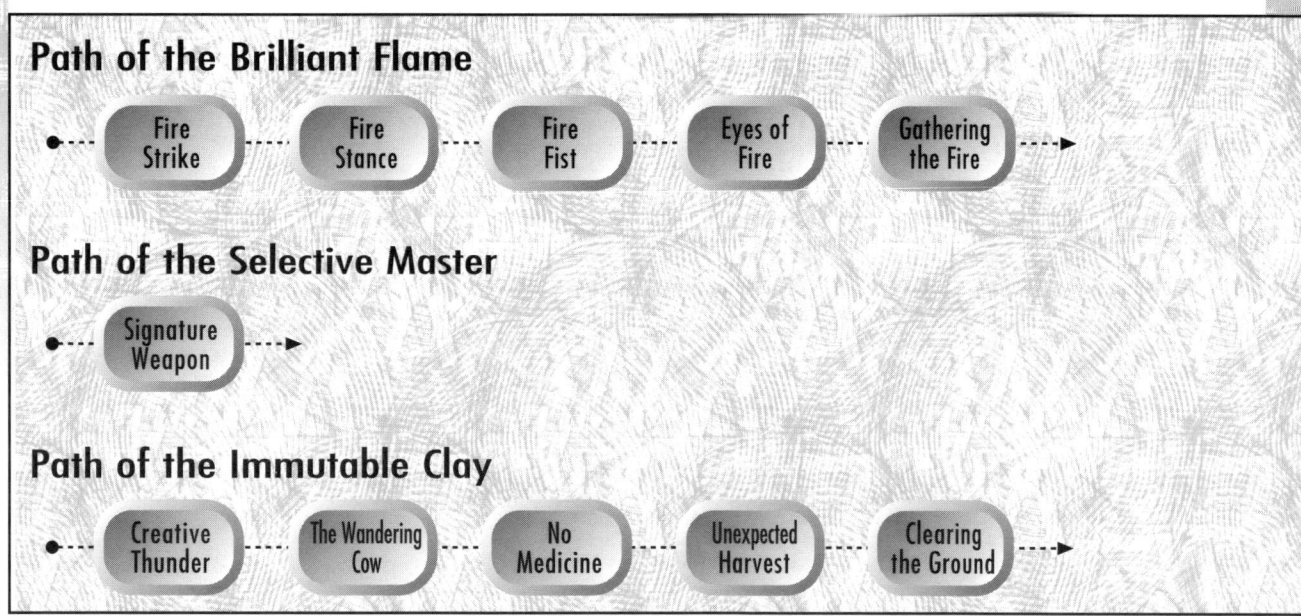

Chapter 5

Illustration by Grey Thornberry

Fu Powers

Unexpected Harvest Chi: 0 / Shots: 0

If you have just completed a successful use of the No Medicine fu power, you may convert the dissipated arcanowave energy into a one-time store of chi energy. Make a Martial Arts task check, using the same Difficulty as the No Medicine check. If successful, you gain a number of Chi equal to that Difficulty; once the Chi is spent, it cannot be recovered. These bonus Chi points remain with you until spent, but they do not add to your Chi attribute rating. *Prerequisite: No Medicine, Path: Clearing the Ground*

Clearing the Ground Chi: 8 / Shots: 15

Cure a willing subject who has been mutated by arcanowave exposure, returning the subject to his state before any mutation due to mutation checks occurred. To do so, take the character's current value on the Mutation Outcome Chart (p. 124), treat it as a positive rather than a negative number, and make it the Difficulty for a Martial Arts check. If you succeed, the subject is cured. If you fail, the subject remains in his mutated condition, and you yourself must make a mutation check at the end of the session, adding the Difficulty of the check you have just made to the Difficulty of the Mutation check. *Prerequisite: Unexpected Harvest*

Path of the Empty Bottle

Drunken Stance Chi: 1 / Shots: 1

As a continuous action, weave and trip drunkenly about. Your opponent must make a Perception check in order to attack you; making this check uses up one of your opponent's shots. Difficulty of the Perception check equals the number of servings of alcohol you have consumed in the last half hour; a beer counts as half a serving for this purpose while a dose of wine or liquor counts as a full serving. When Drunken Stance is used, any Martial Arts Action Value penalties due to alcohol consumption are ignored until end of sequence. You are also a master of the ancient and esoteric art of speed-drinking. You can consume two servings of alcohol per shot by using Drunken Stance. The alcohol hits your bloodstream immediately, taking full effect on you as soon as you chug it down. *Prerequisite: none, Path: Drunken Fist*

Drunken Fist Chi: X / Shots: 3

Strike an opponent barehanded, subtracting X (an amount of Chi you elect to spend) from his Dodge Action Value for your Martial Arts check. In order to use this power, your character must have consumed a number of beers equal to his Constitution rating, or a number of servings of wine or liquor equal to half his Constitution rating, no more than half an hour before the beginning of the fight. *Prerequisite: Drunken Stance, Path: Wily Stupor*

Wily Stupor Chi: X / Shots: 1

Add X (an amount of Chi you elect to spend) to your Toughness when a successful attack is made against you. Using Wily Stupor is a defensive action. In order to use this power, the character must have consumed a number of beers equal to his Constitution rating, or a number of servings of wine or liquor equal to half his Constitution rating, no more than half an hour before the beginning of the fight. *Prerequisite: Drunken Fist, Path: Aberrant Spasm*

Aberrant Spasm Chi: 3 / Shots: 1

Duck and weave unpredictably in combat as a defensive action. After your opponent's Martial Arts check, make one of your own and select any character within 3 m as the possible target of his attack. Your Difficulty is your opponent's Action Result plus half of the new target's Dodge value, rounding up. The new target suffers Damage equal to your Outcome plus the damage rating of your opponent's weapon. In order to use this power, the character must have consumed a number of beers equal to his Constitution rating, or a number of servings of wine or liquor equal to half his Constitution rating, no more than half an hour before the beginning of the fight. *Prerequisite: Wily Stupor, Path: Spasmodic Leap*

Spasmodic Leap Chi: 3 / Shots: 1

Until end of sequence, any opponents wishing to draw a bead on you with guns or other ranged weapons must make a successful Perception check. If they fail the Perception check, they must spend 6 shots firing at you without hope of success. The Difficulty of the check is the number of servings of wine or liquor, or half the number of beers, your character has had in the past six hours. Opponents who fail the check may not act for 3 shots, after the 6 shots of firing end. *Prerequisite: Aberrant Spasm*

Path of the Empty Bottle

Drunken Stance → Drunken Fist → Wily Stupor → Aberrant Spasm → Spasmodic Leap

Path of the Healthy Tiger

Claw of the Tiger Chi: 1 / Shots: 3
Strike an opponent barehanded; damage value for the strike is your Strength +3. *Prerequisite: none, Path: Tiger Stance*

Tiger Stance Chi: 1 / Shots: 0
Immediately after you are damaged by an opponent in hand-to-hand combat, you may launch a free Martial Arts attack on that opponent. This has no effect on your current Shot. *Prerequisite: Claw of the Tiger, Path: Unyielding Tiger Stance*

Unyielding Tiger Stance Chi: 2 / Shots: 0
When you are attacked in hand-to-hand combat, you may respond with a simultaneous Martial Arts attack. This has no effect on your current Shot. *Prerequisite: Tiger Stance, Path: Vengeance of the Tiger*

Vengeance of the Tiger Chi: 4 / Shots: special
When you are wounded in hand-to-hand combat, you may immediately launch a Martial Arts counterattack against the opponent who just wounded you, using any Wound Points you suffer from that one attack (after reduction for Toughness) as a bonus to your Action Value. You must then make a Constitution check with the Wound Points you have just suffered as your Difficulty; if the Outcome is negative, you are exhausted and cannot act for a number of shots equal to that Outcome. If you pass the check, you must wait 3 shots before acting again. *Prerequisite: Unyielding Tiger Stance, Path: Storm of the Tiger*

Storm of the Tiger Chi: X / Shots: 0
X is any amount of Chi you elect to spend. Add X twice to the Damage of a bare-handed strike you have just made. *Prerequisite: Storm of the Tiger, Shadowfist*

Flow Restoration Chi: 0 / Shots: 1
Release a subject affected by the fu power Point Blockage from paralysis; you must be able to touch subject. *Prerequisite: none, Path: Corners of the Mouth*

Corners of the Mouth Chi: X / Shots: 1
Spend any amount of Chi (X) while touching subject; subject gains that amount of Chi and may spend it at any time during the current sequence. At the end of the current sequence both your Chi total and the subject's return to normal, and any unspent Chi is wasted. *Prerequisite: Flow Restoration, Path: Healing Chi*

Healing Chi Chi: special / Shots: 10
In a lightning-quick series of moves, jab crucial acupressure points of a wounded patient in order to dramatically speed up his natural healing process. Make a Martial Arts check and subtract the Action Result from the patient's current Wound Point total; there is no such thing as negative Wound Points and no way to save up healing to apply against future wounds. If you are damaged yourself while performing a Healing Chi, apply any Wound Points you suffer during this period as a penalty to your Action Value. If your Action Result is negative, recipient suffers a further 5 Wound Points. See p.137 of the Fights section for general rules on Medical Assistance. *Prerequisite: Corners of the Mouth, Path: Point Blockage*

Point Blockage Chi: 5 / Shots: 3
Strike an opponent in unarmed combat in such a manner as to block the flow of chi through his body and paralyze him. You must make a successful Martial Arts check, and then must make a Chi check with your opponent's Chi rating as the Difficulty. If you make both checks, opponent is paralyzed and remains paralyzed for a number of shots equal to the Outcome of the Chi check. The victim retains all of his senses while under this effect. If he realizes that an attack of any sort is aimed at him while paralyzed, he can make a Chi or Kung Fu check (his choice) with your Chi or Kung Fu rating (whichever is higher) as the Difficulty. If successful, he is freed. *Prerequisite: Healing Chi, Path: Shadowfist*

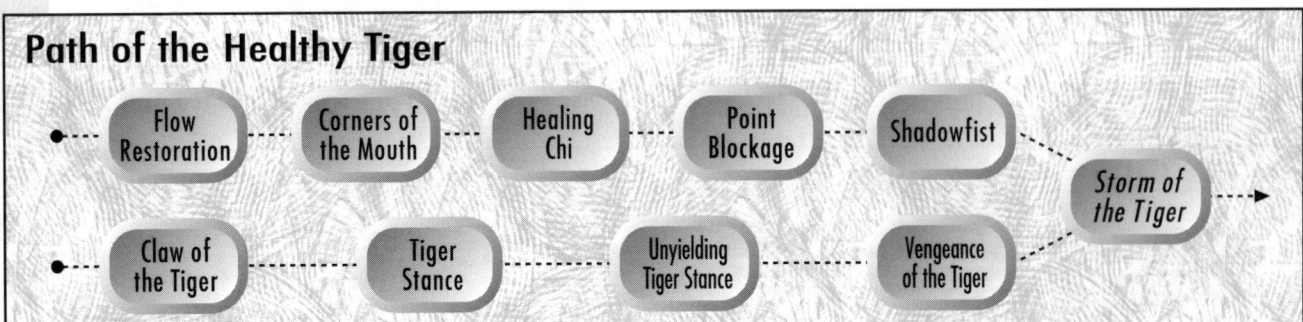

Path of the Healthy Tiger

Fu Powers

Shadowfist Chi: special / Shots: 3
Strike an opponent barehanded. If you succeed at a Martial Arts task check, you do not do normal damage. Instead, make a Chi or Kung Fu task check with opponent's Chi, Kung Fu, or Will (whichever is highest) as the Difficulty. If this check succeeds, permanently reduce your Kung Fu and Chi ratings by 1; opponent's Martial Arts Action Value is permanently reduced by 5 and opponent permanently loses the ability to use a fu power of your choice. Prerequisite: Point Blockage, Path: Storm of the Tiger

Path of the Storm Turtle

Clothed in Life Chi: 1 / Shots: 1
Until end of sequence, Damage done to you by characters with lower Chi ratings than your own is reduced by 2 per strike. *Prerequisite: None, Path: Armored in Life*

Armored in Life Chi: 3 / Shots: 3
Until end of sequence, add 3 to your Toughness for the purpose of determining Wound Points suffered from successful attacks. *Prerequisite: Clothed In Life, Walk of a Thousand Steps*

Inner Strength Chi: 1 / Shots: 1
Substitute your Kung Fu secondary attribute for your Magic secondary attribute when determining the difficulty of magic spells cast against you. Applies until end of sequence. *Prerequisite: none, Path: Eye of the Storm*

Eye of the Storm Chi: 2 / Shots: 3
Neutralize the lingering effects of any single magic spell cast against you. Does not affect Wound Points caused by spells up to that point but halts any further damage from occurring once the spell is neutralized. *Prerequisite: Inner Strength, Path: Gift of the Storm*

Gift of the Storm Chi: 1 / Shots: 0
As you use another fu power, you may designate another character as the beneficiary (not the target) of its effect. Treat that character as "you" in the fu power's description. That other character must be a willing participant, and must be within (3 m x your Chi rating) of you. In the case of Drunken Stance and the fu powers on its path, it is the user of Gift of the Storm who must be drunk, not the new beneficiary. *Prerequisite: Eye of the Storm, Path: The Storm Reverses*

The Storm Reverses Chi: X / Shots: 1
Specify a new target for a magic spell cast at you by an opponent. X equals the opponent's Magic rating. Using The Storm Reverses is a defensive action. *Prerequisite: Gift of the Storm, Path: Tornado of Shelter*

Tornado of Shelter Chi: 7 / Shots: 3
You are immune to damage from magic spells or arcanowave devices until end of sequence. *Prerequisite: The Storm Reverses, King on the Water*

Willow Step Chi: 1 / Shots: 0
Your Dodge Value increases by 2 for the duration of the shot. *Prerequisite: none, Path: Walk of a Thousand Steps*

Walk of a Thousand Steps Chi: X / Shots: 3
Until the end of the sequence, you add X (the amount of Chi you elect to spend) to the Action

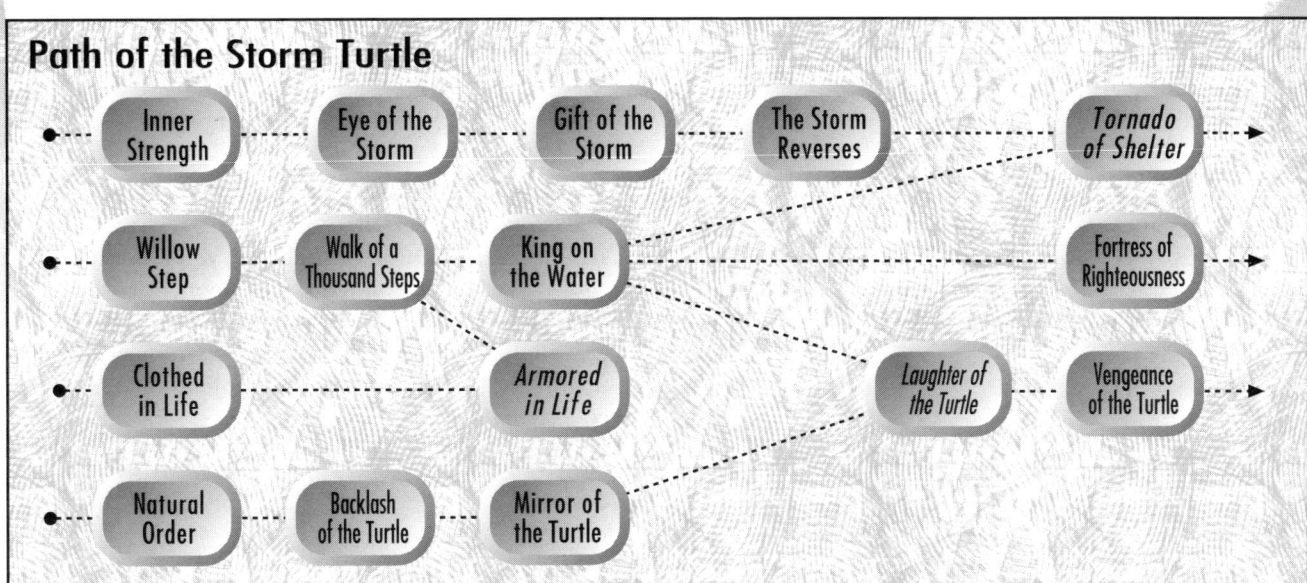

Path of the Storm Turtle

(85)

Value of your Martial Arts rating whenever you make an active Dodge. *Prerequisite: Willow Step Path: King on the Water, Armored in Life*

King on the Water Chi: 3 / Shots: 3
If your Charisma rating is greater than your opponent, the next attack he makes against you automatically fails. *Prerequisite: Walk of a Thousand Steps Path: Fortress of Righteousness, Laughter of the Turtle, Tornado of Shelter*

Fortress of Righteousness Chi: X / Shots: 3
A fu power used by an opponent in striking you is neutralized. X is the Cost of the neutralized power. Opponent still spends chi and shot costs of neutralized power. Using Fortress of Righteousness is a defensive action. *Prerequisite: King on the Water*

Natural Order Chi: 3 / Shots: 1
You take no damage from a single strike from a gun or arcanowave device. Using Natural Order is a defensive action; declare it when you're targeted for attack but before the check is made. *Prerequisite: None, Path: Backlash of the Turtle*

Backlash of the Turtle Chi: 3 / Shots: 3
A gun or arcanowave device which has just done Wound Points to you is destroyed. Signature weapons are immune to this effect. *Prerequisite: Natural Order, Path: Mirror of the Turtle*

Mirror of the Turtle Chi: 3 / Shots: 3
Make a Martial Arts check with the number of Wound Points (after any reductions for Toughness) you have just suffered from a single hit from a gun or arcanowave device as your Difficulty. If you succeed, the opponent that wounded you takes an equal amount of Wound Points which are not reduced by Toughness. *Prerequisite: Backlash of the Turtle, Path: Laughter of the Turtle*

Laughter of the Turtle Chi: 7 / Shots: 3
You are immune to damage from guns until the end of the sequence. *Prerequisites: Mirror of the Turtle, King on the Water, Path: Vengeance of the Turtle*

Vengeance of the Turtle Chi: 4 / Shots: 3
If you succeed in striking a non-living vehicle barehanded or with a kick, that vehicle is destroyed. *Prerequisite: Laughter of the Turtle*

Path of the Leaping Storm

Gathering of the Clouds Chi: 1 / Shots: 0
Maintain a continuous action without adding to the shot costs of other actions you take. *Prerequisite: none, Path: Awesome Downpour*

Awesome Downpour Chi: 1 / Shots: 3
Using a single Martial Arts check, attack two named characters who are within 3 meters of one another, using the highest of the two Dodge values as the Difficulty. Both opponents take the same amount of Damage. *Prerequisite: Gathering of the Clouds, Path: Rain of Fury*

Rain of Fury Chi: 2 / Shots: 0
Immediately after making one attack on an unnamed opponent, you may make another attack on the same opponent with no shot cost. *Prerequisite: Awesome Downpour, Path: Torrent of Fury*

Torrent of Fury Chi: 8 / Shots: special
Spend all of your shots at once to launch a series of attacks against a number of opponents. Each time you succeed at a Martial Arts task check, you can immediately make an additional attack on another opponent. You may attack each individual opponent only once per sequence. *Prerequisite: Rain of Fury, Vertical Charge, Path: Integration of the Clouds*

Integration of the Clouds Chi: 1 / Shots: 0
Combine the use of two fu powers into one action; affected powers must share a word in their titles (such as "Fox" or "Fire"). Fu powers with contradictory conditions may not be combined. Pay chi cost for both, but only the highest shot cost. *Prerequisite: Torrent of Fury*

Prodigious Leap Chi: 1 / Shots: 1
Leap twice your normal Move rating. The leap can be horizontal or vertical. *Prerequisite: none, Path: Abundant Leap, Flying Windmill Kick*

Flying Windmill Kick Chi: 7 / Shots: 5
Make a normal kick attack with the Martial Arts skill. If the task check is successful, you may make another kick attack on the same opponent at 0 shot cost. You may continue doing this until you fail a task check, so the number of attacks you may launch against this single opponent is theoretically unlimited. *Prerequisite: Prodigious Leap*

Fu Powers

Abundant Leap Chi: 2 / Shots: 3
Leap four times your normal Move rating. The leap can be horizontal or vertical. *Prerequisite: Prodigious Leap, Path: Flying Sword*

Flying Sword Chi: 3 / Shots: 3
Strike an opponent by flying at him with sword outstretched; if you hit, add your Move rating to Damage dealt. *Prerequisite: Abundant Leap, Path: Loyal Steel, Vertical Charge, Water Sword*

Water Sword Chi: 5 / Shots: 1
Make a display motion in which your sword seems to become springy and flexible. Until end of sequence, opponents suffer a -2 penalty to their Dodge values, but only for attacks made by you. *Prerequisite: Flying Sword*

Loyal Steel Chi: 1 / Shots: 3
Throw any hand-to-hand weapon at an opponent; opponent may be as far away as (3 meters x your Chi rating). Make a normal Martial Arts check to see if you hit; if you do, Damage is calculated as if you had hit your opponent with that weapon in normal hand-to-hand combat. Whether you hit or not, your weapon immediately flies back through the air to return to your hand. *Prerequisite: Flying Sword*

Vertical Charge Chi: 3 / Shots: X
Run up a vertical surface, such as a tree trunk or wall. You choose a shot cost for the action; add this shot cost to your Martial Arts Action Value for a sword attack made immediately after using this power. *Prerequisite: Flying Sword, Path: Torrent of Fury*

Path of the Leaping Storm

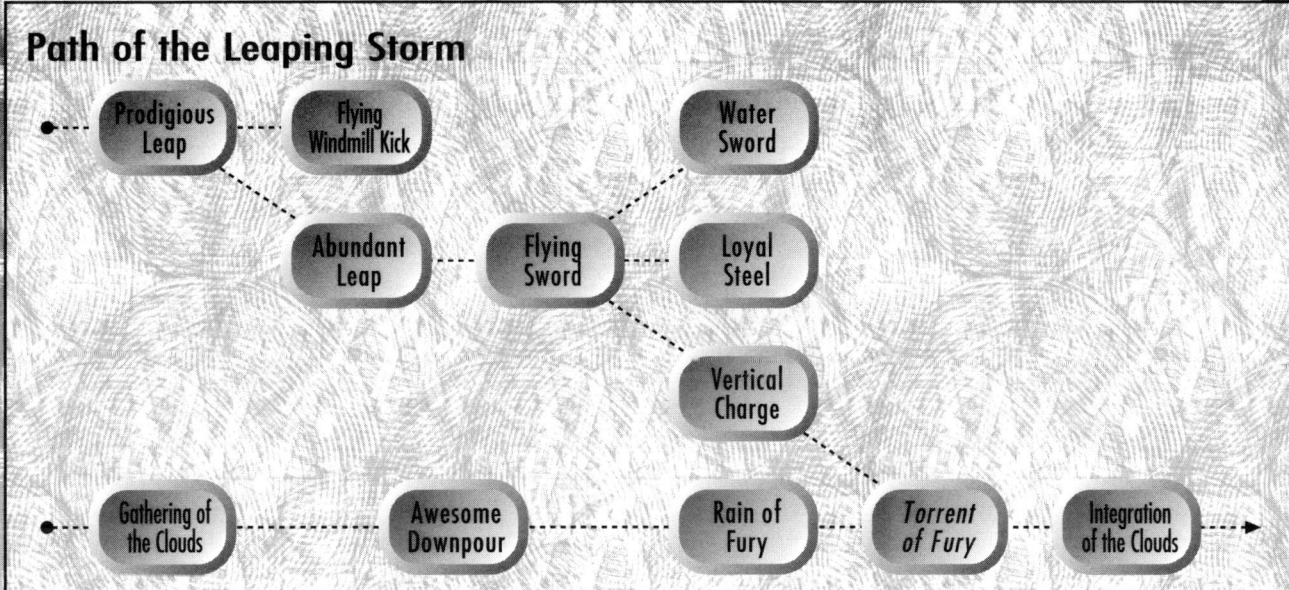

CHAPTER 6

Magic

THE WAY OF THE SORCERER

You need to read this section only if you're a GM or are playing a character with the Sorcery skill. It provides some general rules on the use of magic, and then describes the different magic schticks available to characters.

SPELLCASTING IN THE WORLD OF *FENG SHUI*

When casting spells, sorcerers are gesticulating, chanting, and undertaking other ritual actions. These might include using a brush and ink to form particular Chinese characters on paper, burning incense or paper, or spreading powders in mystical patterns.

To prevent a sorcerer from casting spells, you must gag him, bind his hands, or separate him from his supply of inks, papers, and powders.

SPELLCASTING IN THE GAME

Casting a spell is a complex action with a shot cost of 3. It requires a task check against the spellcaster's Sorcery skill. Difficulties for various magical actions are listed in the magic schtick descriptions given later in this section.

Example: Yuan Guo is casting a Movement spell. According to the Movement description, the Difficulty of the spell depends on the size of the object being moved. In this case, he's moving a rock with a corresponding Difficulty of 10. Yuan's Action Value for Sorcery is 15. He rolls a +2, yielding an Action Result of 17 and an Outcome of 7. According to the schtick description, he can move the rock a distance equal to the Outcome x 3 m–in this case, 21 m.

Whatchacallit?
Sorcerers in Hong Kong action movies often have funky names for their spells. The names for the special effects in *Feng Shui* are basic and explanatory; you should choose a new name for each special effect that is the name your character knows it as. Instead of "Chucking Things About" for example (a Movement special effect), your character might call it "Wind of Eagle's Wings" or "Unseen Hand." You don't need to re-name every special effect right from the start, but if you think of one during play you should jot it down on your character sheet and try to use that in the future. Sorcerers often call out the name of their spell if it would be dramatic, so using a funky name for your spell is both cooler and also prevents your enemies from knowing just what you're doing.

The rituals required for spellcasting are not so exacting that a few extraneous movements will spoil them. It is possible to passively or even actively dodge while spellcasting, although an active dodge means that the spell will go off on a later shot than originally planned. As with other actions, it is possible to shave shot costs on Sorcery checks by taking a negative modifier on your Action Value—see "Snapshots," p. 130.

Instead of dividing magic up into dozens of minutely differentiated little spells, *Feng Shui* gives sorcerers a few basic types of effects to perform; each is a schtick. The schticks provided in this

Magic

book include Blast, Divination, Fertility, Heal, Influence, Movement, Summoning, and Weather. Each schtick lists a variety of **special effects**. These are broad subcategories that define what spells look like and how they behave. A character can use any of the special effects given under a schtick he has; they are more like guidelines and suggestions rather than individual spells you have to learn and so they're all available to you. The one exception to this rule is for the Blast schtick; you only get 3 Blast special effects at first. This is covered under "Learning New Schticks" on p. 92.

As a player with a sorcerer character, when you want to use your Sorcery skill to do something you should first look at the schticks you have chosen for your character. If the desired effect is explicitly listed in the schtick description (probably as a special effect), there's no problem—even the Difficulty of the spell will be ready and waiting for your GM. If it is not listed—and many common and useful effects will not be—figure out how your schtick could be used to create the effect you want. Then convince the GM that the desired effect falls within your schtick. You have to be able to do this in a straightforward sentence or two. *Feng Shui* leaves no time for complicated wrangling between you and the GM. If the GM buys your line of reasoning, she'll secretly assign a Difficulty to the attempt and tell you to make a Sorcery task check. If she doesn't, she'll tell you that the attempted effect is impossible given your schticks. If you prove particularly argumentative, she'll pretend to be assigning a Difficulty to the attempt and let you make a task check, even though she's decided that the attempt will be an automatic failure. This is especially risky if you roll boxcars, since such failures still allow for Backlash—see below.

GMs should use the examples provided under each schtick to arrive at sample Difficulty numbers. For example, the Difficulty of any spell effect which directly targets a being with attributes is the victim's Chi attribute or its secondary attribute Magic, whichever is higher.

When you do this, you might want to jot down notes on what you just did and consider that to be a new special effect that you can readily use during future games. If so, then consult with your GM after the session and make sure you both agree on how this new special effect works. This doesn't cost you any experience points, since it's just a different way of using something you already have.

Again, though, the Blast schtick is different: You can always do a basic blast without any special effects, but you can't make up a new Blast special effect on the fly.

Example: Peter and Avis are both playing sorcerers. Both of them want to persuade a distrustful bartender to reveal some information. Peter's character's schticks are Blast, Heal, and Movement. Avis' PC's schticks are Blast, Influence, and Weather.

Peter says: "Movement should apply to the desired effect because I want to move his opinion."

The GM says: "Nice try, but Movement is about moving physical objects. Won't work."

If Peter persists, the GM—instead of slowing down the game by getting involved in a lengthy session of rules-lawyering—can let him make a Sorcery check that secretly has no chance of success.

Avis then says: "I'll use the Inspiration special effect of Influence to give the bartender the idea that he trusts us and can tell us what we need to know."

The GM figures that this is right on target, and assigns the standard Difficulty rating for this kind of spell, as given in the schtick description: the Chi or Magic rating of the affected character. In this case, the Chi rating of the bartender is 4. He also assigns a +5 modifier to the Difficulty because the effect is subtle, and subtle effects are always harder than obvious ones in the world of Feng Shui. *(See the Spellcasting Difficulty Modifiers chart, p. 90.) This means that Avis needs an Action Result of 9 to convince the bartender.*

Avis makes a Sorcery check for her character, who has a rating of 12 in Sorcery. Her roll is a -4, giving her an Action Result of 8. The bartender isn't convinced and won't help the characters.

Peter is antsy. "I'm going to use Blast to knock the guy against the wall, and I want it to leave him feeling woozy and willing to talk."

Again, the GM says nix. Peter can Blast the bartender and hope that's persuasive enough by itself, but he can't tack on the willingness-to-talk effect onto his Blast; that's really a new special effect, and he can't make up a new Blast special effect on the fly.

Combining Schticks

Some magical effects will fall between the definitions of the various schticks. Sorcerers can combine the schticks they know to create complex effects. Again, how well this works depends on the player's persuasive powers and the GM's judgment. The GM may allow for partial successes when one part of the combination seems much harder to attain than the other.

Example: Lew wants his sorcerer character to reanimate the corpses of some dead henchmen he wants to interrogate. This doesn't seem to fall directly within any of the schticks he knows. But he proposes to use both Heal (to bring the corpses back to a semblance of life) and Summoning (to retrieve their souls and

Spellcasting Difficulty Modifiers

Nature of Desired Effect	Modifier
completely derails the plot	automatic failure
helps move plot along	-3
is boring or expected use of schtick*	+1
is especially entertaining	-2
is necessary to advance the plot	automatic success
is obvious and flashy	-2
is subtle	+5
slows down the story	+5

*Doing damage to an opponent is never penalized in this manner.

Spellcasting Juncture Modifier Chart

Juncture	Sorcery Action Value Modifier
69	+2
1850	-2
Contemporary	-2
2056	+1
Netherworld	+1

consciousness from their journey to the underworld) together to create the effect. Lew's GM buys the argument and lets him try it. However, she thinks it should be pretty tough to bring characters back from the dead. She decides that he needs a 15 on his Sorcery task check to get the corpses moving again, and a 20 to get the right souls back in their bodies. If he gets an Action Result above 14 but under 20, the GM decides that the revived corpses will simply stumble about mindlessly, causing trouble for the PCs. Since Lew has mentioned nothing about Influencing the reanimated goons, the GM also decides that the spirits of the henchmen will be considerably less than cooperative even if Lew's character does get them stuffed back into their old bodies.

SPELLCASTING DIFFICULTY MODIFIERS

GMs have to come up with Difficulties for Sorcery checks off the cuff. They should determine what all of the relevant factors are and then mush them all together to get a final Difficulty rating. The chart below has some standard Difficulty Modifiers to consider

JUNCTURE MODIFIERS

Magic is easier to work in some junctures than others. In some junctures, factions or individuals hostile to the use of magic control most of the feng shui sites. In game terms, this means a penalty to your Sorcery Action Value; see the Juncture Modifier Chart at the left.

If the balance of feng shui control shifts in a juncture, these modifiers will change as well, at the discretion of your GM. For example, if the Ascended get control of the 69 or 2056 junctures, the modifiers for those junctures will become the same as the 1850 and contemporary ones. On the other hand, if a group that relies on magic (like the Lotus) takes control of the later junctures, those junctures will match the modifier of the 69 juncture.

The Sorcery check modifier of the Netherworld changes too, to balance out the modifiers of the open junctures. The total Action Value modifier of all open junctures plus the Netherworld is always 0. If another juncture changes its modifier value, the modifier for the Netherworld is whatever number is needed to make the total of all juncture modifiers equal 0.

Example: The 69 juncture changes to a -2 Sorcery Action Value modifier. The total of all open junctures is: -2 -2 -2 +1 = -5. The modifier for the Netherworld is now +5 to make the total equal 0.

Hong Kong and Juncture Modifiers

For some reason—various theories have been proposed to explain it—contemporary Hong Kong and the New Territories is not subject to the usual Sorcery Action Value Modifier. Its modifier is 0.

We suggest Hong Kong as a starting point for *Feng Shui* series. Among other things, this cuts the sorcerers in the group a little slack to start out with.

SORCERY AND STUNTS

Sorcerers, like fu experts and gun maniacs, can achieve useful results by employing stunts as they make Sorcery checks. This is most relevant to spell effects that have an obvious, physical result.

Multiple Targets. Sorcerers can hit multiple targets with the Blast schtick, at an Action Value penalty of -1 per additional opponent.

Magic

Called Shots. Like other forms of attacks, Sorcery attacks allow for the use of Called Shots. See p. 137.

Ancillary Effects. Sorcerers can create funky additional effects as well. For example, you might want to singe a mook with a fiery Blast spell, and at the same time ignite a drum full of gasoline behind him. The Action Value penalty for such attempts will not typically exceed -2.

DODGING WITH BLAST

Sorcerers with the Blast schtick can passively or actively dodge using their Sorcery value as the Dodge score. They do so by erecting a barrier of magical energy around themselves; it serves to deflect incoming attacks directed at them. Juncture modifiers to your Sorcery Action Value also apply to sorcerous dodging.

PARRYING WITH BLAST OR MOVEMENT

Certain schticks allow spellcasters to use their Sorcery skill as the basis for a Parry attempt—general rules on parrying appear on p. 133. Characters with the Blast schtick can fire counter-blasts which intercept incoming ranged weapon attacks, spells, and hand-to-hand blows. Characters with the Movement schtick can interpose large, solid objects as shields against ranged weapon attacks and incoming spells. Needless to say, such objects must be available to the sorcerer. Parrying with a spell has a shot cost of 1.

DESPERATE EFFORTS

Spellcasters usually draw on the chi energy of the world around them to power their supernatural effects. However, it is possible to put extra energy into a spellcasting effort by expending your own personal mystic energy. Sorcerers can spend points of their Magic secondary attribute during combat to increase their Sorcery Action Values.

For each point of Magic that you expend, you may increase your Sorcery Action Value by 1; this applies to one task check only. You may expend multiple Magic points on one check.

Immediately after the check on which you've spent the point(s), subtract them from your Action Value for Sorcery. When determining the Difficulty of spell effects used against you, the GM uses your current Magic total, not your usual maximum. Remember, since Magic is the base attribute of the Sorcery skill, your Sorcery Action Value goes down too as do any other skills you have that use Magic as the base attribute. So does the damage you do with Blast. Obviously, you cannot spend more points than you have.

Magic points return to normal at the beginning of each game session.

Example: Yuan Guo is really PO'ed now, so on his next shot against his rival, he decides to spend a Magic point to increase the Action Value of a Blast attempt. He is at his normal Magic rating of 7. He reduces his Magic to 6 for the remainder of the session and adds 1 to his Action Value, so that it goes from 15 to 16. His roll is a +2, for an Action Result of 18. That oughta singe his opponent's robe!

Some spell effects require the expenditure of Magic points; these do not count as Desperate Efforts in determining Backlash (described in the very next section). Magic points spent in this way also return at the beginning of a session.

BACKLASH

Magic is a means of forcing chi energy to obey your will, and chi energy does not like to be forced. Sometimes a sorcerer ends up channeling more energy than he can handle. This makes magic inherently dangerous in a way that using fu powers or firing guns is not. When a character fumbles and fails any Sorcery check, he suffers a magical Backlash. Backlash effects vary from spell group to spell group, and are explained in the schtick descriptions later in this chapter.

Example: Yuan Guo is casting a Blast spell at a rival sorcerer. He makes a Sorcery check with a Difficulty of 13. His Action Value is 15. He gets boxcars on his first roll. He then rolls a -3, for an Action Result of 12—a failure. This failure following double sixes means that he suffers a Backlash. In the case of a Blast spell, that means that he suffers 10 Wound Points.

If you get boxcars when shaving the shot cost for a spell attempt, or employing a desperate effort (see above), you automatically suffer backlash, whether you succeed or not.

LEARNING NEW SCHTICKS

Some character types come with magical schticks. Types without such schticks may not take any at the beginning of the game, but can learn them in the course of play.

Characters with the Sorcery skill can acquire new magic schticks at a cost of (16 + x) experience points per schtick. X = the number of magic schticks they will have when they gain the new one. Learning a new schtick requires no time on-stage during the game. It is assumed that they have been studying the tricks of the schtick between scenes while accumulating those experience points.

When you learn a new magic schtick, you automatically can use all of the special effects for that schtick unless it's Blast. You only gain 3 of Blast's special effects. To buy another Blast special effect, you have to spend 3 experience points. You can create a new Blast special effect and spend 3 points to gain it, but this should be done between game sessions since it involves some work on the part of your character. The GM can let this occur during a game, but not if it's going to slow things down and make everyone wait around while you and the GM hash out the new Blast special effect. New special effects for other schticks don't cost anything and can be created on the fly if possible.

LEARNING THE SORCERY SKILL

Any character may learn the Sorcery skill in the course of play. To do so, one must spend two years as an apprentice to an experienced master of Sorcery: one with a Sorcery rating of 15 or more. Such apprenticeships generally involve lots of demeaning manual labor, boring rote learning, and general boot-licking. During such a period of apprenticeship, the character must obey every command of his master, even to the point of risking his personal safety. The master has the unquestioned right to control every aspect of the apprentice's personal life. At the end of two years, the apprentice must make a check with his Magic secondary attribute; the Difficulty of the check is 10. If the apprentice passes the test, he may then spend experience points on the Sorcery skill, and may choose two schticks. If he fails but wishes to try again, he must spend at least another 6 months of apprenticeship, after which he may make another Magic check, this one with a Difficulty of 8. Failing characters may continue to make new checks every six months; for each additional six month period of apprenticeship, the Difficulty decreases by 2. Note that masters concerned with saving face may boot out apprentices who fail more than once; keeping on an obviously shoddy student reflects poorly on the master.

MAGIC SCHTICKS

Here are the basic schticks of sorcery. Some Difficulties listed below require you to divide. Always round up fractions in Difficulty ratings.

BLAST

Blast spells do damage to opponents and/or objects. No *Feng Shui* spellcasters worth their ritually-burnt tortoise shells lack this schtick. Because Blast is such a powerful effect in the game world, involving a violent force of chi flow, it's hard to make Blast do funky things—in other words, you can't make up new special effects on the fly. Creating new Blast special effects is covered in "Learning New Schticks", above.

The base Damage value for a Blast is your character's Magic rating + 2. The Difficulty of a Blast spell is the opponent's Dodge, Magic, or Sorcery rating, whichever is higher. Blast spells work like any other attack form. Backlash for all Blasts is 10 Wound Points suffered by the spellcaster.

Example: An evil eunuch with a Magic score of 10 and a Sorcery skill of 15 tosses a lightning spell at Yuan Guo. Yuan Guo's Dodge rating is 12; his Magic and Sorcery ratings have been decreased by 1 since Yuan just spent a Magic point: they're 6 and 14, respectively. His Sorcery rating is highest (14), and is therefore the Difficulty of the Blast attempt. The eunuch rolls a +4, for an Action Result of 19. This beats the Difficulty of 14 with an Outcome of 5. The Outcome of 5 is added to the Blast's Damage of 12, and then Yuan's Toughness of 6 is subtracted. Yuan suffers 11 Wound Points. Ouch!

Blast Special Effects

Acid. Creates a stream of liquid or a cloud of gas that eats away tissue and other material. Also useful for removing serial numbers from contraband items, damaging evidence, and poisoning small water supplies.

Chi. Too much raw chi energy can burn and sear opponents, and wither objects. When cast within a feng shui site it will sever or disrupt the connections between the site and those attuned to it. When done successfully, those attuned to it lose any benefits of attunement until they re-attune. The Difficulty of severing a chi connection is 3 x the number of attuned characters. You can't de-attune some characters and not others. Desperate Efforts with this blast type yield an Action Value bonus of 2 per Magic Point spent.

Conjured Weapons. You create from thin air a glowing, magical weapon or weapons—for example, a sword, spear, or rain of knives—which hurls towards your opponent. Useful for damaging things that are immune to most normal attacks; it's also particularly upsetting to opponents previously unfamiliar with magic.

Disease. A particularly nasty way of harming someone, one which works only over a long period of time; more suited for use by villains than by player characters. Instead of delivering instant Wound Points, the Damage determines the severity of the illness caused. Subtract the victim's Constitution from the Damage. The result is the disease rating. For every 5 points of disease rating (rounding down) the victim suffers 1 point of Impairment until cured. The disease can be cured by conventional medicine if the doctor makes a successful Medicine task check with the disease rating as the Difficulty. It can also be cured by the Sorcery schtick Heal, or by the fu power Healing Chi.

Disintegration. Causes affected matter to simply disappear. Also useful for simulating vanishing tricks and destroying evidence. At the GM's discretion, characters damaged by disintegration blasts—particularly called shots—may suffer injuries that can only be healed with magic or arcanowave tech. If he adopts this as a general rule, add 2 to the Difficulties of all disintegration blasts.

Fire. An old favorite. This damages opponents by burning them. Also useful for setting fires, lighting cigars and cigarettes in an impressive manner, heating up coffee, increasing room temperature, and thawing out frozen foods.

Ice. Applies severe freezer burn to opponents. Also useful for making ice cubes, freezing or chilling food, making water solid enough to walk on, and cooling the temperature in a hot room.

Lightning. The discharge of electrical energy. Also useful for recharging car batteries and overloading electronic equipment.

Steam. Scalds opponents and causes water damage to some materials. Also useful for fogging up car windows and eyeglasses, as well as opening envelopes,

Transmutation. Turns one type of matter into any other type of your choice. Damages tissue by turning it into one substance, like stone, water, or primordial ooze. The new substance is a very rough approximation of the real thing; this power can't be used to create gold pure enough to sell, or manufacture objects durable enough to be used without breaking. It's only good for hurting people and wrecking stuff. This one is very demoralizing, as characters damaged by it can only be healed by magic or arcanowave tech. Transmutation blasts suffer a +3 Difficulty modifier.

DIVINATION

The magician gains information through mystical means. The backlash for Divination is bad luck. The GM assigns your character an additional negative die on your next three important task checks. The GM gets to decide what constitutes an important check.

Divination Special Effects

Revelation. On a successful Sorcery task check, the caster can identify illusions as false or divine the true forms of supernatural creatures who are using the Transformation schtick (p. 107.)

Prediction. Gives the caster good, if somewhat obscure, advice or information about the future. Most traditional Chinese mages will employ the I Ching (pronounced Yee Jing), the ancient Book of Changes. This is a book of cryptic verses; one finds the relevant verses by dividing yarrow stalks into odd and even patterns, arriving at a pair of trigrams. Trigrams are parallel broken or unbroken lines arranged in threes. Even more traditional mages will tell fortunes by throwing tortoise shells into the fire and then interpreting the patterns of cracks that appear on them after they are burned.

When a sorcerer PC uses Prediction, the GM should provide a cryptic answer to the question the sorcerer seeks the answer to. This answer should be designed to a) make the player work to puzzle out its meaning and b) move the plot along by providing a clue that gets the characters to the next scene. The Difficulty of such attempts depends on how good the GM thinks her clue is. If all she can think of is an obvious clue, the Difficulty is high. If she is confident in the ingenious nature of her clue, she can make the Difficulty low.

If the GM is familiar with I Ching—good translations can be found at any decent bookstore—she can choose in advance an applicable trigram, and assign a Difficulty of 8 to the divination attempt. If the attempt fails, the sorcerer gets a random trigram instead. (The I Ching being what it is, the players may well find just as good advice in the random trigram!)

When enemy sorcerers succeed in using Prediction, they get warning of the PC's plans and are ready and waiting to counter them. Difficulties for such divination attempts equals the highest Chi or Magic rating in the PC group.

Warning. The sorcerer draws a chalk outline on the ground around an area she wishes to secure from intrusion, making a Sorcery task check as she does so. There is no limit to the size of the area, but the chalk outline must be unbroken. She may name any number of specific intelligent beings who may cross it without triggering the alarm. Any intelligent being not so named causes a palpable shiver to run down the spine of the sorcerer if the being crosses the line. Secretly make a Magic or Sorcery check (whichever is higher) for the intruder; if the Action Result beats the sorcerer's original Sorcery Result, the warning is not sent.

If the sorcerer using Warning also knows the Blast schtick, she can combine the two effects to create a mystical booby-trap. She makes two Sorcery checks: the first for Warning, the second for a Blast. If an intruder triggers the warning, he gets to make another Magic or Sorcery check besides the shiver check; if it is lower than the sorcerer's original Blast check, he suffers the effect of a blast. This blast is a surprise and cannot be dodged. The sorcerer does not know when or if the Blast booby-trap goes off; only the basic Warning provides the shiver of awareness that the line has been crossed.

The warning effect remains in place as long as the chalk line remains unbroken. It is not possible for an intelligent intruder to brush away the line without also triggering the warning, but there are many natural effects that will destroy it without causing a warning.

FERTILITY

These effects all depend on the core ability to measure and modify the flow of chi in the natural environment. A Backlash with any Fertility effect decreases the sorcerer's Constitution rating by 1 until the end of the session.

Fertility Special Effects

De-Attunement. You can sever an individual's link to all of his feng shui sites, forcing him to re-attune to them in order to continue getting their benefits. Difficulty is the highest of the following: victim's Sorcery or Magic rating, or (the number of feng shui sites he is attuned to) x3.

Germination. Creates powders and potions to make plant seeds germinate even in very barren soil conditions, or to increase milk production in cows and goats. Neither of these effects requires a task check.

This can also be cast on people or animals to make them more likely to conceive offspring. Base Difficulty is 5. If the subject of this latter effect is unknowing or unwilling, add its Magic or Chi rating to the Difficulty. If the check is successful, the GM makes a special check the next time the subject engages in activities likely to lead to procreation, adding the Outcome to an open roll. If the end result is positive, the female partner conceives. If the end result is over 15, animals get larger litters and human subjects will have twins or even triplets.

The sorcerer can also create potions of reversed effect that will retard plant growth, sour cow's milk, and make animals and people temporarily infertile.

Growth. Creates a potion which causes all plants in the vicinity to immediately increase their size. Vicinity means within 5m of the point where the potion is poured onto the earth. For each 5% size increase desired by the sorcerer, Difficulty goes up by 1.

Example: To create a potion that will increase the size of corn stalks in a field by 5%, the Difficulty is 1. If the increase is 25%, the Difficulty is 5. If the increase is 75%, the Difficulty is 15. If the increase is 150 percent, the Difficulty is 30.

Harvest Chi. The sorcerer may spend a Magic point to add an extra positive die to any task check she attempts.

Observe Chi. Allows the sorcerer to see the flow of chi in an area. The stronger a place's chi, the easier it is for the sorcerer to see. She can immediately identify feng shui sites. She can identify the particular features in a natural formation or building that either channel or retard the flow of chi. The sorcerer can precisely peg the Chi rating of any character she can directly observe for more than thirty seconds. She can also see any lingering magical or arcanowave effects: these both deform the flow of chi in distinctive ways. None of these actions requires a task check.

Steal Chi. The sorcerer may spend a Magic point to add an extra negative die to any task check attempted by any other character she is currently observing. Seeing someone through remote viewing aids such as binoculars and video cameras counts as observing.

Restore Chi. The sorcerer can restore chi flow where it has been disrupted or altered by sorcery or arcanowave technology. This cancels any currently-active magic or arcanowave effects. Difficulty equals the Sorcery or Arcanowave Action Value of the character who caused the effect. The fertility sorcerer need only equal or exceed the Difficulty in order to completely neutralize the effect. If the Restore Chi attempt is made at the same time as a Sorcery or Arcanowave check and is successful, it prevents the Sorcery or Arcanowave effect from taking effect in the first place.

HEAL

This is the ability to restore individuals to good health and repair objects. If the character is a Chinese sorcerer, she is in all probability an alchemist. She whips up her cures by mixing various powders and potions she carries on her person; these are then either applied externally or taken orally. Laying on of hands to heal is a special effect more appropriate for Western characters. Backlash effects vary by special effect, but generally will do the reverse of the desired effect to the sorcerer and not help the target.

Heal Special Effects

Cure Diseases. Difficulty varies depending on the severity of the illness. A cold virus would be Difficulty 6; pneumonia, Difficulty 8; chronic heart illness, Difficulty 12; cancer, Difficulty 15; AIDS, Difficulty 20. Nasty arcanowave biohazards engineered by the Architects cause diseases of at least Difficulty 15. In a Backlash, the sorcerer contracts the illness she is attempting to heal. If the sorcerer is trying to cure herself and suffers a Backlash, she infects a friend or loved one, usually one nearby or recently encountered.

Heal Wounds. Make a Sorcery task check and subtract the Action Result from a wounded person's total Wound Points. This may not be performed during a fight or other ongoing injury-inducing crisis. In a Backlash, the sorcerer suffers a number of Wound Points equal to the patient's current total. See p. 137 of the Fighting section for general rules on Medical Assistance.

Immortality. The holy grail for Western alchemists was the ability to transmute lead into gold; for Chinese alchemists it was the secret of immortality. With this effect, you can reverse a year's worth of the aging process in yourself or others. Difficulty is the actual age of the recipient divided by 5. Recipient must permanently decrease her Magic secondary attribute by 1; it is not possible to go below 0. In a Backlash, all benefits from previous Immortality effects reverse themselves; if the recipient is past normal life expectancy, he dies. This seems like more of a problem for the recipient than the sorcerer, but recipients usually make arrangements for servants and allies to slay sorcerers incompetent enough to blow their immortality checks.

Material Restoration. Repair any broken or damaged inanimate object. Difficulty increases with the size and complexity of the item. A small, simple item like a pair of scissors would be Difficulty 4. A small and complex item like a gun, or a large and simple item like a brick wall, would be Difficulty 8. Small and very complex items like a palmtop computer would be Difficulty 12, as would large and complex items like cars. Very large and very complex items, like jet fighters, would be Difficulty 16. It is not possible to repair arcanowave devices with this or any other purely magical spell. On a Backlash, the item is permanently destroyed and cannot be repaired by any means.

Poison Antidotes. Formulate potions to neutralize the effect of toxins in the body. Difficulty is the Damage Value of the poison. If the Sorcery check exceeds the Difficulty, all Wound Points done by the poison are canceled out. On a backlash, the sorcerer suffers a number of Wound points equal to those done by the poison. This effect also works against the lingering effects of the supernatural creature schtick Corruption (p. 103); in this case, Difficulty is the Creature Powers Action Value of the creature that did the corrupting. Backlash: sorcerer becomes corrupted.

Chapter 6

INFLUENCE

This schtick allows the spellcaster to affect the emotions, thoughts, and sensory input of humans and other intelligent beings.

Influence Special Effects

Emotion Potions. Allows the sorcerer to create a potion that fosters a desired emotion in any thinking being who consumes it. The love potion is the most famous example of this type. The sorcerer may also specify the object of the emotion, which need not be another thinking being. For example, a potion could inspire hatred of a truck or lust to own a jewel. A sorcery check is made when the potion is created. When the potion is consumed, the Action Result is compared to the Difficulty—which is the subject's Chi or Magic rating. If the Action Result exceeds the Difficulty, the subject is affected for a number of days equal to the Outcome. On a Backlash, the sorcerer comes under the influence of the potion.

Enchantment. Allows the sorcerer to impose her will on a subject. The subject must be within earshot of the sorcerer: It is possible to work the spell through a telephone, prerecorded sound or videotape, or other long-distance communications methods.

The subject will obey a single instruction, following its spirit as well as its letter. Difficulty is based on the subject's Chi, Magic, or Will rating, whichever is higher. Modifiers are added to the Difficulty based on how likely the subject would be to follow the instruction without magical influence. Instructions that he would follow anyway have no modifier; those he would be only mildly averse to fulfilling are +3. Instructions he would be actively unwilling to follow are +6; those he wouldn't follow without extreme coercion are +9. Instructions that the subject would sooner die than follow are +12. Instructing a mook character to attack one of his comrades usually falls into the "not without extreme coercion," or +9, category.

On a Backlash, the sorcerer becomes extremely susceptible to suggestion and must obey the next instruction he is given. The source of the suggestion might be a friend, an enemy, or even a billboard or TV commercial.

Illusions. Allows the sorcerer to send false sensory signals to a subject's mind. The subject sees, hears, smells, feels or tastes something that isn't there. The sorcerer must be within (3m x sorcerer's current Magic rating) of the subject.

The nature of the illusion is entirely up to the sorcerer. Difficulty is the subject's Chi or Magic rating, whichever is higher. Add +3 Difficulty for each sense after the first affected. Note that this spell alone does not make the subject particularly disposed to believe what his senses are telling him. For example, a sorcerer conjures up in the mind of a security guard an image of a smiling, felt-covered purple dinosaur toting a Heckler & Koch MP5. The guard may well assume that he is hallucinating or that his eyes are otherwise deceiving him. Refusal to believe does not make the false sensory input go away, however; even a false image of Barney's evil twin can be quite distracting in the midst of a gunfight. The illusion lasts for a number of shots equal to the Outcome of the Sorcery check.

On a Backlash, the sorcerer experiences the desired illusion.

Inspiration. Allows the sorcerer to plant a thought or idea in the mind of a subject. The sorcerer may be any distance from the subject, but must have either an intimate item owned by the subject or a former piece of his body, such as a lock of hair or fingernail. Difficulty equals the subject's Chi or Magic rating, whichever is greater. Subject will think he had the idea himself, or interpret the message as a sending from the sorcerer, as the sorcerer desires. If the character thinks it's his own thought, there is no guarantee that the subject will consider the idea to be a bright one or be in any way impelled to act out its instructions; this is not mind control.

On a Backlash, the sorcerer suffers a -1 penalty to his Mind rating for the next 8 hours. He will also be unable to sleep during this period.

MOVEMENT

Allows the spellcaster to move objects around from a distance.

The Backlash from any movement effect causes the sorcerer to be violently hurled a number of meters equal to the Difficulty of the check in a random direction. This will likely entail taking some Wound Points, the exact number being up to the GM. It should be based on what the sorcerer lands on.

Movement Special Effects

Chucking Things About. The sorcerer must be able to see the target object at the time that the spell is cast. Visual aids such as binoculars and remote video cameras work just fine in this regard, but a photograph of the object wouldn't work. The Difficulty is the weight of the affected object(s) in kg, divided by 5. A 50 kg rock would be Difficulty 10; a 100 kg rock would be Difficulty 20. The maximum distance that the object can be moved equals the Outcome of the Sorcery check x 3m. Objects under 5kg can be moved automatically, without the need for a Sorcery check.

Sometimes it is possible to move larger objects by applying just enough force to get them rolling under their own steam. For example, a sorcerer might want to move a tractor trailer parked on the side of a hill. After using Remote Manipulation (see below) to take care of the parking brake, 50 kg or so of pressure in the right place would get the truck rolling down the hill.

Flight. The sorcerer can fly through the air at her usual Move rate. This does not require a Sorcery check. However, the sorcerer will need to make checks when doing complicated things like picking up other people, making active Dodges, zipping through small openings, and so forth.

Remote Manipulation. The sorcerer can perform tasks based on the Manual Dexterity secondary attribute without touching the objects involved. As with Chucking Things About, the sorcerer must be able to somehow see the objects at the time the spell is cast. The Difficulty of the Sorcery check is the same as the Difficulty to perform the task normally; the Sorcerer must succeed both at the Sorcery check and the relevant skill check for the effect to work.

Speed. The sorcerer can increase her Speed rating, or that of another character, for 1 sequence. The Difficulty is the subject's current Speed plus 5. The Outcome is the number of additional Speed points the subject gains for the duration of the subsequent sequence. The sorcerer must be able to somehow see the subject. Characters who don't want to be speeded up can resist with their Dodge, Magic, or Chi ratings.

The sorcerer can likewise decrease the Speed ratings of other characters. Difficulty is the target's Magic or Chi rating, whichever is higher. If the target is aware of the spell and elects to actively Dodge, the Dodge rating becomes the Difficulty. The Outcome is the number of additional Speed points the subject loses for the duration of the subsequent sequence. The sorcerer must be able to somehow see the subject.

SUMMONING

The sorcerer can perform a range of spells and rituals relating to supernatural creatures. For the purpose of this spell description, "supernatural creatures" are defined as any characters with supernatural creature powers (as described on p. 100 of the Creature Abilities chapter) or arcanowave mutations (as described in the Arcanowave Devices chapter). Unless otherwise indicated, the Difficulties for all effects listed below are the Willpower ratings of the target creatures.

Summoning Backlashes involve the sorcerer summoning all manner of unintended, vile creatures who usually proceed to attack him and his buddies.

Summoning Special Effects

Banishment. The sorcerer may drive supernatural creatures from her presence. The sorcerer must be able to see the creature and vice versa. If the Sorcery task check is successful then the subject creature must—for a number of sequences equal to the Outcome—travel at its top speed away from the sorcerer in any direction it finds convenient. The creature may stop to defend itself from actual attacks, but may take no other action (other than attempting to flee) while the spell remains in effect. It must attempt to overcome any barriers in its path by any means including the selection of a new route. It is not obliged to endanger itself in surmounting these obstacles, however. If a creature is banished but cannot leave (because it's in a small enclosed area, for example), it will cower as far away as it can and will avoid the sorcerer until the effect of the spell ends.

Corruption. The sorcerer can ritually desecrate an area, making it especially amenable to supernatural creatures. Doing so requires a Sorcery check with a Difficulty of 8. The area corrupted is a sphere centered on the sorcerer, with a radius equal to the Outcome in meters. The area is stationary; once cast, it does not follow the sorcerer. The area remains corrupted for a number of days equal to the Outcome; if the sorcerer spent a Magic point before resolving the check, the effect is permanent. Supernatural creatures within the area of effect gain a +2 bonus on all Action Values.

Corruption only works on an area of space, not an item. You could cast Corruption in a room of a building, but not on a medallion.

A successful Corruption can cancel out the effects of a Purification (p. 99), but the Difficulty of such attempts is the Action Result of the original Purification check.

Domination. The sorcerer may impose his will on a supernatural creature, forcing it to obey spoken instructions. The sorcerer must be able to see the creature; the creature must be able to hear the caster. If the Sorcery check is successful, the creature must obey the letter of the sorcerer's instructions to the best of its abilities for a number of sequences equal to the Outcome. If the Sorcerer spends a Magic point immediately before the check is made, the creature must obey for a period equal to the Outcome in hours.

Exorcism. The sorcerer may remove the taint of the monster from a living subject, such as an individual suffering from possession or arcanowave muta-

Illustration by Thomas Manning

tion. If the condition was created by a supernatural creature or user of an Arcanowave Device, use that being's Action Value in the relevant skill as the Difficulty. If you're curing arcanowave mutation, the Difficulty is the victim's current mutation point total. In an unwilling subject, the effect lasts for a number of sequences equal to the Outcome. In a willing subject, the effect is permanent. This can't be used on supernatural creatures, abominations, or other beings in order to stop them from being monsters or to suppress their powers.

Invocation. The sorcerer can seize a supernatural creature through time and space and bring it into her presence. The sorcerer must have in her possession a former body part of the creature, such as a claw, piece of hair, scraping of skin, or severed hand. Or the creature must be one that the sorcerer has successfully used the Domination effect on in the past. The base Difficulty is the creature's Willpower; add 7 to the Difficulty if the creature is in another juncture or the Netherworld when the spell is cast. Add 5 to the Difficulty if the creature has had an arcanowave device installed since the sorcerer's last encounter with it. To perform a summoning, the sorcerer must spend 2 Magic points. If the Sorcery check is successful, the creature immediately materializes in front of the caster. Merely summoning a creature does not ensure its cooperation. In fact, in most cases it is a guarantee of the creature's displeasure.

Purification. The sorcerer can ritually cleanse an area, making it very difficult for supernatural creatures to enter it. Doing so requires a Sorcery check with a Difficulty of 8. The area purified is a sphere centered on the sorcerer, with a radius equal to the Outcome in meters. The area is stationary; once cast, it does not follow the sorcerer. The area remains purified for a number of days equal to the Outcome; if the sorcerer spent a Magic point before resolving the check, the effect is permanent. Supernatural creatures attempting to enter an area of active purification must succeed at Willpower checks, with the Action Result of the sorcerer's check as the Difficulty. If they fail, they are not only unable to enter the area, but suffer a point of Impairment for a number of sequences equal to the Outcome of their Willpower checks.

Purification only works on an area of space, not an item. You could cast Purification in a room of a building, but not on a medallion.

A successful Purification can cancel out the effects of a Corruption (p. 98), but the Difficulty of such attempts is the Action Result of the original Corruption check.

WEATHER

The sorcerer can manipulate weather effects. Difficulties for all of these effects depend on the degree of change between current, normal weather conditions and the desired condition. The Difficulty for slight weather changes is 5; dramatic changes, 10; and extreme changes, 15. The Backlash from any Weather effect causes the sorcerer to take a -1 penalty to his Chi rating for the duration of the session; however, the sorcerer's Chi cannot go below 0 due to this backlash.

Examples: Causing rain to fall on a heavily overcast day would be a slight change. Causing rain on a partially cloudy day with a low chance of precipitation would be a dramatic change. Causing a downpour on a cloudless day would be an extreme change. Similarly, turning rain into snow would be a slight change on a cold day, a dramatic change on a mild day, and an extreme change on a sweltering day.

Weather Special Effects

Cold. Sends people inside in search of shelter. Forces opponents to don awkward and constraining heavy coats, scarves, gloves. Causes guards to huddle together around heaters and garbage-can bonfires, abandoning their posts. (No, this isn't mind control; these are things that might naturally occur as a result of cold weather.)

Heat and Humidity. Causes suffering to opponents wearing armor or heavy coats to conceal their portable arsenals. Makes exertion difficult. Makes others thirsty enough to drink that potion- or poison-laced but ice-cold glass of lemonade.

Fog. Obscures vision. Provides partial cover for yourself. Creates a sinister atmosphere and creeps out the easily-spooked.

Lightning. As per the Blast special effect of the same name; see p. 93.

Rain. Mires enemy vehicles in mud. Clears the streets of pesky bystanders. Demoralizes foes.

Snow. Snarls traffic. Causes flight cancellations. Obscures vision.

Thunder. Impresses mooks and other underlings. Obscures sounds.

Wind. Knocks opponents over or slows them down. Blows away light objects. Damages buildings, knocks down trees and power lines. Creates sandstorms, which obscure vision and demoralize foes.

CHAPTER 7

Creature Abilities

THE WAY OF THE BEAST

This section lists abilities available to supernatural creatures; you only need to read it if your PC is one of these beasties, or if you are a GM. For the purpose of this section, "supernatural creature" refers not only to the character type of that name, but any other type that gets creature abilities as a schtick.

BASIC CREATURE STUFF

All characters who have creature schticks have certain things in common. These are qualities, mostly unhelpful, that they all get no matter how they choose to spend their schticks.

HORRIFIC APPEARANCE

All supernatural creatures, in their natural state, look somehow horrific. Exactly how your character looks is up to you, unless your type description specifies otherwise (but it has to be awful). The most popular forms are walking corpses and gigantic ogre types. They may have wild frizzy hair, horns, strangely-colored skin, pulsing veins, gigantic fangs, or whatever. Supernatural creatures are immediately recognizable as such and arouse fear and dread in any normal person. This can sometimes be quite useful: for example, when you want to intimidate or frighten someone. Supernatural creatures gain the Intimidate skill at +2 when in horrific form, even if they do not normally have it.

However, a horrific appearance does prevent you from moving easily in normal society as many other PC types are able to do without a second thought. Most regular folks will immediately organize efforts to hunt down and destroy supernatural creatures wherever they are on the loose. Abominations still attached to buro military missions in the 2056 juncture are not considered to be "on the loose."

In this natural state, a supernatural creature's Charisma secondary attribute is effectively 2 when trying to make a positive impression. If you have spent more on Charisma and want to be able to use it in this manner, you must take the Transformation schtick for your character—see below. If you're trying to look menacing (as with Intimidation checks) or make a negative impression, Charisma is as normal.

DECEPTIVE SPEED

All supernatural creatures, except for ghosts, look much slower than they really are. They look like they stumble or hop along at a rate equal to half of their Move rating, but they still move at their full Move rating. They can shamble along at a seemingly lumbering pace and still keep up with prey running at top speed. Ghosts, however, look as fast as they are, if not faster.

Creature Abilities

JUNCTURE MODIFIERS

The feng shui sites of the various open junctures are controlled by different groups, some of whom want the chi flow to make it easy for supernatural creatures to operate, some of whom want to suppress them. This means that characters with creature schticks get modifiers to all of their Action Values depending on which juncture they are in. Note that the abomination character type has different modifiers in some junctures than do other supernatural creatures. This reflects the fact that they have been reconstructed with arcanowave technology, which works better in 2056 than in other junctures.

The Netherworld is neutral as far as supernatural creatures are concerned. Supernatural creatures do not suffer a modifier in contemporary Hong Kong for reasons no one has been able to learn.

Supernatural Creature Juncture Modifiers Chart

Juncture	Creature	Abomination
69	+2	+1
1850	-2	-2
Modern	-2	-2
2056	-1	+2
Netherworld	0	0

HEALING PROBLEMS

Supernatural creatures can't be healed by practitioners of the Medicine skill, unless the practitioner is from the 69 juncture. They have no problems being healed by the fu power Healing Chi, the Heal schtick of Sorcery, or arcanowave Slap Patches.

SCHTICK ACQUISITION

Supernatural creatures may acquire creature schticks both during character creation and in the course of a series. You are considered a supernatural creature if:

- you started play with one or more creature schticks
- you have failed a mutation check due to arcanowave exposure; see p. 118.

ACQUIRING MULTIPLE SCHTICKS

Each character type that gets supernatural creature schticks gets to pick only a certain number of them. Some creature abilities allow you to spend multiple schticks on them, giving you extra benefits in exchange.

Example: Scot wants his supernatural creature, Mujiang Xugou, to have the Armor schtick, and has 5 schticks to spend. The Armor schtick allows his character 2 points of Armor per schtick spent. Scot spends 3 schticks on Armor, giving his character 6 points of Armor. This leaves him with 2 schticks left to pick up other abilities.

ACQUIRING NEW SCHTICKS

In the course of play, supernatural creatures can gain any new creature schtick. Getting an additional schtick costs $(8 + x)$ experience points; x being the number of Creature Abilities schticks you will have when you gain this new one. This takes no time in the game world; new powers simply arise spontaneously. Creatures may buy entirely new schticks, or increase the benefits of schticks they already have. The latter is done just as if the player was spending an extra schtick on a power during character creation.

Example: Scot plays Mujiang Xugou for a while and ends up with 16 experience points. He wants to spend another schtick in Armor, to bring him to a new total of 8 points of Armor. Mujiang already has 5 schticks; gaining the Armor will take him to 6. That means that it costs 14 points to get another schtick in Armor: the flat rate of 8 plus 6, the number of schticks Mujiang will have once he gains the new schtick. Scot then wants to acquire the Transformation power. This would be his seventh schtick, so the cost would be 15 experience points; he'll have to wait a while.

CREATURE SCHTICKS

All creature abilities that require task checks use the Creature Power skill (see p. 70) unless otherwise indicated.

CREATURE SCHTICK LIST

ABSORPTION

When you are attacked by an opponent using a fu power, make a Creature Power task check. The Difficulty is your opponent's Martial Arts Action Result. If you succeed, the Outcome equals the number of sequences for which you may use the fu power in question. Your opponent is unable to use this fu power for that number of sequences. If you absorb a fu power/schtick using the Absorption schtick, you get to use the normal Chi of Fu rating (whichever is higher) of the martial artist whose fu schtick you've absorbed. If you absorbed an Old Master's fu schtick that costs X, go to town!

ABYSMAL SPINES

You are covered with sharp, bony spines. For each schtick spent on this power, add 2 to your Damage values for unarmed hand-to-hand attacks. You may not gain more than 8 Damage in this way.

If you have some natural weaponry in mind other than spines—jagged teeth, wicked claws, whatever—describe how it looks accordingly. The game effect remains the same no matter what form of extra damage you pick. We just thought "abysmal spines" sounded cooler than "extra damage."

AMPHIBIAN

You can easily move and breathe underwater. If you wish, you can reduce your Move attribute by any amount on land in order to increase it by the same amount when underwater; this decision is made when you take the schtick.

ARMOR

You are covered in thick, hairy plates. For each schtick spent on this power, gain 2 points of Armor. You may not gain more than 8 points of Armor in this way. See p. 138 for armor rules.

BLAST

You have an ability much like the magic schtick Blast. For each schtick you spend on this power, you may gain one of the special effects presented in the description for Blast on p. 90. Use Creature Power as the skill to make task checks with, not Sorcery.

BLOOD DRAIN

You gain additional vitality by drinking the blood of human beings. You have a specialized body feature that allows you to draw blood from living victims. Examples might include hollow fangs, rasping mouths on the palms of your hands, or dozens of little suckers on your torso. If you have the creature abilities Abysmal Spines or Tentacles, these can be your feeding equipment.

When you hit an opponent with a Martial Arts attack, you may elect to make a Creature Power task check, with the Chi or Magic rating of the opponent as your Difficulty. If you are successful, you forgo the usual damage in favor of an effect listed below.

For each schtick you spend, you can take one of the following effects:

Action Value gain. Choose a skill you and your victim have in common. You gain a +1 bonus to your Action Value for this skill until the end of the session; your opponent suffers a -1 penalty to his Action Values for the same period. This effect may be used repeatedly on the same victim.

Fortune drain. You gain one of the victim's unspent Fortune points; victim loses a point. May be used repeatedly on the same victim. Has no effect on characters who currently have no fortune points.

Memory drain. You acquire the memories of the victim. These fade at the end of the session. Until the end of the session, your victim is haunted by disturbing nightmares, becomes emotionally distraught, and is subject to unpredictable memory lapses and horrific hallucinations. There is no point in doing this to the same victim twice in a session.

Voice gain. You can now mimic the voice of your victim with complete accuracy, and may continue to do so until the end of the session. There is no point in doing this to the same victim twice in a session.

BRAIN SHREDDER

You can provoke in other intelligent beings a fear response so intense that they suffer brain damage. In order to activate this power, you must be within range of your intended victim. Range equals your Chi or Magic rating in meters. Your victim must be able to clearly see you and vice versa. You may not use this ability and Transformation (see p. 107) at the same time.

Your base Damage rating for Brain Shredder is 7; increase this by 3 for each additional schtick you spend on this power. To use the power, make a Creature Power task check; Difficulty is the victim's Dodge rating. Instead of Toughness, the victim subtracts his Chi (or Fortune or Magic, her choice) rating from the damage to get the Wound Points suffered.

CONDITIONAL ESCALATION

You temporarily gain a point in a single, specified primary attribute (that is, Body, Chi, Mind, or Reflexes) each time a particular condition is met. Gained points last until the end of the fight. You may add another specified primary attribute by spending another schtick. No check is needed to activate this power; it just kicks in whenever a particular condition is met.

When you spend your first schtick on this ability, pick one of the conditions below. You may add conditions by spending one schtick per condition.

- When you take more than 10 Wound Points from a single attack.
- When you cause more than 10 Wound Points in a single attack.
- When you are the target of a successful Sorcery task check.
- When you are the target of a successful Arcanowave task check.
- When you are hit by an opponent using a fu power.
- When you are hit by an opponent using a gun or other ranged weapon.

CORRUPTION

You infect your victims with your own supernatural essence; if this taint is left unchecked they become supernatural creatures as well. Any victim who suffers, in the course of a single fight, more than 25 Wound Points from your non-weapon hand-to-hand attacks is in danger of slowly transmuting into a creature of the same type as yourself. The victim must make a Constitution check with a Difficulty equal to the number of successful attacks you have scored against him. If the check fails, the victim will change into a monster after the passing of three midnights.

The victim's game statistics change: Take your attributes and subtract 1 from each to get his new attributes. The victim gains the skill Creature Power. He retains all of his previous skills, although these are refigured based on his new attributes. At first, he retains his original will and consciousness. But whenever confronted by an opportunity to act in a savage or monstrous manner, he must make a Willpower check with a Difficulty equal to your Magic rating. If he is a PC, the GM temporarily takes control of the character whenever he fails a check, forcing him to act contrary to his player's desires. Once he has failed three of these checks, his old personality is forever lost, and a new bestial personality takes over. If a PC, he becomes a GMC. This happens even if the creature that infected him appears to be a "good" entity; by definition, any creature willing to use Corruption is tainted by the foul spiritual essence of the Underworld.

Corruption remains reversible until the third Willpower check is failed. Extensive blood transfusion or the Poison Antidotes effect of the Sorcery schtick Heal will both reverse its effects.

For each living and active character you have corrupted, you gain 1 Corruption Point. A Corruption Point can be spent at any time during a session for a +1 bonus to any Action Value for one action only. Multiple Corruption Points can be spent on the same action. Your pool of Corruption Points returns to maximum value at the beginning of each session.

If you spend an additional schtick on Corruption, you gain the ability Domination (see p. 105) at a +6 bonus to your Creature Power Action Value; this specialized form of Domination can be used only on characters who have become supernatural creatures due to your Corruption ability.

DAMAGE IMMUNITY

You are immune to a particular form of damage, and suffer no Wound Points from such attacks no matter what. For each schtick you spend, you become immune to an additional form of damage. You may not spend more than two schticks on this ability during character creation. New schticks in this ability gained during the course of play cost four times the usual number of experience points.

The available forms of this ability are:

- Immune to normal bullets. Exceptions: magic or silver bullets.

Chapter 7

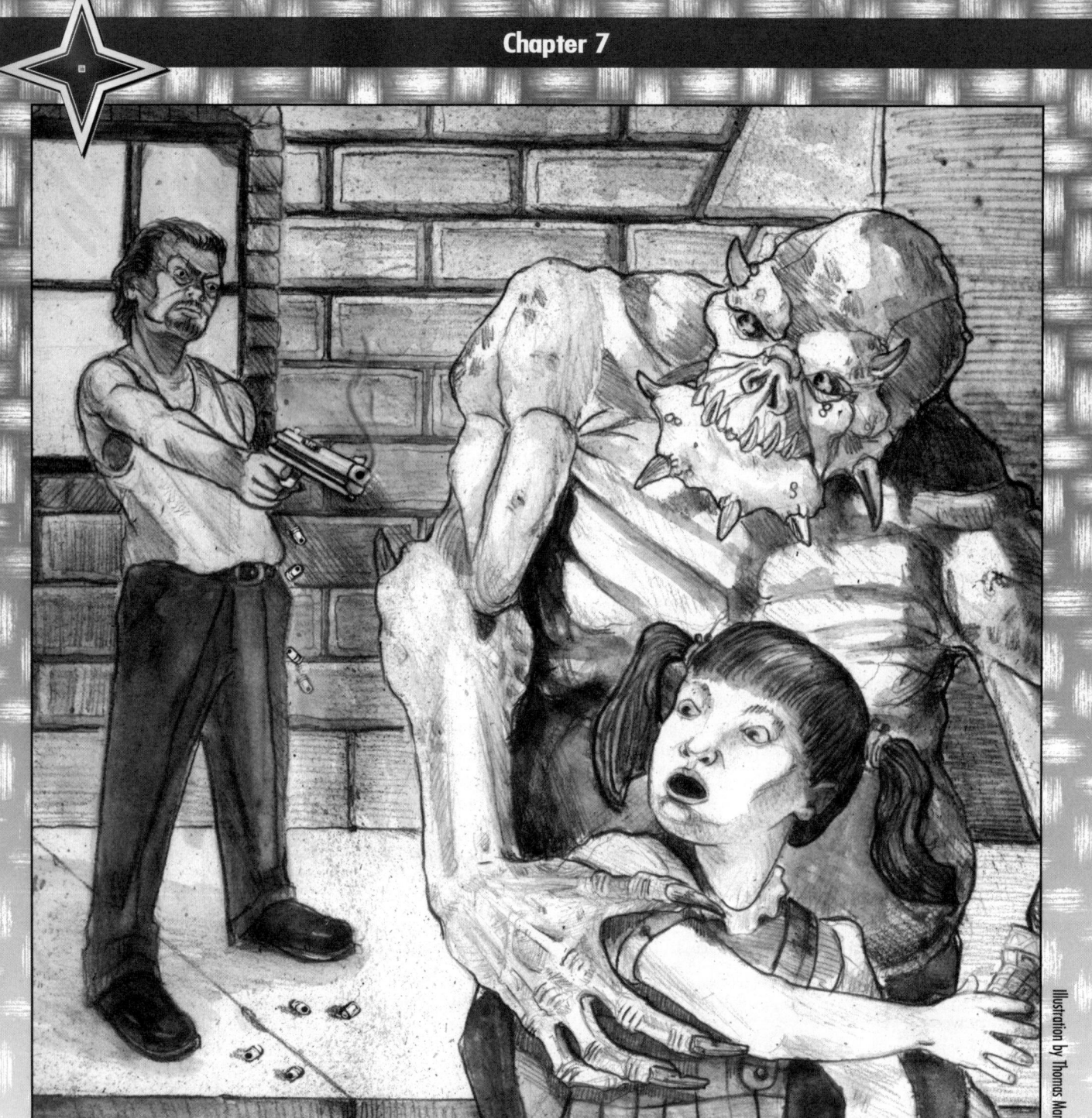

- Immune to hand-to-hand weapons. Exceptions: magic weapons, and one type of mundane weapon of your choice. Examples of the latter might include wooden stakes, blowgun darts, or pole arms. The GM may require you to pick a new exception if she deems the one you pick to be too rare or ineffectual.
- Immune to unarmed attacks. Exception: attacks using fu powers.
- Immune to damage from the Blast sorcery schtick. Exception: one effect of your choice; see Blast on p. 92.
- Immune to the effects of all sorcery schticks except for Blast, and one other of your choice.
- Immune to the effects of all but three creature schticks described in this section. You pick two schticks that affect you; your GM picks the third. You cannot be immune to schticks that do not cause harm of some sort to you, for example those that are purely defensive in nature.

Creature Abilities

- Immune to fire. Exception: magical fire.
- Immune to falling damage.
- Immune to damage from things falling on you.
- Immune to poisons, except for one type of your choice and one type of the GM's choice.
- Immune to damage from suffocation or drowning.
- Immune to damage from explosions.
- Immune to damage from vehicles and vehicle crashes.

DEATH RESISTANCE

For each schtick you spend on this ability (up to a maximum of three) you gain a +3 Action Value bonus when making Death checks.

DOMINATION

You can overcome the wills of others and force them to do your bidding. You must be able to see the victim of the Domination attempt, and he must be able to see you. (A two-way video link is acceptable, for example.) You make a Creature Power check and spend a Magic point; your victim's highest Action Value is the Difficulty. If you succeed, then your victim makes a check with his highest Action Value; the difficulty is the Outcome of your just-made Creature Power check. If your victim succeeds, then your Domination attempt fails.

If you succeed, your victim must follow your orders for a number of sequences equal to the Outcome. These orders need not be voiced; the victim will intuitively understand what you want him to do and attempt to fulfill the spirit as well as letter of your commands. The victim will not engage in directly suicidal actions, but will follow other commands that involve severe risks.

You may gain the following benefits by spending additional schticks on this ability:

One extra schtick: Victim will recall being dominated but will not remember specific actions undertaken while dominated. These memories can be recovered through hypnotic regression, or inventive use of the Sorcery schtick Influence.
Two extra schticks: Victim will have no memory of being dominated, but will be aware of a chunk of "missing time." Memories can be recovered, as above.
Three extra schticks: Victim won't even know about the missing time until prompted through hypnotic regression or Influence.

Four extra schticks: Victim's memories of domination can't be recovered, period.

FLIGHT

You can fly through the air at your normal Move rating. For each additional schtick spent, add 2 to your Move rating while flying.

FOUL SPEW

You can spew a nasty substance from your mouth at will, firing it a number of meters equal to your Creature Power Action Value. Choose one substance for each schtick you spend on this ability.

Glutinous Goo. You emit a sticky substance. Anyone hit by it or stepping in it must make a Strength task check with your Creature Power Action Value as the Difficulty in order to free himself from it.
Nauseating Chunks. Your vomit causes disabling nausea to all within 3 meters of it. Activating this power takes 6 shots; you spew on the sixth shot. For those 6 shots, your Dodge rating is halved. Anyone within range must make a Constitution check with your Creature Power Action Value as the Difficulty. Those who fail the check spend the next 6 shots throwing up themselves, and may take no actions other than passive dodging with their ratings halved; actions they are engaged in when the effect begins are stopped.
Slippery Slime. You emit a slippery substance. Anyone trying to climb a wall or walk along a floor covered in it must make an Agility task check with your Creature Power Action Value as the Difficulty. Those who fail slip and fall. A successful Agility check is required to get up and away from the slime.

There are other creative uses for this power, such as the obscuring of car windshields, psychological warfare, and so forth.

INEVITABLE COMEBACK

When you fail a Death Check, you instantaneously die in the middle of the combat. Or so it seems to any outside observer. Make a Magic check with the same Difficulty of the death check you would otherwise have to make—see p. 135 for death check rules. If you fail, you go on to make a normal death check, adhering to the normal rules for dying. If you succeed, you return to life 10 sequences later, with your current Wound Points reduced to 5. You may do this once per session per schtick spent on this ability. However, your Wound Point total when you recover increases by 5 each additional time you use Inevitable Comeback in the course of a session. If your Wound Point total after returning to life equals or exceeds 35, you must again make a Death Check. If you fail this Death Check, you may again attempt to use Inevitable Comeback if you still have any uses of it left to you.

Example: Mujiang Xugou has already used Inevitable Comeback four times this session when it again fails a Death Check. It makes a successful Magic check against its death check Difficulty of 7. After 10 sequences, it returns to life, with 25 Wound Points already racked up.

INSUBSTANTIAL

You may pass through solid matter by making a Creature Power check. The Difficulty is 1 for each inch of thickness of the matter you are passing through. You must specify four types of matter you cannot pass through; your GM picks a fifth type. For each additional schtick you spend, you may reduce the number of types you must choose. It is not possible to buy off the GM's choice. Note: This power does not make you immune to damage; buy the Damage Immunity schtick for that.

POISON

You secrete a toxic venom with a Damage rating of 10. For each additional schtick you spend on this power, the Damage rating of the poison increases by 2. Victims subtract their Constitution ratings rather than their Toughness from the Damage in order to determine Wound Points suffered.

Select one means of delivery:

Fangs. You have long, cobra-like fangs. You must bite your opponent; in combat this requires a successful Martial Arts check.
Gland. You can milk a gland in one of your extremities to produce a poison which must be ingested to take effect.
Skin. Your skin is poisonous, but you must rub your skin against the victim's for several minutes for it to have any effect (a handshake won't do it).

This poison cannot be communicated in combat, but there is also no obvious sign of it.
Stinger. You have a scorpion-like stinger somewhere on your body. See "Fangs" for rules.

RANCID BREATH

When you want, your exhalations damage people and objects. You must successfully hold an unwilling opponent to subject him to your reeking breath; this requires a Martial Arts stunt action. Base Damage rating for your breath is 10; add 3 for each additional schtick you spend on this ability. Victims subtract their Constitution ratings rather than their Toughness from the Damage in order to determine Wound Points suffered.

REGENERATION

Your Wound Point total decreases by 1 at the beginning of each sequence for each schtick you have spent on this power. You are limited to 5 schticks in Regeneration. Wound Point totals may not be reduced below 1. This ability stops working when you fail a death check until you are restored to 0 Wound Points by other means.

SOUL TWIST

Your touch ruptures the normal pattern of chi energy within a healthy person's body, doing great harm. The base Damage rating of this ability is 7; add 2 for each additional schtick spent on the power. You can have a maximum of 4 schticks in Soul Twist. To activate it, you must make a successful Martial Arts check against your victim.

Victims subtract their Kung Fu ratings rather than their Toughness from the Damage in order to determine Wound Points suffered.

Damage suffered from a Soul Twist cannot be healed by normal means. Only the Heal magic schtick or the Flow Restoration fu power can cure this damage. Flow Restoration heals all Wound Points suffered as a result of Soul Twist.

TENTACLES

You have long tentacle(s) attached to some part of your monstrous anatomy; you can use these to attack enemies in hand-to-hand combat while keeping your own vital parts out of harm's way. Your tentacles are elastic, and can stretch a maximum distance equal to your Creature Powers Action Value in meters.

Use your Creature Powers skill to hit opponents with your tentacles, rather than your Martial Arts skill.

The number of tentacles you have is equal to the number of schticks you spend on this ability. You can grow new tentacles at any time by buying additional schticks with experience points.

Opponents engaging you in hand-to-hand combat are normally unable to hit anything other than your tentacles, unless they inventively use stunts or a movement-oriented fu power, like Prodigious Leap. Your tentacles can each take 20 Wound Points before being severed; these Wound Points are not added to your normal total and do not cause Impairment or otherwise affect you in any way. They do not grow back when severed, unless you also have the Regeneration schtick—see p. 106. If you do have the Regeneration schtick, you may at any time apply the Wound Point reduction to one of your tentacles instead of to your normal total. Tentacles can fully regenerate after being severed.

TRANSFORMATION

You may adopt another form. For each schtick you spend on this ability, you may assume one predetermined form. That form may be an animal, person, other type of supernatural creature, or even an object such as a table, an elevator, or a motorcycle. If you become an object, you gain all usual abilities of that object. Your GM gets final say on what the usual abilities of any object might be. You return to your normal form whenever you make a Creature Power check; this limitation can be eliminated by spending an extra schtick. You get to determine any visual characteristics of the form you adopt—if you want a human form, you may specify its hair color, height, apparent weight, facial features, and so on. A transformation takes 9 full shots.

If you spend an additional schtick on this ability, you may adopt hybrid forms, halfway between your own form and that of the chosen person or object. For example, if one of your selected forms is a motorcycle, you could become a motorcycle with your usual monstrous head between the handlebars. If you have the tentacles schtick, the motorbike would have tentacles, and so on.

You may assign different attributes to each form you take. Use the base attributes given in your type, and assign the additional attribute points differently for each form. You can't alter Mind from form to form, though. If you choose to give your transformed self different attributes, your transformations are more lengthy and painful than the norm: you suffer 1 point of Impairment per changed attribute for 3 sequences after you transform.

If you improve your attributes with experience points in the course of play, all of your various forms' attributes are altered by the same amount.

Chapter 8

September 5

One minute I was in a forest at midnight blowing away hopping vampires, and the next I found myself alone in a desert at high noon. Well, that's not exactly accurate. In between those two moments was a split second featuring excruciating pain radiating out from the back of my head, and my vision turning to mush. I woke up feeling like I must have consumed an entire year's output of the Jack Daniels distillery the night before. But I felt back behind me and found a big bandage and immediately knew that it was another form of self-destructive behavior that was responsible for my cranial agony.

I struggled to stand, losing my footing in the soft and shifting sand. I was right smack dab in the middle of a sand dune. None of my colleagues were anywhere in sight. This was a bad thing. Assuming I was even in the same juncture I got conked out in, I was in ancient China, circa 69 AD. This was not a place I wanted to be without the others. I didn't know diddley about the ground rules here. Back when I was supposed to be a good little schoolboy learning all about history, I was busy putting together my first extortion ring.

So I was worried. My best bet was to find a portal to the Netherworld and make my way back from there to my Hong Kong. Finding a gateway was definitely going to be in the easier said than done category. But before I could even start on that, I had to attend to my first priority: finding my left shoe, which was no longer on my foot.

I saw something dark sticking out of the dune a little further up. So I trudged over, struggling with the lousy traction. I leaned over to grab it, and then pulled my hand back right quick. There was a sleeping snake coiled inside the shoe. At least, it had been sleeping: now it had twisted around and was baring some nasty fangs at me, like it was ready to strike any second. I had no idea what kind of snake it was or whether it was poisonous, but I was not itching to star in my own little nature documentary, so I reached for Mr. Browning. I wasn't giving much thought to the hole that would end up in my shoe if I plugged the snake.

Then all of a sudden I'd dropped the gun and my hand was stinging with pain. Somebody had thrown something at me, and hit me good right on the back of the hand. I spun around. There was maybe the most beautiful woman I'd ever seen, all done up in silks of white and powder blue. She was holding this little throwing club in her left hand. I glanced down to see its twin lying in the sand, right next to Mr. Browning. She spoke.

But not to me. She talked to the snake. She walked over to it and picked it up, and said something I could barely decipher at the time. I think it was somewhere along the lines of: "He will not hurt you and you will not hurt him. Now go; I will tend to this."

"You are far from home," she said. In English. Bingo. Another innerwalker. How convenient. Probably— seeing as I knew zero about the circumstances of my being conked and ending up on a sand dune—much too convenient.

I nodded and stretched my hand out to her. I gave her a name. Not my real name or anything. But hey, I didn't want to seem unfriendly. I didn't want to get whacked with that other club, for example. She put her hand in mine. Not a handshake really, more of a caress. Her skin felt funny: very dry and very smooth. At the same time I was busy falling into her eyes. There was something odd about them. They were green—but there was something else I couldn't even start to put my finger on. That just made her even more stunning, of course.

I figured there was no point waltzing around the whole deal, so I asked her:

"You're not with the Lotus, are you?"

"The Lotus are our foes. Sorcery is our bane."

I was about to ask who she meant by "our", but then the words of the Prof came back to me: "If you meet someone mysterious and beautiful who fears magic, she may not be what she seems."

So she didn't just talk to snakes, she was one. I'd fallen in love with her anyways.

CHAPTER 8
Transformed Animals

THE WAY OF THE ASCENDED

This chapter describes the special abilities of transformed animals and the drawbacks of their existence. Unless you are a GM or are playing a transformed animal PC, you do not need to read this chapter.

PICKING PACKAGES

Unlike other character types, transformed animals do not get to mix and match from an unlimited list of schticks. Instead, they must choose their schticks from within a single package of abilities corresponding to the animal type that the character once belonged to or is descended from.

These packages provide attribute bonuses and penalties, which you combine with the baseline attributes provided with the transformed animal type on p. 45. Including these modifiers does not count against your limit for raising Action Values with character points at the beginning of play. You get these attribute modifiers automatically; they don't count against the number of schticks you have to spend on abilities. Sometimes a package will reduce a primary attribute while increasing one of its secondary attributes, or vice versa. Changes to primary attributes do not effect a secondary attribute if a modifier is separately listed for that secondary attribute.

Example: The spider package requires a Body reduction of 1 and a Move increase of 2. When recalculating Body and its secondary attributes, don't reduce Move, because it is listed separately; instead, just add 2 to its value. The base Body score for the transformed animal type is 5. With the modifier, Body and its unlisted secondary attributes (Strength, Constitution, and Toughness) are reduced to 4. Move is increased to 7.

Within each package is a list of abilities. Each ability you select counts as a schtick. You may spend multiple schticks on certain abilities in order to get cumulative benefits.

When determining the cap on raising attributes during character creation, use the attributes you get after incorporating the package modifiers as your base attributes.

USING TRANSFORMED ANIMAL ABILITIES

Some special abilities of transformed animals require no task checks; the crab's armor is a good example of this. Those that do require task checks either require Martial Arts checks, or Chi checks. The Difficulties of any checks are described under the descriptions of the various abilities.

Some abilities require the use of Chi points. The number of points you must spend to activate an ability is its **chi cost**. Each sequence, a transformed animal may use any abilities so long as their total cost is not greater than her Chi rating. Higher secondary attributes of Chi, such as Kung Fu or Magic, do not contribute to the number of points you can spend in a given sequence. When an ability description refers to your Chi rating, however, that means your usual attribute rating—whether or not you have currently spent any chi points in this sequence.

Each power also has a **shot cost** that tells you how long it takes to use the power. For more information on shot costs, consult the Initiative rules on p. 129.

GAINING NEW SCHTICKS

New schticks in a transformed animal ability cost (8 + x) points per schtick gained, where x = the number of Transformed Animal Schticks you will have when you gain this new one. There is no time or training requirement involved; the character simply gains these abilities through off-stage sustained meditation.

REVERSION

Transformed animals are not werecreatures; they do not, and cannot, switch back and forth from their human and animal forms. They are human beings with a few odd powers and animal chromosomes in their DNA. To a transformed animal, changing back to an animal is a very bad thing indeed because it's pretty much a one-way trip. And who wants to spend the rest of his life as a snake?

The transformed animal is always in danger of being reverted to its original form through exposure to chi energy which has been altered through sorcery. In the 1850 and contemporary junctures, a great organization of transformed animals called the Ascended has seized control of the Earth's pivotal feng shui sites in order to suppress the widespread use of magic for this very reason.

Indirect exposure to magical energy can wreak havoc with a transformed animal's ability to retain human form. Transformed animal characters from AD 69 are more used to the influence of magic in the world and are better at resisting this than those from other junctures. For each twenty-four hours (consecutive or otherwise) a transformed animal character from 69 AD spends in an environment with a Sorcery Difficulty Modifier of +3 or more (see chart, p. 90), that character acquires a reversion point. Transformed animals from junctures other than 69 gain a reversion point for each twenty-four hour period spent in an environment with a Sorcery Difficulty Modifier of +1 or more. Note that this includes 69, 2056, and the Netherworld. At the end of each session, a character with reversion points must make a check using his highest Action Value; the current reversion point total is the Difficulty of the check. If the check fails, the character reverts permanently to animal form.

The character's original form is determined by the package you take for him during character generation. If he reverts to that form then he becomes an elephant, a spider, a fox, or whatever. You don't need game statistics for these forms because the character is effectively out of play when he becomes an animal. GMs may create plot devices that allow the transformed animal to be returned to its original form after a short period of reversion. But in general, once your character becomes an animal, it might as well be dead for the purposes of a *Feng Shui* series: you have to start over with a new character.

Characters can reduce their current reversion point totals to 0 by spending at least twenty-four consecutive hours in an environment with a Sorcery Difficulty Modifier of 0 or less.

OTHER DRAWBACKS

Transformed animals who learn and use Arcanowave Device schticks gain 1 reversion point for each sequence in which they use an Arcanowave Device schtick (in other words, sequences that count towards a mutation check also count towards reversion points). They cannot learn Sorcery.

THE PACKAGES

The animal packages appear on the following pages. For each one, we first present the attribute modifiers and then the schticks for each ability.

BEAR
Attribute Modifiers: Body +4, Will +4

Bellow Chi: 4 / Shots: 1
If you've been wounded, you can make an enraged, blood-curdling bellow. Make a Martial Arts check with an opponent's Willpower as the Difficulty. If successful, opponent suffers Impairment equal to your current Wound Points ÷ 5 until end of sequence. You may target an additional opponent for each extra schtick spent on this power; take the highest Willpower among your targets as your Difficulty.

Fortitude Chi: 8 / Shots: 3
Use this power when you have reached 35 or more Wound Points. You may forgo making a death check until the end of the fight. Each time you

receive more Wound Points during the fight, you must use Fortitude again or immediately make a death check.

Slap   **Chi: 1 / Shots: 3**
Hit an opponent with a backhanded slap by making a Martial Arts check. If the check is successful, your opponent is hurled backwards a number of meters equal to the Outcome. He must make a check on his Dodge Action Value with your Action Result as the Difficulty, or suffer normal damage from your attack in addition to being knocked back.

Rage   **Chi: 5 / Shots: 1**
Until end of sequence, you have an Armor rating equal to your current Wound Points ÷ 5.

CRAB
Attribute Modifiers: Toughness +3, Will +3, Reflexes +3

Impervious   **Chi: 3 / Shots: 1**
After you are hit by gunfire, you may elect to take no Wound Points and instead convert the Wound Points you would normally have suffered into Chi Points, which you must spend by the end of the sequence. Any unspent Chi points become Wound points again at the end of the sequence, so use them up quick. Imperviousness only applies to gunfire damage.

Pincer   **Chi: X / Shots: 3**
Hit an opponent bare-handed with a Martial Arts check; if successful, you may add X (any amount of Chi you elect to spend) to the Damage rating for your attack.

Scuttle   **Chi: X / Shots: 1**
Add X (any amount of Chi you elect to spend) to your active Dodge rating until end of sequence.

Shell   **Chi: 4 / Shots: 1**
You gain 2 points of Armor until end of sequence. Each additional schtick spent increases the Armor gain by 2. The maximum armor that any transformed animal can gain through any combination of transformed animal schticks is 8.

DRAGON
Attribute Modifiers: Body +4, Fortune +3, Mind +4, Reflexes +4

It costs all 5 available schticks for a starting transformed animal character to take the dragon package. However, a transformed dragon can, in the course of the game, acquire any schtick available to any other transformed animal package. These cost the dragon character (12 + x) experience points, where x = the number of transformed animal schticks the character will have once he acquires the new one.

Dragons are particularly vulnerable to reversion. They adopted human form because they require levels of magic found only in legendary times to survive in their original forms. A transformed dragon who reverts in an environment with a Sorcery Difficulty Modifier of +4 or less dies immediately because the magical energy in that environment is not enough to support their dragon form.

ELEPHANT
Attribute Modifiers: Body +5, Will +3

Armor   **Chi: 3 / Shots: 1**
You gain 1 point of Armor until end of sequence. Each additional schtick spent increases the Armor gain by 1. The maximum armor that any transformed animal can gain through any combination of transformed animal schticks is 8.

Herd   **Chi: 3 / Shots: 1**
Add 1 to the Action Values of all transformed animals within range until end of sequence. Range equals your Chi rating in meters. You can spend additional schticks to increase the range, adding to it your Chi rating in meters for each schtick spent.

Trample   **Chi: X / Shots: 3**
Launch a flurry of kicks to a prone opponent with a Martial Arts check; if the check is successful, add X (any amount of Chi you elect to spend) to your Damage Rating.

Trumpet   **Chi: 3 / Shots: 1**
You can send a psychic signal to any and all transformed animals in your vicinity. That signal may be either a request for aid, or a warning to flee the area. No more sophisticated messages can be transmitted. Range of the ability equals your Chi rating in meters. Each additional schtick spent on this ability doubles the range.

FOX
Attribute Modifiers: Fortune +3, Mind +3, Will -1, Reflexes +2

Borrow   **Chi: 3 / Shots: 1**
You may gain a single transformed animal schtick from any willing transformed animal within range, and use it until the end of the sequence. Range equals your Chi rating in meters. You can spend

additional schticks to increase the range, adding to it your Chi rating in meters for each schtick spent.

Embezzle   **Chi: 3 / Shots: 3**
Strike an enemy bare-handed and make a Martial Arts check. If successful, you may choose to gain the opponent's rating in any primary or secondary attribute until end of sequence; your opponent has your rating in the attribute for the same period.

Mockery   **Chi: 3 / Shots: 3**
You may verbally deride any intelligent being who can understand your words, distracting that being. Make a Charisma check with the target's Willpower as the Difficulty. If successful, the target is unable to attack any character other than you until the end of the sequence. In the unlikely event that two characters are using Mockery at the same time on the same target, the one with the higher Outcome becomes the object of the target's rage. Range equals your Chi rating in meters. You can spend additional schticks to increase the range, adding to it your Chi rating in meters for each schtick spent. You can also spend additional schticks to target one additional opponent for each schtick spent; take the highest Willpower among your targets as your Difficulty.

Swindle   **Chi: 3 / Shots: 1**
While in unarmed combat, strike a character who has used an ability during the current sequence. If your Martial Arts check is successful then you may—on your next shot—use that ability against any target, using the character's relevant Action Value in the skill to make any task checks. You may use the ability only once for each successful use of Swindle. Choose a single type of ability you can swindle when you take this schtick: either arcanowave devices, creature powers, fu powers, or skills other than Sorcery. You can spend additional schticks to add another type of ability. If you want to add Sorcery to your list, however, it will cost you two schticks to do so.

MONKEY

Attribute Modifiers: Fortune +2, Charisma +4, Reflexes +3

Bounce   **Chi: 3 / Shots: 3 + X**
Make X number of Martial Arts checks, in which you bounce off available vertical surfaces such as trees, pillars, or walls (one bounce per check). Each bounce has a shot cost of 1 and a difficulty of 10. When you stop bouncing, you may launch a Martial Arts attack against any available target. Add 2 to your Martial Arts Action Value for that attack for each bounce you have just made. If you spend an additional schtick on this ability, add 3 for each bounce. If you spend an extra two schticks, add 4 for each bounce. You may not spend more than two additional schticks on this ability, ever. If you are somehow stopped from bouncing against your will, you gain no bonus for any attacks you subsequently launch.

Caper   **Chi: 3 / Shots: 1**
You skitter wildly about—executing cartwheels, flips, and somersaults—when targeted by a ranged weapon or throwing weapon attack. The attacker makes his Guns or Martial Arts check, as appropriate; then you make a Martial Arts check. If your check exceeds that of your opponent, you may select any other character within range of you as the actual target of the attack. Range is your Chi rating in meters. For each additional schtick you take in this ability, add your Chi rating in meters to the range.

Diversion   **Chi: 3 / Shots: 3 + X**
Execute a series of dazzling acrobatic maneuvers using your Martial Arts skill. The Difficulty is the Willpower rating of an opponent of your choice. If you are successful, the target stands slack-jawed in astonishment, unable to do anything until one of two conditions is met:

1. You stop. You may continue the use of Diversion until the end of the sequence, or stop at any time.
2. The target is the subject of an attack. He may then Dodge normally, and your hold on him is broken.

You may spend extra schticks on this ability to add to the number of targets you may affect, at a rate of one schtick per target. When used against multiple opponents, use the highest Willpower among your targeted opponents as the Difficulty.

Throw   **Chi: X / Shots: 3**
Add X (the amount of Chi you elect to spend) to any Martial Arts check using a thrown weapon.

RAT

Attribute Modifiers: Fortune +2, Perception +3, Reflexes +3

Disorienting Strike   **Chi: 5 / Shots: 3**
Make an unarmed attack against an opponent, striking at a crucial nerve point in order to induce dizziness and blurred vision. If successful, then you not only do normal Damage to opponent, but you may also add your Outcome to the Difficulty

of the next attack check he makes. The opponent may counter this latter effect by doing nothing but reorienting himself for the next 3 shots. The target may still passively Dodge, however. For each extra schtick you spend, the amount of time to clear the disorientation increases by 3 shots.

Infect Chi: 3 / Shots: 3
Make an unarmed attack against an opponent with a Martial Arts check. If successful, the opponent suffers (in addition to normal Damage) 1 point of impairment for every 5 Wound Points suffered; round fractions down. Wound Points delivered through an Infect attack do not heal naturally: They must be treated with antibiotics or healing magic.

Lurk Chi: 8 / Shots: 1
You can make yourself invisible to others by hiding behind even the most inadequate of cover. Make a Martial Arts check with the Perception of target character as the Difficulty; if successful, the target simply cannot see you. If you are anything but perfectly still while lurking, the GM adds at least 2 to the Difficulty of the check; the exact penalty depends on how much you are moving. For each extra schtick you spend on this ability, you may affect an additional target. When used against multiple opponents, use the highest Perception as the Difficulty. Once you've made the lurk check, you may continue lurking as long as desired. You only need to make another check if you move, if you want to affect an additional target, or until someone you can't target enters the area and spots you (in which case failure is automatic).

Squeeze Chi: 3 / Shots: 8
You can contort your body in order to squeeze through holes as small as 12 cm in diameter. Spend another schtick to make the limit 6 cm in diameter. You can't increase this ability beyond 6 cm.

ROOSTER

Attribute Modifiers: Move +3, Charisma +3, Speed +3

Crow Chi: 5 / Shots: 3
You can emit a piercing wail which causes temporary deafness to characters within range. Make a Martial Arts check; all within range must beat its Action Result with a Constitution check in order to remain unaffected. If affected, they suffer 1 point of Impairment for a number of sequences equal to their Perception ratings. Range is a radius equal to your Chi rating in meters, centered on you. You can spend extra schticks to add your Chi rating in meters to the range for each extra schtick you spend. Or you can spend extra schticks to exclude one individual from the effect per schtick spent. Transformed roosters, including yourself, are immune to the effects of this ability.

Display Chi: 4 / Shots: 1
Raise your arms in a stylized movement of size and intimidation directed at an opponent. After you've done this, you gain a bonus to your Martial Arts Action Value, provided that your Charisma is higher than that of your opponent. The bonus equals the difference between the two Charisma ratings. The bonus lasts until the end of the sequence. If you spend extra schticks on this ability, you can target an additional opponent per extra schtick spent.

Flight Chi: 8 / Shots: 3
You can become airborne, and remain airborne until the end of the sequence. You may reach a maximum vertical height equal to your Move rating, and travel horizontally up to twice your Move rating. Each extra schtick adds a Move rating to vertical flight and two Move ratings to horizontal distance.

Peck Chi: 3 / Shots: 3
Make an unarmed Martial Arts attack on an opponent, ignoring any armor he may have.

SNAKE

Attribute Modifiers: Intelligence & Charisma +2, Reflexes +3

Coil Chi: 3 / Shots: X
Remain inactive for X number of shots, and then make a 3 shot Martial Arts attack on an opponent. Add double the number of shots you were inactive to your Action Value for the attack.

Shed Skin Chi: special / Shots: special
You may abandon your old human form in favor of a completely new human appearance of your choice. You may never return to your former appearance. Doing so costs 8 chi points; these points do not return until 12 hours have elapsed. The transformation itself takes 1 hour; no residue (scales, flesh, etc.) is left behind. If you spend an additional schtick on this ability, you can recreate the appearance of specific people you have studied carefully for at least a week immediately prior to your use of the schtick; this means that even with two schticks spent you still can't go back to your old form.

Strike Chi: 4 / Shots: 1
Make a normal Martial Arts attack with a shot cost of 1.

Warning   Chi: X / Shots: 1

Make a fierce display of rapid martial arts moves while hissing and baring your teeth. Make a Martial Arts check with target opponent's Willpower as the Difficulty. If you succeed, your Dodge rating against that opponent increases by X (any amount of Chi you elect to spend) until end of sequence. For each extra schtick you spend on this ability, you may target an additional opponent. When used against multiple opponents, use the highest Willpower among your targeted opponents as the Difficulty.

SCORPION
Attribute Modifiers: Move +3, Reflexes +3

Dance   Chi: X / Shots: 1

Execute a series of hypnotic dancing movements, directing them at an opponent. Make a Martial Arts check with opponent's Willpower as the Difficulty. If successful, opponent is distracted and suffers X points of Impairment, X being any amount of chi you elect to spend. The effect lasts only while you are actively maintaining it; you must spend X chi each shot and devote all of your attention to the dance. You may target an additional opponent for each extra schtick spent on Dance; take the highest Willpower among your targeted opponents as your Difficulty.

Sting   Chi: X / Shots: 3

Hit an opponent with an unarmed attack. If your Martial Arts check is successful, you do not do normal damage. Instead, opponent suffers 3 Wound Points at the beginning of each sequence for X sequences.

Surprise   Chi: X / Shots: 3

Hit an opponent who is unaware of your presence in hand-to-hand combat, adding X (the amount of chi you elect to spend) to your Action Value.

Scuttle   Chi: X / Shots: 1

Add X (any amount of Chi you elect to spend) to your active Dodge rating until end of sequence.

SPIDER
Attribute Modifiers: Body -1, Move +2, Agility +3, Speed +3

Leap   Chi: 2 / Shots: 3

Leap up to twice your normal Move rating, either horizontally or vertically. The multiplier increases by 2 for each schtick you spend in this ability: for two schticks you get to leap four times your normal Move rating; for three schticks, you can leap six times your Move rating, and so on.

Scuttle   Chi: X / Shots: 1

Add X (any amount of Chi you elect to spend) to your active Dodge rating until end of sequence.

Tingle   Chi: 1 / Shots: 1

You can check to see whether anyone you have successfully hit with the Web ability is in the area. You must have used Web on the character within the last 24 hours. The area of effect is a circle with a radius equal to your Chi rating in meters. You can spend additional schticks to increase the range, adding to it your Chi rating in meters for each schtick spent. You can also spend an extra schtick to be able to accurately locate the character within the area of effect.

Web   Chi: X / Shots: 3

Weave an invisible web of chi energy, which you can use to entangle your opponents. Make a Martial Arts check against the target's Dodge or Parry rating. If successful, the opponent suffers X points of Impairment for a number of shots equal to the Outcome. The standard version of this ability requires you to be engaged in hand-to-hand combat with the opponent. For an extra schtick, you can make it a thrown weapon attack; the range equals your Chi rating in meters. You can spend additional schticks to increase the range, adding to it your Chi rating in meters for each schtick spent.

TIGER
Attribute Modifiers: Strength +1, Reflexes +2

Bite   Chi: 7 / Shots: 3

Make a successful called shot (see p. 137) with Martial Arts to bite your opponent's windpipe. If successful, derive the Outcome of the attack using the opponent's Constitution instead of his Dodge or Parry value. If you spend an extra schtick on this ability, you also ignore any Armor the opponent may have when making this attack.

Mark Prey   Chi: 3 / Shots: 3

Strike an opponent bare-handed, making a Martial Arts check with the opponent's Chi rating as the Difficulty. You do not do normal Damage. Each time you successfully hit an opponent with Mark Prey, you gain a +1 Martial Arts Action Value bonus on further attempts to hit that opponent. These bonuses are cumulative. If you spend one schtick on this power, any bonuses last until the end of the fight. If you spend two schticks, bonuses last for a week. If you spend three schticks, they last for a

Transformed Animals

month. If you spend four schticks (the maximum for this ability), they last for a year.

Pounce   Chi: X / Shots: 3

Leap upon your opponent from a distance. Make a Martial Arts check. If successful, you hit your opponent, adding X (the distance in meters between you and your opponent before making the leap) to the Damage value.

Surprise   Chi: X / Shots: 3

Hit an opponent who is unaware of your presence in hand-to-hand combat, adding X (the amount of chi you elect to spend) to your Action Value.

TORTOISE

Attribute Modifiers: Constitution & Toughness +4, Move -1, Intelligence +2, Reflexes -1

Rebuke   Chi: 3 / Shots: 3

Strike a sorcerer bare-handed with a Martial Arts check; if successful, sorcerer is unable to use the Sorcery skill for a number of shots equal to the Outcome. You may multiply the Outcome by the number of schticks you spend on this ability. You may spend an additional schtick to apply this ability to the Arcanowave Device skill as well.

Reflect   Chi: 5 / Shots: 1

When you are successfully targeted by a Sorcery check, you may reflect the spell effect back upon the caster. You are not affected by the spell. If you spend an extra schtick on this ability, you may choose to reflect the spell effect on targets other than the caster. These targets must be no further from you than your Chi rating in meters. You can spend further schticks to increase the range, adding to it your Chi rating in meters for each schtick spent. You may spend an additional schtick to apply this ability to the Arcanowave Device skill as well.

Shell   Chi: 4 / Shots: 1

You gain 2 points of Armor until end of sequence. Each additional schtick spent increases the Armor gain by 2. The maximum armor that any transformed animal can gain through any combination of transformed animal schticks is 8.

Wise Fist   Chi: 3 / Shots: 3

Strike an opponent bare-handed, using Intelligence rather than Manual Dexterity as the base attribute for your Martial Arts check. For each additional schtick you spend on this ability, increase the Damage rating of your punch by 1.

Illustration by Thomas Manning

Chapter 9

October 17

The Prof called me into her little cubbyhole under the Junkyard and told me that the future guy and I were going to go back to the real world and blow up this stone garden.

You remember me mentioning the future guy, right? With the funky gun and the clue dispenser? He'd dropped out of the picture for a while, but now he was back.

So me and the future guy, we headed out. The Prof had found a gate that would open pretty close to where we wanted, but it was a fair hike to get to. So on the trek me and the future guy had a while to talk. He even trusted me enough to give me his name: Concourse Godard. I didn't figure it was his real name or nothing, but a handle was at least a starter. Those guys from 2056 are paranoid to the bone.

As I was talking to him, I couldn't shake the idea that there was something different about him this time. His voice was just a little different, and his body language had changed. I was curious why, but seeing as I don't exactly care for people poking into my business, I wasn't about to butt into his.

Then this gang of Netherworld Rabble popped out behind a turn in the corridor and tried to shoot us down.

I found myself in the mood for a series of calm and collected one-shot takedowns, so I selected Mr. Browning instead of the MP5. But Concourse didn't appear to be into the subtlety thing: he hauled out a great whacking gun with these weird skulls and insect-type parts embossed on it. He sprayed its glowing beam of pure nastiness at the Rabble and sent them packing pronto—those that didn't just melt on the spot, that is.

I'm always interested in checking out a new piece, so I asked him if I could take a look before he stowed it again. I could tell he was a little reluctant, but he didn't say no, so I started to turn the baby over in my hands. Damn, it was heavy. Then I got tangled in something—I realized that it was attached to the guy! There was this fiber-optic type cord leading from the stock and feeding into this bone-like ring implanted in his upper arm. He was busy gritting his teeth and yanking the cord out of this socket thing. There was a jack on the end of the cord, looked like a copper alloy of some kind. I looked up at him hoping for an explanation of some kind. His facial muscles were twitching something awful, and I could swear that his eyes turned bright yellow. He lurched over, covering his head in his hands. I put my hand on his shoulder to see what was the matter, and he batted it away. He turned on me, yelling for me to get away from him and leave him alone.

His skin had turned a purplish green, and all of these warts had broken out on it. They kind of bubbled and shifted around on the surface of his skin. His eyes were glowing yellow, and his hair was growing at about an inch a minute. He opened his mouth and howled, revealing several rows of serrated teeth. They looked plenty sharp for my taste, and I wasn't sure just how far he was planning to take his freak-out. So I made sure Mr. Browning was back in my hand without him noticing it.

And just as abruptly as it started, it was over. He tumbled over onto the floor of the passageway, and started throwing up. But the green skin, the warts, the glowing eyes, the teeth: all gone without a trace. Once he'd finished spilling his lunch and got his breath back, I told him that he'd better get straight with me. I was putting my life in his hands going out with him, and if he wasn't up to it, he'd better let me know. He told me that what I'd just seen was a Mutation Episode. Apparently if you use that freaky Architect gear, it sends bent magic into your system, kinda like a virus. If you use it too much, you get subject to seizures, and if one of them seizures goes really wrong, you end up turning into an Abomination. You know the Abominations... those altered demons the Buro uses to fight its wars.

I wasn't too enamored of the idea of going out with somebody who could turn into a twisted freak on me at any moment, and I told him so. He said he'd never let anyone down yet, that he could handle his own problems. Okay, I thought, I'll trust you. But Mr. Browning, he's going to keep an eye on you. Just call Mr. Browning a suspicious guy.

CHAPTER 9

Arcanowave Gear

THE WAY OF THE FUTURE

This section details the schticks that may be chosen by characters who receive arcanowave schticks. You only need to read it if you are a GM or if you are playing such a character.

WHAT ARCANOWAVE GEAR IS

The items described in this chapter are all products of the unnatural science of the Architects of the Flesh. They have discovered the connection between magical theory and the scientific method, and have put this knowledge to the worst possible use. Although it may mimic the form of common items like guns, goggles, or armor pieces, arcanowave gear is alive. Arcanowave gear is created by growing living matter in the lab, and then infusing it with the spiritual essence of ritually-slain supernatural creatures or captured spirits. This living matter is then placed in housings of high-impact plastic, to which it fuses. The resultant material is called **arcanowave resonating biopolymer**, or ARB. Arcanowave gear is so visually distinctive that it is recognizable at a glance to anyone even remotely familiar with it. It is often moist or slimy to the touch, or it may be a hard and bone-like substance covered in a chalky residue. The outer shells of arcanowave gear are invariably decorated with arcane sigils, and are covered with forms that seem vaguely skeletal, or resemble the shells of crustaceans. There is something profoundly unnerving about these devices; those who stare too long at the tiny details of their housings can become nauseous or even psychologically unstable.

Most pieces of arcanowave gear must be physically fused to their users in order to work. To be able to operate a piece of arcanowave tech, you must have an **arcanowave input/output port**, or **AI/O port**, surgically installed somewhere on your person. These ports are about the size of a dime, and appear on the surface of the skin as small rings of typical chalk-white arcanowave matter, decorated with a number of occult signs. A specially-adapted form of coaxial cable is connected from the arcanowave device to the user's AI/O port. The AI/O port itself extends below the surface of the skin; it terminates in a microscopic piece of optic fiber which penetrates one of the nerves. The AI/O port translates electronic and magical impulses from the arcanowave device into chemicals which can be rapidly transmitted and read by the brain. Any AI/O port can accept data from any arcanowave device, but typically only one device can be connected to any port at the same time. Some Buro agents and soldiers have jury-rigged splitters to allow them to plug more than one device into the same port in the field. These are recommended only for emergency use, such as when one AI/O port is damaged and a remaining one must do the work of two: see "Malfunctions," p. 119.

Plugging an item into an AI/O port has a shot cost of 3 unless otherwise indicated.

Arcanowave tech has a viral quality to it. The magically-charged chemicals that the AI/O ports transmit can alter the DNA of those exposed to large doses. This can lead to mutation, birth

Chapter 9

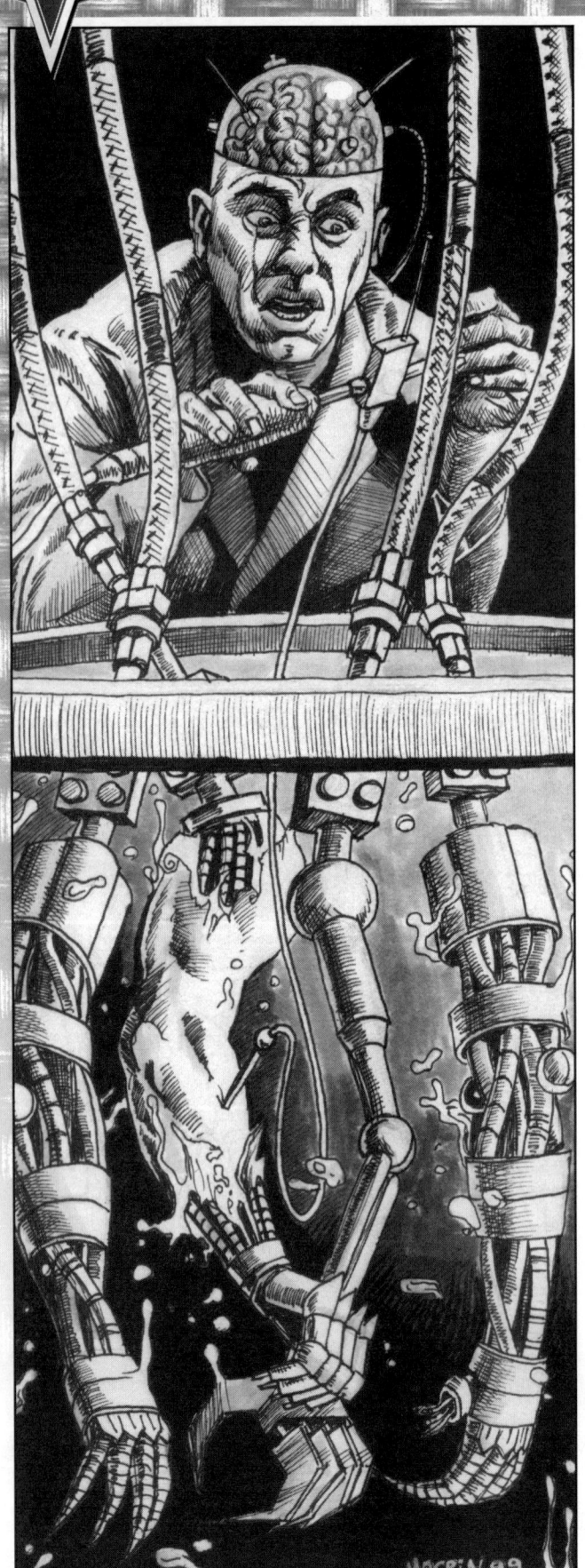

Illustration by Toren Atkinson

defects, and personality disorders. Consequently, human users of arcanowave tech employ it only sparingly, plugging it in only immediately before action, and unplugging it immediately afterwards. Abominations, the biologically altered supernatural creatures that the Architects employ as shock troops, are already infused with magical energy on the cellular level, and are immune to further harm from the devices.

Any character who begins the game with arcanowave schticks can have as many AI/O ports as desired.

ARCANOWAVE MUTATION

Human characters using arcanowave tech must keep track of the number of sequences (or portions thereof; always round up) they spend with one or more arcanowave devices plugged into an AI/O port during each session. At the end of each session they have had an arcanowave device plugged in, they must make an Arcanowave Device task check, with the number of sequences as the Difficulty. This is made on a closed roll. This check is called a **mutation check**. If a character fails the test, take the Outcome of the check and consult the chart on p. 124.

These changes are cumulative; you automatically get all results above your result on the chart if you have not already suffered them. When a mutation result changes an attribute, all secondary attributes (except for Magic) also change accordingly, as do related skills.

Once you have failed a check, add the Outcome of the last check to the Outcome of all subsequent mutation checks (make a note of this somewhere on your character sheet). There is a plus side to this—you can now gain the Creature schticks on pp. 102-107.

Example: Antonio Jawara has had an arcanowave device plugged into one of his AI/O ports for a total of 16 sequences this session; this is the Difficulty of the check. His Arcanowave Device rating is 15. At the end of a session, he makes an Arcanowave Device check to see if he suffers any side-effects from this prolonged exposure to arcanowave energy. His roll is a -2, for an Action Result of 13 and an Outcome of -3. A ring of small tattoos, each of them a tiny mocking face, spontaneously appears on the back of his left hand. The next time he makes a mutation check, he will add -3 to the Outcome of the check.

If any primary attribute other than Chi is reduced to 0 as a result of mutation, the character is retired from the game; time to create a new one.

"YIKES, NO WAY I'M PLAYING THIS!"

Although the ever-present threat of arcanowave mutation looks nasty at first, keep in mind that fights in *Feng Shui* rarely take more than three sequences from the first shot to the last punch. And the average session rarely involves more than three fights. So your mutation check Difficulty should only rarely hit the double digits.

For GMs who run marathon sessions, allow characters to add their Constitution ratings as a bonus to their Action Values when making a mutation check.

GAINING NEW ARCANOWAVE SCHTICKS

Because they are inherently magical, arcanowave devices cannot simply be picked up and used by anyone with an AI/O port. A character who wants to use a new arcanowave device in the course of the game must pay (8 + x) experience points to attune the device to her aura. X = the number of arcanowave devices you will be attuned to once you're attuned to this one. Attunement takes about fifteen minutes. There is no limit to the number of arcanowave devices you can be attuned to at any one time. When you become attuned to one device, you attune to all other devices of that type.

In order to gain a new device, one must also acquire it in the course of the storyline. Arcanowave devices are not exactly easy to come by. They exist only in the 2056 juncture, and even there are tightly controlled by the Buro authorities, who only disburse them to soldiers and top agents. The best way to get these devices is to capture them in battles with Architect forces.

Characters with no arcanowave schticks who wish to acquire them in the course of play must also acquire AI/O ports. Doing so means finding a PC or GMC who knows how to surgically install them. The installation requires the doctor to make successful task checks with the Medicine and Arcanowave Device skills, each at a Difficulty of 10. The doctor must know the Surgery subskill of Medicine, and must have access to a lab full of Architect biomedical equipment. If the Action Results of both checks are negative, the patient suffers 6 Wound Points. If one succeeds and one fails, the operation is a failure but the patient suffers no ill effects. There is no other ill consequence of a botched installation.

A character receiving his first AI/O port must then make a Magic check in order to attune himself to arcanowave energy. The Difficulty of the check is 10. If this check fails, the character is not only unable to use the AI/O port, but is never able to use arcanowave technology; he simply doesn't have the spiritual aptitude for it. This may reflect well on the character. GMs should add to the Difficulty if the character is particularly virtuous or spiritually advanced, and subtract from it if the character is especially wicked or depraved.

DESPERATE EFFORTS

Arcanowave device users usually draw on the chi energy of the world around them to power their supernatural effects. However, it is possible to put extra energy into an arcanowave device effort by expending your own personal mystic energy. Charaters can spend points of their Magic secondary attribute during combat to increase their Arcanoave Action Values.

For each point of Magic that you expend, you may increase your Arcanowave device Action Value by 1; this applies to one task check only. You may expend multiple Magic points on one check.

Immediately after the check on which you've spent the point(s), subtract them from your Action Value for Arcanowave devices.

Magic points return to normal at the beginning of each game session. (See "Desperate Efforts," p. 91.)

MALFUNCTIONS

Arcanowave devices are notoriously delicate; even a sudden change in the emotional atmosphere of a room can make them harder to operate. Much of the skill in using arcanowave devices is adjusting for the nuances of the spiritual environment. No matter how skilled the user, however, arcanowave

Chapter 9

devices are more likely to malfunction than mundane gear.

Whenever the die roll on an Arcanowave Device task check comes up snake-eyes—ones on both negative and positive dice—you fail to compensate for a sudden change in the occult background radiation of the area and suffer a malfunction. You suffer 12 Damage, add 3 to the Difficulty of your mutation check at the end of the session, and have a device which is temporarily inoperable.

You can then attempt to impose your will on the device and force it to operate again. This action has a shot cost of 8; you must make an Arcanowave Device check with a Difficulty of 10 in order to get it working again. If you fail, you can take another 8 shots to try again. There is no limit to the number of times you can try to fix a malfunctioning device.

If you are using two devices at once, attached to a single AI/O port through a splitter, you suffer a malfunction not only on a roll of snake eyes, but also when you roll twos on both negative and positive dice.

An AI/O port can become damaged, although it is small and therefore hard to hit. (Any check to hit an AI/O port with a Called Shot takes a -3 Action Value penalty.) If one of your AI/O ports is hit with any kind of force, it is rendered inoperable and you take 15 Damage. An AI/O port can't be repaired; it must be replaced under surgical conditions, as described earlier in "Gaining New Arcanowave Schticks."

JUNCTURE MODIFIERS

Arcanowave devices work better in the 2056 juncture than in other junctures or the Netherworld. (See the chart on this page for details.) As the Architects conquer feng shui sites in other junctures, the magical atmosphere of those junctures will increasingly support their twisted blend of technology and magic.

Arcanowave Gear Juncture Modifier Chart

Juncture	Modifier
69	-1
1850	2
modern	-1
2056	2
Netherworld	0

ARCANOWAVE SCHTICKS

On the following pages are the various devices available to characters with arcanowave schticks. Note that arcanowave guns do not use conventional ammo but instead draw arcanowave energy from the environment, employing the user as a conduit. They therefore do not have ammo capacities and need not be reloaded. They do have Concealment ratings, however. See "Concealment," p. 63.

AERIAL MOBILITY UNIT

Or—to translate the burospeak—wings. These are huge (3 meter wingspan) wings composed of a number of metallic struts, over which an ultra-thin elastic fiber sheet is stretched; the sheet is made of an ARB derivative. Visually, the effect is a combination of bat and robot. When plugged into an AI/O port, the Aerial Mobility Unit allows you to fly. When first plugged in, make an Arcanowave Device check with your Move rating as the Difficulty. The Outcome is added to your Move score when airborne. This value is valid for a number of sequences equal to the Outcome; then you must make another Arcanowave Device check to remain airborne. This check may alter your Move score while airborne. Characters must also make a new check if they land and then wish to take off again.

AGONY GRENADE

This looks like a grenade with an ARB casing and a clawed demonic hand for a pin. To charge it up, plug it into an AI/O port and leave it there until you suffer a single attack. You then unplug it and keep it handy until you want to throw it. (Multiple attacks do not charge the grenade multiple times; it only charges once.) Use a Strength check to throw the grenade, as per the throwing rules on p. 142. When it hits the ground, it emits arcane energy over an area. Make an Arcanowave Device check against a Difficulty of 6; the Outcome is the radius of the effect in meters. The radius is centered on the grenade. All within the affected area suffer Impairment penalties. Impairment is equal to the number of Wound Points you suffered from the blow which you used to charge the grenade divided

(120)

by 3 (round down). Affected beings do not suffer any actual injuries from this effect; the arcane energy is stimulating the pain centers in their brains. Only living beings are affected by agony grenades. The effect lasts for a number of shots equal to the Outcome of the Arcanowave Device check.

There is a mystic link between the character charging the agony grenade and the grenade itself; if anyone else attempts to throw an agony grenade, it is a dud. There is no addition to the Difficulty of a mutation check for throwing a grenade, but there is one for charging it up in the first place—the single shot in which you took damage from an attack and thus charged the grenade.

Agony grenades retain their charge until the end of the session; at the start of the next session, any charged grenades have lost their charge completely.

If you take this schtick, you have an essentially unlimited supply of grenades, but can keep only one charged for each Agony Grenade schtick you've taken. Of course, you can always be separated from your bag full of the things if you get captured or fall out of a plane or something like that.

FEEDBACK ENHANCER

This looks like a tiny radio receiver dish made of ARB and covered with howling faces. Any Sorcery spell which targets you while you have a Feedback Enhancer plugged in causes an automatic backlash (see "Backlash," p. 91) to the sorcerer. This does not negate the effect of the spell, which goes off as usual.

HELIX RETHREADER

This large rifle emits a beam of arcanowave energy which temporarily scrambles the portion of the victim's DNA that allows for the normal flow of chi energy. A character hit by it is affected for a number of shots equal to the Outcome of the attack. While affected, the victim takes 5 Wound Points for each Chi point he spends to activate fu powers. These Wound Points are not reduced by Toughness or Armor. For every 5 Wound Points of Helix Rethreader damage a character suffers, he also suffers 1 point of Impairment until the end of the fight.

Concealment rating: 6. See the Guns chapter for rules on concealment.

HELIX RIPPER

This large rifle emits a beam of arcanowave energy that tears apart living victims on the cellular level. Its Damage rating is 15, and its Concealment rating is 7. Hits from a Helix Ripper take out unnamed characters on an Outcome of 3 or more. Medicine task checks do not reduce Wound Points caused by Helix Rippers. It cannot be used to destroy inanimate objects. The Helix Ripper's beams are dissipated when they hit more than 12 cm of solid matter; they pass lesser thicknesses without effect on the beam or the matter. The beams thus ignore non-living armor. A Helix Ripper weighs close to 20 kg when unplugged from your AI/O port, but, due to the bizarre nature of arcanotech, is a more manageable 6 kg when plugged in. It is not capable of autofire.

JUICER

This is an insect-shaped casing of ARB filled with a soupy green broth of magical gunk. It does not plug into an AI/O port. Instead, it is attached to the body with a small tube which is permanently implanted through surgery. (The game mechanics for this are identical to having an AI/O port implanted; see p. 117.) When activated by pressing a button on the casing (a one-shot action), it negates any Impairment you might otherwise suffer for the rest of the session except impairment incurred due to arcanowave shticks. Use the highest Impairment you would have suffered during the session as the addition to the Difficulty for this session's mutation check.

NEURAL STIMULATOR

This is a coil of wires attached to a rectangular 3 inch by 5 inch ARB battery pack which can be strapped or taped to any sufficiently large portion of your outer anatomy. When plugged into an AI/O port, the ARB pack writhes obscenely, generating energy that stimulates your nervous system, making you artificially faster. Make an Arcanowave Device check when you first plug it in, with your Speed rating as the Difficulty. Add the Outcome of this check to your Speed for the purpose of making Initiative Checks. This effect lasts for a number of sequences equal to the Outcome. Having your nervous system hopped up in this way is debilitating; at the end of any sequence in which you've had your neural stimulator plugged in, you suffer 1 point of Impairment.

Impairment is cumulative. Unplugging and then immediately replugging a neural stimulator is especially debilitating, adding 2 points of Impairment each time it is done.

PULSER

This broadcast device takes the form of a small skull of a reptilian creature packed with wires and diodes; it can be attached to a band which can be adjusted for wear on the forehead, arm, thigh, or can be strapped to the torso. When activated with a successful Arcanowave Device check against a Difficulty of 5, it alters the magical atmosphere of a small area so that its Arcanowave Device juncture modifier is replaced by that of the 2056 juncture. See "Juncture Modifiers," p. 120. This occurs within a circular area centered on the user, with a radius equal to the Outcome in meters. The duration of this effect is equal to the Outcome in sequences. The effect is terminated prematurely if the device is unplugged from the user's AI/O port.

REINFORCER

This device is a three-foot skeletal hypodermic needle filled with foul-smelling green ectoplasm. The user injects it into any intelligent subject and makes an Arcanowave Device check with the subject's Magic rating as its Difficulty. The subject then grows a temporary hard, insect-like shell which provides 3 points of armor protection (see Armor, p. 138) and levies an Agility penalty of -1. The armor lasts for a number of sequences equal to the Outcome of the Arcanowave Device check. At the end of the session, the subject must make a mutation check, with the Outcome as its Difficulty. If the subject would have to make a mutation check anyway, the Outcome is added to the Difficulty.

The user does not have to have the reinforcer connected to an AI/O port when injecting the needle. However, to refill it with summoned ectoplasm, the hypo must be plugged in. Refilling the device has a shot cost of 8 and requires an Arcanowave Device check with a Difficulty of 6. If an attempt fails, it can be immediately repeated with no ill effect.

ROBOT LIMB

You have an arm or leg made of an alloy that mixes steel and ARB. (You can buy up to four schticks in robot limb, one for each limb.) The limb moves in accordance with your will just as a real arm would, and even has a sense of touch. When relying exclusively on this limb, your effective Strength rating is 12. This is the base Strength used for determining damage of hand-to-hand attacks made with this limb, or by weapons held in this limb. If you have two robot legs, your Move rating is 12.

The limb is attached to an AI/O port in your shoulder or hip. When unplugged, it moves under the power of an onboard battery pack; the battery is a product of mundane technology and does not contribute to your mutation point total. When running from the battery, your attribute ratings are not boosted by the Robot Limb, and any Manual Dexterity-based check using the limb suffers a -2 Action Value penalty. Add 1 to your end-of-session mutation check difficulty for each fight in which you power up your robot limb or limbs, and for each out-of-combat check you make using an attribute boosted by a robot limb. This includes skill checks.

SLAP PATCH

This first aid device is a palm-sized rectangular chunk of ARB with a powerful adhesive along one side. When you want to use it, tear the waxed paper covering off the adhesive and glom it onto a wounded living being. The character applying the slap patch makes an Arcanowave Device check; subtract the Action Result from the patient's Wound Point total. There is no such thing as negative Wound Points and no way to save up healing to apply against future wounds. The patient heals immediately, as the arcanowaves emanating from the ARB patch temporarily reconstitute his DNA for rapid healing. This can be a shock to a weakened system; the patient must make a Constitution check with the number of Wound Points healed as Difficulty; failure means that the patient suffers an additional 4 Wound Points instead of being healed.

The patient must make a mutation check with a the Difficulty of 3 at the end of the session; this is cumulative with other additions to the mutation check Difficulty.

The user of this schtick gets a kit which allows for the manufacture of slap patches. It includes a growing vat, tiny crystals of "seed" ARB which grow into the full chunks, a supply of chemical broth for the vat, a jar of adhesive, and a supply of wax paper covers. Don't worry about how the character gets replacement material when it runs out; like a gunman's constant supply of highly illegal weaponry, this should never be an issue in an action movie context. It is possible to grow one slap patch per day in

Arcanowave Gear

this manner. A character adds 1 to the end-of-session mutation check for each slap patch he grows.

SPIRIT SHIELD GENERATOR

A spirit shield generator is a harness of ARB material and lycra, which can be worn over clothing or armor. It stretches across the torso and down the legs. When plugged into an A/IO port, it activates a number of spirits trapped in the ARB. These invisibly circle your body, on the alert for incoming ranged attacks. When you are the subject of such an attack, you may make an Arcanowave Device check with no shot cost. If your check exceeds the attack check that has just been made against you, a tiny, grotesque spirit partially materializes and devours the projectile or thrown object; you are not hit and take no damage. The spirit, on the other hand, is then released from its bondage and abruptly vanishes. Spirit shield generators provide no protection against Sorcery or hand-to-hand attacks.

When your character first gets a spirit shield generator as a schtick, it has eight captive spirits. This is the generator's maximum capacity. To replace a spirit, you must spend four hours exclusively engaged in a ritual; then you make an Arcanowave Device check with a Difficulty of 7. If you succeed, you have replaced the spirit. If you fail, you have wasted four hours. Since *Feng Shui* characters should never be wasting time while on-stage, expect your GM to make this as inconvenient as possible.

SUCKER ROUNDS

These are bullets for regular handguns (.22, .38, 9 mm, .44, .45) made of ARB. They reduce a gun's usual damage rating by 2, but any victim hit by a sucker round must make a mutation check at the end of the session, adding the number of Wound Points suffered from sucker rounds to the Difficulty. Sucker rounds always malfunction (see p. 64 of the Guns section for relevant malfunction rules) when used by a character who has not taken them as a schtick; one must be attuned to them to allow them to fire at all. Characters with the sucker rounds schtick always have more rounds handy, though they still reload normally. They add 1 to their mutation check Difficulties for each clip or revolver they fill with sucker rounds.

Illustration by Toren Atkinson

THREAT EVALUATOR

This is a wet, insect-like compound eye encased in a ring of ARB material. It can be implanted in your forehead or in any large muscle on your body. (The eye has been involuntarily donated by a flesh-eating demon.) It does not use a normal A/IO port; instead you just hit a button on the casing to activate it. When activated, make an Arcanowave Device check with the number of targets you are scanning as the Difficulty. If you succeed in the check (which takes one sequence), the GM gives you the current Wound Point total of each scanned target. There must be a clear line of sight between the Threat Evaluator and the targets; it's no good keeping it hidden under your clothing, for example. If you suffer a fumble on the check, you note only the Wound Point total of the most wounded target, but must immediately attack that target. Unless somehow restrained, you will attempt to devour the target raw, as your natural instincts are overridden by those of the demon whose eye you now use as a cybernetic enhancement.

A Threat Evaluator also allows you to use your Arcanowave Device rating instead of your Perception rating when making Perception checks.

TRACER RESIN PROJECTOR

This small rifle fires hollow, soft-shelled ARB bullets full of magically-charged gummy stuff. Any target hit by them is then additionally vulnerable to hand-to-hand attacks launched by abominations and attacks of any sort using arcanowave weapons: the victim's Dodge and Parry values against them is lowered by 2. This reduction is cumulative with multiple hits from the device. When firing a tracer resin projector, you must have it connected to an AI/O port, and must make an Arcanowave Device check to hit. The effect lasts for a number of shots equal to the Outcome of the attack. The pellets do no actual damage.

WAVE SCANNER

This set of goggles made of hard, unyielding ARB makes you appear to onlookers as if you have a set of demonic, fiery eyes. With these goggles you can detect and evaluate sorcerous, chi, and arcanowave energy. When they are plugged into your AI/O port, you gain a +2 bonus to your Dodge rating when targeted by sorcery effects, fu power attacks, and arcanowave weapons. You can also detect the presence of unusual amounts of magical, chi, or arcanowave energy on a successful Arcanowave Device check. This includes the identification of feng shui sites.

WAVE SUPPRESSER

This is a grenade launcher that fires globes of foul blue ectoplasm. Any supernatural creature, ghost, or abomination hit by it becomes paralyzed for a number of sequences equal to the Outcome of your attack. If the victim of a wave suppresser hit suffers Wound Points while paralyzed, it can make a Willpower check (with your Arcanowave Device score as the Difficulty) to attempt to end the effect prematurely, adding the number of Wound Points suffered to the Action Value of the check. It makes one check per Wound Point-dealing attack. Its concealment rating is 6.

Mutation Outcome Chart

Outcome	Symptom
-1 to -3	minor cosmetic blemish, such as small patch of discolored skin, spontaneous appearance of stigmata or occult tattoos, lengthened fingernails
-4 to -6	noticeable cosmetic blemish, such as large patches of discolored skin, sharpened teeth, considerably lengthened fingernails
-7	as immediately above, plus minor psychological disorder such as chronic insomnia, propensity to abuse addictive substances, compulsive behavior
-8	unmistakable monstrous features appear; more serious psychological symptoms such as hallucinations and violent impulses begin; character is now considered an abomination for the purposes of effects that specifically target abominations
-9	subtract 1 from character's Mind; add 1 to Body
-10	subtract 1 from character's Mind; add 1 to Body
-11	subtract 1 from character's Chi; add 1 to Magic
-12	subtract 1 from character's Reflexes; add 1 to Body
-13	subtract 1 from character's Chi; add 1 to Magic
-14	subtract 1 from character's Reflexes; add 1 to Magic

Arcanowave Gear

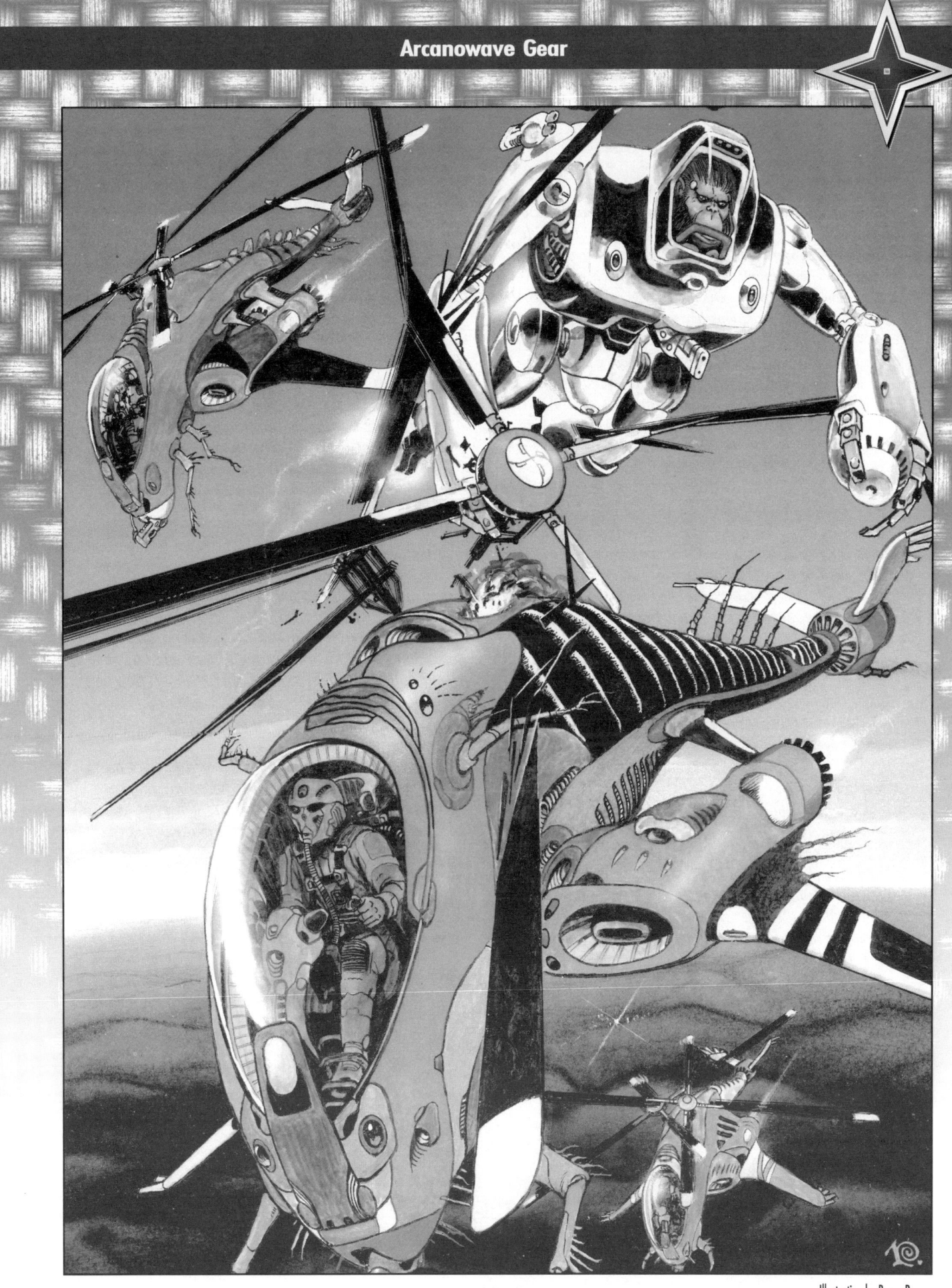

Illustration by Roger Raupp

Chapter 10

November 30

The kid was wounded, and I was having a hard time driving with one hand and shooting out the window with the other. I counted at least eight motorcycles roaring after us. They weren't having quite so much trouble firing from their moving vehicles, seeing as they were shooting in the same direction they were driving. Since I was dealing with the Ascended, I couldn't expect help from the cops. Fifty-fifty, these were the frigging cops. And they didn't give a rat's ass that the kid would likely bite it if I took a bullet and the Jag went outta control. That's the Ascended for you. A few dead kids—even dead kids of Lodge honchos—well, they'd be sad and all, but they consider it the cost of doing business.

I looked over at the kid. She'd lost so much blood she no longer had the energy to cry or even to look scared. A few more seconds and she'd be completely passed out. I used the rearview to judge a shot and removed one of my pursuers from the equation. But that still left seven or more, and the kid was well on the way to being dead. Well, maybe they didn't care, but I did. She was my responsibility now. But a quick mental review of the hospital locations on the island put me squarely in the outta-luck category. My chance of getting both of us alive to any emergency ward was less than zero.

Then it clicked: the Yanjing Building was only two streets over. If I could get the kid into the elevator of the Yanjing in one piece, I could pop into the Netherworld and get her to the Ice Pagoda. The Queen's attendants could do their magic thing and she'd be better than new in no time.

Now that I knew I only had to go a short distance, I could stop trying to peg the Pledged and concentrate purely on evasion. I managed to lose two of them in traffic. One of them blew over the guardrail and into a ravine. That left somewhere around four of them still to go by the time I roared onto the pavement in front of the Yanjing. I did a one-eighty, bringing the driver side around to face the oncoming bikers. I kicked the door open to give me enough of an angle of fire to hit all four— and hit all four is exactly what I did. Their bikes kept going, smashing into the mirrored glass of the building and sending office workers diving for cover in the lobby.

That was fine with me; I didn't want any competition for that elevator. I scooped up the kid and ran to the lobby doors. A security guard was cowering in the foyer, having thrown down his gun and put his head on his hands. Smart guy.

I jabbed the down button on the elevators. Looked over at the display that tells you where the different elevators are: they were all up, way up. Looked down at the kid. She was slipping away, I could tell. Looked back up at the display. Time got real slow.

But finally the elevator arrived, and I stepped inside. I glanced over at the panel. The special button appeared, the one that only innerwalkers can see. I stabbed at it, and it lit up. You know that normal pit of the stomach feeling you get in a bad elevator? Well, the elevator to the Netherworld is a thousand times worse. Switching dimensions can do that to you.

The doors slid open and I was back in that weird realm, with its dusty air and wet walls and endless tunnels. Someone had reshaped the elevator corridor since I'd been there last. Now it was all covered in shiny ceramic tiles with lettering on them that looked halfway Arabic, halfway Chinese. That meant that the Fire Warriors had claimed this particular gate for their own. There were a couple of them on duty, admiring a newly commissioned fire sled. I shot them and took it.

A fire sled is a magical vehicle, but it handles pretty much like a snowmobile. Not that there's any snow in the Netherworld—not unless you create some, that is. Anyhow, all we need to know for this particular story is that it's one kick-ass vehicle, and it took me from the elevator portal under the Yanjing building to the Ice Pagoda real fast like. I had to scatter some Netherworld Rabble here and there, but the sight of Mr. Browning convinced them not to mess with me.

The kid made it all right. A sorcerous transfusion kept her alive. Of course, being a descendant of the Lodge and all, the exposure to magic has transformed her into half kid, half tiger. But that's the Prof's problem. I just deliver 'em, I don't sort 'em out afterwards.

CHAPTER 10

Fights

FAST AND FURIOUS

Fights are something your characters will be getting into frequently in *Feng Shui*. Here are the rules to help you figure out who wins and who loses.

STUNTS

The most important thing about *Feng Shui* fights is this: they should be stylish, fast-moving, and wildly improbable. Most PCs have reached a jaw-dropping level of accomplishment in one or more of their skills, invariably including skills that are useful in knocking the bad guys around.

When your character is in a fight, you should always be visualizing the scene and thinking up exciting and unexpected maneuvers that your character can execute. These maneuvers are called stunts. A stunt is any attempt to use a physical skill in a dramatic way, doing something especially difficult in order to get an especially effective result.

When asked by the GM what your character is doing in combat, saying "I try to shoot the guy" is not very interesting. It is also not a stunt. However, saying that "I aim for the barrel of his rifle, trying to squeeze off a perfect shot so that it runs up the barrel and blows it up" describes a stunt. It is also much more fun.

Likewise, saying "I try to hit him" when you're playing a martial artist is not a stunt, and is not very interesting. To say "I open the desk drawer with one hand, grab him by the scruff of the neck, shove his face into the open drawer and then slam it shut" is an interesting stunt.

A stunt for a sorcerer might run something like this: "I conjure up a ball of fire and whirl it into the shape of a burning rope; then I lasso him with it, so that his holsters are burned off and his extra guns drop to the ground."

A cyborg with an Aerial Mobility Unit could perform a stunt that goes like this: "I swoop down on them, grabbing one of them in a scissor lock with my legs, and then carrying him high up into the sky. Then I threaten to drop him if he doesn't talk."

A player of a supernatural creature with the Foul Spew power might say, "I discharge a river of slippery slime under his feet; then I punch him so that he slides backwards into the elevator shaft."

We don't want to present you with an exhaustive list of every stunt possible with every skill or schtick; like one-on-one fighting video games, discovering cool moves for yourself is a big part of the fun of the game. But we do want to emphasize that the game will be a zillion times more enjoyable if you make this the focus of your fight scenes. Otherwise they're just an exercise in dice-spinning and time-killing.

Stunts can be used in many situations; both combat and non-combat stunts will be described in this chapter. Stunts can be used both offensively and defensively.

ADJUDICATING STUNTS

Whenever a character is doing something extra to try to get a better-than-normal result, the GM should very quickly decide how tough the maneuver is to perform and what its additional benefit might be. The player's description should include the hoped-for special result. Any stunt attempt reduces the Action Value of the skill used.

Sample Difficulties for Stunts

Attempted Stunt	Difficulty
barefoot water-skiing	5
dodge explosion by doing head-first long jump	10
hang onto bottom of speeding sports car	10
hang onto edge of cliff with fingertips	12
hang onto wing of airborne plane	10
jump vertically more than 1 m	+9/meter
jump horizontally more than 2 m	+6/meter
lay flat on road to avoid being run over by truck	10
lay flat on train tracks to avoid being run over	12
remain balanced on high wire	10
run along vertical surface	18
swing on chandelier	5
walk on wing of airborne plane	15

In combat, a popular stunt is trying to hit multiple opponents in one go. Hitting two opponents at once imposes a -2 modifier to the relevant Action Value. This is the benchmark stunt against which you should measure the challenge factor of other stunts.

Likewise, an attempt to hit three opponents warrants an Action Value penalty of -3. Four opponents means a penalty of -4, and so on.

Except for attempts to hit more than two opponents in one strike, -2 should be a sufficient penalty for the vast majority of stunt actions. We want to encourage stunts so that they are the norm rather than the exception during any fight scene. In your imagination, you should be seeing something as frenetic and exquisitely choreographed as the most exciting action sequences to come out of Hong Kong or Hollywood—so don't make stunts too hard.

The one exception is stunt attempts that are repeated with no variation again and again and again in the same fight. If a PC insists on sticking to a small repertoire of stunts, his opponents can get wise to him; as GM, increase the Difficulty for tired stunt attempts. However, even a little variation in the player's description should exempt him from any such penalties.

Example: "With a Tokarev clutched in each hand, I roll across the tabletop, shooting the two nearest mooks as I pass" is sufficiently different from "I jump onto the dolly and go shooting across the warehouse floor, kneecapping two mooks as I whiz by" so as not to incur any Difficulty increase beyond the standard -2 Action Value penalty for doubled attacks. Sure, it's not much of a surprise that our hero is going to try to take out two mooks every time he gets the chance to squeeze his triggers, but what he's doing while he's firing is a surprise each time and varies by the situation in which the fight occurs.

If the character makes his task check at the reduced Action Value, he successfully executes the stunt and achieves the desired result. In some rare situations, if the GM considers the desired effect impossible even by *Feng Shui* standards but the stunt is still cool, she can describe to the players an equally useful but different result.

Important Note: Since we want to encourage flashy attack descriptions, the GM should not assess an Action Value penalty to attacks that seek no extra benefit, even if they sound more difficult than a basic attack.

For example: Troy's character, maverick cop Jack Donovan, is in a tussle with an unnamed character, a lone pirate left to stand guard on a derelict ocean freighter Jack wants to search. All Jack needs to do is knock the guy out. Troy could just say, "I slug him," but that would be boring. So instead Troy says, "I grab a life jacket from a nearby lifeboat, slap it down over his arms to trap them, and then pummel his face with a flurry of blows." Since the end result of this attack—one mook out of action—would be the same with or without the added description, the GM should not apply a penalty to the Action Value for the attempt.

NON-COMBAT STUNTS

We hate to bring it up in a chapter devoted to fighting, but characters can also perform stunts out of combat. A stunt is any extremely difficult physical action requiring whole-body agility. Characters most often use Martial Arts as their skill to check for such attempts. Stunts which do not aid in the damaging of an opponent do not suffer an Action Value penalty; instead, the GM just decides on a straight Difficulty for any given stunt.

Some examples of stunts and the Difficulties associated with them appear on this page. If the players aren't coming up with stunts that don't appear here, they're not thinking hard enough.

UNNAMED CHARACTERS

Many of the opponents you will be facing are of low skill; their only advantage is numbers. Heroes in action flicks mow through cheap henchmen with little trouble. In *Feng Shui*, we call these opponents **unnamed characters**. If the GM hasn't bothered to give them a name, they're not really important to the plot. They're set dressing, basically, but more fun to beat up. (Don't get too overconfident, though—they can still do damage to you when the GM rolls high.) Unnamed characters follow a different set of rules than named characters, as explained later in this chapter.

It is also possible that you will have unnamed characters fighting on your side; these too will go down like tenpins when the bad guys attack them.

Sample Unnamed Characters
Here are a couple of standard unnamed characters.

Modern Mook
Attributes: Bod 5, Chi 0, Mnd 4, Ref 5
Skills: Guns 8, Intimidation 8, Martial Arts 6

Ancient Henchman
Attributes: Bod 6, Chi 1, Mnd 4, Ref 6
Skills: Intimidation 8, Martial Arts 8

NAMED CHARACTERS

Named characters are harder to take out in a fight, because they are sufficiently important to the story for the GM to have given them names. PCs are all named characters, as are the main bad guys your characters will be fighting.

Named GMCs may be created using the same character creation process as PCs. Or the GM may just pick attribute and skill ratings based on her requirements for the character in the storyline, without bothering to match them to a type. There are lots of possible characters who don't correspond to the types available to PCs. Non-combatant supporting characters and bystanders are prime examples.

RUNNING FIGHTS

Each fight is divided up into a number of **sequences**. A sequence is supposedly around three seconds of real time, but will take longer to play out, just as three seconds in a movie fight takes longer on screen due to slow motion sequences, cuts between simultaneous actions, and so forth. A scene is made up of as many sequences as are required to resolve the fight. It is up to the combatants to decide when the fight ends. They can stop a fight either by running away, or by whacking on the other side until they all keel over or run away.

Each sequence is divided into a number of **shots**. The number of shots in a scene is variable, and depends on the initiative check of the characters at the beginning of each sequence.

INITIATIVE

At the beginning of each sequence, each participant in the fight makes an **Initiative Check**. This is a roll of one die, to which the character's Speed is added. Sixes are not re-rolled. The resulting number is the shot at which the character first gets to act. A sequence starts with the highest Initiative Check Result of any character participating in the fight.

Example: Kar Fai (Spd 8), Johnny Tso (Spd 7), Jacqui Daniels (Spd 6) and The Silver Mask (Spd 7) are involved in a fight. Each rolls Initiative at the beginning of a sequence. Kar Fai rolls a 5, and adds his Spd of 8; his first shot will be 13. Johnny Tso rolls a 6 and adds his Spd of 7; his first shot is also 13. Jacqui rolls a 1 and adds her Spd of 6; her first shot will be 7. The Silver Mask adds a roll of 2 to her Spd of 7, and acts at shot 9. The highest shot is 13, so there will be 13 shots this sequence.

Once the highest shot has been determined, the character with the highest shot gets to act. The GM counts down shots from highest to lowest to see who gets to act next. When a character's shot comes up, he can act. The complexity of the action he chooses to make determines how many shots elapse before he can act again. Even the slowest characters generally get to act several times during a sequence.

Actions that take place during the same shot occur in the order of the GM's preference.

Shot Cost of Actions

Most complex actions cost three shots. In three shots a character can (for example) attack in hand-to-hand combat, aim and fire a weapon, draw and nock an arrow, pick up an object, or throw an object. At the same time, he can also travel a distance up to his Move rating in meters. If just running, he can travel twice his Move rating in meters (this can't be a snapshot). In a sequence in which he rolled initiative, he can move a total of three times his Move. (If not in combat, he could go four times his Move.)

Some simple actions take only one shot. In one shot a character can, for example: parry or block an attack, resist a wrestling maneuver, draw a weapon from a holster, reload a clip-fed gun, duck or dive flat, or catch a thrown object.

Example: On shot 13, Kar Fai decides to boot Jacqui Daniels in the head. This is a complex action with a shot cost of 3. He will next be able to act on shot 10. Assuming he continues to make three-shot complex actions, he will also get to act on shots 7, 4, and 1.

Once the GM has counted down through the shots, and resolved all actions that take place on shot 1, a new sequence starts with a new round of Initiative Checks. There is no shot 0.

Running Out of Shots

At shots 2 and 1, characters may take actions that cost up to 3 shots even though there aren't enough shots left. There's no penalty for this, and the unaccounted-for shot cost is not carried over to the next sequence.

Actions with a shot cost higher than 3, however, do carry over. See "Extra-Long Actions" (at right) for more information.

Defensive Actions

It is possible to take defensive actions any time you are attacked, as long as your next shot is greater than 0. Defensive actions include dodging or parrying incoming blows and dodging incoming missiles such as bullets or arrows. Reduce your next shot number by 1 unless otherwise specified.

Example: Jacqui Daniels decides to dodge Kar Fai's boot to the head. This makes it harder for him to hit her, but has a shot cost of 1. She reduces her next shot by 1, from 7 to 6.

If your opponent is significantly faster than you, it is possible to spend all of your shots on defensive actions and not ever get to take an offensive action. Hint: you're in big trouble.

When attacked, often the best thing to do is to execute a stunt to not only prevent your opponent from attacking you, but to give yourself an advantage of some sort over that opponent. See the discussion of Stunts earlier in this chapter.

Snapshots

It is possible to decrease the shot cost of an action by doing it recklessly. An action performed in this manner is called a **snapshot**. To reduce the shot cost by 1, subtract 2 from your action value for the task check. To reduce the cost by 2, subtract 5 from the action value. You can't reduce your action value any further.

For those of you who really like putting things into categories, a snapshot can be considered to be a type of stunt. You could combine a snapshot with other stunts for an even greater Action Value penalty but a cooler result.

Continuous Actions

Sometimes your characters will be doing one thing throughout a sequence while also trying to perform other actions. These are called **continuous actions**. Examples of continuous actions include driving, attempting to remain balanced on a precarious or slippery perch, or using certain fu powers. These do not have a shot cost, but increase the shot costs of all other attempted actions by 1.

Extra-Long Actions

Some actions in a sequence take more than 3 shots. Certain fu powers require more time than it takes to make a standard attack. Or your character might also be engaging in non-combat action, such as defusing a bomb or frantically trying to repair an out-of-control vehicle, while her pals and enemies are furiously hammering on one another.

Characters who wish to take actions that take 4 or more shots subtract the remaining number of shots from their first shot of the next sequence. This result gives them the shot on which their current action is completed and a new one may begin.

Example: Using the fu power Healing Chi, Kar Fai is bringing an injured Mad Dog McCroun back from the brink of death during a raging battle with a passel of Gnarled Exploders. Healing Chi takes 10 shots. It's shot 2 of the current sequence. This means that 8 shots carry over to the next sequence. Kar Fai's player makes an initiative check and gets a result of 12. He subtracts the carryover of 8 from that result to get the shot on which he'll next be able to act: shot 4.

Fights

Illustration by Heather Hudson

Chapter 10

Keeping Track of Shots

It is your job, as player, to keep track of the next shot you get to act on. It is the GM's job to keep track of which shot it is. At the beginning of each shot, the GM calls out the shot number. He then asks each player whose character gets to act on that shot to hold up her hand. The GM goes through the players whose hands are up clockwise by their seating position. Then he resolves the actions of GMCs who get to act on the current shot. All actions in a given shot occur in the order of the GM's preference (usually by seating order).

Example: Jose, the GM, is running a fight scene with his players Avram, Barry, Chris, Dana, and Elsie. He's in the middle of the fight and has just finished up describing the events of shot 8. Then he calls out "Shot 7, who gets to go on shot 7?" Avram, Chris and Dana's characters all get to act on shot 7, so they put up their hands. He has each of them resolve the actions they're attempting, in an order based on their seating arrangement. He also has three GMCs acting on shot 7; he resolves their actions, and then calls out shot 6. Barry's character gets to go on shot 6, so Barry puts up his hand. And so on. Butt is kicked in an orderly fashion.

HITTING YOUR OPPONENT

When you want your character to hit another character in combat, you make a task check using the appropriate combat skill. If you are hitting in hand-to-hand combat, the relevant skill is Martial Arts. If you are hitting an opponent from a distance with a missile weapon, the relevant skill is Guns. If you are attempting to hit an opponent with a spell, use Sorcery. Some attacks can be made with the Arcanowave Device or Creature Powers skills; if you have a schtick that requires that these skills be used, this will be indicated in the schtick descriptions.

If your opponent is stationary and does not defend against you, the Difficulty of the task check is 0. If the opponent is dodging or parrying, the Difficulty equals the Action Value of the opponent's dodge or parry attempt (this is covered in the next section). Your opponent might also successfully execute a reactive stunt that prevents you from attacking him at all.

Other factors such as range, cover, and impairment from wounds can alter Action Values and Difficulties during combat.

Example: Mike the Ninja is about to clobber an unsuspecting Buro mastermind. Mike has crept up behind his opponent, who is nonchalantly drinking a can of cream soda from the office pop machine. The hapless buro official therefore is a stationary target, and the Difficulty to hit him is 0. Mike hits him automatically.

HOW NOT TO GET HIT

Few characters who know that they're in the middle of a fight are going to stand stock still waiting to be creamed. Any character engaged in combat is assumed to be moving about; this is considered to be a **passive dodge** and has no shot cost. If a character is making a passive dodge, the Difficulty of any attempt to hit her equals her Dodge Action Value.

A character's Dodge Action Value equals her highest Action Value from the following list: Arcanowave Device, Creature Power, Guns, Martial Arts, Sorcery (if they have Blast), or the Agility secondary attribute. You should always have the Dodge Action Value for characters you are running available for easy reference.

Example: After socking the Buro official, a security guard comes around the corner. Mike leaps at him. The guard sees him and combat begins. The guard's Dodge Action Value, and therefore Mike's Difficulty rating for a Martial Arts attack check, is 8.

Characters may also choose to make an **active dodge** against any attack. This means that the character is, for the moment, concentrating entirely on not getting hit. An active dodge has a shot cost of 1. Making an active dodge increases your Dodge Action Value by 3.

An active dodge counts as a defensive action, as does a parry (explained next).

Example: Mike makes short work of the security guard, but the fight attracts the attention of an abomination also on security patrol. Mike, seeing the size of his opponent (and of his opponent's gun, which is firing), decides that an active dodge would be in order. His Dodge Action Value is 15, to which is added the +3 bonus for an active dodge. This has a shot cost of one; Mike's next action will take place one shot later that it would have had he not chosen to make an active dodge.

The abomination's Guns Action Value is 12; it rolls and gets a final Action Result of 16. But Mike's Dodge is now 18, so the abomination's attack fails. By expending a shot, Mike avoided getting hit by his opponent.

Fights

In especially close quarters, dodges—whether passive or active—may be especially tricky: your GM will reduce your Dodge Action Value accordingly.

A *parry* is a kind of active dodge, in which you are placing a hard object such as a shield or sword between you and the incoming blow. Or maybe you're grabbing the guy's sword arm or otherwise forcefully preventing him from going upside your head. Your Parry Action Value is always equal to your Martial Arts Action Value (though Sorcerers can use Blast or Movement schticks instead if they have them). There is no rules difference between active dodging and parrying, but the result is described differently by GM and players. It is merely a matter of style. GMs may rule that parrying is inappropriate in certain circumstances, and insist that characters dodge instead.

Example: It makes more sense to dodge a hail of machine gun fire than it does to try to parry it. If an ordinary mook with a sword and a Parry Action Value of 8 were facing off against the abomination in the above example, it would not make sense for the mook to try to parry the shots from the gun with his sword. Even dodging, he'd get hammered by the abomination's ungodly Action Result of 16. It would be especially ridiculous for him to try to avoid getting hit just by sticking up his little ribbon of steel.

Mike, on the other hand, is on a completely different plane of achievement. His active Parry Action Value of 18 is just a hair short of Frigging Astounding! (See Sample Action Values, p. 10.) With this kind of Action Value, he can perform highly improbable actions while parrying. As the abomination's bullets come raining in on him, he whirls his gleaming katana in a blazing circle of reflected light, slicing the bullets into ricocheting shrapnel with dazzling grace.

Likewise, if he'd chosen to have simply dodged the abomination, he would have done so with eye-popping acrobatic aplomb. It's up to the player to describe this action in suitably entertaining detail. Perhaps he would have, from a standing start, executed a backwards double leap up onto the Coke machine. The abomination's bullets would have ripped through the machine, sending a dam burst of carbonated beverage cascading into the room. The more collateral property damage you can describe when filling out the details of such maneuvers, the better!

At this level of skill, whether you choose to parry or dodge is merely a style preference.

Active Dodges and Fortune Dice

It is possible to expend a Fortune point and roll a Fortune die while making an active dodge; simply roll the die and add it to your Dodge rating for a single attack. If you are subject to more than one attack in the same shot, you must specify which attack you're spending the Fortune die on. You can spend more than one Fortune die per shot if you're being attacked more than once during that shot, but make it clear before you roll which die roll goes with which attack.

GETTING HIT

Despite your character's best efforts, there will come a time when she will get hit. She'll also want to be hitting her opponents on a regular basis. The result of a hit depends on whether the victim is a named or unnamed character. Both instances require you to arrive at the Outcome of the attack. As with any Outcome, this is the difference between the Action Value of the attack check and its Difficulty: In this case, the Difficulty is the dodge or parry ratings of the target.

When Unnamed Characters Get Hit

If an unnamed character is hit and the Outcome of the attack was 5 or more, he is out of the fight. If the Outcome is between 1 and 4, the GM may elect to describe various ill effects of the fight that the unnamed character might be suffering, but this is simply a style thing: The character suffers no impairment or other game consequence.

Named characters using attack skills in which they have an Action Value of 10 or more are so good at fighting that they can choose exactly how unnamed characters they hit are taken out. They can therefore mow their way through gobs of unnamed GMCs without committing mass murder, if they wish, or decapitate every single baddie in a massive bloodletting.

Characters using Martial Arts can either knock out or kill unnamed opponents, as they desire. Characters using Guns don't have to kill their enemies either: They can incapacitate with well-placed shots that the mooks can recover from after a lengthy hospital stay. The same is true of Creature Powers, Arcanowave Device attacks, and Sorcery.

Example: As Mike is dealing with the abomination inside the Architect complex, another security guard accosts his partner, Brenda Chang, who is waiting outside by the getaway vehicle. Brenda wins initiative and gets to go first. The guard's dodge Value is 8; he decides to actively dodge for a total Action Value of 11.

Brenda's player says: "I try a forward aerial somersault; I'll catch the guard's neck between my legs as I come down, driving his face into the dirt."

She gets an Action Result of 17 on her Martial Arts task check. That beats the Difficulty (the guard's dodge of 11) with an Outcome of 6. Since the guard is an unnamed character, he's out of commission.

"So did you want him dead, or what?" asks the GM.

"Nope, just conked out," says Brenda's player.

And so the unnamed guard is knocked unconscious by Brenda's move.

To save time, the GM should ask a player how hurt he wants a mook to be only after the attack is resolved and it is clear that the mook is going to be taken out by it. There's no need to ask before every attack against a mook is made. Or, to save even more time, just ignore the whole thing unless it's important to make an issue of it, just like the movies do; bodies fall left and right, and unless a fallen mook could crawl over to the bomb and set it off, who cares if they live or die? That's life in the movies.

PCs should only fail to deliver the desired sort of harm to unnamed characters when they are using attack skills they are comparatively unfamiliar with (those in which they have an Action Value or 9 or less), or when believability absolutely demands it. For example, if the player has already specified that he has jumped up from a table to shove the barrel of an M-16 down a thug's throat and fill his innards with lead, the player can't then specify that he wants to deliver only incapacitating wounds. In a case like that, the thug's survival would be too improbable even for a *Feng Shui* episode.

When Named Characters Get Hit

Here's the basic formula for determining the result of a successful hit on a named character: **Attack Outcome + Damage - Victim's Toughness = Wound Points suffered**.

Here's how this works: when a character hits an opponent, take the Outcome of the attack check; this is the difference between the attacker's higher attack Action Result and the defender's lower Dodge or Parry Action result.

Add this figure to the ***damage*** value of the attack form. Each type of attack does a different amount of damage: see Damage Values Chart, p. 139.

Then subtract the victim's Toughness value.

The result of the equation is the number of Wound Points that the character suffers. If the result is 0 or less, the character suffers no Wound Points. However, just because the character suffers no damage in game terms doesn't mean that he won't *look* like he's been hurt. Describe some superficial bleeding and bruises, or mimic the crunching sound of fist hitting flesh even if there is no game effect of a solid blow. (The willingness to return to childhood and do goofy sound effects is the hallmark of a good *Feng Shui* GM.)

Example: After Mike parries the abomination's bullets with his katana, he moves in for a strike. "I'm just going to jab him in the chest to see how tough he is," says his player, deciding to test his opponent before trying any fancy stunt attacks.

Mike's player makes a Martial Arts attack check, with an Action Value of 15. The Difficulty for the action is the abomination's passive Dodge value of 10. Mike's roll is 2, for an Action Result of 17. The Outcome of the attack is therefore 7. If the abomination were an unnamed character, it would be out of the fight, and Mike's player could decide whether he were dead or incapacitated.

However, as it happens, the abomination is a named character called Gnarl. So the damage resolution system for named characters kicks in.

The damage rating for his katana is 7. The abomination's Toughness is 12.

The formula is Outcome + Damage - Toughness = Wound Points. 7 + 7 - 12 = 2.

The abomination suffers 2 Wound Points as a result of Mike's hit.

Now it's Gnarl's turn. He opens up on Mike with his machine gun at close range. Mike decides to make another Active Dodge with a rating of 18. Gnarl tops out on his positive die roll, re-rolling sixes multiple times, for an Action Result of 27. That's an Outcome of 9. Gnarl's massive machine gun has a damage rating of 14. Mike's Toughness is 7.

Outcome (9) + Damage (14) - Toughness (7) = 16 Wound Points.

Ouch! Mike is in big trouble now!

Being Wounded

Unnamed characters don't worry about wounds. They're either in the fight or out of it. Named characters do need to worry about wounds; they

Fights

must keep a running total of their current Wound Point value.

Impairment

When a character has 25–29 Wound Points, he suffers 1 point of **impairment**. Impairment is a penalty applied to all of the character's Action Values. When a character has 30–34 Wound Points, he suffers 2 points of impairment. Other things (like certain schticks) can cause impairment, also.

Example: Ta Yu is a villainous GMC in the midst of a furious battle with our heroes. He has already taken 14 Wound Points in the course of the fight. Johnny Tso pegs him with a rifle blast, and he takes another 14 Wound Points, for a total of 28 Wound points. He now suffers a point of impairment; all of his Action Values decrease by 1. That includes his Sorcery skill rating. This means it is both harder for him to hit his opponents and easier for his opponents to hit him, since his Dodge rating is based on his Sorcery Action Value.

Although it is possible to keep going with 36 or more Wound Points (see below), The character's impairment can never exceed 2 from Wound Points. Other factors can raise this above 2, however, as noted earlier.

Death

When a named character has suffered 35 or more Wound Points, he is in danger of dying. To avoid doing so, he must make a special Constitution check called a **death check**. The Difficulty of a death check is the difference between 35 and the character's current Wound Point total. Impairment does not affect a character's Constitution Action Value for the purpose of death checks.

An Outcome of 0 or more means that the character remains upright and conscious and can keep fighting or doing other things, albeit with the impairment penalties explained above. But, assuming that the character's Wound Point total remains higher than 35, the character has to make another death check every time he suffers another wound.

An Outcome of -14 or less means immediate and instantaneous death—well, instantaneous as of the end of the fight, anyway. Any dying *Feng Shui* character should live long enough to deliver a properly melodramatic death speech and see his fellow characters weep and wail over him. After death, there is a pause in the action for a slow-motion flashback montage featuring the highlights of the character's career as a sad pop ballad unfolds on the soundtrack. (The player should describe this.)

An Outcome of -13 to -1 means that the character collapses and will soon die unless some kind of intervention is made. To see how long the character can cling to life in the meantime, consult the chart below.

Shuffling Off Mortal Coil Chart

Outcome	Time Before Snuffing It
-13	15 minutes
-12 to -10	30 minutes
-9 to -5	1 hour
-4	2 hours
-3	3 hours
-2	4 hours
-1	6 hours

Example: Johnny Tso is hit several times during a firefight at a warehouse controlled by the Ascended. The last of these hits takes his Wound Point total from 33 to 43. He must now make a death check. His Action Value for the check is his Constitution rating of 7. The Difficulty of the check is 8, the difference between his current Wound Point total and 35. Johnny rolls a -2, for an Action Result of 5. Subtracting the Difficulty of 8 from the Action Result yields an Outcome of -3. Consulting the chart, we see that Johnny has 3 hours to live.

Every time an already-dying character is hit in combat, the time before he snuffs it is decreased by one increment. (No Death Check occurs.) If the end result is less than 15 minutes, the character dies at the end of the fight and cannot recover.

Example: A security guard takes an easy shot at Johnny's prone but conscious body as the warehouse battle continues: the guard beats the required Difficulty of 0 on his attack check. This decreases Johnny's time left on this earth by one increment, from three hours to two. In other words, if someone's down and you want to be safe, pop them seven times and they're toast.

Medic! Medic!

Dying characters can be stabilized if given proper medical attention—specifically, a successful Medicine task check, a Sorcery check using the Heal schtick, or a Martial Arts check using the Healing Chi schtick. The Difficulty of the check is the difference between 35 and the character's current Wound Point total.

If the character delivering the medical assistance succeeds at this check, he can then go on to attempt to reduce the patient's Wound Point total. This is described below, under "Medical Assistance."

Chapter 10

RECOVERING FROM WOUNDS

Okay, now the fight is over and the heroes are lying about, their fine suits perforated and bloodstained, their vital fluids slowly leaking out onto the pavement. Now the rules for recuperation from injuries come into play.

When your character has survived a fight but is wounded—whether still standing or laid out on a stretcher waiting for the ambulance—you'll want to know how recuperation from injuries works. Fortunately, Feng Shui characters heal much more rapidly than people in the real world, enabling them to get out and risk getting wounded again in no time at all.

Characters recuperate naturally from injuries. At the beginning of each session, their Wound Point totals drop to 0.

GMs may decide to suspend this rule in one of two situations:

The end of the session is a cliffhanger. If you break in the middle of a fight, or in some other situation in which it completely defies credibility for the characters to be healed up the next time you get together and start playing, the GM may rule that you have yet to heal. Note that when we say completely defies credibility, we mean *completely defies credibility*—not just strains it. The "full healing at beginning of session" rule simulates the way in which action movie heroes rarely have to worry about debilitating injuries from one fight to the next. Sure, they may have a fashionable bandage or arm sling to carry with them for the rest of the movie, but that's just a style thing. If you're a GM, you should always give the PCs the benefit of the doubt when it comes to healing. They'll have plenty of opportunity to get grievously injured again during the next fight.

Example: In order to end the episode on an exciting cliffhanger, the GM decides to stage an explosion in the PCs' headquarters. She describes the ticking sound, allows the PCs to try fruitlessly to defuse the bomb, and then describes the massive explosion that they're all caught in. She tells them how many Wound Points they've suffered from the blast, and ends the session. It wouldn't make any sense for the characters to heal up between this session and the next week's, so the GM doesn't permit the PCs to do so.

A suitable break in the action occurs in the middle of a session. GMs should do their best to time their games so that one session is a coherent episode in the ongoing series, with a distinct beginning, middle, and end. This isn't always possible, though, because the players' decisions determine the length of scenes as they play out. If you reach a point in the course of a session which feels like the end of an episode but you're going to keep on playing, declare it the equivalent of the end of a session for recuperation purposes, and allow the characters to reduce their Wound Point totals to 0.

Example: Later in the same series, the GM ends on another cliffhanger: the final confrontation with the enemy the PCs have been doggedly tracking for session after session. The next week, she realizes she's got a pacing problem on her hands: the big climactic battle is going to be over in an hour, and then she's going to have to start a new storyline. Indeed, it takes about twenty minutes of real time to play out this scene. The PCs then start cleaning up and poking about looking for another plotline. The PCs want to spend a couple of weeks doing research and taking care of loose ends. It doesn't make any sense for the PCs to finish up this long period of rest as wounded as they started it, just because the game session isn't over. So the GM declares that the PCs heal over the course of their slack time.

DYING CHARACTERS AND RECOVERY

Characters who fail death checks should have a rough time recovering from their injuries. Whether they are dying as of the end of a session, or were dying but have already been stabilized, they should not automatically start the next session at 0 Wound Points.

A character who is dying at the end of the session still needs to be stabilized before the time period indicated on the Shuffling Off the Mortal Coil chart (p. 135); otherwise he dies when the time elapses.

A character who was dying should spend a realistic amount of time in intensive care in the hospital. His buddies should get to stand around and look at the tubes up his nose, pace down the hospital corridor in a worried manner, and so on. To determine how many days the character needs to spend in the hospital, turn the Outcome of the death check into a positive number. That's how many days it is.

Having characters languishing in intensive care while the others are hot to get out and nail the bad guys before they get away is a real pacing problem for the GM. Try to encourage them to wait for their pal to recuperate before moving the plot along. A good way to do this is to encourage the players to think that they need to guard their fallen comrade from attack; for that matter, if you can stage the next big action scene right there in the hospital (like in *Hard Boiled*) then go for it!

Characters who have failed death checks can forgo the lengthy hospital stay if healed by unconventional means such as magic or fu powers; these fantasy elements neatly sidestep the believability issue.

MEDICAL ASSISTANCE

It is also possible for characters to reduce their Wound Point totals during the course of a session. To do so they need to seek out healers. Doctors or other characters with the Medicine skill are healers. So are characters with the Heal schtick of the Sorcery skill, and characters with the fu power Healing Chi. All of these abilities allow the healer to subtract the Action Result of the relevant task check from the patient's Wound Point total.

A healer may heal any given recipient only once for each scene in which he suffers damage. If characters deliberately harm themselves or allow themselves to be harmed merely in order to qualify for further healing, the GM should display appropriate contempt and mockery for the player attempting this weaselly stunt. And, needless to say, rule that any attempts to heal that damage automatically fail.

Example: Johnny Tso and Kar Fai have concluded a rather rough fight with a passel of Mutoids. Johnny is barely standing, at 39 Wound Points. Kar Fai's Martial Arts Action Value is 19. First he performs Healing Chi on Johnny, getting an Action Result of 21. Subtract this from Johnny's previous Wound Point total to get his new one: 39 - 21 = 18. Johnny is now at 18 Wound Points. If there were someone else with a Healing ability, like Healing Chi, the Sorcery schtick Healing, or the Medicine skill, that person could also attempt to reduce his Wound Point total. But Kar Fai won't be able to try again until Johnny gets damaged in another fight, falls off a moving freight train, gets hit by lightning, or whatever.

ASSORTED FIGHTING RULES

Now that we've covered the basics, we're going to go back and fill in some details that relate to particular situations that commonly arise in combat.

AIMING

When using guns or other ranged weapons, characters can take extra time to aim. If a shooter is just using the regular combat rules given above, the assumption is that she's taking quick, opportunistic shots. For each shot a character spends aiming at a target, she gains a +1 Action Value bonus. The maximum bonus for aiming is +3.

Example: Rick "Water" Rachned wants to make sure he pegs the special ops guy who shot his pal Johnny in the warehouse firefight. His normal Guns Action Value is 14; his next action is on shot 3. He decides to aim for two shots; he will make a Guns task check on shot 1, with an Action Value of 16.

CALLED SHOTS

In a called shot, an attacking character attempts to hit a particular body location of an opponent, or a particular inanimate target. This is considered a stunt; the GM imposes an Action Value penalty, usually -1 or -2, depending on how hard it would logically be to hit the exact spot the attacker wants.

Feng Shui characters often use called shots to disarm opponents; the target of the called shot is the enemy's gun or sword or whatever. GMs are free to fiddle with this for dramatic effect, but here's a guideline to use for this common situation: on an Outcome of 7 or less, the weapon is undamaged but is knocked from the opponent's grasp. On an 8 or more, the weapon is damaged. Signature weapons are, of course, immune to this effect.

Rather than give you a chart listing what Outcomes are required to bust particular items, we're going to leave the exact results needed for massive property destruction up to GMs to gauge as they go along. It should be easier to wreck things in *Feng Shui* than it is in real life. Remember: in action movies, props exist in order to be spectacularly destroyed.

COVER

It is often wise, when a hail of bullets is coming your way, to get something nice and solid between you and said bullets. When you are behind cover, your opponent's Difficulty goes up when trying to hit you. How much the Difficulty increases depends on how much of you is behind a solid barrier: If you are exposing yourself by poking out to fire your own weapons, the Difficulty reflects the percentage of you that is covered during your most exposed moments.

These values are halved when the barrier reduces visibility but is not solid enough to deflect incoming bullets: barriers of this type would include heavy fog, smoke, shrubbery, and so on.

Example: Rick is standing behind a row of oil drums, which come up to about his waist. This gives him 50% cover; opponents targeting him with ranged weapons face a +2 Difficulty modifier. If he was in fog that obscured visibility by about half, there'd be a +1 Difficulty modifier instead.

Cover Chart

Percentage of Target Covered	Difficulty
25%	+1
50%	+2
75%	+4
90%	+6

DAMAGE

Here is some more information on dishing out and taking damage.

Damage Values of Common Attacks

When choosing your character's preferred mode of attack, the amount of damage she can deliver is a crucial factor.

The Damage delivered by Martial Arts depends on the type of attack; your characters' Strength rating is added to the value given for that attack.

Example: Rachelle Tzeto's Strength rating is 8. Rachelle's player, Paul, wants to know her Damage Value for a punch. Checking on the chart (p. 139), he sees that a punch has a Damage Value of "Strength + 1." That means that her base Damage for a punch is 9.

He then checks on her Damage Value with a sword. It is Strength +4, or 12.

The base damage of Guns attacks is fixed for each weapon, and is given in the chart on page 139.

Other Sources of Damage

There are lots of other ways to take Damage than getting hit in combat. When a character suffers damage outside of combat, simply subtract the character's Toughness from the Damage to get the Wound Points suffered.

Example: Oscar Balbuena is thrown through the front window of a restaurant and falls to the sidewalk. According to the chart on the next page, getting tossed through a plate glass window does 15 damage. Oscar's player subtracts his Toughness from this value to get the Wound Points suffered. Oscar's Toughness is 7, so he takes 8 Wound Points.

GMs will inevitably have to come up with Damage values for situations not covered here. They should keep in mind that Damage values should reflect how dangerous things are in action movies. Whatever you do, don't let reality get in the way! Nearly everything that does damage in *Feng Shui* hurts more in real life.

Armor

Most *Feng Shui* characters will be lightly armored if at all. Any type of armor that is at all useful against the deadly weapons and powers that are continually being tossed about in the typical *Feng Shui* fight also impedes movement and makes it harder to hit opponents. In other words, you don't often see armor on action movie heroes, so we've made it a rather unattractive option in game terms.

Armor Protection Values

Type	Toughness Bonus	Agility Penalty
light vest	+1	-1
heavy vest	+2	-2
police shell	+2	-1
military shell	+3	-3

Armor adds to the Toughness rating of characters wearing it, and reduces their Agility ratings. There are two common types of armor: **bulletproof vests** and **polymer shell** uniforms.

Bulletproof vests are available in both the modern and 2056 junctures: they come in light and heavy grades. Light vests can be hidden under clothing; heavy vests are obvious and not concealable.

Fights

Damage Values Chart - Weapons

Attack/Weapon Type	Damage Value
punch or chop, tonfa, nunchaku	Strength +1
kick, knife	Strength +2
staff, club, dagger	Strength +3
spear, sword	Strength +4
throwing star	5
thrown dagger	6
arrow, crossbow bolt	7
small handgun (.22)	8
medium handgun (.38)	9
big handgun (9 mm/.45)	10
really big handgun (.357/.44)	11
BFG (.50)	12
hunting shotgun	10
combat shotgun	13*
medium rifle (5.56 mm)	13**
heavy rifle (7.62 mm)	13†

* Damage value is 14 for pump action shotguns if you spend a shot to dramatically go "KA-CHINK!"
** Unnamed characters hit by this weapon go down on an Outcome of 4 or more.
† Unnamed characters hit by this weapon go down on an Outcome of 3 or more.

Damage Values Chart - Other Sources

Injurious Situation	Damage
Hit by a cruising Chevette	15
Hit by a cab	17
Hit by a speeding bus	22
Falling one story	15
Falling two stories	19
Falling four stories	27
Falling five stories	40
Falling ten stories	41
Falling twenty stories	42
Falling forty stories	43
Soaked in Gasoline and set on fire	15*
Drowning	5**
Having a television dropped on you	13
Having a support beam fall on you	18
Having stone temple ceiling fall on you	22
Being thrown through a plate glass window	15
Jumping from a speeding vehicle	15
Jumping on grenade	23
In middle of big explosion	27
More than 3 meters away from big explosion	12
Mild poison	12
Strong poison	17
Extremely toxic poison	22

Car Accidents

Driving into a telephone pole	17
Wiping out at 80 mph	20
Driving off a cliff	22

* Damage is inflicted each sequence for as long as the condition lasts.
** Damage doubles each sequence for as long as the condition lasts.

Opponents can ignore the Toughness bonus of vest armor by making successful called shots (see p. 137) to unprotected parts of the target's body.

Polymer shell uniforms are worn by military and police forces in 2056; this is basically high-tech plate mail made of a comparatively light, high-impact combination of steel and plastics. They are not concealable, and make their wearers look like contemptible Architect goons ripe for a bullet in the head in a dark alley.

Some fu powers, magic spells, and creature schticks also simulate armor.

Example: Celia Mui has a Toughness of 6 and an Agility of 8. Anticipating trouble, she dons a heavy bulletproof vest. While she wears it, her Toughness is effectively 8 and her Agility 6.

Chapter 10

Illustration by Heather Hudson

EXPLOSIONS

Things blow up a lot in *Feng Shui*, but you shouldn't sweat the details of explosions in game terms too much; they're just a big special effect.

The Damage chart on p. 139 provides sample values for jumping on a grenade (23) and being in a big explosion (27 in the middle, 12 if you're at least 3 meters away). Use these values to judge the Damage ratings of other explosive situations. If a character is more than 3 meters away from a grenade, you might assign a Damage rating of 9 or 10. If a character is across the street from an exploding building, it might just be 6 or 7. In general, explosions shouldn't do a lot of damage to characters unless the characters are right in the thick of the blast; otherwise, it's mostly just a cool special effect and a way to do property damage.

HAND-TO-HAND MANEUVERS

Sometimes characters fighting hand-to-hand will want to grab, pin, hold, or throw an opponent instead of just thumping on him. To adjudicate any result other than injury to an opponent, use the stunt rules that lead off this chapter.

INANIMATE TARGETS

When firing at inanimate targets, GMs should determine Difficulty ratings based on the size of the objects. Anything larger than a TV set has a Difficulty of 0. A paperback book would have a Difficulty of 6; a wallet would have a Difficulty of 10; a coin would have a Difficulty of 15. Adjust for range (see p. 141) if needed.

If the objects are moving, use the "Moving Target Difficulty Conversion Chart" on page 141.

MOVING TARGETS

The Difficulty to hit a moving target is based on how fast it's going—see the chart on page 141. Fast-moving characters can use the Difficulties below instead of their Dodge ratings. Note that most *Feng Shui* characters will be better off dodging, unless they're in speeding vehicles.

SIGNATURE WEAPONS

Certain schticks allow you to designate a single weapon of a given type as a ***signature weapon***. For example, a martial artist may be allowed to select a hand-to-hand weapon, a gun user gets to pick a gun, and so on. More specific information for each option is found in the relevant schtick sections. Players should, if possible, tie the signature weapon to their characters' melodramatic hooks.

A character with a signature weapon gets a +3 Damage rating bonus with that specific weapon. Note that this applies to a single, actual weapon, not all identical weapons.

Example: Johnny Tso's signature weapon is a particular Walther PPK, one given to him as a gift by his fiancée four years ago. His fiancée was killed in a restaurant hit meant for him just minutes after giving him the gun as an engagement present. Johnny has sworn to use the PPK as his instrument of vengeance against the gangsters who ordered the hit, and never lets it out of his sight.

Signature weapons are never destroyed: They're not literally indestructible, but the GM should contrive the plot so that they always survive mishaps, no matter how grave. They can be damaged or lost, but only when this becomes a major focus of the storyline. Characters should never lose the use of signature weapons due to casual or random events.

Example: A bomb goes off in Johnny's bedside table while he is in the bathroom brushing his teeth. The GM has decided to have this happen, but it is not a big deal in the story–just another routine hazard for any secret warrior. Although the Walther is on the table, the GM decides that, because it is a signature weapon, it survives the blast: It is thrown across the hallway to land, smoking, at Johnny's feet.

However, the next session the GM decides to make Johnny's melodramatic hook the center of the action. She plans to reintroduce the gangsters who killed his fiancée, and have one of them steal his precious PPK as a means of taunting him. Getting his signature weapon back becomes the primary motivation for Johnny in this session, so it is okay for the GM to separate him from it.

RANGE

It's easier to hit nearby targets with guns and other ranged weapons than it is to hit faraway targets. The same is true of magicians casting spells. Range increases the Difficulty of Guns and Sorcery task checks.

Sometimes range becomes very important; most of the time it's just a pain in the butt. GMs should ignore range modifiers unless there's a special situation that seems to demand it. When believability or a special tactical circumstance makes range significant, use the chart below. Otherwise, just forget about it for heaven's sake.

Moving Target Difficulty Conversion Chart

Move	Speed	Description	Difficulty
2	7kph	walk	3
4	15kph	jog	5
8	25kph	fast sprint	7
12	50kph	fast animal	9
25	90kph	cruising car	11
50	180kph	speeding car	13
100	350kph	race car	15
200	700kph	jet plane	17

Range Difficulty Table

Description	Range	Difficulty Modifier
Short	20m	0
Medium	40m	+2
Long	80m	+6
Extreme	160m	+14

Example: You've been running an exciting shoot-em-up scene without bothering to worry how far the combatants are from one another. But now you want one of the bad guys to get away; he's a ghost with the Flight ability. You describe him as rocketing away from the scene. One of the characters has a sniper rifle and wants to bring down the villain so he can't get away and wreak further havoc later. Now range matters; the ghost is fleeing at high speed, and it's important to know how hard it is for the PC to hit him, and when he'll get far enough away that the range penalty is prohibitive.

Each doubling of the range after 160m doubles the Difficulty Modifier.

LIFTING STUFF

On occasion, especially-strong characters will be called upon to lift especially-heavy stuff. This is resolved with a Strength check against a Difficulty corresponding to the mass of the object, as given in the chart on the next page. There are more interesting things in the world than a comprehensive list of what things weigh, so play it by ear using these benchmarks as a guide. Increase the Difficulty for especially awkward objects. If a character's Strength exceeds the Difficulty for an object's mass by 2 or more, no check is required; the character automatically succeeds.

Lifting Stuff Difficulty Chart

Example	Mass	Difficulty
average person	60 kg	5
piano	250 kg	14
compact car	1000 kg	16
van	2000 kg	20
semi truck	3000 kg	27

Throwing Stuff Table

Type of Stuff	Penalty
bar bells	-3
book shelves	-3
large dog	-2
parking meter	-3
TV set	-2
wooden chair	-1
wooden table	-2

THROWING STUFF

Sometimes your character will want to throw stuff in the course of a fight. This requires a Martial Arts check. If the object is heavier or more unwieldy than your normal designed-for-throwing object, throwing it counts as a stunt action. The GM determines the penalty to your Martial Arts rating based on the type of object, as follows.

If the object is really heavy, the GM will require a successful Strength check as well as a successful Martial Arts check. Double the Difficulties given in the Lifting Stuff chart on this page for thrown objects.

If you throw an object and miss the target—in other words, you've failed the Martial Arts check—that object will still land somewhere. This sometimes matters. Like with grenades, for example. One of the cardinal rules of action-adventure is that thrown objects, especially explosive ones, never land anywhere boring if they can possibly help it. When you fail a check, all characters closer to you than the target of your throw make a Fortune check. The object lands near or on the character with the lowest Action Result. If there are no relevant characters nearby then the thrown object—if at all possible—lands on and damages something you don't want damaged. You shouldn't have missed the roll, sucker.

UNDER THE INFLUENCE

Adventure heroes are sometimes known to knock back foolhardy amounts of alcohol. Sometimes they have to impress rough bandit chieftains; other times they have to impress decadent high-society types. Perhaps they're getting an informant drunk to loosen his tongue. Or maybe they're world-weary, secretly-troubled types who just *like* to get soused. The effect of drunkenness (or being under the influence of other hard drugs) is measured in points of impairment. For every serving of alcohol the character has imbibed in the past 6 hours, the character receives a -1 penalty on all Action Values. A serving is considered to be two beers or one drink of wine or liquor.

Characters with the fu power Drunken Stance (p. 83), oddly enough, do not suffer any drunkenness penalty to their Martial Arts Action Values no matter how plastered they are. That's why, if they live long enough, they become known as Drunken Masters.

CHAPTER 11

GM Tips

STYLE AND SUBSTANCE

This section contains tips for the GM running a *Feng Shui* game. If you're not a GM, there's not much here to interest you. The material in this section is meant as advice, not as a series of commandments. We've found that we have more fun running our *Feng Shui* games a certain way. The rules of the game have been set up to support a fast and loose style of play, so we thought it would be a good idea to give you some pointers on running a game in this style. However, everyone's tastes vary, and we're not obsessive enough to think that what works for us is going to work for everyone.

GETTING STARTED

Any action movie worth the price of admission starts things with a bang. Many flicks will even open with a completely irrelevant action sequence just to get the adrenaline pumping: For an example of this technique, check out almost any James Bond picture. It's dramatically neater to start with a relevant fight scene, but savvy directors know that gratuitous action is better than no action.

On the other hand, most opening sessions of roleplaying series creep along with painful sluggishness. Players have to be introduced to the setting, taken through character generation, have to sit around thinking of the characters they want to play, and then spend hours minutely polishing game statistics. When you're finally ready to start the action, it's almost time for everyone to go home.

In *Feng Shui*, we've tried to keep the inevitable pencil-scratching to a bare minimum. We want groups to be able to go from arrival in the game room to actual play in less than half an hour. That's one of the reasons why we use a character type system, and why the game statistics for each type allow only a few finishing touches instead of allowing players to build characters entirely from scratch.

Although it doesn't hurt if players have read this book ahead of time, it is by no means necessary for them to do so. If your players are coming into the game session cold, here's how you should prepare them for the road ahead.

INSPIRATIONAL MATERIAL

Tell your players that the game is based on wild action movies, especially fu movies and Hong Kong action flicks. Advise them to leave any pernicious notions of "realism" at the door.

The best way to get players operating from the right frame of reference is to show them a clip from one of the movies that inspired this game. If you have a VCR and can show them a sequence from *The Killer, Savior of the Soul,* or *Chinese Ghost Story,* you're cooking with gas. If you have to settle for your fave sequence from a Hollywood action flick, that's okay too.

Chapter 11

RULES WALKTHROUGH

Once the players know the basic territory of the game—but before they start creating their characters—you'll need to introduce them to a few of its basic concepts. Skim through Chapter One, "KIII-YAAAHHH!," selectively paraphrasing its contents. Skip all of the introductory setting material; the players can learn about the various groups involved in the secret war during the course of their adventures. Start on p. 8, with task checks. Explain the difference between a closed and open roll. Tell them what an Action Value is, reading off entries from the Sample Action Values Chart to give them an idea of what they should be shooting for in character creation. Explain Difficulties and Outcomes; read off a few entries from the Sample Difficulties chart. (Alternately, if you have access to a photocopier you can run off a handful of the *Feng Shui* rules summary sheets found at the back of this book.)

Then tell your players to read through the Types section and pick the type they'd like to play in the game. Once everyone has a type picked, but before they start to juggle their attributes & skill bonuses or buy schticks, flip to the Characters chapter and walk them through the rules presented there.

If they're inexperienced roleplayers, give them some tips on personalizing their characters. Inexperienced or not, tell them about melodramatic hooks and ask them to think of ones for their characters. Then explain what the various attributes are and what they do. Explain skills and skill bonuses. Use the Skill Summary section to run down the available skills. Explain schticks and how they are chosen. Quickly gloss over possessions and wealth levels. Tell your players that, depending on which type they select, they have a choice of time frames from which their characters may come: ancient China (69 AD), China in the imperial age (1850), the contemporary world, or a dark future (2056.) If you are insisting that all PCs start from one juncture, tell them that they must pick types that appear in those junctures.

Then give your players time to paw through the rule book and finish up their characters. If things begin to drag, politely but firmly prod the stragglers to make their decisions.

Creator's Remorse

Some players poke along because they want to cover all of the angles and are afraid of making a mistake they'll have to live with for the duration of the character's career. So tell the players that they can, before the next session, shift the details of their characters around if they want. Let them change the ways they tweaked their attributes, the skills they buy, and even their schticks. After all, it's pretty easy to miss a trick or two when starting out. Only after they've played the character in one or two sessions should the details be set in stone. Fiddling around early on isn't going to hurt anyone, is it?

GENRE STYLE

Before you actually start the adventure, you should emphasize to your players a couple of points about genre style. *Feng Shui* combats will be much more fun if players get into the proper spirit. Explain the stunt attempt rules to them, and tell them that the rules are set up to reward them for trying wild maneuvers.

It's also kind of jarring if the PCs turn the first fight into a slaughterhouse. Explain to your players that, when fighting vastly inferior opponents, they can always decide whether to kill or simply to incapacitate them.

Finally, point out that the characters in a *Feng Shui* game should be essentially altruistic. They may posture as cynical types or mercenaries, but when it comes down to it they fight in the secret war because it's just the right thing to do. We also assume that the heroes get together after kicking the first bad guy butt they see and then hang around together without giving their sudden coherence as a group very much thought. Veteran roleplayers may consider this a creaky, implausible device. But it's a creaky, implausible device that works, dammit!

JUNCTURES

When players choose any juncture other than the contemporary one, you should give them a capsule description of their home juncture, paraphrasing the following:

69: You come from ancient China, in the year 69, during the last years of the Han Dynasty. China is already a complex civilization with large cities; it's supposed to be run by a bureaucracy of officials appointed according to merit. Unfortunately, the dynasty is in a downward spiral. Officials are corrupt, and the eunuchs who attend the Emperor have secretly taken over the administration of the empire. What's more, hauntings and monster infestations are on the rise: demons, evil spirits, and hopping vampires are so common that it's not safe to go into the forest alone at night.

1850: It's the height of the Imperial Age of the European powers, and China is facing humiliation. Foreign powers, especially the British, have humbled the Emperor through gunboat diplomacy, demanding trade access to China. They sell opium from India to the Chinese, and use the money to buy tea to sell to their home markets. The result is a shamed populace and legions of addicts.

2056: A totalitarian world government, called the Buro, controls the Earth. Citizens are carefully monitored by a sophisticated surveillance state. Uprisings are controlled through the military deployment of abominations, bioengineered creatures of mysterious origin. These beings were created after the discovery of arcanowave technology, which blends science and magical principles.

You will also have to explain how the characters got from their home juncture to the contemporary world; we're assuming that this is where your series will be set initially. So you'll have to describe the Netherworld, too:

"You got to this time by traveling through a strange hole in space. You walked for many days through a peculiar underground land filled with strange people. You witnessed many peculiar wonders there, as if it were a massive inhabited junkyard filled with the refuse of all of history, and some imaginary histories as well. After wandering its gray passageways, you saw daylight, and stepped into this strange new world."

Temporal Confusion

Players whose characters come from a juncture other than the one in which the first adventure is set should get a few hints about how to play their confusion level. In time travel movies, characters from the past tend to be momentarily confused by their new surroundings, but soon pick up the important details about the need to duck when guns are fired or cars come barreling at them. However, this doesn't stop them from playing more mundane encounters with modern technology for laughs.

The rule of thumb is: when the result is funny, your character is confused by the new juncture. When the result would be disaster for the character, or a tedious halting of the plot, the character is a phenomenally fast learner and knows just what to do.

Illustration by Roger Raupp

Chapter 11

THE FIRST ADVENTURE

Before your players show up to begin a *Feng Shui* series, you'll have given some thought to the first adventure their characters will star in. We'll get into plot construction in more detail later in this chapter. The important thing about the first adventure in particular is that it should get off to a running start. It should open no more than a few minutes before a big fight breaks out.

The PCs don't need to know each other before the action begins. Open by telling them they're all at whatever the location you've chosen for the first fight. Describe the location, and tell them to suggest reasons why they happen to be there; you can help players who can't think of a good reason to be on the scene. Then have a bunch of bad guys who need their butts kicked show up and start causing trouble. Since you'll also be using the first fight to introduce players to the way combat works in *Feng Shui*, it's best if these initial enemies are mostly unnamed characters, with maybe one or two named characters thrown in for spice. If you do use named characters, try to see that they survive the fight, so that the PCs will have someone to look forward to defeating later. You'll note that we use exactly this formula in "Baptism of Fire," the introductory adventure in this book (page 228).

In your backstory, connect the bad guys to a broader mystery, with more influential villains waiting in the wings for the PCs to confront. Cooperating to find and then stomp on these miscreants should give the separate PCs a motivation to band together and figure out what's going on.

If a PC seems inclined to avoid joining the group or getting involved in the plot line, use that PC's melodramatic hook to reel him into the story.

Example: Greg sees no reason why his character, Shinobi Izawa, should hang around with a couple of maverick cops, a sorcerer, a ghost, and a big bruiser just because he helped them put down a bunch of bullies who were threatening an honest business owner. He tells the GM that Shinobi is immediately leaving the scene. If the other PCs can't convince him to hang around, the GM should make sure that his melodramatic hook eventually leads him back into the storyline.

Shinobi's melodramatic hook is as follows: he's searching for his missing teacher. Greg has specified that Shinobi is in Hong Kong, where he was last seen. He says he's looking for another student of the master. You, as GM, use this opportunity to turn Shinobi back towards the plotline. The student he contacts, a GMC, tells Shinobi that the master was last known to be in the service of Fast Eddie Lo. Fast Eddie Lo is a GM character you have already decided to use in your storyline. When Shinobi talks to Fast Eddie, he'll learn that his master disappeared while checking out the very bad guys who he helped fight in the first scene. Presto, he now has a motivation to find the other PCs and join them in resolving the storyline.

RUNNING FIGHTS

Fighting is a common activity during *Feng Shui* sessions. You should take special care that fights never become boring or routine. The more inventive your combat descriptions are, the more fun everyone will have.

In order to be at your peak of head-crunching creativity, you need to have as few other things to think about as possible. This means reducing the number-juggling to a minimum.

KEEPING TRACK OF SHOTS

The shot cost system for combat is useful because it creates the sensation that all sorts of things are happening at once, and that people are bouncing around the fight doing different things. It can be a bit distracting to keep track of, however. There are two ways to make the shot cost system more manageable:

Use a shot cost keeper, as shown on the next page. (It also appears in the handy photocopy appendix at the back of the book.) At the beginning of a sequence, when you determine the highest shot for that sequence, place a coin, bead or other counter on the corresponding number. Starting with the first player on your left, go around the room, letting all players whose character acts on that shot resolve an action for their characters. Then resolve the actions of any GMCs who act on that shot. Then move the counter to the next number, and call out that number to see which players have characters who act on that shot. Repeat until you hit "end sequence." Then start again with a new round of initiative rolls.

Delegate the duty of calling the shots to another player, preferably the player to your immediate right. Give the player a shot cost

SHOT COST KEEPER

① ② ③ ④ ⑤ ⑥ ⑦ ⑧ ⑨ ⑩
⑪ ⑫ ⑬ ⑭ ⑮ ⑯ ⑰ ⑱ ⑲ ⑳

keeper, or let her keep track as she prefers. (She has less to keep track of than you do.)

ATTACK RESOLUTION

You should also leave much of the math involved in attack resolution up to the players, as described in the next three sections.

Fighting Unnamed Characters

When a player attacks an unnamed character, just tell him the number he needs to down the mook: the unnamed character's Dodge value plus 5. The player tells you that he either got or missed the number, so the mook is either still in the fight or out of it. This means that, instead of doing basic adding and subtracting, you're thinking of a cool way to describe the attack. It also means that the player will know the relative ability of his character's opponent, but that's a small price to pay for offloading the math duties. *Feng Shui* characters are so combat-proficient that they should be able to size up their opponents at a glance anyhow.

Example: Greg's character, Shinobi, is going up against an unnamed character—a walking corpse, to be precise. "Shinobi dashes towards the chain link fence, bounces back, and on his way back slashes at the zombie with a backhanded katana blow. It's just a corpse, so I want to take its head off."

You're Greg's GM. The corpse's Dodge value is 7. Greg needs an Outcome of 5 to take out the Mook when he makes Shinobi's Martial Arts check. In other words, he needs an Action Result of 12. So you say: "Tell me if you get a 12 or more."

Greg makes his check and gets a 14.

"Got it."

"You execute the fence maneuver perfectly. The zombie's head flies off, shooting crypt dust everywhere and conking another of his undead companions on the noggin. It shakes its head in fury and pain and dives for you."

Fighting Named Characters

When a PC takes on a named character, tell the player his opponent's Dodge score. If the player fails to match that score on his attack check, he should just say, "I miss." If he does get the score, he should subtract the Dodge score from the Action Result to get the Outcome, add the Damage rating of his weapon to this number, and give you only the result, the final Damage of the attack. That leaves you with only one calculation to perform: subtracting the character's Toughness from the Damage of the attack to get the Wound Points suffered.

This approach lets the players know which characters are named. But *Feng Shui* characters should be able to easily identify the truly capable among a throng of opponents, so it's no big deal.

Example: "Shinobi stands his ground, waiting until the corpse gets close, and then tries to deliver a cleaving blow to the top of his skull," Greg says.

This walking corpse happens to be a named character, Four Deaths.

You tell Greg: "You need to get a 13 to hit it. If you do hit it, give me the Damage of the attack."

Greg makes a Martial Arts check, getting an Action Result of 16. Not bothering you with the steps, he calculates the Outcome (16 - 13 = 3), adds the Damage rating of his katana (3 + 11 = 14) and gives you only the final result of 14.

You then subtract Four Death's Toughness of 6, to get the Wound Points it has suffered: 8.

Chapter 11

Fighting Player Characters

At the beginning of each session, jot down the Dodge values of the PCs, in the seating order of the players. You'll find this very convenient when you have to make attack checks for GMCs against PCs. This way you won't have to ask the player each time what his Dodge value is, slowing the combat down and breaking the mood by calling out additional numbers. If some characters have changing Dodge values (for example, those who can increase their Dodge values with fu powers), make sure the player knows to notify you when her Dodge value has gone up or down.

THE MAP IS NOT YOUR FRIEND

Traditionally, roleplaying has been fixated on maps. This goes back to the earliest roleplaying games, which were fantasy games in which plot development was confined to clearing out room after room of monsters who lived like apartment dwellers in underground complexes. Many people still enjoy this style of play and we don't want to knock them for it. It does enforce a certain mind set which can bog down a *Feng Shui* game, though. Specifically, the problem is using two-dimensional maps as the main way of visualizing the action being described in a scene.

If you haul out a map at the beginning of a fight scene and lay it on the table, you're causing your players to stop focusing on the action scene in their heads and instead directing them to a dead, lifeless piece of paper; now they're like a bunch of football players planning a play on a chalkboard instead of a bunch of football players running like crazy and tackling like mad. It may be extremely useful to you to have a floor plan among your notes, so you can judge where all of the combatants are. Just don't show it to the players! And don't treat it as gospel: a map should be, like any of your other rough notes in preparation for an adventure, subject to revision as you go along.

Illustration by Heather Hudson

GM Tips

Revealing your map locks you into a precise conception of the area in which the characters are fighting. If you just describe the place with words instead of plunking that map down, you can keep your options open. In *Feng Shui*, you want to be able to decide on the spur of the moment that there just happen to be awnings hanging over that walkway between buildings, or there is indeed a ledge big enough for that hoodlum to jump off of.

Sometimes you're going to have to give in and show your players some kind of floor plan or diagram to help them visualize where they are. Never show them a nice, neat map from one of our adventure books. Or a nice neat map of your own creation, for that matter. Instead, whip up a rough sketch that conveys the bare minimum amount of information. That way, if you decide in the midst of a fight you need a spiral staircase complete with banister in the middle of that ballroom, you can add one just by sketching as you go. The messier and more incomplete the map, the more room there is to fill in the blanks.

If you are forced in this way to slap that map on the table, it's best to have miniatures on hand. Although they're harder to find than fantasy figures, you can find 25mm metal figures of contemporary characters at well-stocked game and hobby stores. There are problems with miniatures, too, since they rarely match the players' conceptions of their characters exactly. But at least they're three-dimensional and more lively than a nasty old map.

An alternative to maps are color pictures from magazines. Travel or architectural magazines often have excellent photos which you can use as the basis of your set design. You can show these to your players to help visualize where their characters are, and they will stimulate the imaginative process instead of hampering it.

TONE

Although I've inserted jokes here and there in this book in an effort to keep the rules as non-boring as possible, *Feng Shui* is not a comedy game. There's a big difference between a tongue-in-cheek approach and outright spoofery. There's nothing wrong with moments of laughter in a *Feng Shui* adventure, but it's *not* meant to be a parody of action movies.

We've drawn some inspiration from Hollywood shoot-em-ups, but our big touchstone for this game are the wild action movies put out by the Hong Kong studios. (See Hong Kong Action Movies, p. 243, for an introduction to these terrifically entertaining flicks.) One big way in which HK movies differ from Western genre flicks is the way they veer abruptly from one mood to the next. In the typical HK action flick, you'll go from fast and bloody action in one scene to outright low comedy in the next, and then on to over-the-top melodrama. Then it returns to low comedy for the next scene, and so on. To someone accustomed to Western movies, which tend to stay within the same emotional box from beginning to end, this can be rather startling at first.

Accordingly, humor is just one element in a *Feng Shui* series. For one thing, sympathetic characters can die permanently and hideously. This includes the PCs: They may be capable of superhuman feats, but they are still quite mortal, despite their ability to soak up hideous levels of physical punishment before keeling over. In fact, just as Hollywood screenwriters mangle believability in order to make sure that the hero survives and finds true love at the end, HK movies often contrive their scripts to arrive at unhappy endings. The violence in a *Feng Shui* adventure may be cartoony and unreal, but it should also be bloody and final. When a named character finally does take enough damage to die, don't flinch from the consequences. Describe the scene in all of its terrible detail, allowing sympathetic characters to gasp out a few final, touching lines before dying.

Bad guys go much further in HK movies than Western sensibilities allow. For example, villains kill little children and even babies. As GM, you're going to have to carefully weigh the scenes you choose to include in your series, especially if your players are unfamiliar with the Hong Kong style. But if the mood does get too silly and spoofy, this is the kind of sudden shock you can throw at them to show them they're not in Kansas anymore.

Our culture has a curious ambivalence about action movies, which are really just our high-tech versions of the hero myths celebrated by all cultures since the dawn of time. Even people who really enjoy them sometimes feel they have to show that they're really above all that. Try not to condescend to the material or think of it as cheesy. Sure, these stories are stylized and highly exaggerated, but that doesn't mean that they don't satisfy a real emotional need. Depending on who makes them, action movies can be sleazy and brainless, or they can excite something vital and primal in the audience. In creating *Feng Shui*, we're shooting for the latter, and we hope you'll join us for the ride.

SELF-REFERENTIALITY

There's one particular type of spoofery which is especially damaging to the mood we're trying to create. Given the way that the *Feng Shui* rules simulate movies and not real life, some groups may be tempted to play their characters as if they're aware that they're characters in an action movie. You can run things any way you like, but I'd recommend drawing a strict line between what your players know about the way the *Feng Shui* environment works and what their characters know.

On one hand, it helps to imagine what a scene would look to your group if they were sitting in theater seats staring up at it on the big screen. You should now and then describe things in cinematic terms: "This would be a slow-motion sequence, with the shell pumped out of the shotgun and bouncing across the top of the bar." "Imagine a panoramic widescreen shot of the entire mountain vista." Anything that stimulates the visual imagination during a roleplaying session makes it more vivid and exciting, and you can do so quickly and sharply by using movie references as shorthand.

On the other hand, you don't want to distance the players from the scene in their imaginations. Any suggestions that their characters are played by actors, that they can see klieg lights or cameras in their peripheral vision, that they are in danger of tripping over dolly tracks, or that the characters can look down and read the subtitles superimposed on their chests, are a damaging violation of the illusion that *Feng Shui* is trying to create. Although the best *Feng Shui* characters will be fairly simple and based on genre stereotypes, they should also have an emotional reality to them. It's okay if the players sometimes comment on the cinematic nature of the proceedings, but their characters should think that they're real people.

PACING

Pacing is the art of time management when creating a story, of devoting the most time to the most important things and little time to irrelevancies. A session in which the characters spend three hours buying a car and then ten minutes driving the car off a cliff is not going to meet most players' definition of an entertaining evening. Although the following advice is generally applicable to any roleplaying game, it is especially important in *Feng Shui*, which tries to create a cinematic feel.

The difference between a roleplaying game and a movie is that roleplaying sessions don't allow for screenplay rewrites and film editing. You and your group will be creating a story on the spot, as the players react to the adventure outline you've created. This typically means that many scenes which would be cut from the first draft of a screenplay will be played out in full in the course of a roleplaying session. As GM, you should do your best to keep the session paced like an adventure movie by trying to cut off tedious scenes whenever possible. Think of yourself as a film editor, always impatient to cut to the next scene when the tension of the current one begins to flag.

The top sources of roleplaying boredom include:

Dithering. Some groups of players can get bogged down trying to plan what to do next. Some players are cautious to a fault, and become paralyzed into inaction by the fear of failure. Sometimes entire groups are made up of ditherers, but even one player who persuasively shoots down every plan the others come up with can turn a game session into an exercise in frustration. There are a number of ways to handle this.

One is to reward action over inaction. Remind players that their characters exist in a world where "go get captured and try to figure out what the enemy is up to" is actually a pretty good strategy. Make sure that every fight advances the plot by pointing them to an important clue.

Another way to handle this is to remember the words of the great hard-boiled writer Raymond Chandler. He is reputed to have said that whenever he got stuck for a plot development, he just had a guy come through the door with a gun. If your players are dithering and refuse to go to the action, have the action come to them. This should teach the players to have their characters take a more active approach to their problems; it's always better to blow up the bad guy's hangout than to have them blow up yours.

Irrelevant Scenes. We've done our best to structure the rules so that the characters don't need to spend a lot of "on screen" time taking care of trivial tasks such as buying guns, training in their fu powers, and acquiring equipment. If a scene doesn't advance the plot, glide over it in a few sentences. Some players like to act out every encounter with a bit player in excruciating detail. Don't let these guys turn a stop at the gas station to ask directions into a sequence longer than the balcony scene

GM Tips

in *Romeo and Juliet*. Let them save their roleplaying skills for the scenes that really count.

For example: Jake is an incorrigible scene dragger who grabs every second of time in the spotlight he can, whether the result is of any interest to anyone else or not. He is playing a techie character who is cruising junk shops in search of parts for an invention. The only thing that matters to the plot is whether Jake's character gets what he needs and successfully creates his gadget, and you've already decided to let him. If this were a TV show, there's no way the scriptwriter would devote fifteen minutes to discussions with irrelevant junk shop dealers, so you're ready to cut this tangent off before it starts.

Jake: I head into the first junk shop I see. I look for the proprietor. "Howdy, pardner," I say, "Would you happen to have any power tools?"

You, the GM: Okay, after going to a number of junk shops you find the stuff you need and create your invention. Make a Fix-It task check.

Jake: But, but—

You, the GM: Now, is there anything anybody else does before the raid on the Tea Gardens?

Digressions. Everybody breaks character in the course of a roleplaying session. You shouldn't be a conversation cop, snapping at anyone who brings up an unrelated topic. But you should gently steer people back on course rather than allowing the action to turn into a panel discussion. You should also be prepared to cut off rules discussions. When faced with a player who wishes to convince you to adjudicate something differently, decide quickly and stick with your decision. If the player wishes to discuss it further, ask her to wait until after the session is over. As GM, you're in charge of building suspense and a sense of momentum. Don't let extraneous yakking throw you off your game.

Dead Ends. In order to keep this momentum going, it's up to you to allow easy movement from one big plot sequence to another. Make sure that the clues that tell the PCs who to beat up next are fairly easy to get. There should always be several alternate ways of advancing the plot line. There should never be a clue that can only be obtained in one particular way, or that relies on the success of a single task check. After all, if that task check happens to fail then you'll be stuck in a dead end, and the whole group will be in for an evening of butting their heads against the metaphorical wall. You should also always allow the PCs to succeed if they come up with a clever way to advance the plot that you hadn't thought of. Remember, the adventure outline—whether it's one we've published or one of your own creation—is not the important experience. What's important is what happens during the game session, and you should be prepared to juggle things around to keep them interesting.

In-Character Chat. Sometimes the players will be so into their characters that they'll spend hours just shooting dialogue back and forth. This is not always a bad thing, so you have to exercise your judgment before cutting it off and insisting that the players start working on getting to the next scene. After all, how much fun would *Pulp Fiction* have been without Vincent & Jules shooting the bull about Big Macs in Paris?

Remember that the whole point of a roleplaying session is entertainment. Some of the most entertaining game sessions I've spent as a GM have involved my simply sitting back and watching the players riffing while in character. But there's always a point where such a scene starts to wind down. It's up to you to cut it off just as it starts to trail off, so that everyone remembers the fun bits instead of the last fifteen minutes of going in circles.

To sum up, you should try to develop "a sense of the room," just as an actor or stand-up comic does in performance. If you pay attention, you can tell whether your players are excited and engaged by the story, or if they're getting bored. When they're getting bored, do whatever you can to get the story out of whatever track they're on that's causing them to tune out. Jolt them back into the story by shifting gears, introducing a new element, or simply throwing in some gratuitous violence.

PLOTTING

The main objective of *Feng Shui* is to create a roleplaying experience that feels like an action movie. However, one advantage that movie screenwriters have over GMs is that their characters are guaranteed to cooperate with them. A GM is only a collaborator in creating the story in a roleplaying game; the players also want to influence the course of events through the decisions they make for their characters. Some GMs use a dictatorial style in their effort to make roleplaying stories resemble those told in other media: they decide exactly how the story should proceed and then mess with the PCs whenever their choices deviate from a predetermined structure. We suggest that you avoid this approach. Roleplaying has its own demands as a form; a storyline that we might find enjoyably airtight as audience members in a movie theater can be frustrating and confining when imported whole into a gaming context.

While it's important to plan things in advance,

you should always be prepared to go with an entertaining tangent that one of your players' actions might suggest. Set out story goals for a session, but be prepared to get to them in a number of ways. Leave yourself room to react to what the players do. The result will seem fresher and more natural. As an added bonus, you get to be surprised by the direction of the plot, and get just as much of a feeling of suspense as your players. Like your players, you are an audience member as well as being one of the creators of the story.

Creating a plot line for a roleplaying series involves a certain amount of advance preparation. Exactly how much varies from GM to GM. Personally, I tend to rely heavily on my ability to improvise; I'll start a game session with a few basic ideas of where the story may head, but little else. Other GMs are more comfortable when they've prepared copious notes for themselves. Still others rely almost entirely on adventures written by others, like the "Baptism of Fire" adventure that begins on p. 228 of this book. We'll be publishing a line of *Feng Shui* supplements containing adventures for those who like to use them. At any rate, you'll soon learn just how much advance planning you need to feel comfortable when running a game.

It might be a good time for you to check out the "Baptism of Fire" adventure and then return to this section. It will give you a concrete example of a typical *Feng Shui* story. This will help you to understand the more general advice given below.

SET PIECES

It is helpful to look at a *Feng Shui* storyline as being like a movie screenplay. Think about your favorite action movies and what you find memorable about them. Most popcorn-crunching movies feature a number of **set pieces**. These are the big scenes you remember and talk about with your friends on the way home from the film. The rest of the script is usually connective material that leads the characters from one set piece sequence to the next.

When creating a *Feng Shui* story, decide first of all what your set pieces will be. Given the genre we're emulating, each set piece is going to be a fight of some kind. Each fight should build on the last one somehow, to give a feeling of rising action. One obvious way to do this is to increase the strength of the opposition from one set piece battle to another. The bad guys in the first set piece can be almost exclusively unnamed characters; the final confrontation might be entirely with named characters. Another way to up the ante is to make the setting of the fight more interesting each time out. You can go from your basic street fight to a battle in a warehouse full of explosives to a fight on the wing of a taxiing jumbo jet.

Since *Feng Shui* depends heavily on fighting for its excitement, it's up to you to make sure that each fight has something special about it. I've played roleplaying games where the supposedly life-and-death struggles of the main characters have been the most boring element, duller even than the characters sitting around chatting. Don't let this happen to you!

First of all, use the tips given earlier in "Running Fights" to turn each task check into a vivid visual image that everyone can picture in their imaginations.

Second, prepare in advance to have cool things happen in the fight. Figure out where the fight will take place, and imagine cool stunts that might take advantage of its features. Memorable film fights are never just a straightforward exchange of blows. Props get smashed. Fighters go flying. Movement and high energy are paramount. Think of yourself as a movie fight choreographer making preliminary notes towards planning a sequence he can show to his stunt performers. Even if you tend to wing things like I do, you'll find it worthwhile to jot down a list of ideas.

For example: You decide that one of your set pieces is a fight on the loading docks at the waterfront. Think for a moment about what cool things could happen during a loading dock fight, and make a list:

- *somebody could get beaned with an oil drum*
- *or have an oil drum clang down on him, trapping him*
- *or roll an oil drum at an opponent, so the opponent has to jump out of the way*
- *somebody should get thrown in the water*
- *someone should get hit by a crane hook*
- *someone could run up the side of a docked ship and jump on an opponent*
- *a freight hook would make a great impromptu weapon*
- *a really vicious mook should be crushed by the fall of a massive crate*

The more things you can think of, the better. Obviously, you don't control the actions of the PCs, so it will be the bad guys making most of these maneuvers at first. Soon, however, your PCs will catch onto the idea and start trying to think of similarly cool things to do. Note that your notes

GM Tips

don't tell you what must happen; they just give you some ideas to use or not, as the situation dictates. If the PCs come up with ideas that hadn't occurred to you, go with them! Don't punish players for creativity, even if it means slightly revising your visual image of the "set" that the characters are fighting on. If a player needs a prop or building feature to execute a slick move and asks if that prop or feature is there, your first instinct should always be to say "yes." Unless you're worried that it would completely strain believability and break the illusion of the fictional world, let fun stuff happen.

Continuity and Structure

Roleplaying games are usually a serial form of entertainment, like TV shows, movies with strings of sequels, or comic books. A *Feng Shui* series is made up of episodes or adventures. The player characters, and probably some basic plot elements as well, will continue from episode to episode. These recurring elements are referred to as your continuity. After a

Illustration by Thomas Manning

while, you will find that it is the continuity that keeps your players coming back for more. They want to find out what happens to their characters. Does Shinobi find his master? How will Justin Lee adjust to that robot arm? Will Hamish MacPherson discover the true secret of his family castle? If you're creating an entertaining story, they'll also care about the fates of the GMCs: Will Carina sell the restaurant? Will Gao Zhang finally be cast out of the Emperor's Palace? Is Desdemona Deathangel really dead, or will she come back to fight another day?

The continuity of a roleplaying series tends to take on a life of its own, especially if you are attentive to your players' interests. If they all seem to enjoy interacting with a bit player you've created on the spur of the moment, elevate the importance of that bit player so he comes back again and again. If they're all interested in achieving a certain goal, make sure your plots allow them to get a little closer to that goal each episode. Continuity should evolve naturally over time. Once you've got a bunch of plot threads on the boil, you'll find it easier and easier to keep the story going from session to session.

In the meantime, you need to create the episodes that will develop your continuity. That means thinking a little bit about structure: the way in which your scenes are connected to one another, and the overall pattern they adhere to.

Most movies have three acts; most action movies have about three big fight sequences. It's an arbitrary number, but I tend to create adventures with three set piece battles. One opens the story, one occurs in about the middle of the story, and the last is the final climax. This is an easy framework to start out with, anyway: You can vary things as you get the hang of running your *Feng Shui* series.

How many sessions it takes to play out an episode is up to you. Ideally, each session will involve one major fight. Preferably, this fight will take place at the end of a session in order to create a sense of climax. Of course, the biggest factor in working out how long it takes to play an episode is the length of your sessions. A three-hour session works best for me, so I tend to have episodes that last for three sessions. If your group gets together and plays all day, you might be able to cover an entire episode in one session.

Backstory

Once you've come up with your three set pieces, you should figure out how to connect them. This generally means coming up with a **backstory**. This is a term screenwriters use to describe events that have occurred in the characters' pasts before the actual narrative begins. Since in action stories heroes are usually reacting to the terrible things that villains do, the backstory will largely concern the plans and activities of the bad guys you've chosen to feature in the current episode.

First decide who your PCs will be fighting. We've created the various factions in the secret war in order to give you a choice of antagonists for your characters. When you're first starting out, it's best to use bad guys whose methods are big and obvious and evil, like the Architects of the Flesh or the Eaters of the Lotus. Once your players have their feet wet and have a handle on the nature of the world, you can start to throw in the more subtle operators like the Guiding Hand and the Ascended.

Once you've picked your villains for the episode, figure out what they're up to. This should relate in some manner to the locations of some or all of your set pieces. It may be that the later set piece battles occur in the hideouts of the bad guys, which may or may not directly relate to whatever devious plot they're hatching.

For example: In "Baptism of Fire," the first set piece battle occurs in the Eating Counter restaurant. This couldn't be more directly related to the bad guy's plot: They want to take it over because it is a feng shui site. The second set piece—the construction site fight—doesn't relate directly to their plan. It's just a hideout that the heroes raid; they could equally well be headquartered in an old power plant or warehouse. The last set piece relates back to the main plot, though, because the bad guys capture Carina Shen and hold her hostage in order to get the restaurant.

When deciding what the bad guys are doing, it's best to stick to simple ideas at first. If you can't sum up their goal in a sentence, it's probably too complicated. Again, you can move on to more complex plots later, when your players are more comfortable with the ins and outs of the secret war.

Having decided what the basic goal of the bad guys is, you can decide what they've done already to move towards it, and what they plan to do during the course of the action to finally achieve it. Their plans should, of course, be the sort that can be foiled by the PCs and their butt-kicking abilities.

For example: You're looking through a book of photos of Hong Kong seeking inspiration for your set piece battles. You find one photo of a man standing in a bank vault full of safety deposit boxes. A photo of a ferry catches your eye. Finally, you see a picture of the small sampans of Yaumatei's boat city (see "Yumatei," p. 214).

GM Tips

You decide that these three places would make great locations for your set pieces.

Now you have to come up with a way to tie these three places together in a way that will bring the PCs head-to-head with the bad guys.

The safety deposit boxes provide obvious inspiration: the bad guys want something in one of the deposit boxes. What might they want? Maybe there's a magically-charged jade ring in one of the boxes, one that will provide the user with additional power in the secret war.

There's one group that would especially want magical artifacts: the sorcerous Eaters of the Lotus. Since they come from the past, this gives you a nifty idea. The main eunuch bad guy (who you'll name later) already has this jade ring back in 69 AD. If he can come forward into our time and grab the same ring, which has changed owners throughout the centuries, he'll be able to double its usefulness back in the 69 time juncture.

So he sends modern goons—maybe the remnants of the Thorns of the Lotus, from the Baptism of Fire episode—to hold up the bank in a daring daylight robbery and grab the jade ring. Later you'll figure out how to make sure the PCs are in the bank when the robbers come in, so you have all the ingredients in place for the first fight to erupt.

You decide to save the ferry for last, because it has the most spectacular potential for blowing up. That leaves the sampan community.

What if the owner of the ring is a rich eccentric who has retired to a life among the poorest of Hong Kong's people, the residents of the boat city? He's actually left a phony copy of the ring in his deposit box for insurance purposes, and has kept the real one. The sorcerer quickly realizes that the one his goons have grabbed from the bank raid is a fake, and uses divination to lead him to the sampan city. He and the goons attack—and again, later you'll figure out how to make sure the PCs are there when the fight breaks out.

Okay, now you have to get the plot to the third set piece, the ferry battle. Maybe that's where the ring really is, you figure. The eccentric owner of the ring has given it to a young boy, one he feels has magical potential. The young boy happens to be the son of the ferry pilot. The sorcerer and his allies fly over to the ferry to attack it. If the PCs are there, you have your big climax.

So, presto: instant backstory! The bad guys want a magical ring which they at first think is in a safe deposit box, then in the sampan city, then on the ferry. Straightforward, simple, and with lots of action potential. As you get used to the game you can go for more complex plots; but this is a great way to get started.

Opening Scene

Now that you've chosen your set pieces and the backstory that connects them, all you have to do is get the main characters—the PCs—involved in the action. The trick is getting them to the first battle. Then leave enough clues and motivation to carry them from that set piece on to the remaining ones.

Getting PCs involved in stories to begin with is one of the biggest pains in the posterior a GM faces in all of roleplaying. You at least have an advantage over the writers of published adventures, in that you know the PCs you're creating your episode for.

For *Feng Shui*, we advise you to put the burden of motivation on the players as much as possible. Very few action-oriented TV shows or movies begin with the heroes getting up in the morning and trying to figure out what to do for the day. Instead, they start just a few moments before the action begins. So don't start a new episode by asking the players where they are and what they want to do with themselves. Instead, say: "As the action opens, you're at [insert desired location]. Incidentally, why do you think you would happen to be there?"

You should, however, be prepared to work with the players by suggesting reasons why their characters are where they are when the action begins. This is where melodramatic hooks come in handy; try to weave these into the opening scene to give the players a reason to get involved.

For example: You start the episode outlined above. You want the PCs to be at the bank already when the action starts. So you say to them: "You're at the main branch of the Hong Kong and Shanghai Banking Corporation. Why are you there?"

Ian pipes up with a suggestion: "Hamish [Ian's character] had some money wired to him from Scotland, and he's here to pick it up. He invited the others to come along, since there's a good restaurant nearby. After I do my banking, we're planning on sitting down and trying to figure out how to protect the feng shui site we just attuned ourselves to."

That seems reasonable enough, so you use Ian's suggestion. You've just skipped about half an hour of boring shilly-shallying.

You do have to strike a balance between keeping your opening scenes sharp and depriving the players of control of their character's fates. Don't open scenes assuming that the PCs have done something stupid, reckless, or blatantly out of character. A good rule of thumb to use is this: Does your opening require that the players imagine important intervening scenes between this session and the last?

If these intervening scenes would have been dramatized in a movie or TV show, you should play them out in your game session, and allow the players to make choices that might influence their outcome. If they would have been left out, then don't feel bad about kick-starting the story and skipping right past them.

For example, the scenario outlined above is a good one because it doesn't assume too much about the character's actions between the last session and this one. No one is going to feel unduly put out when they're told that they're waiting for one of their buddies to make a bank transaction before getting some chow. But if you tell them that they've all awakened in chains, stripped naked, and deprived of their weapons, they're going to be rightly upset since they didn't have a chance to prevent this unpleasant situation. This isn't to say that PCs should never be captured, but you should open this episode with the bad guys creeping up on them to capture them, rather than presenting the result as a fait accompli.

Finding the Next Fight

Once you've gotten the PCs into the story, your job is to make sure that they get from set piece to set piece with a minimum of boring stuff in between. Several pointers for managing this are presented earlier, under "Pacing."

You can also prepare in advance to get the PCs from one pivotal scene to the next. This involves the creation of **clue paths**. A clue path is simply a chain of information that the PCs can trace to find out what they really need to know. Virtually every TV cop show is structured along a clue path. The detective talks to one witness, who gives him a piece of information that leads him to another witness, which leads him to a piece of physical evidence, which leads him to consult an expert, who gives him a clue that sends him to another witness, and so on, until the puzzle is solved.

For each set piece that leads to another, come up with a number of possible clue paths. Never make the episode's success rely on the PCs doing one exact thing. They shouldn't depend on a PC having a single skill either: if the player fails a task check—or worse yet, isn't able to make it to the session that night—your story comes to a standstill. Instead, make sure there are several challenging routes to every set piece. It's okay to have clue paths that converge at some point. You might also want to make them simpler than the average cop show clue path, at least at first.

If your PCs happen to come up with yet another way you hadn't anticipated, so much the better—provided it makes some sort of basic sense, naturally. Just create a few obstacles for them to overcome on this unexpected path, and let them go with it.

Example: You have figured out a couple of clue paths for the PCs to pursue to find the owner of the jade ring in the boat city.

One is for the PCs to weasel their way past bank officials into their confidential records to find out who the safe deposit box belongs to. You know that there are numerous ways the PCs could use to get to this clue path: The cop could bend the rules and use his credentials to convince the bankers to cough up the info. The ninja could use intrusion to enter the bank at night and examine the files. The techic could use his computer expertise to hack into the bank's database via long distance. If any of these attempts succeed, the PCs learn that the box belonged to a man named Walter Tau.

Another clue path starts with a check of local experts on ancient jade artifacts. One of the PCs got a good look at the ring as it was being stolen, and finds a picture of it in a book. Any knowledgeable expert knows that it belongs to an eccentric collector named Walter Tau.

The two clue paths have converged; they might then follow various means of tracking Mr. Tau after he left his last known residence. Finally, they end up in a meeting with Tau in his new sampan home—and moments later, a fight with attacking Lotus goons.

Note that the second clue path above seems less difficult than the first. If the PCs are proceeding too quickly along any clue path, you should always throw extra obstacles into the mix. Perhaps one of the antique experts the PCs contact has been bought off by the Lotus sorcerer. Depending on how much trouble you want to throw at the characters, he may send the PCs on a wild goose chase, or even arrange for them to be ambushed by the bad guys.

USING THE SECRET WAR

The setting of *Feng Shui*, with the secret war and the various groups that fight it, is designed to give you an easy way to link your plots together. They provide you with a variety of antagonists who might be doing all manner of sneaky things that can connect your set pieces together into episodes, and your episodes together into a series. Here are some hints on integrating the secret war into your series.

GM Tips

Don't throw the whole big mess at the players from the first session. Start off slowly, introducing one element at a time. That way you'll still have some surprises for later. If your players learn one thing about the secret war every couple of sessions or so, you're pacing out the grand continuity at a good pace.

For example: "Baptism of Fire" involves villains from only one of the factions in the secret war, the Lotus. A character connected with the Ascended appears in a supporting role, but the Ascended themselves play no part in the story. After running this episode, you could reveal more about the Lotus and where they come from, or you could switch to providing the first few hints about the nature of the Ascended.

As your series progresses and the PCs learn more about what's going on, they can gain greater influence over events that have an impact on all of history. They can go from pounding on minor Lotus goons to confronting Gao Zhang, the Center of the Lotus himself. They can explore the Netherworld, shake up the groups fighting the secret war, and even change history. This will be all the more dramatic if they started out slowly, rather than finding themselves in the thick of earth-shattering plot lines right from the get-go.

Should all *Feng Shui* storylines relate to the secret war and feng shui sites? Should the only villains your PCs encounter be representatives of the factions? Certainly not. Throw in independent operators as bad guys once in a while. Create stories that don't involve the secret war at all. This will keep your players on their toes: there's no one so easy to fool as a player who thinks he has the setting memorized inside and out. It will also add a sense of variety to your series. The PCs should face the classic "So many bad guys, so little time" dilemma. They can face mobsters, terrorists, stray monsters, petty dictators, serial killers, and more.

Dealing with Background

The contemporary time frame is ideal if you want to start out with a normal-seeming action framework and then gradually introduce the fantasy and science fiction elements. You can start the series as if it's typical modern shoot-'em-up fare, so that the players only discover several sessions in that their characters' enemies are actually eunuch sorcerers or evil agents of a future police state. Naturally, your success at keeping this a surprise depends on how familiar your players are with this material.

If they've all read this book cover to cover or extensively played Shadowfist, there isn't much point in maintaining the pretense: you might as well just plop them down in the middle of the time wars right away. On the other hand, your players might savor a slow, steadily-paced introduction to the various plot elements that they're looking forward to interacting with. You'll have to gauge the tastes of your group and adjust accordingly. See the next section, "Customizing the Setting," for more suggestions on this topic.

If none or only a few of your players know the whole background, it'll be easier for you to introduce the material to them slowly in the course of play than dumping it on them all at once.

If you have a mixed group—some players who know the setting well and others who are new to it—you might take the experienced players aside and ask them to cooperate with you in presenting the secret war background. Ask the new players to choose from the contemporary archetypes. Allow the others to pick archetypes associated with the other junctures. This latter group of characters already knows about the Netherworld, having used it to get from their home junctures to the contemporary one. They also know about the secret war, although they may not know much: Perhaps all they are aware of is that something big is going to happen in the contemporary world, and they should be there to take part in it. You can engineer a way for the experienced players' characters to meet up with the other PCs: Starting them in the same location as a big fight breaks out is always a classic approach. Then the experienced players can take on some of the burden of providing exposition about the background to the others, so that the introduction of this sizable wad of information seems smooth and natural.

Customizing the Setting

If your players are old hands at *Feng Shui* by the time you start your series, you might want to adjust the published material so that their assumptions aren't always correct. You could invent entirely new factions or alter existing ones. What if Gao Zhang, leader of the Lotus, were slain and his organization taken over by a former member of the Guiding Hand? What if the twisted scientists of 2056 overthrew the Buro? What if an overtly sinister transformed animal were elected as the Ascended's Unspoken Name?

You can also have new junctures open up. Pick your favorite historical period and invent an organization to go with it.

Chapter 11

Of course, changes to history from actions in past junctures can greatly alter circumstances in your setting, making it as alien and unfamiliar as you can handle. See Time War, p. 190.

If you do alter continuity in this way, you'll have to alter material in future *Feng Shui* supplements to match events in your series. But if you're inventive enough to change things in the first place, this shouldn't be a problem for you.

DIRECTING THE PLOT

Different GMs and groups have their own preferences as to how much the GM should be dictating the pace and direction of a series' plot.

Some player groups expect the GM to construct a complete plan in advance; they show up and expect to be led through a set **scenario** with a pre-established beginning and ending as well as a clear set of victory conditions. They are content to use published adventures—such as the ones later in this book and in future *Feng Shui* supplements—pretty much as-is. Connections between scenarios don't matter much; they're just opportunities to spend character points and buy new equipment. If this sounds like your group, the secret war is an excellent backdrop for you to use to keep your players supplied with clear, separated missions. Have them meet a patron character fairly soon in their adventures who will explain to them what is going on. The patron might be a powerful Netherworld potentate, like the Queen of the Ice Pagoda, or an in-the-know political operator from their home juncture. The patron will provide them with a safe base of operations, as well as access to needed equipment and other support, if they will agree to take assignments on her behalf. Since your group doesn't expect a whole lot of allegedly-realistic shilly-shallying when it comes to getting their adventures started, they'll be content to start each session with a briefing from their patron, outlining the juncture they'll be traveling to, and the feng shui site they'll be either protecting or trying to capture. When using published adventures, you can simply replace the suggested means of getting into the adventure with the standard briefing from the patron. Although *Feng Shui* can support all sorts of political intrigue and background weirdness, it is primarily about kicking butt. If your group wants to punt posterior without all of the frills, on no account should you be shy about letting them

do so. In this simpler style of play, you may want to emphasize only one group of bad guys at a time. The characters can fight the Eaters of the Lotus for a while, then switch to pounding on the Architects and their abominations, take a breather to fight the Jammers, and then return to the Lotus for a repeat engagement. If your group is not interested in complex plotlines or involved intrigue, keep the interaction and rivalry between the various groups squarely in the background.

Other groups are more interested in forging a long-term storyline, and don't like to think of their series as being divided up into more or less interchangeable episodes. They want subplots to develop from one session to another. They also expect to have more control over the storyline, by choosing what it is that their characters want to do. This type of group demands a more reactive style from you; *Feng Shui* is also well-suited to this approach.

In this style, you can spell out the situation in the secret war without dangling a reliable patron in front of the characters: they will likely want to act as free agents, or set up their own group. Perhaps they will become heirs to the mantle of the Dragons (see p. 178); maybe they will remain freelancers. Maybe their agenda will be heroic, but you can't assume that it will.

Your job as GM is not to direct the characters towards any particular outcome, but to provide interesting consequences for decisions that the players make on behalf of their characters. You'll want to give them access to lots of information about the time war and how it works, so that they can make the kinds of tough decisions that make this kind of play exciting. You can present them with dilemmas that have no obvious or definitive solution.

For example, they could discover, at the same time, plans for the Lotus and Architects to mount major offensives in different junctures. They have the manpower and resources to thwart one of the two groups — provided they're brave and smart and lucky — but not both. Let the characters know what the negative consequences of each of the possible choices is, and then let them make their decision. The results may not be rosy — after all, if everything was perfect in the world of *Feng Shui* there'd be no reason for the characters to be whacking on each other, and then where would we be?

If your players enjoy feeling that they're directing their character's destinies, they'll be happier with this relatively messy structure. The neatness of the story is less important to them than their identification with their characters. So feel free to emphasize political interaction, factions within factions, possibly insoluble tactical problems, and other relatively-complex plot points. Instead of choosing a single juncture and feng shui site to be the center of an evening's play, decide before each session what's going on in a number of fronts of the secret war. Then let the players decide which one they're going to dive into. The challenge of this style is that it requires you to think on your feet; the benefit is that after a while the story will seem to run itself, as the players pick up previously dropped plot threads and follow them.

Of course, in any group of players you're going to find a mix of preferences. Some will want a clear episodic structure and others will want a sprawling and self-directed style. It's up to you to find the balance between the two approaches in the way you handle the secret war.

PLAYING THE ROLE

When creating and playing GMCs, remember that simplicity is the key to action-adventure. When you think of the great heroes and villains of pop fiction, most of them are elementally simple. The kind of brilliant simplicity behind Tarzan, Sherlock Holmes, and Batman is actually very difficult to do well. A character based on a single strong idea is always more memorable than one created from a laundry list of minor quirks and complex life experiences. This latter kind of characterization can work splendidly if you're an actor in a kitchen-sink drama, but it's misplaced in *Feng Shui's* action movie context. You can labor over the biography of a GMC for hours, but if you don't play him vividly in the actual game session, all of your work is wasted.

If a character is going to be on-stage a lot during an episode, try to come up with a single defining quirk that your players can use to identify him. It might be a distinctive speech pattern: stutters, repeated words, catch phrases, a particular vocabulary, an accent or a funny voice. Eunuchs should all have high, squeaky voices, for example, because they've lost their... uh... well, they're eunuchs.

Props also help to define a character. An unlit cigarette can do wonders in changing your persona from narrator to sleazy informant. You don't need to go overboard here, but a simple visual cue or two can be very useful.

Once you've picked a gimmick to help you differentiate a character, the most important thing to know about her is what she wants. If you know what her most important goal is, you'll know what she tries to do in the course of the story. And what a character actually does in interacting with the PCs is much more interesting and important than all of the preparatory notes you can scribble.

LANGUAGE

Language barriers can be a big impediment to character interaction in roleplaying. Just having a fight with an ancient bad guy isn't as much fun as trading quips with him as you try to clobber him. Realistically speaking, few characters from the modern world would be able to converse in an appropriate dialect with an ancient Chinese general. Or with an evil cult priest from the backwoods of contemporary Thailand.

So to heck with realism. Just like in Hong Kong movies, everyone in the world speaks perfect contemporary Cantonese, wherever and whenever you go. Ancient Egyptian pharaohs speak Cantonese, the Prime Minister of Belgium speaks Cantonese, bio-engineered abominations from the future speak Cantonese. Of course, in your games everything is being automatically translated into English, including the puns...

CHAPTER 12

Getting Even Tougher

POWER AND GLORY

Feng Shui characters are already outrageously competent when they begin the game. However, it's fun to see your character improve as time goes on. Here are rules to pump up your character in the course of play.

AWARDING EXPERIENCE POINTS

Experience points are awarded during the course of play by the GM. Experience points accumulate over time; when you have enough of them, you can spend some to increase one of your character's game statistics. They don't really correspond to anything concrete in reality or even in action-adventure sources. But players like them anyway, so what the heck.

At the end of each session, the GM awards 0 – 6 experience points to each character.

Characters earn 0 experience points if they horribly mess up, sending the storyline to a complete and crashing halt. (Note that this is quite different from the players' surprising you by sending the plot off in a different direction than the one you expected—you should *reward* them for entertaining you!) They earn 0 experience points if they act completely out of character for short term gain, or if they act in a manner contrary to the spirit of *Feng Shui*. For example, if they spend an entire evening dithering over what to do next instead of getting out there and making something happen, they deserve a goose egg. Getting a 0 should be a rare occurrence; if it happens regularly, there is obviously a two-way communication problem between players and GM. If you're a GM giving out a 0, be sure to explain why.

Characters should almost always get at least 3 experience points. If the players show up, have a good time, and contribute to everyone else's good time, they get the 3 points. Gaming is a recreational activity, not a physics test.

Characters can rarely earn up to 6 experience points. To do so, they must both score an outstanding success in the plot line, and entertain the heck out of the GM and other players in the process. If you're awarding over 3 experience points each time out, you're being too generous. This award is reserved for play outstanding by your group's standards. If you have the most avid, entertaining group on the face of the planet, even their characters should only get the big 6 when they outdo themselves. It's a scale relative to your group, not an absolute scale that applies to everyone.

SPENDING EXPERIENCE POINTS

Rules on acquiring new abilities or increasing old ones appear in the sections relevant to particular schticks: fu powers, skills, creature powers, and so on. To recap, experience points can be spent on the areas below; "schticks you will have" means the total schticks for that area of ability, so if you've got 3 schticks' worth of Carnival of Carnage, it counts as 3, not 1.

New Arcanowave Devices. If you acquire a new arcanowave device in the course of play and have the AI/O port necessary to operate it, you may spend (8 + x) experience points to attune yourself to it. This allows you to use the new item. X = the number of arcanowave devices you will have attuned once you have attuned to this one.

New Creature Abilities. If you are considered a supernatural creature, you may acquire new creature ability schticks or increase the benefits of old ones. Getting an additional schtick costs (8 + x) experience points; x = the number of Creature Abilities schticks you will have when you gain this new one.

New Fu Powers cost (3 + x) experience points per power. X = the number of fu schticks you will have when you gain this new one.

New Gun Schticks cost (8 + x) points per schtick; x is the number of gun schticks you will have once you acquire the new one. You can't get new Guns schticks if your Action Value in the Guns skill is less than 12.

New Magic Schticks. If you already have the Sorcery skill, you can acquire new magic schticks at a cost of (16 + x) experience points per schtick. X = the number of magic schticks you will have when you gain this new one.

New Blast Special Effects for your existing Blast magic schtick cost 3 experience points apiece above the 3 effects you get at first.

New Skills can be acquired by spending (8 + x) experience points; x = your rating in the base attribute of the skill. In order to learn a new skill, you must undergo a training montage, as explained on p. 51. The rules for acquiring the Sorcery skill are different; see p. 92 for those.

Skill Bonuses. You can increase by 1 a bonus in a skill you already know by spending experience points equal to the new Action Value you will have once you have learned the skill.

New Transformed Animal Schticks. These cost (8 + x) points per schtick gained, where x = the number of Transformed Animal Schticks you will have when you gain this new one.

ATTUNEMENT TO FENG SHUI SITES

Characters who have attuned themselves to feng shui sites advance much more rapidly in their abilities, as positive chi flows to them from the site and gives them phenomenal abilities to learn and grow. Attunement and maintaining attunement are described on p. 165.

BENEFITS OF ATTUNEMENT

Characters attuned to one or more sites gain additional experience points at the end of each session. The number of additional points is equal to three times the number of feng shui sites the characters are attuned to.

Example: The PC group is attuned to one feng shui site. They gain an additional 3 points per session. When they attune to another site, they will gain an additional 6 points per session.

Attuned characters may also increase attributes in the course of play. Raising a primary attribute by 1 costs a number of experience points equal to four times the new rating in the attribute. Raising a secondary attribute by 1 costs a number of experience points equal to twice the new value of that secondary attribute.

Example: Jack Donovan is attuned to a feng shui site. His player, Troy, wants to pump up Jack's ability to shrug off hits from opponents. Jack's current Body rating is 7; he has no secondary attributes. If Troy wanted to raise Jack's Body to 8, it would cost him 4 times the new attribute rating in experience points, or 32 experience. If he just wanted to raise Jack's Toughness, it would cost him 16 experience points, which is twice the new value.

Some major feng shui sites provide other benefits to those attuned to them; the precise nature of these additional goodies is up to you. Use this leeway to hook players into your plots.

When you raise a primary attribute, its secondary attributes increase only when they are less than or equal to the primary attribute.

Example: Ting Ling's Chi rating is 1. Her Kung Fu secondary attribute is 6, her Fortune is 1 and her Magic is 0. If she raises her Chi to 2, her Kung Fu rating remains at 6, because it is already higher than the primary attribute. Her Fortune and Magic ratings each go up by 1 because they are equal to or less than her Chi.

Chapter 13

May 22

I still don't think I really understand this whole business with the feng shui sites and how they change history. The way I'd had it figured, the world wasn't hard to understand. There were the guys who had the power, and if you wanted the power, you had to bump those guys off. Then you took over their operation, and tried to stop everybody else from bumping you off. In other words, all that mattered was what you did, whether you were smart enough, and whether you had the operation required to get things done on the street.

But now I find out that nothing like that matters at all. The only thing that matters is how many of these feng shui sites you control. If your feng shui sites are the right kind of sites in the right kind of places, the chi of the world will flow to you, and things will go your way. The guys you want to bump off will fall easily beneath your bullets. Their assassins will always fail to smoke you. The cops you want to bribe will be honored and delighted to kiss your glorious behind. No one will ever beat the odds at your gambling houses. All of your Little Brothers will be loyal to you. Money will stick to you like it was glued there. All because of them feng shui sites. They're the only thing you got to protect; they'll drop everything else into place for you.

But if you lose a site, look out. That means your chi flow is screwed up. And screwed up chi means things will start to go wrong for you and good for whoever grabbed your site. Which means it will be all the harder for you to defend your remaining sites. So it's like a snowball effect: the more sites you lose, the more vulnerable the rest of your sites become. Which means one slip-up in the feng shui protection department and you can go from sittin' on top of the world to sittin' at the bottom of the world's garbage chute.

Okay, so that's tough enough to swallow if you've always believed in yourself and self-reliance and all of that. The next thing is the kick in the head. If you lose sites, you may not just end up getting smoked—I mean, in my line of work we all expect that sooner or later, that's part of the deal—but you can get totally erased from history. If you have a bunch of sites and they get taken from you, it doesn't just change your present and your future: sometimes it will change your past too. They keep explaining it to me, and I keep trying to understand: time is not a river, it is an ocean. It does not flow in one direction, ever onward. It is simply a big body of stuff, stuff that can be shaken and changed by big tidal waves of chi.

I really can't say I understand what that really means, except that with this Netherworld thing connecting up all different periods in time, nothing is certain. One day I can be top of the world, have a bunch of great feng shui sites lined up, and be the Big Brother to everyone I know. Then someone can go back to 1850, nail the sites that I control in 1996, and arrange things so that I'll never have a shot at grabbing the site in the first place, in 1990 or whenever I first snagged it. Not only that, but grabbing that site in 1850 might mean that I wasn't born to the same parents, or that they ended up getting snuffed in the Cultural Revolution, or that maybe I never got born at all. So if I'm on top and want to stay on top, I not only gotta protect my feng shui site in the present, I gotta protect it in the past, too. Not to mention the fact that what I do with my site now affects what kind of future there's gonna be, and people from the future are gonna be coming after me to grab my site so they can end up with the kind of present they want!

And then after that it gets kind of confusing.

CHAPTER 13

Feng Shui Sites

WIND AND WATER

As you've noticed by now, the pursuit of feng shui sites is the default plot hook of *Feng Shui* adventures and the secret war. This doesn't mean that every story has to revolve around them. But when you do want to use this device, you'll need some tips.

WIND AND WATER

Feng shui is the oriental art of geomancy; it literally means "wind and water." It is devoted to harmonizing one's environment for the most beneficial flow of chi energy possible. Although referred to as geomancy, or earth magic, by Westerners, it is neither confined to matters of the earth, nor considered a form of magic.

GEOMANCERS

Chinese geomancers see themselves more as wise men or scientific practitioners than as magicians. In game terms, this means that it is possible to tell whether a place has good feng shui or not without resorting to the Fertility schtick of the Sorcery skill. The Info/Geomancy skill gives characters familiarity with the principles of feng shui as handed down by geomancers throughout the ages. It isn't necessary or desirable to get into the complex mechanics of feng shui in *Feng Shui* adventures. Just keep in mind that geomancers have memorized a whole passel of complex rules about what features of a place affect its feng shui.

Two factors are especially important in geomancy: angle and shape. Geomancers always carry devices for measuring angles in the landscape or in architectural features. These may be traditional wooden devices with flip-up sides and a system of pegs used in the abstruse calculations of the geomancer, or they may be modern orienteering compasses. Geomancers know which angles have positive aspects and which ones are negative; the relationships between angles in a site are also very important.

Shapes are also important; if the shape of a feature resembles an animal, this is very auspicious. This applies especially to natural features of the landscape. For example, a village nestled among a series of hills that looks like a dragon's back has good feng shui. However, you want to make sure that you're positioned on the right side of such a formation. If you're at the tail of a dragon, you're doing very well for yourself. But if your village is positioned at its head, you are in metaphorical danger of being eaten. And that means bad feng shui, which brings misfortune and ill health to those who live there.

The rules of feng shui apply to more than the features of buildings and natural formations. They can be applied to the shape of a lot you own, the arrangement of furniture in a room, or even the positioning of pens on a contract you are about to sign.

Some families have ongoing relationships with particular geomancers who they call on again and again throughout their lives. Geomancers are consulted when new properties are purchased, or when buildings are built or extensively renovated. They can warn their customers away from sites with bad feng shui, or recommend against particular architectural features that will either choke off chi flow or send too much of it blasting into the building's inhabitants. Too much chi energy is as harmful as too little.

Improving Feng Shui

Geomancers wouldn't be in high demand if you couldn't do something to change a site's feng shui. When believers start to feel that they are the victims of bad luck, they call on the local geomancer for help. In such cases, the geomancer's job is to adjust the chi flow of a place so that it becomes beneficial to its owners or inhabitants. Sometimes this is as simple a matter as rearranging the furniture.

Small octagonal mirrors called **tangrams** play an even bigger role in adjusting chi flow. Chi bounces off of mirrors, so tangrams are often placed on inauspicious angles in order to modify them. Unfortunately, tangrams can be removed as easily as they can be placed, and are ripe for sabotage. Outdoor tangrams are also vulnerable to being knocked down by strong winds, which are common during Hong Kong's typhoon season.

In the case of buildings, extremely bad feng shui can be fixed through renovations. For example, in a home it's bad feng shui to have an upstairs hallway that ends right at the front door of the house. All of your chi will flow out of your house, taking your money and good health along with it. There's no way to fix such a severe problem with mirrors alone; instead, the geomancer will recommend calling the contractor to completely alter this feature of a home.

Property lots with weird or irregular shapes can be adjusted by bringing them into harmony with the natural world.

For example: A fishmonger's shop is located on a strange lot with a shape like this:

The geomancer will want to take this odd shape and make it look like something recognizable. He tells the owner to put two green poles at the round "head" of the lot to make it look like a shrimp. Now that it looks like a shrimp, it will go from generating poor chi to generating superb chi.

Not all bad feng shui can be adjusted. In particular, formations of the landscape (especially big ones) are very difficult to adjust. If an entire system of hills looks like a tiger ready to pounce on a village, the villagers should probably just give it up and move to another area.

Harming Feng Shui

If it is possible to accidentally ruin the feng shui of a site, it stands to reason that it is possible to do so intentionally to a site you want to sabotage. This is something that PCs will want to do to their enemies in the secret war at the same time as they avoid having it done unto them. In the world of *Feng Shui*, blowing stuff up is an excellent response to any situation, and it applies to enemy feng shui sites as well as anything else. But there are more subtle ways to hose your enemy's chi flow than the direct application of pyrotechnics (though the Jammers prefer blowing stuff up anyway).

Geomancers are just as adept at harming the feng shui of a site as they are at improving it. This ability comes in handy when clients refuse to pay their bills. For example, it is very bad feng shui to have any kind of shape jutting out towards you. In one amusing case described in Sarah Rossbach's book *Feng Shui: The Chinese Art of Placement* (Dutton, 1983), a feng shui master who was not paid due respect by the callow new head of an old family decided to take some geomantic revenge. He bought the lot next to his victim's property and stuck a bunch of bamboo poles into the earth in a pattern representing an arrow aimed at the heart of the offender's estate. Needless to say, the family suddenly fell victim to a run of extremely bad luck. Finally realizing the importance of feng shui, the family head sought out another geomancer, who solved his problem for him by suggesting that he place lawn statues of rabbits on his property. The fast and tricky rabbits would symbolically catch the arrows that the irritated geomancer was shooting into the family's chi flow.

You'll note from this story that feng shui depends a great deal on sympathetic magic. In other words, it uses physical representations of abstract ideas to change reality.

Example: The owners of the shrimp-shaped lot paint the poles red, and their luck turns bad. They run to the geomancer for help, and he tells them that now their business is like a cooked shrimp! They repaint the poles green, and things return to normal.

Your PCs' enemies can use the symbolic aspects of feng shui against them. If they suddenly realize that they have lost their connection to their chi source—as described later—it might not be so easy for them to discover why. Is it the glowering face on that new billboard across the street from their home? The excavations being carried out by the archaeological team on the property next to theirs? Or the slightly new arrangement of furniture they may not even notice the next time they return to their headquarters? Yes, this is a world in which a team of geomantically-trained ninja interior decorators could wreak great havoc on their opponents...

ATTUNEMENT

Characters who receive the chi flow benefits of a place are said to be **attuned** to it. People whose chi is being constricted by connection to a place with bad feng shui are also attuned to that place. The average person is probably attuned to a place, or even several places, without knowing it. Your most important place for chi flow purposes is your home, the place where you live. You may also draw chi from your place of work, or from your city or village.

Secret warriors can also attune themselves to sites other than those in which they work or reside. Doing so requires what is called a **ritual of attunement**. This is a simple matter for those who know how to do it, and is explained in the next section. They now gain the experience benefits of attunement, as outlined on p. 161 of the section Getting Even Tougher, and they now have a vested interest in keeping the site safe.

HOW TO ATTUNE

To attune yourself to a feng shui site, you must be a member of a group that controls that site. You must occupy the site for at least twenty-four hours. You must keep enemies and uninvited individuals from entering its boundaries for a period of at least one week after this. Then each member of the group must simultaneously participate in a simple ritual in which they meditate on the inherent beauty and power of the site. Each character must spend 1 experience point to attune herself to it. All characters who do so are then eligible for the benefits of attunement, as described in the previous chapter. Characters present at the initial meditation ceremony can bring others into the attunement by repeating the ceremony (but not the initial occupation); only newly-attuning characters have to spend the experience point.

MAINTAINING ATTUNEMENT

It is not necessary to occupy a site indefinitely in order to remain attuned to it. It is, however, necessary to prevent anyone else from attuning themselves to your site. If they do so, your attunement is nullified. (It's okay for someone else to attune to your site if they're on your side, and you're there with them when it happens.) Characters may wish to be attuned to more than one site at a time; they'll also want to be out having adventures rather than just sitting at home with a shotgun guarding their sacred grove or hidden grotto. However, they will need to take measures to ensure the security of their sites. They can hire guards, install automated security measures ranging from primitive traps to land mines, or employ magical protective measures. As long as no one else has attuned to the site, their attunement remains in effect.

Sharing Sites

It's certainly possible for more than one person to attune to a site; in fact, it's common. But as stated in the text, anyone who wants to attune to a site must have a strong claim to it. If some random mook wants to attune to a site the PCs control, he can't do it. But if the mook later joins the PCs and becomes a player character from that point forward, he could. Someone who controls a feng shui site can allow someone else to attune to it, but that other person must in some way be tied to the controller. A powerful Ascended honcho, for example, could allow his bodyguards to attune to one of his sites.

It's impossible for people who aren't allies of some sort to share attunement. If one of that Ascended's bodyguards later turns traitor, she will automatically de-attune and suffer the loss of benefits. On the other hand, if the bodyguard pulled a coup and kicked her former master out on the street to starve somehow, she would become the controller of the site and he would be de-attuned.

NOTES ON ATTUNEMENT

We recommend against starting the PCs off already attuned to a powerful feng shui site. Sure, there's a chance that their apartment or warehouse headquarters has good feng shui, but it's a pretty low chance. GMs should declare it a zero chance; this gives the PCs a motivation to get out and get attuned to a site. And motivation is a good thing for a group to have, especially in the early stages of your storyline.

Chapter 13

It is not possible to attune to a site you do not have a strong claim to. However, the meaning of "strong claim" is somewhat nebulous depending on the situation. If you can defend a site from others who want to attune to it, or have a reasonable expectation that you will be able to do so, you have a strong claim. Just waltzing into a building and taking it over at gunpoint does not usually confer this strong claim, because you have to expect a swarm of SWAT teams to swoop down on the area to try to bring you to heel. The strong claim must seem relatively permanent. Legal ownership counts as a strong claim only if you are able to enforce your legal rights. However, it is not necessary in the event that the legal owner is unable to enforce his rights. In other words, it is much easier to take over and attune to sites in lawless areas than in civilized ones.

For example: Your PCs want to attune themselves to an Alabama truck stop they know to have powerful feng shui. They can't do so simply by walking into the place, ordering some hamburgers, and commencing to meditate. They would have to achieve some degree of ownership, legal or otherwise, over the place. They could buy shares in the property (assuming the proprietor was willing), or they could intimidate the owner into signing it over to them. They would not be able to attune to the site, however, if the owner was likely to go to the cops or call on some other source of help in retaking the truck stop.

Some groups in the secret war are better able than others to enforce their claims to sites. The Lotus and Architects can't call up the police when one of their secret bases in the modern world is taken: they don't want to have to explain the walking corpses or the bioengineering vats, respectively. On the other hand, the Ascended have police connections up the wazoo and maintain a policy of aggressively retaking any installations seized by opponents. (Such are the advantages of being the secret masters of the world.)

Although all sites have feng shui of some sort, there is little point in attuning to a site with simply average feng shui. Most buildings, villages, and natural formations have only average feng shui. Only a small minority have strong enough chi to become tactical goals in the secret war.

Illustration by Ralph Horsley

It is possible to attune to a site with negative feng shui. Characters can't accumulate or spend experience points while attuned to a site with bad feng shui. They can't use fortune dice. It's extremely unlikely that PCs smart enough to consult a geomancer or sorcerer will attune to a bum site, unless they've been fooled in some extraordinary way.

DE-ATTUNEMENT

It is possible to lose the game benefits of being attuned to a site; this is called **de-attunement**. This happens when someone else attunes to your site, or when the site ceases to provide an above-average chi flow.

When characters become de-attuned, they feel it immediately. They may break out into a cold sweat, automatically fail a task check or trivial action, feel that someone has walked over their graves, become nauseous, or otherwise suffer an unpleasant gut reaction. Depending on their experience with feng shui, they may or may not identify these as the symptoms of de-attunement.

Other characters can attune to one of your sites when they have a stronger claim to it than you do. This means that they must be physically occupying the site for at least a day, and must reasonably believe that you have little or no chance of taking it back from them. An armed takeover is the obvious scenario, but your PC's enemies may take sneakier measures in pulling their feng shui sites out from under them. For example, a Pledged government official might arrange for the government appropriation of their property, and install Order of the Wheel agents to attune themselves to it.

Sites most often cease to provide chi flow when tampered with. (See earlier for ways in which the PCs' enemies might do this.) Chi flow from sites that have been tampered with returns when the source of the tampering is neutralized. This might be as mundane a matter as repairing a blown-out wall, or as mystical as putting symbolic statues on your property to ward off similarly metaphorical injuries.

It is not possible to voluntarily de-attune oneself from a site simply by meditating. Someone else must willingly take over the site and attune to it, or the site must be destroyed, to sever the mystic link of attunement. Characters attuned to a bad feng shui site can't just snap their fingers and erase the bad luck.

DEFENDING MULTIPLE SITES

PCs will want to become attuned to more than one site. The more sites they attune to, the harder they are to defend. As GM, you don't want the campaign to degenerate into an exercise in **turtling**. Turtling occurs when your players adopt an entirely defensive posture and behave like turtles, rarely poking their exposed bits out where their enemies can get at them. Since this is supposed to be a game of cinematic action, this is a bad thing.

You can discourage turtling by first of all making sure that the PCs only have the chance to attune to relatively minor feng shui sites. These are sites—like the Eating Counter restaurant in the "Baptism of Fire" adventure—which are powerful enough to provide game benefits to the PCs but not so powerful that they make a difference in the grand progress of the secret war. There are lots of minor feng shui sites all over the world. The groups who are on top in any given juncture gain no real benefit from capturing them; they already have much better ones impregnably protected. Only hungry or disadvantaged groups—in other words, groups with resources roughly equal to the PCs—will have a reason to go after them. For example, in Baptism of Fire the Eaters of the Lotus have just begun to investigate modern-day Hong Kong; they have only a sorcerer and some street punks at their command. They're small enough to have a reason to want to capture a minor site like the Eating Counter, which means they're also small enough for the PCs to have a chance at taking them down.

As the series progresses, you can allow the PCs to attune to major sites at the invitation of the honchos who control those sites. This gives them a good reason to seek out patrons who will draw them into the major events of the secret war plotline. If they please the Queen of the Ice Pagoda, she might let them attune to one of her chi-producing sites in the Netherworld—maybe even the Ice Pagoda itself. In these cases, they can enjoy the game benefits of attunement without having to worry about spending all of their time guarding the site itself. The servants of their patron will do that for them.

Chapter 13

BURNING SITES

In the jargon of the secret war, permanently destroying a feng shui site is referred to as **burning** it. For a site to be permanently destroyed, its potential to generate positive chi for its owners or inhabitants must be forever eradicated.

Example: If you blow up a building with great feng shui, it is not considered permanently destroyed so long as there is a chance of rebuilding it. But if you blow up the building and manage to destroy all available means of reconstructing it, such as all copies of the original plans, then you're cooking with gas.

Characters who burn a site get a temporary rush of chi energy, as it flows from the site to its destroyers. In game terms, that means an additional 5 experience points per participating PC at the end of the session. This bonus is not multiplied by the number of feng shui sites the characters are attuned to at the time. It is not possible to gain the bonus for burning a site you are currently attuned to, or have been attuned to at any time in the past. Any rush of chi energy is canceled out by an accompanying psychic shockwave upon the loss of a site.

Small players in the secret war often capture a site they can't themselves defend and turn it over to a more powerful patron in exchange for information, logistical support, loaned henchmen, equipment, or other favors. This is also called "burning," because the minor group gets a one-time advantage for taking a site it knows it can't hang onto.

SPECIAL SITES

Not all feng shui sites are created equal. Some of them are so resonant with chi that they become crucial stakes in the secret war. The primary owners attuned to such sites get a major chi charge from them. PCs shouldn't have a shot at attuning to them. If such an event happens at all, it should be reserved for a pivotal moment in the campaign in which the current PCs retire as active characters to adopt roles as behind-the-scenes string pullers.

More within reach of the PCs is the situation in which a major patron allows them to attune to the site as a reward for service. In this case, the PCs receive only the standard benefits of attunement to a feng shui site.

In addition to such sites, there are lesser sites that offer different benefits. Some sites might offer bonuses to Sorcery AVs rather than experience points, for example. You may create any such sites you like, but don't go overboard.

Illustration by Roger Raupp

CHAPTER 14

Monsters

FOUL AND FORBIDDEN

Although they will often be mowing down human mooks, gunsels, and lackeys, *Feng Shui* PCs should also be prepared to go toe-to-toe with a variety of monsters. These include ghosts and demons from the 69 juncture, and bioengineered abominations from 2056. The supernatural creature and abomination types and their associated schticks allow GMs to create custom monsters, and we encourage you to do so. However, a few pre-determined creatures of the night never hurt anybody, did they?

The statistics given for these creatures are not set in stone, they should vary from individual to individual. All schticks are creature powers unless otherwise indicated.

Special rule: If, when you introduce one of these monsters into your series, any of your players ever say anything like, "Oh, I know this monster, its Action Value is X," you should immediately increase all of the creature's Action Values by 5 against that player's character.

GNARLED MARAUDER

This demon from the Underworld resembles a walking sea anemone with dozens of flailing tentacles, each of them with a barbed hook on the end. Its flesh is warty and, well, gnarled. Despite their appearance, these things are intelligent, and in fact have a taste for poetry and fine calligraphy. Unfortunately—especially for poets and calligraphers—their taste for the flesh of the living is even greater. Gnarled marauders are on good terms with Gao Zhang and the Eaters of the Lotus, who have fed many screaming victims to them since coming to power.

Gnarled Marauder
Attributes: Bod 8, Chi 4, Mnd 6, Ref 5
Skills: Creature Powers 8, Martial Arts 8
Schticks: Abysmal Spines x 2, Amphibian, Conditional Escalation (Body increases by 1 whenever targeted by successful Sorcery task check), Tentacles x 6
Weaponry: tentacle barbs (12), bite (9)

Chapter 14

HOPPING VAMPIRES (JIANGSHI)

The most famous Hong Kong movie monster is the jiangshi, or hopping vampire, who manages to be vaguely ridiculous and extremely deadly at the same time. These undead creatures aren't really bloodsuckers in the literal sense, but they do have a contagion power that turns their victims into more hopping vampires. Those affected by its Corruption schtick always turn into jiangshi themselves.

Hopping vampires look like somewhat decomposed humans, wearing the robes of ancient noblemen. Their eyes glow red and their fingernails are frightfully long and sharp. Although they can move only by hopping, that doesn't slow them down any. Jiangshi aren't intelligent: they can't speak, think, or employ complex strategies in pursuing their prey. But pure determination and single-mindedness can be scary, too: These things never give up.

The best way to deal with a hopping vampire is to slap onto its forehead a piece of rice paper with mystical calligraphic symbols on it. Any character with the Summoning schtick of Sorcery can create these paper amulets as a trivial action; no task check is required. Any character, sorcerer or not, can deactivate a jiangshi by slapping the paper firmly to the creature's forehead. This requires a Martial Arts check with the Difficulty being the jiangshi's Dodge rating. Once the paper is fixed to the thing's head—it's a good idea to stick some glue to it before slapping it on—the jiangshi goes into dormancy, standing at attention and unable to move.

Jiangshi are unable to hop across a solid line of uncooked sticky rice. Make sure your rice dealer isn't cheating you, though, because lower grades of rice don't do squat against them. A pure diet of sticky rice can also cure you if you're part-way through the process of turning into a hopping vampire yourself. It usually takes 3 or 4 days of rice-eating to purge your system of their Corruption effect.

As far as can be determined, hopping vampires don't wear black very often and only rarely suffer from angst. They're too busy menacing square-jawed action heroes and turning the hero's best friend into an undead creature of the night.

THE RECONSTRUCTED

These cybernetically-altered ogres are the standard-model abominations sent out by the Buro to put down insurgencies throughout the Third World in 2056. They are reasonably intelligent, and genuinely enjoy maiming and killing. Each Reconstructed is implanted with a Cerebral Grepper, a device that causes it an instant brain hemorrhage if it knowingly disobeys the orders of a superior officer. The Buro tends to lose Reconstructed every so often, because they have low impulse control and sometimes lash out at their officers anyway. But it's better than losing perfectly-good human officers.

The Reconstructed are enormous humanoids with monstrous features and gleaming metal implants. They don't all look alike. They come in a variety of bright flesh colors: red, green, and purple are common. Some have horns, others are covered with coarse hair, bubbling blemishes, or other repulsive features.

The Reconstructed
Attributes: Bod 12, Chi 0 (Mag 5), Mnd 3, Ref 7
Skills: Arcanowave Devices 8, Creature Powers 8, Guns 8, Martial Arts 8
Schticks: [Arcanowave Schticks]: Juicer, Spirit Shield Generator, [Creature Powers]: Armor, Inevitable Comeback
Weapons: punch (13), kick (14), Buro Godhammer (13/4/5), Buro Hellharrower (16/8/20)

Hopping Vampire
Attributes: Bod 8, Chi 0, Mnd 0, Ref 5
Skills: Creature Powers 10, Martial Arts 8
Schticks: Abysmal Spines (well, claws, actually) x 3, Corruption, Damage Immunity: Blast (one exception of your choice), Damage Immunity: bullets, Regeneration x 2
Weapons: claws (11)

SNAKE MEN

Snake Men are demons from the Underworld (the place where demons come from, not the Netherworld), and are sometimes mistaken for Ascended-style transformed snakes. They are humanoid in appearance, appearing as muscular men or women wearing a weaving, writhing tunic of live snakes. They fight unarmed, relying on martial arts abilities and fu powers to defeat their opponents. Snake men are not very bright or motivated, and usually fight only when dominated by a powerful sorcerer. Left to their own devices, they want only to attack and eat helpless prey, and to avoid attacks from stronger beings.

Snake Men
Attributes: Body 6, Chi 8 (For 0), Mnd 4, Ref 6
Skills: Creature Powers 8, Martial Arts 8
Schticks: [Creature Powers]: Poison (fangs), Regeneration, [Fu Powers]: Eyes of the Snake, Slither of the Snake, Strike of the Snake, Coil of the Snake, Lunge of the Snake

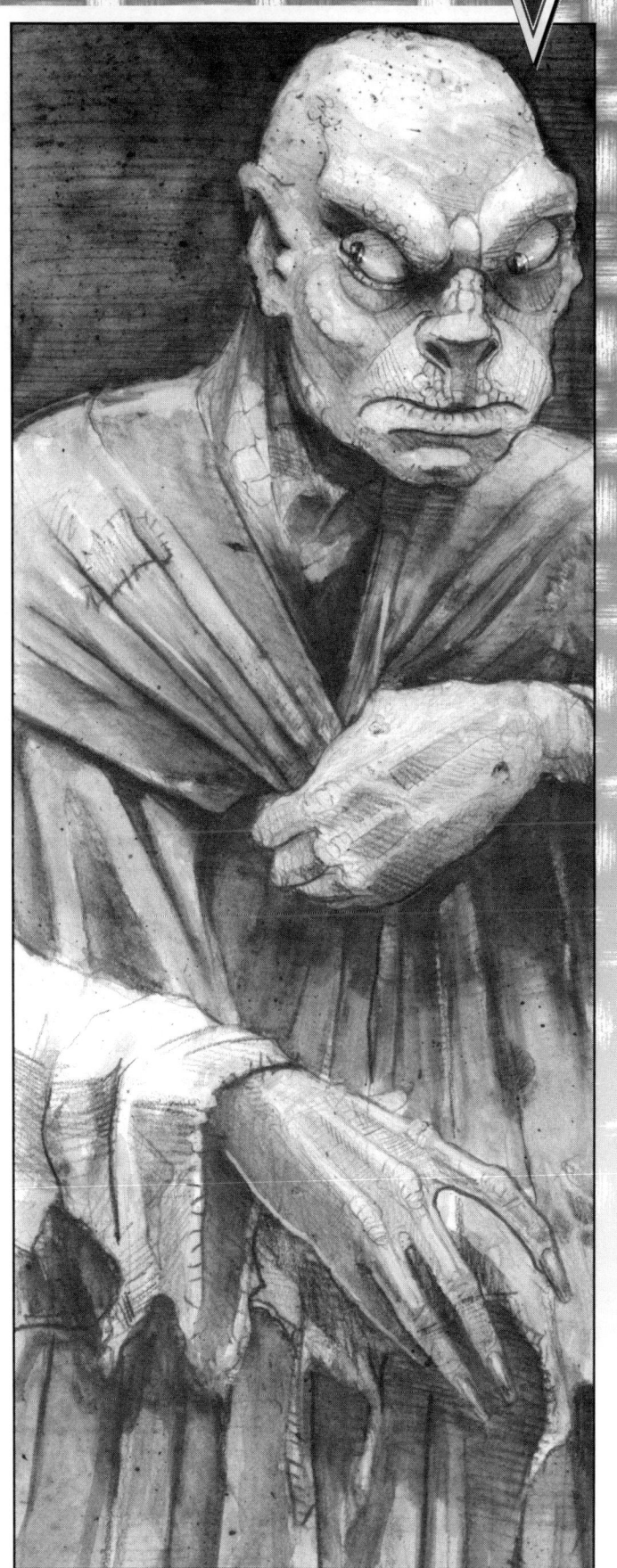

Illustration by Thomas Manning

Chapter 15

December 20

I gotta admit it was pretty cool to have a genuine old British type manor house bequeathed to me. Well, us really: Johnston-White deeded the thing to the whole bunch of us after he pushed off. Imagine, guys like me, McCroun, Donovan... lords of an estate, so to speak. The only one of us who looked properly noble was Mané; I guess he really was descended from African royalty. Least, he looked good in tweed.

Kar Fai came by for the housewarming shindig and taught us to do something he called "attuning." Yeah, more hocus pocus. Let me see if I got it straight. J-W's place had powerful feng shui, Kar Fai said, and as long as we did some basic things, it would focus chi energy towards us. And of course the chi energy would make us smarter, luckier, stronger, faster, give us better fashion sense, the whole nine yards. The basic things we hadda do to maintain this were: a) do this funky attuning deal and b) defend it against anyone who tries to take it away from us. Well, I didn't know from a), but b) has been the cornerstone of my philosophy since I first climbed outta the crib.

The attuning bit was kinda weird, actually. He just had us sit all around in a circle like yoga boys and think on this word over and over. And suddenly I felt like this enormous block of stone had been lifted off of my shoulders. The whole guilt thing with Steve and what happened to him, all the bad things I'd done, all the new worries with all of this crazy secret war stuff going on—poof, it melted offa me like steam off a kettle. I felt like I was high or something, but I swear I hadn't had more'n a couple beers. I felt almost like dancing.

We used J-W's place as a base of operations from then on in. In between going off and shooting bad guys and blowing stuff up, we'd stop off there for rest and recuperation—recuperation being a frequent need of ours. J-W's old family retainer, Broomfield, stayed on to keep the place tidy and to administer first aid whenever we blew in. Turns out he'd been a Dragon himself, just like J-W, back between the wars. His info wasn't up to date anymore, but he gave good strategic advice.

So it was pretty distressing when we got back that one night and found him hanging from the chandelier. Not dead: he'd been duct-taped to a chair and hung by chains from the ceiling. Also taped to him were about fifty sticks of dynamite. Walking in the door must have triggered some kind of sensor mechanism, because the big red LED letters on the bomb started ticking down, and they started at 00003. I had just barely enough time to whip out Mr. Browning and shoot through one of the teeny tiny wires on the bomb before it went off. Good thing I picked the right one.

Unfortunately, the scumbags who'd gotten the drop on Broomfield—turned out later to be the Lotus—had planted more bombs. We heard this awful blasting noise, and rushed to the back of the house. The entire wall was blown right out.

Soon as this happened, all of us who'd been attuned to the place felt this gut-churning sensation, like an entire platoon was walking over our graves. I felt like curdling up into a ball, and I could tell the others were feeling identical. Jeez, I'd swear Mané turned pale.

I gotta hand it to Broomfield: he was cooler than the rest of us put together. And he'd been the one hanging in the breeze with TNT strapped to his butt! He just muttered something about the Thorns of the Lotus being amateurs compared to the Gestapo, and got on the cell phone to a building contractor. He explained to us that Ta Yu and his punks were trying to mess with us by cutting off our chi flow from our feng shui site. The feng shui of the building depended on its special architectural properties—and here he got into all this rigamarole about lines and angles and placement and stuff. Which meant that what went down could come up: All we had to do was make sure that the builders reconstructed things according to the identical plans drawn up by J-W's ancestors back in the 1850s.

Broomfield told us not to sweat the details. The contractors he could handle. He suggested that there might be a certain eunuch sorcerer and some leather-clad thugs we might want to track down and hurt really badly. After a very brief moment of reflection, my fellow gentlemen and I concurred with our retainer's assessment of the situation.

CHAPTER 15

Groups

THE SECRET WAR

In this chapter you'll find introductory descriptions of the groups taking part in the worldwide battle for control of Earth's feng shui sites. As players reading this material, keep in mind the fact that your characters may not know everything you know about the setting, especially at the beginning of the game. Very few people in the contemporary world know about these groups, or about the existence of the time-spanning conflict they're waging with one another. Even though your characters might not know this stuff, we're giving players enough info about the world to know what kind of game you'll be playing. Knowing a bit about the enemies your characters will be facing, and the reasons behind all of the fights they'll be getting into, will help you decide what kind of character you want to pick and how you choose to play them. Different types of characters will start with different degrees of knowledge. Once you've picked your character, you and your GM can figure out just how much, if any, of the following information she has at her disposal at the beginning of the game.

ARCHITECTS OF THE FLESH

The **Architects of the Flesh** are the mad scientists whose perverse creations—spawned by an unholy combination of biotechnology and magic—support a worldwide police state in the year 2056. Not content with international domination of their own juncture, they have decided to use time-twisting technology to conquer all of human history, working backwards from their own period.

The group that would eventually become the Architects first formed in 2014 as the CDCA, or Cross-Disciplinary Convergence Association. This group was founded in order to pursue possible connections between recombinant DNA research, quantum physics, and parapsychology. The main figure behind this movement was **Dr. Anita Dao**, a physicist who became convinced that there was a scientific basis to many paranormal claims. Her study of quantum mechanics led her to identify an energy pattern which she labeled as the **arcanowave**. Dao believed that this was the form of energy which was manipulated in the past by individuals claiming to work magic. She further identified **high-end** and **low-end** arcanowaves: high-end arcanowaves were used in powering magical spells. These wave patterns occurred only rarely in nature, and were difficult to create in the lab. Low-end arcanowaves, on the other hand, flowed through all living things at various rates. They were even amplified by certain geological and architectural patterns. Her Chinese heritage and knowledge of feng shui principles provided her with the frame of reference to understand what she had found: a scientific means of identifying and measuring chi energy. This breakthrough was hailed by young workers in a variety of scientific disciplines: they found the basic mathematical patterns of arcanowaves mirrored in their own fields. Astrophysicists, chemists, geologists, mathematicians, and especially biotech researchers found Dao's theories easy to incorporate into their research. The scientific establishment was less than enthusiastic about the arcanowave theory, and blocked

Chapter 15

attempts to fund research into it. Dao and others created the CDCA to break free of these constraints, and to try to find applications for the surprising implications of their studies.

This innocuous academic organization was gradually transformed into a powerful and malevolent political force. A decade after her ground-breaking studies, Dr. Dao vanished from her lab. The new president of the CDCA, a DNA researcher named **Dr. Curtis Boatman**, soon displayed much wider ambitions than his predecessor. He successfully lobbied to attach the CDCA to the United Nations as an official sub-agency, thereby assuring a steady flow of funding. By 2025, the UN had become the industrialized nations' primary instrument for imposing their will on the Third World. Restructured to allow greater control by the great powers, it had formed a standing army to handle so-called peace-keeping missions around the globe. As tensions increased between the have and have-not nations, the UN shifted its role from troubleshooter to occupying power. In order to secure unlimited funding for his project, Boatman yoked it to the military interests of the Bureau of Tactical Management.

The BTM was the Security Council-dominated military command, referred to in institutional slang as the **Buro**. Working closely with a then little-known German functionary named **Johann Bonengel**, Boatman turned the CDCA into a huge operation dedicated to turning Dr. Dao's arcanowave discoveries into military technology. Together, the two quietly established CDCA bases at crucial feng shui sites throughout the world. As they acquired more such bases, their political opposition within the UN faded away—the CDCA had the flow of chi on their side, and as a result things just went their way.

A top priority of the project was the creation of a new breed of soldier. The industrialized nations had a big disadvantage in fighting the third world: the high casualty rates of the various wars of subjugation were politically unpopular with their electorates. Boatman promised to find a way to fix the "body bag problem," as it was called. At first, his researchers experimented with ways to clone super-soldiers using arcanowave techniques to accelerate their growth and give them abilities far beyond human norms. But this was nixed by Boatman's political controllers: the creation of a superior species of humankind was even more disturbing to the electorate than the battlefield deaths of their sons and daughters. Boatman then switched to a program to try to convert laboratory-bred primates into DNA-enhanced fighting machines. But this failed too: the chimpanzees and gorillas used were unwilling to engage in senseless combat.

The problem was solved in 2037 when the CDCA's quantum mechanics division discovered a means of artificially opening a gate to the **Netherworld**, a timeless quasi-dimension adjacent to our own reality. They sent heavily-armed exploratory teams into the Netherworld, capturing a number of supernatural creatures. When these entities were studied back in the lab, Boatman knew he had found his test subjects. He would use the various ogres, snake men, walking corpses and hopping vampires as the basis for his super-soldiers. They were already violent, and the results would be in no way superior to humankind. The first **abominations**, the results of DNA/arcanowave alterations to the physical structures of these supernatural beings, rolled off the assembly line and onto the battlefield in 2042.

The abominations, monsters of old reinforced by the latest in killing technology, were brutal in combat and highly demoralizing to the enemy. The military successes scored by abomination-backed UN Forces were impressive. Boatman's political mentor, Johann Bonengel, was appointed head of the Buro, and became known as **Buropresident**. The rebellious nations of the Third World surrendered to the UN, especially after the BTM instituted a policy of directly attacking enemy heads of state with abomination guerrilla squads. The UN then had to figure

> Does the UN/Buro's subjugation of the world seem improbable? Remember that the key was their seizure of crucial feng shui sites; those who control the flow of chi find that history unfolds to their benefit. Actions that the world would find unthinkable without this chi influence came to seem acceptable and even commonplace because of it. The flow of chi throughout the world subtly turned the minds of the populace into accepting the dictates of those who controlled the chi. The rise of the Architects is a dramatic example of the power of chi: without it, they would never have gotten anywhere.

out how to administer their victory. They were afraid of instituting democracies in these nations, and so instead they reintroduced colonialism. The UN would directly administer the governments of the defeated countries.

This was a difficult matter at first, until Bonengel and Boatman arranged for the construction of Buro or CDCA installations on the major feng shui sites of the conquered nations. They then used arcanowave technology to warp the chi of these sites, so that its benefits would flow only to them. Soon the rebellious populaces of the Third

World began to see the Buro as their natural leadership.

It took the arcanoscientist and the politician little time to realize that the abominations they had created were only halfway responsible for their victories. The occupation of the feng shui sites made it possible to consolidate their military victories by giving them influence over the nations' chi forces. The next step was obvious: gain a similar stranglehold on the chi of the industrialized nations. The final stages in the Buro's plan for world domination were accomplished with relative ease. Bonengel appropriated the key feng shui sites of the major powers through political and bureaucratic means. Since only a few of their most trusted colleagues were aware of the full significance of feng shui sites, none of their potential opponents even knew enough to fight them for the sites. In 2051, a series of votes in the legislatures of the industrialized countries dissolved the United Nations and made the Buro the legal authority of a new world government. The triumph of Boatman and Bonengel seemed complete.

Boatman retreated to his lab in order to further pursue arcanological research. Bonengel, on the other hand, became restless. Despite their lock on the world's most resonant feng shui sites, pockets of rebellion still existed. The extreme chi of the Buro was enough to sway ninety-eight percent of the population. But the remaining two percent dogged Bonengel's thoughts. He became obsessed with complete domination of all of mankind, creating an all-encompassing police and propaganda state. The hunt for dissidents became a top priority for the Buro. Today the Buro spends much more on the hunt for subversives than it could possibly lose by leaving them alone. Its heavy-handed tactics sometimes even work against it, creating anti-Buro sentiments in people who would otherwise be lulled into unquestioning obedience.

Seeing that Bonengel was in danger of polishing the gilt off his own golden egg, Boatman proposed a more challenging and rewarding project: the conquest of all of human history. After a rigorous analysis of historical patterns and their relation to chi concentrations, Boatman's strategists have come up with a theory to target specific points in the past to concentrate on conquering. According to this theory, there are certain crucial turning points in history. If you take over the world at one of these junctures, your control of history is guaranteed up until the next breakpoint. If they go backwards in time from breakpoint to breakpoint, they can conquer all of history with a minimum of effort. The Architects have further concluded that the best timeframe to attack first is our very own present. Their activities in our timeframe have only just begun, with the capture of a few innocuous feng shui sites. They have yet to figure out that most of the sites are currently controlled by one group, the Ascended.

The Architects also use the Netherworld to make extensive forays into the ancient past, in search of supernatural creatures to use as raw materials for their abominations. There they have come into conflict with the Eaters of the Lotus, who need supernatural creatures for their own schemes. The Architects are also opposed by a group from their own timeframe, the Jammers. Much of the Architects' anti-subversion activity is directed at rooting out Jammers. The Architects are victims of substantial disinformation about these rebels, much of it of their own devising. In their paranoid imaginings, the Architects believe their enemies to be twice as organized and pervasive as they really are. However, in one central area they underestimate their foes: they do not know that the Jammers are aware of the significance of feng shui sites and are pursuing their own cross-time strategy to make them useless.

THE ASCENDED

Paranoids the world over develop wild theories about an international hidden conspiracy secretly in control of all world events. Usually these deluded idiots point the finger at ethnic or religious groups they don't like; sometimes they accuse institutional leaders like the Queen of England or the Pope of secretly pulling all the strings. These bigots and loonies are truly to be pitied. But if they really knew who was in charge of the world, they'd be beside themselves with fear and anxiety. A highly elusive secret society known as *the Ascended* has been unobtrusively directing world affairs for hundreds of years. It now commands a truly staggering amount of power and influence. Influential individuals from every walk of life—from government to big business to the media—are either members of the Ascended or willing servants owing unswerving allegiance to them. But even those who serve them are unaware of the true nature of the inner circle of the Ascended.

These mysterious individuals are the descendants of animals who magically transformed themselves into humans millennia or more ago. The blood of various types of creatures—tigers, tortoises, cranes, snakes, dogs, bulls, cats, spiders, and even dragons—still pulses in their veins. During China's

Chapter 15

In the distant past, when magic was still commonplace in the world, animals were as fully intelligent as humans and as capable of reason and emotion. While many animals were happy with their lot, a few envied the society of humans and sought to join it. This was not without peril: it was widely—and falsely—believed that such creatures were innately evil. In reality, a transformed animal can choose between right and wrong just as well as any human can. Despite this fact, these beings were hunted by magicians and Taoist monks, who considered their pretense to be an affront to the natural order. Evading the efforts of these supernatural watchmen, many animals did succeed in fooling humans into accepting them. They interbred with true humans, spawning various lineages which continue to this day. Although most of the early transformed animals were found in China and elsewhere in the East, they quickly dispersed through the globe. As they traveled, they sometimes used their knowledge of magic to assist native animals of these unfamiliar regions in the world to become human as well. The ancestors of the Ascended are the inspiration for the myths found in most cultures about humans who sometimes assume animal form: the werewolf of Eastern Europe, the bearwalker and other shapechangers of native North America, and so on.

Genetically, the current Ascended are mostly human, with only a trace of their supernatural and animalistic origins in their biological makeup. However, this trace element gives them a potentially disastrous flaw: if magic ever again becomes as common as it was in ancient China, they will be reclaimed by their animal natures. Although they enjoy certain benefits from their animal heritage, the Ascended quite like being human, and therefore expend much effort to make sure that the contemporary world remains mostly magic-free. In order to keep it that way, they need to control a large number of feng shui sites. If the feng shui sites were to fall into the hands of a magic-using organization like the Eaters of the Lotus or one of the Four Monarchs, magic would become much easier to teach and use. This return would threaten the Ascended with exposure, and the Ascended therefore view these groups as their worst enemies.

The group has been active for centuries, quietly acquiring a large number of feng shui sites; they control the majority of the most powerful sites in the modern world. In order to acquire these sites, they needed to marshal great resources, both political and financial.

The early history of the Ascended is obscure even to those few who have learned of the organization's existence. Study of the group is no doubt hampered by the fact that those scholars who stumble onto it have an odd habit of suffering fatal accidents shortly thereafter. It seems to have been founded in the eleventh century, at a period of time when the number of magicians in the world was beginning to dwindle for some unknown reason. Within decades of one another, two similar organizations formed, one in Europe and the other in China. The European organization was known as the **Order of the Wheel**; the Chinese equivalent was called the **Jade Wheel Society**. Both were secret societies with elaborate structures and initiation rituals. The Order of the Wheel acquired political influence in feudal Europe by promoting the Crusades. The Jade Wheel Society subverted the ruling Song Dynasty of China, aiding their Mongol enemies. Both seem to have been secretly run by descendants of supernatural animals. In both cases, these organizations manipulated political events to their own advantage, putting their vassals in power and gaining for themselves great wealth and resources. Through the following centuries, both the Order of the Wheel and the Jade Wheel drove deep roots into the power structures of their respective empires.

Both the Order of the Wheel and the Jade Wheel Society exist to this day. The Order of the Wheel is a fraternal order and service organization with chapters throughout the Western world. Most members are small-town businessmen who know nothing of the upper echelon's nature or true influence. The Jade Wheel society follows Eastern traditions, and is found in Taiwan, Japan, Hong Kong, Malaysia, and Singapore. A covert equivalent likely exists as a hidden cadre of the Communist Party in mainland China. As with the more-open Wheel groups, most members of the cadre have no idea what it really is; they just think it's a way of making contacts and getting promoted.

The inner circle keeps a close eye on its recruits, and approaches a very few of them with an offer to rise into a secret hierarchy called **the Pledged**. These individuals swear to take orders from yet a third group, which they know as **the Lodge**. The Pledged agree to further the goals of the Lodge, giving it priority over all other loyalties. They renounce friends, family, religion, and patriotism, casting these aside in favor of promises of wealth and power. The Pledged are typically highly-motivated and skilled people; they're also likely to be less than scrupulous. Once one becomes Pledged, it becomes impossible to back out. Those who have achieved positions of power through their work for the Lodge know that their lives will be ruined if they blow the whistle. The Lodge is careful to reward those who are loyal to it. It is just as quick to ensure that those who turn on it do not remain breathing for long. Members of the Pledged are found in key positions in governments throughout the world, both as elected officials and as bureaucrats. They sit on the boards of major corporations, public and private. They include top doctors, scientists and media figures. The Lodge is especially interested in placing operatives within military and paramilitary establishments, and within police forces. It has also infiltrated all major churches with centralized organizations.

The ultimate promise held out to the Pledged is that they will one day become Lodge members themselves. Although the Lodge is careful to keep its operatives content, this is one promise they never keep. All members of the Lodge are the descendants of transformed animals. Although they never use this name with outsiders, even with the Pledged, the Lodge refers to itself in private as the Ascended. Lodge membership is almost completely hereditary. Descendants of supernatural animals are usually very careful about who they mate with and how they pass their bloodline along. When their sons and daughters come of age, they are inducted into the ranks of the Ascended. Those few descendants who are not actually Lodge members are required to keep in contact with the organization nonetheless. They must update the Ascended on their activities, and swear never to do anything to risk exposure of their collective secret. The Ascended are absolutely committed to preserving their power, and are even perfectly willing to arrange for the assassination of other descendants if necessary.

The Lodge itself works along cooperative lines. Policy questions are settled by semi-annual board meetings, to which each family typically sends one surrogate. Each family has roughly equal influence in the organization, although some members may get more respect than others. The majority of questions are settled by discussion and consensus, with the need for a formal vote seldom arising. Disputes and power struggles within the Lodge are rare if not completely unknown. Most families see eye-to-eye on the issues confronting the Ascended; they've been successful so far and aim to stick with a winning strategy. Every six years, the group elects a chairperson for its board meetings; this individual is given the title of the Unspoken Name. No one but the members of the Lodge know the identity of the current Unspoken Name.

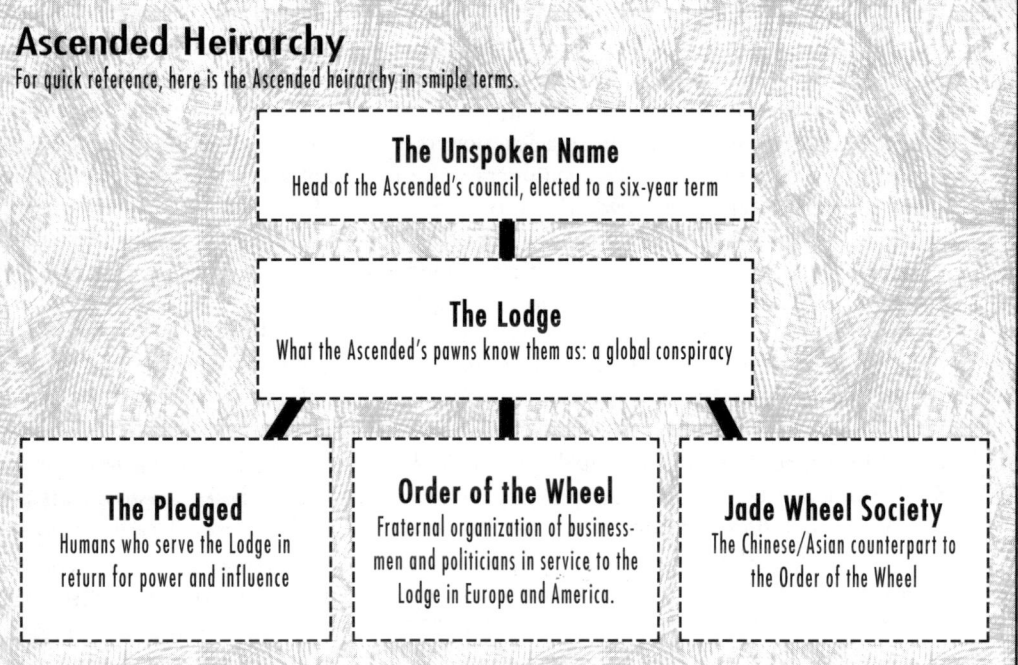

Ascended Heirarchy
For quick reference, here is the Ascended heirarchy in simple terms.

The Unspoken Name
Head of the Ascended's council, elected to a six-year term

The Lodge
What the Ascended's pawns know them as: a global conspiracy

The Pledged
Humans who serve the Lodge in return for power and influence

Order of the Wheel
Fraternal organization of businessmen and politicians in service to the Lodge in Europe and America.

Jade Wheel Society
The Chinese/Asian counterpart to the Order of the Wheel

The Ascended themselves avoid the public spotlight. They would sooner issue orders to office-holders than hold office themselves. When they act, they prefer to do so through several levels of intermediaries. Although the various Ascended families have accumulated great wealth over the past thousand years or so, they do not flaunt their money in public. They do not appear in Who's Who listings, do not show up on the gossip pages, and are rarely, if ever, referred to by name in the news media. They live quietly in dwellings whose modest exteriors attract little attention. The interiors of their homes range from tastefully chic to decadently luxurious. Scattered throughout the world are various Ascended installations, invariably centered around a highly sensitive feng shui site.

The Ascended do not allow their caution and reticence to dull their capacity for action. Their supernatural bloodline provides them with certain powers inaccessible to ordinary humans. They are especially adept at channeling chi through their bodies, and easily learn many esoteric kung fu powers. There are some missions too secret and too delicate to entrust to dupes; these are carried out personally by Lodge members, especially the younger ones. These active types are known as **enforcers**.

Although the Ascended rely heavily on the manipulation of chi, they are vehemently opposed to any use of magic in the modern world. The difference between chi and magic is merely one of degree, but it's a distinction that means everything to the Ascended. When individuals with magical powers appear, the Lodge dispatches Pledged operatives, or even enforcers, to either persuade them to abandon their studies, or to kill them outright. They often instruct their operatives within scientific and media circles to ridicule those making paranormal claims, and use their church contacts to suppress superstition and magical thinking. The witch-burnings that swept Europe during the Renaissance were, for example, a Lodge-ordered effort to prevent a resurgence of magical practice. They are continually on the lookout for Lotus activities.

As the action of the game opens, the Ascended have not realized that their control of Earth's feng shui sites has been targeted by the Architects. The Architects wish to extend their hegemony backwards into the past, and need to displace the influential Ascended in order to do it. The Architects know very little about the exact nature of the Ascended and their organization, but at this point the Ascended know almost nothing about them.

THE DRAGONS

The Dragons are a band of heroes who continually rise from among the humble and the outcasts of the world to fight for freedom, justice, and the right to look extremely cool. Unfortunately, they have a tendency to get wiped out by their enemies. Several times a group has taken on the ancient mantle of the legendary Dragons, only to meet a fate similar to theirs. In Chinese legend, the Silver Dragons were a group of immortals who challenged demons and despotic kings during the days of fable. Although many times they saved the people from slavery and oppression, they themselves met uniformly-grim fates. Despite the sad end of their tales of adventure, many have since adopted their name to fight against the villains and despots of the world.

The Dragons were brought into the secret war by **Kar Fai**, a monk from the 1850 juncture, and **The Prof**, a techie from 2056. Both of them were former members of other factions involved in the war. The hot-tempered ex-monk Kar Fai grew dissatisfied with what he saw as the blinkered, rigid vision of Quan Lo and the Guiding Hand. The Prof rejected the gruesome agenda of the Buro's CDCA scientific organization and fled to the Netherworld, determined to have the discovery of arcanowave science erased from the timeline. The two of them met in the Inner Kingdom, joined forces, and began to look for allies. They found existing Dragon groups in the 69 and 1850 junctures, and encouraged the creation of a similar group in the contemporary world. Kar Fai traveled the earth, finding maverick cops, redeemed assassins, heroic martial artists, and

> ### Operation Killdeer
> Operation Killdeer was a plot launched by the Ascended to crush members of the Dragons and the Lotus. Disinformation was carefully fed to both groups, with the desired outcome. The two factions clashed in a battle over a relatively minor Ascended feng shui site, resulting in several deaths. While the operation served its main purpose, it also served a more important one: a demonstration for the benefit of Ming I and Li Ting of the Four Monarchs (the Queen of the Darkness Pagoda and the King of the Fire Pagoda, respectively). Impressed by the ease with which the Ascended manipulated the other groups into killing each other, the two Monarchs joined with the Ascended and the Jammers in the creation of the Molten Heart, a powerful artifact that would allow the triumvirate of three factions to control all the portals into and out of the Netherworld.
> The Molten Heart was quickly destroyed by a valiant group of secret warriors including the formidable Dragon known as Ting Ting; in your campaign, things may happen differently.

masked avengers. He clued them into the consequences of the secret war and, with the help of the Prof, directed their operations against the various sinister factions in the middle of it.

In a brief span of time, the names of those new heroes became legendary to all secret warriors: Jack Donovan, Iala Mané, and Mad Dog McCroun. Unfortunately, they followed in the footsteps of their legendary namesakes and were recently destroyed in a terrible incident fighting Lotus sorcerers and demons. The Prof has found evidence that the incident was directed by the Lodge as part of something called Operation Killdeer. Torn by grief, Kar Fai and the Prof promised to reforge their team of heroes and to take vengeance upon those who killed their friends.

If your PCs need guidance, perhaps they will be contacted by Kar Fai and the Prof and urged to assume the dangerous mantle of the Dragons. Sure, there's a chance that they'll get toasted in a horrible fashion, just like everyone else who has taken on the name. But they'll be fighting the right fight. And they'll look like a million bucks as they go.

EATERS OF THE LOTUS

The Eaters of the Lotus is a secret society whose members control the Imperial Government of China in 69 AD. Its leaders are eunuchs who are supposed to serve the Emperor but have used cruel sorcery to enslave his will. According to custom, the only males who may live in the Imperial Palace are eunuchs. The will of the Emperor is supposed to be administered by officials who are given their posts according to their proven merit. However, these officials are not allowed to attend the Emperor directly. Because they have direct access to the Emperor, palace eunuchs are sometimes able to twist policy to their own ends. In extreme circumstances they weasel for themselves enough power to set up their own parallel government run by cronies, toadies, and thugs. The unsavory ambitions of the eunuchs should not come as a surprise; being castrated and forced to serve the Emperor is a punishment meted out to enemies. They are then supposed to become former enemies, but the Eaters of the Lotus leave out the "former" part.

It is well-known in the China of 69 AD that the Empire is going through one of its periodic spates of "eunuch trouble." The people know who to blame: **Gao Zhang**, the eunuch who is the senior attendant to the Emperor. The bureaucracy is unable to administer justice or keep the cronies of the eunuchs in check. The eunuchs have equipped strike forces of warriors loyal only to themselves. They use these to raid communities under the guise of "emergency taxation." They're also employed to kill or intimidate anyone who speaks out against the eunuchs. These enemies include functionaries of the official bureaucracy, shamans and village priests, and teachers and political reformers. Not everyone in the official system is an outspoken enemy of the eunuchs. Some of them have also been corrupted and now serve the eunuchs, knowing that this is the way to get ahead. Officials who follow eunuch orders instead of those of their supposed superiors are rewarded with secret payments, and are promoted up the chain of command by other corrupt bureaucrats. The majority of officials simply look the other way, hoping that these bad days will blow over—without their having to take any personal risks to topple the eunuchs. When approaching a government official for aid against the eunuchs, it is therefore very difficult to tell whether one will receive a sympathetic ear

> The Lotus are your basic group of evil, demon-summoning diabolical magicians. Whenever you feel like kicking nasty monster butt or duking it out with some whiny but potent sorcerer, you know it's Lotus time. Their critters are just as repugnant as the Abominations created by the Architects, but unlike the Abominations most Lotus critters don't have firearms or napalm: same great taste, but less technology!

or a prison sentence. Only a few brave souls dare to speak out against Gao Zhang's excesses. They usually end up as fugitives, sheltered by sympathizers in the vast Chinese countryside.

Although everyone knows that times are bad and they know who to blame for it, they do not know that Gao is the head of a secret society of evil magicians; the name "Eaters of the Lotus" is not known to the average Chinese peasant or bureaucrat. Even the majority of the Lotus' soldiers and flunkies don't know the name, nature, or motivations of the organization they serve. Most who follow the eunuchs do so simply for the money and for the pleasure of being able to bully others.

The Eaters of the Lotus were initially founded by Gao simply as an instrument for his own political power. He had been an ambitious provincial official who overstepped his authority and was sentenced to castration by the Emperor. He decided to win the Emperor's trust and use his new position in the palace to rise back to a position of authority. He also decided to employ a new tool in his quest for domination: sorcery. When he learned that a trio of outlaws were to be executed for demon summoning and other occult crimes, he secretly arranged for their rescue. In exchange for their eventual freedom, he demanded that they teach him the darkest secrets of magical manipulation. Gao turned out to have a natural talent for black magic, quickly surpassing the techniques of his masters. He created new spells, and forged new pacts with various potentates of the demonic realms. It is these abilities that provide Gao with his control of the government. He has

Chapter 15

Illustration by Thomas Manning

ensorcelled the Emperor, causing demons to harry him in his dreams. The Emperor, not knowing that it is Gao who is responsible for the hauntings, depends on him for nightly draughts and elixirs that lessen the intensity of the nightmares and allow him to catch fitful moments of sleep. Whenever the Emperor threatens to rein in Gao's political operations, the eunuch threatens to withhold the potions, and the Emperor's protests quickly dissolve into helpless stammers.

Gao Zhang has initiated all of the other palace eunuchs into the Lotus; those who refused to cooperate or were deemed incompetent were murdered. They were either accused of trumped-up crimes and executed, or were simply assassinated. Not all palace eunuchs are sorcerers, but it is necessary to practice magic in order to win high rank in the organization. Not all Lotus members, sorcerers or otherwise, are stationed at the palace. Many more are found in positions of power throughout Chinese society. Not all Lotus members are eunuchs, either, though again all of those in Gao's inner circle are. Some ambitious members have even volunteered for castration in order to be allowed to serve at Gao's side in the palace! There are no women in the Lotus, although they sometimes use the services of female sorcerers, swordswomen, and demons.

The Lotus makes extensive use of supernatural creatures in their effort to terrorize and destroy their enemies. Hopping vampires, walking corpses, ghosts, ogres, evil spirits and demons of various sorts are all part of this hellish legion. Regions which rise up against eunuch domination are soon infested by monsters. After allowing these beasts to run rampant through rebellious areas for a while, Gao sends his cronies in to offer exorcism services. If the rebels knuckle under, the supernatural assault subsides. This is basically a demonic protection racket run under the Emperor's seal. The connection between the eunuchs and the supernatural has not gone entirely unnoticed by the opponents of corrupt government. But so far no one has proven it, and, given the difficulty of getting through Lotus members to get to the Emperor, even direct evidence of such outrages wouldn't automatically end their reign of terror.

Until recently the only real goal of the Lotus was to fiercely maintain its political influence in China. Two years ago this changed. Strangely-equipped warriors began to appear in regions that the Lotus had dispatched its supernatural legions to. These peculiar interlopers were able to hold their own in combat even against the Lotus' best fighters with the help of the strange devices they carried. Their actions were most puzzling: they were capturing the Lotus' monstrous minions and vanishing with them. Eventually Lotus swordsmen were able to track these invaders—until they entered doorways in caverns and trees and disappeared! The swordsmen followed them into these doorways, thus discovering the Netherworld. They reported back to Gao Zhang, who quickly sent some of his most trusted sorcerers to check them out. It didn't take Gao long to learn of the secret war and its significance.

(Incidentally, the peculiar invaders were Monster Hunters sent by the Architects, seeking living raw material for their abominations. They had been monster-hunting in this juncture on a smaller scale for several years before discovery by the Lotus.)

Since learning of the secret war, Gao Zhang has widened his group's mission. Journeying to the modern juncture, his operatives studied up on Chinese history, learning that the eunuchs were eventually to be swept from power by a wave of reform. Armed with this knowledge, Gao has set about capturing feng shui sites owned by the families that the history books say will eventually oppose the Lotus so as to turn the flow of history in the favor of the Lotus. Their entry into the Secret War has alarmed the Architects and Ascended, who, as controllers of later junctures, have a vested interest in keeping history from being changed in a past juncture. Thus both groups have begun to send secret warriors into the past to protect the sites held by these families. The Ascended send Pledged intermediaries, fearing the exposure to magic. At the same time, the Guiding Hand has sent teachers back into the past to form rebel groups bent on overthrowing the corrupt government and replacing it with a benevolent government that will last for centuries. The Ascended and Architects want to stop them too, because this would also change the time stream. Meanwhile, the Lotus have learned about their adversaries and have been sending small teams of sorcerers, swordsmen and supernatural creatures into the other junctures. There they aim to cripple the Ascended, Architects, and Hand by taking from them key feng shui sites. Gao Zhang is also actively recruiting new Lotus members in these junctures and in the Inner Kingdom. If possible, he would like to conquer the feng shui sites of another juncture, thus expanding his empire across chronological lines.

Gao Zhang is a ferociously single-minded individual. From the first thing in the morning until he goes to sleep at night, he dreams about becoming more and more powerful, about having more people bowing before him and afraid of his wrath.

And when he sleeps, he dreams about more power. He is a brilliant planner, able to quickly grasp new ideas and fold them into his long-term aims. His restless mind is always searching out flaws in his own plans, worrying about possibilities he hasn't yet considered. He believes that the chief flaw in any plan is the weakness of his followers; he is not a trusting soul. He keeps close tabs on all of the other Lotus members, always on the lookout for betrayal. This makes him a hard man to fool, but also a man with no true allies. Those who serve the Lotus do so because they believe it best serves their personal ambitions. If Gao ceased to be the most powerful man in the land, he would quickly be deserted by his cronies. The fact that he is quick to execute failures and suspected traitors doesn't endear him to the rank and file, either.

Gao speaks in a funny, high-pitched voice. He is prone to gloating over his enemies and fond of evil laughter. Most of his Lotus servants emulate him in this regard.

THE FOUR MONARCHS

The trackless Netherworld does not have rulers, but if it did, those rulers would likely be the **Four Monarchs**. These individuals—each over three hundred years old—once ruled the Earth, each of them taking a quarter of the globe as his or her unchallenged domain. In a version of the 16th century where magic was commonplace, the future four monarchs were born in the rural backwaters of Northern China. Their names were Li Ting, Ming I, Huan Ken, and Pi Tui. Their father, a sorcerer who had perfected many new magical techniques, had experienced a powerful vision upon the birth of the youngest child, Pi Tui. He saw that, with his help, the four of them could successfully rise to rule the world. His vision also told him that a great calamity would likely befall him just as his children were on the verge of ascending their new thrones. Heedless of the risk, he pursued plans to realize this prophecy. It was a time when the Emperor of China had grown weak, with powerful local lords in the distant provinces challenging his rule. The sorcerer insinuated himself into the service of one such warlord, directing him to capture his enemies' feng shui sites. He spent the remainder of his time teaching his children the secrets of his magical arts. He taught each of them to master a single force. Li Ting learned the ways of fire; Ming I, the secrets of darkness. Huan Ken became one with thunder, and Pi Tui conquered the ways of ice. By the time they were of age, it was a simple matter for them to dispatch the local lord and usurp his forces. The four of them acted in concert, their dread occult powers making them infamous throughout the land. Entire armies surrendered at their mere appearance on the battlefield. Within a matter of years, half of China lay at their feet. Combining their awesome abilities with their father's acute sense of which feng shui sites were best to capture, they continued to roll through Asia and expanded their empire. But their father insisted that none of them could call themselves monarchs until the entire world paid them homage.

The four siblings became increasingly fractious as their successes continued. A series of arguments caused them to split up their forces. Their father remained even-handed, providing each of them with crucial geomantic and strategic advice. Pi Tui expanded northwards, conquering what we would think of as Russia and then North America. Li Ting went south, eventually declaring himself lord of India, the Middle East, and Africa. Huan Ken took Europe. Ming I kept south Asia, and added South America to her holdings. When all of the world was effectively under their sway, they went to their father and insisted that he participate in their coronation: even he could no longer say that they did not deserve to be known as monarchs.

The father then grew nervous, remembering the vision he had witnessed: disaster would befall him when his children became kings and queens. He stalled them, inventing pretext after pretext to avoid crowning them. After a period of years, the siblings gathered for an unusual show of unity. Their father was cheating them of their promised destinies. They came to a grim conclusion: He would never see them crowned. They would have to declare their own titles. Knowing that this would anger him, they decided that they would have to kill him. If they allowed him to live, he would surely swear vengeance upon him. And he was the only person alive who knew the locations of all of their most important feng shui sites. None of the siblings knew of the others' sites but their father, who had identified them in the first place, had the weaknesses of all committed to memory. They all had reason to fear his wrath; until they disposed of him, he held power over them.

The four invited their father to a ceremony of reconciliation, announcing that they had resolved their old differences. The father, overjoyed, should have suspected that only the need to destroy him could unite them so. But he was too filled with fatherly pride to see that this was so. He arrived for a feast and found an ambush. Li Ting burned his flesh. Ming I stole the light from his heart and mind. Huan Ken turned his bones to powder. Pi Tui scourged him with darts of ice.

Even as he lay dying before them, the father gave to them the last nugget of information he had been hoarding. He gasped out the locations of entrances to the Netherworld, and told them that they would have to learn its ways if they were to hold onto the crowns they had won for themselves. He pronounced them the greatest kings and queens that had ever lived, and then died thinking of the truth of his long-ago vision. As life passed from his body, a terrible smile twisted itself across his face.

The four soon staged coronation ceremonies for themselves, during which they officially opened their grand and impossible residences. Ming I demolished the Forbidden City of past emperors, building in its place a towering edifice of pure and solid darkness; she was henceforth known as **Queen of the Darkness Pagoda**. Huan Ken similarly razed the Vatican and replaced it with a castle built of storm clouds: he named himself **King of the Thunder Pagoda** and Pope to boot. In the middle of the Bering Strait, Pi Tui erected a razor-edged city of frozen water, declaring herself **Queen of the Ice Pagoda**. Li Ting replaced Jerusalem with a palace of fire, calling himself **King of the Fire Pagoda**.

The horror of their act of patricide had driven an impaling spear into any hope of unity between the four. Each blamed the others for making the terrible decision and striking the truly fatal blows. They deceived their own hearts, each coming to believe that his or her involvement in the plot had been entered into under protest. Their old rivalries hardened into pure hatred and malice. In the years that followed, the four explored the Netherworld, but only to gain advantage over the others. They waged extensive and utterly pointless wars against one another, expending great resources to temporarily score feng shui sites from one another. Their father had balanced their empires superbly; each of them had an equal amount of chi, and therefore could not prosper against one another. Despite this fact they fought on, continuing in this manner for centuries. Elixirs of immortality given to them by their father enabled them to outlive their subjects and prolong their endless, four-way squabble. Their mutual enmity blinded them to the real meaning of their father's dying warning. They did not think to expand their empire across the timestream by invading other junctures. This was the source of their downfall.

Although they had token forces of innerwalkers, the four monarchs were busy fighting one another when the true threat to their power broke out in an earlier time. Rebels against their rule joined forces with the progenitors of the Ascended in the 13th century to seize certain feng shui sites from their current controllers, setting off a critical shift. The success of the Ascended fostered a series of social changes that led to the Renaissance and the loss of magic in the world. This changed all later junctures, including the 20th century of the four monarchs. They awoke on March 10th, 1988 to find themselves non-entities in a completely-changed world, a bewildering place of automobiles, telephones, and fast-food restaurants. Because they had visited the Netherworld, they still remembered their past identities. But they were shadows of their former selves: the immortality elixir was wearing off, and their magic powers were greatly weakened. Crippled with unnatural age, all four of them made it to the nearest gates to the Netherworld where they began plotting their comeback.

It is in the Netherworld that they remain. As explained on p. 202, the power to reshape the Netherworld to one's wishes depends on the number of feng shui sites one has ever been attuned to. As each of them had been attuned to a quarter of the important feng shui sites of the world, they immediately became forces to be reckoned with in the Inner Kingdom. They created replicas of their magical palaces. They summoned their innerwalking former servants to their sides. They recruited other Netherworlders to join them as vassals. They have been in the Netherworld for eight years now. Although they periodically declare an interest in working together to recapture their erased glories, old habits die hard. Much of the intrigue and danger in the Netherworld itself is a result of infighting between the four monarchs.

Ming I, Queen of the Darkness Pagoda, is a cruel and ominous figure. Although born Northern Chinese, she was strongly influenced by her time spent as ruler of the South American native empires. She became enamored of the Aztec belief systems, and installed in her palace a network of priests to their bloodthirsty sun god; they serve as her advisers and bureaucrats. Human sacrifice is her favorite means of disposing of enemies and punishing disobedient or incompetent minions. Ming I regards palace intrigue as a spectator sport, and enjoys nothing more than to set ambitious priestlings in con-

Chapter 15

tention for her favors. Ming I lost an arm during her early years as a conqueror on Earth, when she still personally led her armies on the battlefield. She replaced this arm with a magical limb of pure darkness; this is the basis of her awesome abilities in physical combat. Like the other four monarchs, she is a whirlwind of destruction in junctures where magic works in its original, uncorrupted form. When she ventures into the juncture of the Architects, the arm manifests as an unpredictable cybernetic device. Ming I has a sharp, acerbic wit, and enjoys playing verbal games with opponents. Her plans are usually subtle or convoluted. She arrogantly regards herself as a brilliant thinker. Although all of the four monarchs want their old timeline back, she is particularly bitter about the loss of her earthly influence. She reserves special hatred for the Ascended; when not plotting against her siblings, she's attempting to undermine the hegemony of the transformed animals. The Jammers are an important secondary foe; a group dedicated to the permanent eradication of magic throughout the timestream is an obvious threat to her plans. The Queen of the Darkness Pagoda maintains an on-gain, off-again alliance with the Eaters of the Lotus. She and Lotus leader Gao Zhang (see p. 179) have a curious relationship in which each joins with the other for temporary benefit while openly declaring an intention to eventually outwit the other. They are bound together by an interesting mixture of admiration and contempt. They betray one another regularly, but seem to bear no grudges.

> The critical shift that erased the Four Monarchs from history is an excellent example of a worst-case scenario (from their perspective, at least), and is exactly what the player characters will be trying to avoid. Should a critical shift occur in favor of the Architects, for example, by 2056 they'd probably be the rulers of a thousand-year-old global empire with high technology beyond our wildest dreams and a totalitarian government that could not be brought down by any means short of another critical shift: bad news all around. Look at the example of the Four Monarchs, secret warriors, and learn…

Huan Ken, King of the Thunder Pagoda, is a tempestuous soul who lives for the recognition of others. Of the four monarchs, he is the one most in love with kingly trappings. His long association with feudal Europe has made him the most Western of the group. He styles his fighting servants as knights and squires, having created an elaborate series of knightly ranks for his minions to vie for. He hosts regular feasts and festivals, complete with jousting tournaments. He pays lip service to the ideals of chivalry, which doesn't stop him from behaving in an utterly ruthless manner when his hold on power is at stake. Huan Ken also pays lip service to medieval Christian principles, claiming for himself the title of Pope as well as King of Europe In Exile. In practice, this means that he is likely to burn his enemies as heretics—after all, opposing the Pope is heresy, isn't it? Huan Ken is quick to anger, and equally quick to forgive an opponent who displays a proper attitude of boot-licking towards him. He is the least organized and thoughtful of the four monarchs; he tends to react to the schemes of the others rather than forming long-range plans of his own. When his honor is insulted or self-image threatened, he will ally with anyone who has a realistic chance of helping him further his ends. In the past, he has associated with the Architects, the Guiding Hand, and even the Jammers. He usually ends up being taken advantage of in such arrangements. In personal combat, he is recognized as the most effective of the four monarchs, which is saying a great deal. He is proud of the fact that no one has survived a one-on-one fight with him.

Li Ting, King of the Fire Pagoda, is the calmest and most collected of the four monarchs. He is proud of the fact that he always acts with rational calculation, never allowing mere emotion to enter into his decision-making. He resolved to cut himself off from all emotional concerns as a way of dealing with his participation in the murder of his father. It could be argued, given his callous and vicious treatments of opponents, that he merely gave in completely to his dark side. Just don't say that to his face. Li Ting denies the existence of all morality, and is a fierce disbeliever in all matters of religion. He is the only thing that matters in the world. He does not bother to disguise this attitude, which makes it hard to attract followers. The typical Fire King follower is someone who has done something terrible and now wants to sidestep all future responsibility by surrendering his will to a charismatic authority—and Li Ting is nothing if not charismatic. He understands human weakness with unrelenting accuracy, and is always effective at exploiting it. Li Ting sometimes lends support to the Jammers, but only when their current strategy will further his own goals. He won't aid Battlechimp Potemkin (p. 189) in instances where they actually have a chance of lessening the amount of magic in the world. Li Ting maintains occasional contacts with top Architect arcanotechnician Curtis Boatman (p. 174); this connection is unknown to Buropresident Johann Bonengel. In combat, Li Ting wields a ferocious array of fire magics. Back on Earth, he was notorious for

Groups

burning entire armies with a single gesture, but his power has ebbed dramatically since that time.

Pui Ti, Queen of the Ice Pagoda, is the only one of the four monarchs who genuinely regrets her father's murder. She sees her mission in life as controlling the excesses of her siblings. She maintains her icy grip on power in order to have a base from which to do this. She also wants to atone for her sins in other ways. She does not actually want the timestream changed to bring the four monarchs back to power on Earth, although she has never shared this fact with her siblings. She thinks the world is better off with the four monarchs ruling only chunks of the Netherworld. She is willing to participate in the secret war, but sees the struggle only as it relates to the fate of her brothers and sister. If an action will thwart one of them, or make it harder for the whole lot to return to their earthly thrones, she'll support those undertaking it. Otherwise, she will not expend her resources. Until their recent destruction, she was an occasional patron of the Dragons. They were routed while on a mission she had declined to take part in. Pui Ti may or may not be feeling deep remorse over this turn of events. Her manner is definitely that

Illustration by Ralph Horsley

of an ice queen, aloof and distant; it is always difficult to tell what she is feeling or thinking. She tends to keep her plans to herself, and can be maddeningly stingy with information or advice.

Although she can seem very unhelpful at times, she is the only one of the four monarchs who will act as a reasonably loyal patron for player characters. As a leader, she is fair and just if not lovable. Her subjects have a right to due process, as well as certain limited rights specified in a written Constitution. They tend to place their loyalty in this document and the principles the queen upholds; she herself inspires admiration and respect but not affection. Although she has not personally entered combat since before the critical shift that brought her to the Netherworld, she is known to employ a sorcerous fighting style which uses thrown ice blades to deadly effect.

THE GUIDING HAND

The 1850s are a trying time for Chinese traditionalists. Long trained to believe that they are the only civilization worth even thinking about, the Chinese ruling class is now face-to-face with imminent defeat. The major colonial powers are on their doorstep, demanding the right to sell their goods in China. They back up these demands with gunships, and the product they most wish to sell is opium. The British in particular are running a lucrative triangular trading enterprise. They ship opium from their Indian colony to China, where they trade it for tea. Then they sell the tea to their domestic customers in Europe. This is making some Britons rich, but it's destroying the lives of legions of Chinese addicts. The Emperor, like most Chinese, wants the practice stopped. But the results of the recent Opium War, with Britain triumphant, has proven him powerless. It doesn't take a prophet to see the beginning of a long decline for the vaunted Chinese empire.

One secret society has decided to do something about this. **The Guiding Hand** was founded in 1810 by a group of monks with political leanings. They foresaw the degradation of their great civilization, and decided to fight to reverse it. They want to see China restored to its former might. Initially, they saw its problems as moral weakness on the part of their own people. They created various cells and study groups (known as Golden Candle Societies) to inculcate the Chinese people, from peasants to merchants to government officials, with the spiritual strength needed to resist foreign domination. Through these recruits they launched diplomatic initiatives, exerted pressure on the Emperor, and even engaged in covert sabotage against the representatives of colonial power. Despite their fervor and clever tactics, they got nowhere.

It was only when a new leader, the Perfect Master **Quan Lo**, took control of the Guiding Hand that they began to make progress towards their goals. Quan Lo, an elderly kung fu master of the Shaolin school, was well schooled in the arts of geomancy. Despite their reverence for ancient Chinese tradition, the previous leaders of the society had regarded feng shui as nothing more than a superstition. But Quan Lo knew better. He had already embarked on some side enterprises of his own, sending his Shaolin students to investigate the ownership of the most potent feng shui sites in China's coastal region. Time after time, they discovered that the feng shui sites were controlled either by European companies, Chinese allies of the Europeans, or members of a venerable secret society known as the Jade Wheel Society. No wonder they had been so successful in undermining the very foundations of Chinese life! Quan Lo realized that no political strategy or covert action would be of any use to the Guiding Hand while these feng shui sites remained in the clutches of the enemy. Upon his election to the top spot in the society, he shifted its strategy to the acquisition of these sites for the Hand. Once they controlled enough of these sites, the tide would naturally turn against the foreign invader, and the Chinese people would return to a golden age of traditional Confucian values.

Unfortunately, the Guiding Hand found that its resources were too limited to mount direct assaults on these feng shui sites. The Jade Wheel Society was even better connected in government circles than they were. When their kung fu warriors did take over a site, government troops were immediately dispatched to retake it. They could not capture the sites through political intrigue, either. The Hand was stymied.

So it set out to investigate the Jade Wheel Society, eventually discovering who was really behind them: the descendants of supernatural animals, a group known as The Ascended. Quan Lo was clever enough not to tip his hand immediately. He kept the Jade Wheel leaders under surveillance, learning many interesting things about them. He learned that many of the most influential European traders were members of a similar secret society known as the Order of the Wheel, and that they were also part of the transformed animal conspiracy. The Ascended were driving the effort to subject the rest of the world to Europe's colonial yoke; they wanted to get the entire planet industrialized as quickly as possible as part of their plan to prevent magic from ever coming back. As they worked to find some way of successfully fighting this centuries-old conspiracy, Quan Lo's operatives stumbled across gateways to the Netherworld.

Guiding Hand members travelled to the other open junctures, appalled by what they saw. The contemporary world was a chaotic and decadent place, where Confucian ideals had been trampled by the Communists in mainland China and the capitalists throughout the rest of South Asia. The authoritarian future of the Architects was even worse. The Guiding Hand came to see themselves as the only hope of civilized values. They changed their goals. Now it was no longer enough to get the foreign invaders out of 1850 China; they had to change the entire timestream to make it an orderly place where scholarly virtues and respect for elders ruled. The greed and villainy that permeated the other junctures would be snuffed out, replaced by wisdom and self-restraint.

Their strategy was twofold. First, they would pursue long-range plans in the normal flow of time. Instead of working for immediate victory in 1850, the Guiding Hand members would emulate the success of their arch-rivals, the Jade Wheel Society. They would slowly build influence, creating a structure that would allow them to grow from generation to generation without being discovered by their enemies. They would use their knowledge of future history to recruit members of families which would eventually become influential. If the history of the future told them that a man would become a prominent official in the Chinese Communist party, or a major figure in Hong Kong business circles by the end of the 20th century, they would recruit his great-grandfather in 1850. So although their influence in 1850 was limited by their lack of feng shui sites, they would use forewarnings gained as innerwalkers to cement their power in the future. Thus the Guiding Hand, like the Ascended, has permanent power bases in more than one juncture. A Guiding Hand secret warrior from 1850 can draw support from Guiding Hand members in our contemporary world—some of whom may be his own descendants.

In the secret war, the Hand targeted the contemporary era as the juncture in which it would be easiest to snatch feng shui sites. Compared to 1850s China, they see our era as lawless. They also see the Ascended of our time as complacent and overextended, compared to those of the heady days of colonial expansion and industrial revolution. They have been able to take a number of important sites from the Ascended, particularly through political manipulation in mainland China. If the Hand has one major impediment to its success in the secret war, it is its Sinocentric view of the world. They still think that only what happens in China really matters. They have little interest in or understanding of the Western world and its way of thinking. They want to wash away every trace of Western influence in both the 1850 and current junctures; they think that this alone will be enough to stem the advance of the Architects and prevent their terrible future, in which all traces of Chinese culture are absorbed into a dreary and oppressive single world culture.

> The Guiding Hand hold twentieth-century Hong Kong in particular disdain, viewing it as a veritable Sodom of the modern world. What bothers the Hand the most about Hong Kong is not that it is a thriving example of Western corruption and lax morality—rather, it's the fact that Hong Kong is a thriving example of Western corruption and lax morality *right in their own backyard*. The Hand dislike Hong Kong in the 1850s enough as it is, and once they saw what the city would become a century later it just confirmed their suspicions that the world was heading right down the toilet. Hand members who encounter the PCs in modern-day Hong Kong will complain constantly about the trash in the streets, the prostitutes, the garish architecture, the smell of the air, the ridiculous "high technology," and how all the translations of Confucius are so shoddy.

The Hand has also made a minor foray into the 69 juncture, which is culturally much closer to them than junctures a mere hundred or two hundred years later. They are setting up small warrior units to take sites from the Lotus. Their plan is to set off long-range social changes that will ripple forward to alter their own juncture, so that its version of the Chinese empire will become spiritually stronger and therefore better able to resist foreign invasion.

Although the player characters may be tempted to think of the Guiding Hand as a potential ally, they will sooner or later discover that Quan Lo and his people are dedicated fanatics with a very narrow world view. Anything that does not fit their definition of virtue is dangerous and bad as far as they're concerned. Extreme discipline is one of their highest virtues. Obedience to superiors and deference to elders is another. Most action heroes (and roleplaying game PCs) are too self-willed to get along in a group like the Hand. Independent thinking is strongly discouraged. Younger operatives are expected to kowtow without question to older ones, to a degree many players should consider humiliating. Even minor screw-ups result in severe punishments, usually of an embarrassing nature. Hand members or allies are expected to not only swallow such measures, but accept them with enthusiasm as improving experiences. The merest sign of disrespect to an authority within the Hand is considered a major screw-up. So is any sign of modern thinking, such as a fondness for technology or pop culture. Sorcerers, supernatural creatures, transformed animals, and cyborgs are all considered to be irredeemably corrupt, and are ineligible to join the Hand, or even ally with it temporarily. It goes without saying that most PCs would not want to live in the perfect society that the Hand is striving for.

The leadership of the Hand also considers itself to be beyond reproach. Although it is by no means as openly and obviously sinister as the Lotus or Architects, it is willing to sacrifice both its own operatives and innocents in the name of what it considers to be a greater good. Quan Lo himself speaks quietly and humbly, but is an uncompromising moralist. He views anyone who does not share his idea of the perfect world as either an enemy to be destroyed, or a dupe to be temporarily used and then tossed aside as befits his lax morality.

THE JAMMERS

The Jammers are a loosely-organized group of rebels and subversives from the year 2056, dedicated to the downfall of the totalitarian world government led by the Architects. Opposition to the thuggish regime of the Buro is surprisingly rare: surprising, that is, to those who do not know the importance of feng shui sites. The Buro maintains power over the masses through its superior supply of the life energy known as chi but almost no one, even in the government itself, knows this. Knowledge of the feng shui secret is what separates the Jammers from the many other isolated revolutionary groups that have popped up to challenge the Buro and been quickly squashed. The Jammers know that attacks against the obvious centers of government power, like the police or the propaganda networks, are futile. Unless they can cut off the Buro from their source of chi power, their efforts are pointless. It is this power that sways the masses, placing them in mental shackles they can't even perceive. No great historical shift can occur without an accompanying shift in chi.

The Jammers are unrepentant rationalists, ignoring the fact that the Buro's research wing (the CDCA) has discovered a scientific underpinning to magic. They find nothing more disturbing than the apparent fact that human free will and independent action mean nothing in the face of the overwhelming power of chi. They liked believing that historical events happened because of the actions of people, not due to the vagaries of some impersonal supernatural force. Unlike the other groups in the cross-time battle that forms the backdrop of the game, the Jammers don't bother trying to possess feng shui sites. In their own timeframe, they know that they haven't a chance against the abomination-packed military installations that the Buro has built on the best sites. They also haven't the resources or patience to occupy feng shui sites elsewhere in the timeline; nor does occupying a site in the ancient past or our present bring them closer to their goal of unseating the Buro. They have decided that their only hope is to go backwards in time and prevent the Buro from taking over the world by making sure there are no feng shui sites for them to build installations on in the first place. This means destroying them outright.

If it succeeds, this plan has a side effect they consider highly beneficial: it will eliminate the role of chi in human history. No longer will the winners of wars or other political conflicts be decided by who has the most chi; instead, success will hinge on who has the most courage, brains, willpower, and inner strength. Or so they believe.

The various members of the Jammers find it easy to support the elimination of chi because almost all of them are part of a very small percentage of the population who are highly resistant to the effects of magic and chi. This explains why they are still able to see the Buro as a repressive monster of an institution when the ordinary citizen, swayed by the Buro's strong feng shui, perceives it as a normal, inevitable part of daily life. If it weren't for this immunity, they'd be saluting the Buro flag and proudly singing the Buro anthem along with everyone else. There are disadvantages to being chi resistant: those with this condition can't learn or wield magic, and can't use exotic kung fu powers requiring chi. For this reason, the Jammers are highly dependent on technology. Some of them are highly-trained fighters who are quite effective without chi powers. But most are dependent on the old-fashioned persuasion capabilities of high-caliber firearms and advanced cybernetics.

The Jammers are by necessity a highly secretive organization. The Buro spends an inordinate chunk of its budget attempting to track them down. Most Jammers have now decamped to the Netherworld, where the influence of the Architects is no greater than any other historical group. The Jammers are philosophically opposed to the use of any of the arcanowave technology of the CDCA (though they readily use non-arcanowave technology), but they make an exception for the GateMaker, the field emission device that creates a temporary entrance to the Netherworld. The Jammers stole one of the original prototypes of the Gatemaker and have since built more; this allows them to move about in and out of the Netherworld and the existing junctures as desired. In their various Netherworld hideouts, they perfect new tech items and scheme to sabotage feng shui sites throughout the timestream. They train themselves in guerrilla tactics, making lightning strikes against feng shui sites and blowing them to bits with high explosives. Their tech items are heavy on offensive power, low on subtlety. Although they abhor the arcane biotechnology of the Architects, they are enthusiastic about purely technological alterations to the human form. Many Jammers are half-human, half-machine. Jammer scientists realize that the elimination of magical life energy from the world will bring about a massive wave of ill-health, and are preparing for this eventuality by developing various drugs and devices to replace chi. Conveniently enough, many of these discoveries are useful in their cross-time assault activities.

Jammers must keep a low profile even in the Netherworld, as it is largely populated by people and beings who rely heavily on magic and chi. In their zeal to prevent the Architects from coming into being, their anti-chi agenda has made them many other powerful enemies. The Eaters of the Lotus, whose power depends on magic and the summoning and control of supernatural creatures, have been hit hard several times by Jammer raids, and are now planning retaliatory measures. The Ascended would be happy if the Jammers destroyed magic, but are heavily dependent on chi; they have had to repel several Jammer raids in the present day. The Guiding Hand sees the Jammers as a force for disorder, finding their anarchistic and libertarian leanings repellent. They believe that the destruction of the Earth's chi would doom it to destruction, and consider the Jammers to be as great a threat as the Architects.

The leader and founder of the Jammers is an odd entity known as **Battlechimp Potemkin**. This genius and combat whirlwind is the result of early abortive experiments by the CDCA to produce super-soldiers by biogenetically altering primates. Formerly a normal chimpanzee, Battlechimp's head was detached from the body he was born with and attached to a formidable eight-foot body of chrome and steel, laden with various implements of extreme violence. However, he was also elevated in intelligence, sufficiently so that he rejected the orders of the Buro to fight on their behalf. He converted several CDCA scientists to his views and figured out the feng shui secret before stealing a GateMaker and heading off to build an opposition to the Buro. Battlechimp is brilliant, but uncompromising. He realizes that his efforts to change historical axioms by destroying feng shui sites will likely cause him, his allies, and countless millions of others to be erased completely from history. This does not sway him from his cause: he believes this is a small price to pay for eliminating the Buro from the timestream. For his own part, he wishes that he was never made sentient or given a grotesque killing machine for a body. This has not stopped him, a firm believer in ends justifying means, from creating other elevated-cyborg chimps. The Flying Monkey squad is one of the most-feared and effective guerrilla units in the Jammer team.

Although most of his forces are refugees from the grim future of the Architects, the weirdly charismatic Battlechimp has succeeded in drawing to his side a number of malcontents, nihilists, and magic-haters from various timeframes. Some of them serve him because they simply like to blow things up; others bear grudges against various groups in the feng shui struggle. Still others are sickly attracted by the thought of destroying Earth's life force; Battlechimp is none too picky about his servitors, figuring that he can always outsmart them when their interests diverge from his. He has managed to bring a sense of unity to his wildly diverse operatives, instilling in them a mighty contempt for the Architects, who the Jammers refer to as **Bobos**. (The term is one of Battlechimp's invention, an insult derived from the names Bonengel and Boatman: they're the top honchos of the Buro and the CDCA.)

Battlechimp runs the Jammers as a benign autocracy, issuing all important orders himself. Many Jammers serve him primarily out of personal loyalty. But he has made arrangements for the organization to continue if one of his many enemies takes him out. His lieutenant, a cyborg gorilla named **Furious George**, is his liaison to the other altered primates. His head of tech research is a defector from the CDCA named Dr. Laura Villaverde, alias **Green Rain**.

One day, says Battlechimp, when the feng shui sites are all destroyed, all people will be equal. History will finally be in the hands of individuals, for good or for ill. Maybe it will be impossible for one person to exercise power over another. Or maybe we'll all shrivel and die without chi, or maybe the world will even explode. Any of these outcomes are better than living as slaves—either to the Buro, or to arbitrary magical powers that control us like puppets.

The Jammers' motto is simple and catchy, a valuable trait given that many members are subliterate at best: "BLOW THINGS UP! BLOW THINGS UP! BLOW THINGS UP!"

Chapter 16

July 19

The minute I woke up, I knew something was wrong. And not just because I banged my head on an upper bunk that hadn't been there when I went to sleep. I knew instantly that I was somewhere else, somewhere really wrong. I heard other people breathing and snoring. My eyes adjusted to the dark, and I saw that I was in some kind of barracks. I reached under my pillow for my old friend Mr. Browning, already knowing that it wouldn't be there. That would be the least of the changes I was going to have to hip myself to real fast-like. It was a critical shift.

A few months ago, I wouldn't have known what a critical shift was. It would have rolled right over me without my even knowing that anything had changed. Just like the rest of the stiffs around me in this barracks. They had no way of knowing that history had just changed under their feet, that they'd just been slipped entire new pasts and identities. Their souls had been zapped into new bodies, and they had a pack of brand-new memories that went back all the way to childhoods that suddenly retroactively existed. But not me. I was an innerwalker now, a secret warrior. Like it or not, I still got to keep my old self, my old memories, be who I always was. Knowing what had happened was going to make it a whole lot more confusing to me than it was to them—to them, nothing had changed. But I've never believed that ignorance is bliss. Give me the real situation and let me deal with that. With or without Mr. Browning.

So the deal obviously was that someone had just captured some serious feng shui sites back in a past time juncture, and the historical changes had rippled all the way to 1996, making it a whole different 1996 than I knew. The first thing was to find the rest of the team, figure out whether this was a shift in our favor or not, and then find an entrance to the Netherworld to confer with the Prof. Somehow I was just naturally assuming that this was not gonna be in our favor, since we weren't expecting it and all. But I'm just a pessimistic kind of guy, you know?

Being in a barracks was not a good sign as far as I was concerned. That meant I was a mook in some big combo—or at least expected to act like a mook. Mooking not being my scene, I decided to split. Barracks being barracks, I was figuring on someone trying to stop me.

I looked down at what I was wearing. Some nasty flannel stuff. Not remotely GQ. More evidence that this was a bum shift. Okay, I had to find an exit, grab some weaponry, and then talk to someone and get myself informed as to the new ground rules.

I slipped out of my bunk, attempting to be as quiet as a mouse. But the guy above me was awake.

"Hey, Rennie, where you going?" the guy whispered.

I had never been a Rennie in all my life, but this guy obviously meant me. Anyway, that wasn't what flash-froze my heart to the rest of my insides. It was the guy's voice.

Steve's voice. I was so freaked I forgot myself completely.

"Steve! What are you doing here? What's with the hair, man?"

"Rennie, what the hell are you talking about? You dreaming?"

"Uh, yeah, right, that's it, I must have been..."

"Who's this Steve character, Rennie?"

Half of my mind had figured out what was going on, but unfortunately it wasn't the half doing the talking.

"You're Steve. Steve, don't you remember me?"

"'Course I remember you, Rennie, but my name ain't Steve, it's Joe."

I jumped out of the bunk to get a look at him. Sure enough, it was Steve. He had a funny haircut and all, but it was Steve. Or at least, history's new version of Steve. It was a case of lateral reincarnation, just like the Prof had told me about. It sounded freaky at the time, but not half so freaky as actually seeing it before my eyes.

"Hey, man, pipe down and get back in your bunk. You know Sergeant Tsien's gunning for your hide already. He catches you even breathing wrong, and it'll be the stockade—"

I felt bad about having to clock Steve like that. As I hotfooted it for a window, I consoled myself that he wasn't really my Steve anymore. And wouldn't be until I helped get the timestream back in order.

Wait—Sergeant Tsien? Oh, man...

CHAPTER 16

Time War

THE UNSEEN WORLD

Feng Shui uses time travel as a device; it allows us to mix and match characters from our favorite Hong Kong movies. Ancient fu masters can stand side-by-side with modern mob-busters and futuristic cyborgs. The price of having all of these characters together is having to deal with the complexities that always bedevil time travel stories. The secret war is a fight in which the combatants are trying to change history all over the timeline, and that can make things complicated. We've tied the whole idea of the war for feng shui sites into our basic idea of how time travel works in a way that we think eliminates most of the paradoxes and hassles of running a time-spanning storyline. That means wrapping your head around some difficult ideas at first, though. Once you get a handle on them, you'll find that the whole time travel deal enables you to keep the setting fresh and surprising. Whenever the following material gets too twisty for you, remember that it's all just a giant justification for characters with all of these funky fu powers, high-caliber firearms, and bizarre futuristic devices to use them on each other.

First we'll explain how time and the universe work, and then we'll give you some pointers for incorporating all of this high-faluting theory into your series.

JUNCTURES

The hidden war for the world's feng shui sites takes place across the boundaries of time. Most people think that time is linear, that events in the past cannot be changed, and that actions in the present lead to an as-yet undetermined future. Really, the timeline is more like a pretzel. The truth is that the course of history can always be changed by those with access to the Netherworld. The secret warrior learns to think of "the present day" in vastly different terms than the unknowing people around him.

You can't just go anywhere you want in the past or future. There are only a few time periods you can travel to at any given moment. Each of these is called a juncture. For the last little while, there have been four of them: 69, 1850, the modern day, and 2056. For participants in the secret struggle, the different time periods connected to one another through the Netherworld are more like different locations than distinct points on a straight line of cause and effect. Going to a different time is like going to a different place.

Example: Dirk Wisely lives in our contemporary world. He finds a portal to the Netherworld in the dumpster behind his apartment building. He can go through the portal into the Netherworld. By traveling through space in the Netherworld, he can go to portals that lead to 69, 1850, or 2056. He can't go to 2,500 BC, 1947, or 2321, because there simply aren't any portals from the Netherworld that will take him there.

Time passes at the same rate within the four junctures and the Netherworld. When a day passes in our juncture, it passes in 69, 1850, 2056, and in the Netherworld. Think of time as a series of parallel lines. You can travel from one line to another, but you can never move backwards on any of the lines. Everyone moves forwards on the lines at the same rate. If something bad happens to you, there's no way for you to go back in time just a tiny bit to prevent it from having happened.

Example: Dirk and his buddies get involved in a fight with Lotus forces in 69 AD. In early March of that year, they are accosted by a sorcerer who kills one of Dirk's friends. Dirk and company can't go to February of 69 and kill the sorcerer to prevent him from being able to kill Dirk's pal in March. Once time has passed in any of the junctures, there's no way to return to that point.

Dirk brings his friend's body back to the current juncture for the funeral. He left for the 69 juncture 12 days ago. When he returns to our time, 12 days have passed. There is no way for him to go back into our time 13 days earlier to warn his buddy not to go to 69 with him, either.

> ### We're Living in the Past
> It's 1996. No, really.
>
> Throughout this book, you'll find references to "the contemporary era," "the modern juncture," and so on. In *Feng Shui*, these refer to 1996. Trust us, it's much simpler for everyone. With the contemporary era set at 1996 we know that we're talking about pre-takeover Hong Kong, for example, and sourcebooks that talk about the modern world won't go out of date every time a banana republic or former Soviet bloc nation falls.
>
> Of course, you don't *have* to make the contemporary era 1996 if you'd rather use whatever year it is now. It's really up to you. If you decide to use another year, though, you'll also have to decide whether the intervening time has passed in the other junctures.
>
> That's right: All of the junctures currently open—AD 69, 1850, 1996, and 2056—move forward steadily as time passes. We're assuming that the specific years referenced in this book (and others) are the point at which your series begins. If a year passes in your series, the junctures will now be AD 70, 1851, 1997, and 2057. We refer to those specific years to identify the junctures, and we'll use the same years in *Feng Shui* supplements. But you should always localize these dates to your own series as needed. If your series has gone on for two years of game time, the first juncture gates will lead to AD 71. If a *Feng Shui* product describes events in AD 69, assume it's referring to AD 71 instead.

Although there are currently four primary junctures connected to the Netherworld, this is not a constant number. Sometimes there are more than four junctures; sometimes fewer. No one, even in the Inner Kingdom, really understands the mechanism behind the opening or closing of particular junctures. They do not remain open for predictable periods, and there is no apparent pattern that explains how the junctures are chosen.

This doesn't stop Netherworlders from trying to come up with theories to explain this basic fact of their existence. Many think that whoever discovers the final secrets of time will be able to conquer all junctures, ending the secret war forever. What is known is that whenever a new juncture opens up, it becomes a battlefield of the secret war, with many opposing groups scrambling to capture and attune themselves to its feng shui sites.

Junctures refer to particular places as well as particular times. Most gates to the 69 and 1850 junctures lead to physical locations within mainland China; gates to our time usually end up in Hong Kong or other bustling urban centers of the Pacific Rim; exits to 2056 most often come out in the highly industrialized Northern Hemisphere. There is no obvious theory to explain this, either. Presumably, there could be a portal to any location and any juncture somewhere in the Netherworld if the GM needs there to be one.

When you become a secret warrior and start traveling from juncture to juncture, your definition of "immediate future" changes. It encompasses events that may take place in the Netherworld or any of the four junctures. You might say "They're going to attack tomorrow!" but be referring to something that happened two thousand years ago.

CHANGING HISTORY

One common strategy in the secret war is to thwart your enemies by changing history out from under them. It is possible to do things in one juncture that change circumstances in later junctures. This can be difficult, because you have to seize feng shui sites in order to do so. The tide of history always flows in the favor of those who control the best feng shui sites. You can change the minor details of what you consider the past, but if you don't cause a new group of people to control those crucial sites, the big trends will remain unchanged.

For example, our modern era used to be one where magic was commonplace. The world belonged to the Four Monarchs, powerful sorcerers who controlled all of the best feng shui sites. But then a new juncture opened up briefly, one that led to the eleventh century. Enemies of the Four Monarchs traveled through the Netherworld to this new juncture. In the 11th century, the Monarchs hadn't yet been born, much less risen to power. Their foes allied themselves with the league of transformed animals that became the Ascended. Together, these groups fought with the various warlords and potentates who controlled the feng shui sites of the 1200s, and grabbed enough sites to change the course of history. They wanted magic to go away, and it did. In order to cement that change, they had to make sure that they held onto the sites for many centuries to come.

The suppression of magic was a significant enough change to alter all of subsequent history, including that of the 20th century. It led to the Renaissance, Enlightenment, and Industrial Revolution. Because of the seizure of feng shui sites in an earlier juncture, the timeline that had the Monarchs in control was erased. They lost their sites indirectly: According to the new timeline, they would never have been able to seize them in the first place.

When vast changes like this ripple through the timestream, only a few individuals even remember the erased version of history. Specifically, only people who have been to the Netherworld retain their memories of past versions of history that have been erased. To them, the historical changes take place instantly.

Example: Li Zheng remembers the days when the 20th century was ruled by the Monarchs, because he was an active visitor to the Netherworld at that time. He didn't participate in the battles that led to the erasure of the Monarch version of history. He just woke up one morning in a vastly different world, one with televisions, cars, and guns. An experienced secret warrior, he immediately recognized what had happened to him. Like any sensible innerwalker, he sprang into action: he started looking for a library so he could quickly catch up on this new version of history.

If he were to stop people on the street and ask them, they would not have noticed what to him was a sudden shift in reality. Those people have lived their lives out in standard, linear time, having been born in this "new" world and lived their every moment in it.

ELASTIC HISTORY

Because they do not alter the flow of chi in the world, activities which do not cause feng shui sites to change hands cannot transform history in any significant way. They may change the personal histories of a few families, but will not alter any great trends. History is made by those to whom great chi flows, and if the chi flow is unchanged, no amount of tinkering around the edges will alter more than a few footnotes in the record books.

Example: Dirk reads a history book which mentions a notoriously corrupt Imperial official whose actions precipitated a bloody uprising in 1862. Appalled by the account of the violent rebellion, Dirk travels to the 1850 juncture, finds the official twelve years before he is to commit his infamous deeds, and shoots him. Satisfied at his exercise of rough justice, Dirk returns to the present day and picks up the same history book to see how much it is changed. To his chagrin, he learns that another official did exactly the same thing as the one he killed, and that the rebellion happened exactly as before. Because his actions did not involve a change in chi flow, they had only a minor effect on subsequent events.

History is elastic. When the timeline is disturbed by actions in a past juncture, history is forced to reshape itself. It does so in the most economical manner possible, creating a new pattern which is as close to the old one as possible given the changed circumstances.

Example: Dirk goes to the library to research the family tree of Adolf Hitler. He wants to wipe out Hitler's ancestors in 1850, thus preventing the dictator from coming to power. He does his homework and commits the grisly deed, reasoning that the ends justify the means. He returns to his home juncture, expecting to find out that World War II and the Holocaust have been erased from the timeline. No such luck: a man with a different name and personal history only slightly different from Hitler's rose to create the Nazi party; history unfolded in a virtually identical manner. Because no feng shui sites changed hands, history has returned as closely as possible to its former shape, despite Dirk's actions.

However, when feng shui sites change hands, the changes in subsequent junctures can be much more dramatic. Individuals who increase their chi energy by participating in successful struggles for feng shui sites will have history altered in their favor. Those who lose feng shui sites may find themselves in radically worse straits when they return to subsequent junctures.

Example: Donald Fong is a reformed gangster of our era who grew up in the squalid Mongkok area of Kowloon. He journeys back to 1850 and participates in a fight that allows local peasants to wrest a major feng shui site from the forces of the Guiding Hand. Unknown to him, the peasant leader is his own great-great-grandfather. The battle concluded, Donald and his allies step back into the Netherworld and into our own juncture.

When Donald gets back, his circumstances are greatly changed. He heads to his crummy apartment in a rancid Hong Kong district and discovers that he is no longer a tenant there. He seeks out the superintendent of the building, who is startled to see him and treats him with fearful deference. After interrogating the man and checking out the business sections of local papers, he discovers that he's the owner of the building, and of many others. At a loss, he must research his own past to find out who he is. Hitting the library, he finds out that his family history has changed. In this unfamiliar version of his life, Donald's great-great-grandfather became prosperous, passing on his success through the generations. Donald grew up not in a filthy brothel, but a wealthy household. He finds out that he has a plush luxury apartment—and a loving wife and children!

Because he has visited the Netherworld, Donald still retains all of his memories of a past that no longer exists. Only his comrades in the secret war remember the old Donald. If he wishes to continue the life of the new Donald, he must bluff his way through it.

Eventually this sort of identity dislocation strikes most secret warriors. Many respond to it by withdrawing into the Netherworld, abandoning lives they no longer recognize. It often makes them withdrawn and reckless, throwing themselves heedlessly into battle because they feel they have nothing to lose. Hence the often-quoted Netherworld proverb: "Only he who is ignorant of time's truth always knows who he is."

On the other hand, some secret warriors learn to fake their way through these new identities and come to prefer them.

Lateral Reincarnation

The classic example of paradox in time travel stories is of the individual who goes back in time to kill his own ancestor so that he would never have been born, in which case he couldn't have killed his ancestor, in which case he was born, in which case he could have killed his ancestor, in which case he would never have been born, yadda yadda yadda. While it's highly unlikely that any of your PCs will want to kill their ancestors, it is likely that your players will ask you how time works by using this example. Well, actually, some players might do it just to drive you nuts...

Although the timestream is elastic, sometimes it just can't recreate itself so that all of the people who existed before a change still exist in the same incarnations after a change. The existence of reincarnation, or soul-recycling as some wags call it, provides a means for the timestream to accommodate these rare events and avoid paradox. Souls are permanent and cannot be wiped out by changes from one juncture to the next. Particular incarnations and personal histories, on the other hand, are impermanent and can be changed. Such changes are called **lateral reincarnations**. When a shift in the timestream causes an individual to be erased from history, that person's soul and consciousness are recycled into a new incarnation.

Let's return to the example of Donald Fong, and assume that the fight for the feng shui site in 1850 has a drastically different outcome. Instead of helping his great-great-grandfather to victory, he makes a stupid error and gets his ancestor killed. When he returns to modern Hong Kong, he discovers that Donald Fong does not exist. His apartment is now registered to a Donald Wong. Upon further investigation, he finds out that he is Donald Wong! He researches his family history, and discovers that he now has an entirely different set of ancestors, and a completely different personal past. However, it is a past that nonetheless leads to his living alone in a lousy apartment in a bad neighborhood of Hong Kong. As before, he has a set of memories belonging to Donald Fong, an individual who now never existed. There are many curious parallels between the lives of Donald Fong and Donald Wong: both grew up in rough straits in Kowloon, both served as street soldiers to the same gangster, both share the same group of friends. But from the point of view of those who are unaware of the Netherworld, Wong exists—while Fong does not and never did.

The curious parallels are a result of the organizing impulse inherent in chi energy, which underlies the timestream and its laws just as it does all other things. Chi energy is not, as far as anyone can tell, directed by any sort of intelligence. But it does tend to arrange messy things into nice, neat patterns. This makes no difference to those unaware of the Inner Kingdom and the secret war; they change incarnations without even realizing that their past lives have been transformed. It is only innerwalkers who have to reconcile their own memories of one incarnation with everyone else's memories of another. Sometimes it is less disorienting for secret warriors to find themselves in entirely new identities than versions of themselves with subtly or greatly changed personal histories.

Thus, innerwalkers returning to a greatly-altered home juncture may find that none of their friends or family members still exist: according to centuries of reshaped history, they were never born, nor were generations of their ancestors. However, if they run into individuals with the souls of their former loved ones, they will instantly recognize them. Their

> Like most parts of *Feng Shui*, you can look at reincarnation from an action-movie perspective. Popular actors who appear in action flicks often play similar characters from film to film; think of John Wayne's many grizzled, grouchy cowboys, or Arnold Schwarzenagger's endless stream of tough guys. You can visualize reincarnation as being a similar circumstance: the same actor is playing the new PC. His name is different, he's got a different history or whatever, but he has that same glint in his eye, the same wisecracking manner, and maybe the same signature phrase he says before he kills someone. In action movies, you're never dead as long as you're popular.

appearances, their mannerisms, their personality traits, and even their favorite catch phrases may recur from incarnation to incarnation. This does not mean that they will recognize the innerwalkers who remember them. But they may feel an inexplicable connection to someone their old incarnation loved—or an unaccountable loathing for a former incarnation's enemy. Such **soul memories**, as innerwalkers call them, are an excellent source of melodramatic hooks. For example, love at first sight is a common occurrence in the world of *Feng Shui*; it is almost always the meeting of two people who were lovers in a previous version of their current juncture.

Feng Shui characters will have plenty of opportunities to get themselves killed outside of their home junctures. Being an innerwalker is no guarantee of immortality. Lateral incarnation does not help secret warriors who are slain outside of their normal place in the time stream. To their loved ones in their home juncture, it is as if they vanished one day and never returned. When characters die in the course of an episode, their players retire their character sheets to the great folder in the sky, and create new characters.

Innerwalkers are never retroactively changed by shifts in history. This means that you don't get to muck around with the PC's abilities! They're still the versions of themselves they remember from the first time they entered the Netherworld. They may discover that others remember vastly different pasts than they do, however—pasts consistent with the new version of history.

Example: Everyone else may think of him as Donald Wong, but Donald Fong has not been altered by the time shift. He still has the same memories and abilities he did before the shift occurred. He does not share Fong's memories and experiences.

Reincarnation and New Characters

The metaphysics of the *Feng Shui* setting allow not just for lateral reincarnation, but plain old ordinary reincarnation as well. When creating a new character after an old one is slain, a player may choose to make the new character a reincarnation of the old one. This has no game benefits; the new character does not share the memories of the old one, is not entitled to use his equipment or other property, and does not carry over any accumulated experience points to the new character creation process. However, some players may think it's fun to play a reincarnation of an old favorite character. The reincarnation may look like the old character and share mannerisms, speech patterns, or other quirks.

A reincarnation cannot be from the same juncture as the original character, but can be from any juncture separated from it by a lifetime or more. If the player chooses to create a new character from an earlier juncture, it will actually be an earlier incarnation of the same character, which there probably isn't a word for. (Preincarnation?) But the idea is the same anyway.

It's up to the GM whether to encourage or allow this. Some GMs try to get their players to play different types each time out. Others will be happy to find an in-game justification to explain why certain players portray their characters the same way every time.

You may also find this device useful to integrate the newly generated character into the ongoing series without stopping to introduce a lot of new subplots; the reincarnation can be drawn, willingly or otherwise, into the old character's melodramatic hooks. Lovers of the previous character might find the new character either compelling or a frightful reminder of their dead sweetheart. Old acquaintances may become confused, and blame the new character for past wrongs done to them by the old incarnation. And of course, sworn enemies of the old character refuse to believe that the new one is a reincarnation and continue to strive for vengeance against him.

CRITICAL AND SUPERFICIAL SHIFTS

The above examples are of relatively minor changes in the timestream. These do not change the fates of millions of people; instead they simply alter the personal histories of a handful of families and their descendants. Inner Kingdom sages refer to such alterations as **superficial shifts**. Such shifts do not overthrow basic political systems or reverse massive movements of history. In the vast majority of cases, the transfer of a single feng shui site from one occupant to another fosters only a superficial shift in later junctures of the timestream, if that. In order for an organization to truly dominate its time period and set the rules of reality, it needs to control hundreds of key feng shui sites. The loss of a single site means little in such terms.

However, there is always a point at which a group that is steadily losing feng shui sites has the balance tipped against it. After a series of defeats, the loss of a particular site can be the final straw, one that sets off a **critical shift**. This is a shift in which the lives of all inhabitants of all later junctures are altered as the rulers of a juncture are ousted, changing history.

For example, when the forefathers of the current Ascended succeeded in driving magic from the world they succeeded in fostering a critical shift. In pursuing their own plans, they also altered all future junctures. Until that point, these were junctures in which magic was a common and vital part of daily life. For example, in changing their own juncture to suit themselves, they wiped out a version of the 20th century ruled by the sorcerous Four Monarchs. Without the help of secret warriors from other junctures or the Netherworld, it is impossible to foster a critical shift: these come about only as a result of outside tampering with the timestream. In the current example, the Ascended who won the conflict were native to the juncture where the change started, but were assisted by other secret warriors, who wanted changes to ripple through the timestream and change their own junctures.

Taking a crucial site does not trigger any changes in junctures prior to the one in which the capture takes place. History starts to diverge from the familiar pattern from the point of capture on. From the point of view of the residents of a given juncture, there are no immediate, shocking changes. History simply moves gradually on in a new course. When the Ascended seized crucial feng shui sites throughout Europe and Asia during the Middle Ages, their opponents did not simply vanish. Their influence and power slowly crumbled over a period of years, allowing the Ascended to step in to fill the vacuum in the various royal courts. It took years for them to solidify their hold on power; from their point of view all changes were gradual, all struggles hard-fought.

However, from the point of view of secret warriors who came from later junctures to participate in the fight, things immediately and dramatically changed back in their home juncture. Most of them had grown up in a world where the feudal era had gone on for a thousand years and was openly ruled by a quartet of powerful magicians (the Four Monarchs). When they returned to their own juncture, they found it radically altered. Instead of a medieval society fueled by magic, they found themselves in a modern world with an industrial revolution hundreds of years in its past. Their sorcerous rulers were gone, replaced by the political rulers of various nation states. Their own personal histories were changed beyond recognition. Some of them found themselves in new identities: as industrialists, scientists, celebrities, or non-entities.

EXILES

Others found out that they no longer existed in the new time frame that they had fought to create: none of the other residents of their transformed time juncture had any recollection of their ever having existed. They still physically lived and breathed and occupied space, and were remembered by other secret warriors, but history had reshaped itself in such a way as to make them castaways in time. In the Inner Kingdom, such individuals are known as **exiles** or **DPs** (distimed persons). Most critical shifts produce some exiles. Exiles are always secret warriors.

Some exiles try to create new identities for themselves in the reshaped versions of their original junctures. This can be trivially easy in the case of low-technology junctures where record keeping is primitive, or phenomenally difficult in authoritarian, high-tech police states like that of the Architects where the movements and activities of all citizens are carefully tracked.

Other exiles retreat to the Netherworld, either thinking of it as a permanent new home or as a temporary base from which to launch operations intended to capture the necessary feng shui sites to return their juncture to its preferred state.

It is possible to get cut off from your home juncture if the connections seal up between a juncture and the Netherworld. For example, a group known as The Unexpected Deliverance Society used to be an influential force in the Inner Kingdom, but most of their leaders and operatives were in a 1457 juncture when all passages between that juncture and the Netherworld sealed up.

FLOW OF TIME IN THE NETHERWORLD

The only place where time flows in an immutable, linear manner is the Netherworld. Anyone who enters the Inner Kingdom even once gains a form of personal immunity from lateral reincarnation. These characters do not change incarnations when their home junctures change. They remain in the incarnation they were in when they first visited the Netherworld. This is true whether they are in the Netherworld, or any juncture, when a critical shift occurs. The character need not understand what is going on to be the beneficiary of this effect. However, those who experience the dislocation of having memories of an erased juncture while trying to live in a new one are likely to view it as a curse or form of insanity if they don't understand what's happened to them.

It is never possible to reverse history within the Netherworld itself. Anything that has happened in the past of the Inner Kingdom has happened, and that is that. The Netherworld cannot be affected even by critical shifts.

Although time is linear in the Netherworld, there is no convenient, agreed-upon way of measuring it. Most Netherworlders continue to use the dating system of their home juncture, as of the moment they first entered their odd new realm. Servants of the Four Monarchs use the same calendar as our contemporary world. From their point of view, their juncture was critically shifted out from under their control in 1988, and they've been in the Inner Kingdom ever since. The Jammers, on the other hand, still operate according to the current year in their still-open home juncture: 2056.

Other former secret warriors from long-erased junctures reckon the passing of time according to their own calendars.

USING JUNCTURES IN YOUR SERIES

Now that we've given you the background material, here are some ideas on how to actually use it in your series. The junctures are a plot mechanism that allows characters inspired by the various types of Hong Kong and fantasy/science-fiction action flicks to interact with one another. It allows your group of player characters to include ancient kung fu masters, slick modern assassins, futuristic monsters, and all of the other wildly-varied archetypes presented in this book. The secret war for the feng shui sites in the various junctures gives them a big goal to strive for.

It's up to you how big a role the time war will play in your series. Our upcoming supplements and sourcebooks for *Feng Shui* assume that it will be central to most GMs' series. It's also a big part of the Shadowfist card game; if your players are fans of that game, they may expect lots of time-crossing action in this one. But it is certainly possible to play *Feng Shui* without using the secret war plot device at all. You may simply want to run a series that simulates one type of action movie without mixing them all together. If you want a game that's entirely based around cops and robbers in the underworld scene of contemporary Hong Kong, all you have to do is restrict the archetypes available to your players during character creation. Do likewise if you want to run a strict fu-and-magic ancient game, or a futuristic series. If you do decide to start out with a narrower scope, you can always keep the whole secret war idea in reserve, ready to introduce it when you feel you've plumbed the depths of your initial setting.

HANDLING CRITICAL SHIFTS

The whole setup connecting the Netherworld to the various junctures of the time stream is designed to make it easy for you to run time travel without dealing with the usual pitfalls of this plot element. The characters can only change history when you're prepared for the consequences. They can't go back and muck around in their own pasts.

They can't replay encounters that go poorly for them. They are limited to a few time periods that you're prepared for them to enter: no need to go rushing to your history reference shelf when they choose a time period at random and head there.

You decide when a battle over a feng shui site is crucial enough to set off a critical shift. You do so in advance, and can in advance work out what the changes will be to later junctures from this shift. If you're reasonably careful, you will never be caught flat-footed trying to work out centuries' worth of changed history from a surprise action the player characters take. Never let your players know for certain ahead of time that the seizure of a particular site will trigger a critical shift—unless you've already worked out what the consequences of that shift will be.

When you do decide to allow a shift, you should work out logically how the events in that juncture will change later junctures, especially the player characters' home junctures. Work out the major issues first, and then deal with the player-level details. Here are some questions to ask yourself when allowing a critical shift:

How does the shift affect the amount of magic in the world? Organizations who are on top in the feng shui sweepstakes get to decide how strong they want magic to be. The Ascended are in charge in the present day, and want magic to be as weak as possible. The Architects want only their own warped blend of magic and technology. The Eaters of the Lotus rely on magic, and want it to be commonplace and easy to perform. The Guiding Hand wants magic weak but chi powers strong. Jammers want to destroy all supernatural energy, while the Four Monarchs want to make it easy for themselves to use magic and difficult for those they would rule. The winners in a critical shift can directly determine the availability of magic in the juncture where the site seizure has taken place, and can influence it in later junctures. For example, when the Ascended tipped the feng shui balance in their favor they made magic scarce for later junctures, including the 20th century, knocking the Four Monarchs from their supremacy.

How does the shift affect feng shui possession in later junctures? In this last example, we see that it is possible to lose feng shui sites you control in your home juncture if someone goes to an earlier juncture and changes history so that the events that led to your controlling those sites could never have happened. This is why it is important for groups like the Architects and Ascended to fight the secret war on a number of fronts, rather than just sitting on their advantage in their own junctures. To return to the example, the Ascended—by making magic difficult to use—made it impossible for the Four Monarchs to have conquered the world's feng shui sites. To seize the sites that guaranteed their supremacy, the Monarchs depended on their powerful sorcerous abilities: abilities that never came into being in the critical shift's new version of history.

Juncture Shift Example

Here's an example of what might happen to the timestream if the current feng shui balance in one juncture were to change in favor of one of the factions. It should not be taken as gospel—what happens in your series is up to you. The point is simply to show how to construct a chain of events that effects later junctures.

The Hand Take 69

The Guiding Hand is training small cadres of chi-based warriors to overthrow the Lotus in 69 AD and institute a just system of government inspired by their neo-Confucian principles. If this group was to win more sites in ancient China than the Eaters of the Lotus now control, the Lotus would fall from grace with the Emperor and be replaced by political advisers loyal to the Hand. The Hand would then use their feng shui control to prevent the Lotus from waging guerrilla war against them by reducing the amount of magic in the world.

The effects of this would ripple forward through the later junctures. With magic already reduced in 69, the transformed animals would never feel the need to band together for that purpose in the eleventh century. They would quietly live out their lives without building the international power network that exists in the 1850s and in our present-day juncture. This would leave the field open for the Hand to create its idea of earthly paradise. They would spread like evangelists across Asia and Europe, influencing followers to capture feng shui sites on their behalf. If their progress went unchecked by other secret warriors, they would eventually come to control the entire world. It would settle into quiet and peaceful stagnation under a world empire, becoming culturally Chinese. Under their guidance, the world Emperor would carefully manage populations and societies.

Illustration by Grey Thornberry

Advances in technology inspired by wars and economic need would be greatly slowed, advancing only imperceptibly from the year 69.

However, the study of chi powers would be greatly advanced. In such junctures, it would be possible for any human character to gain any fu powers described in this book for 1 character point apiece. A whole new range of chi powers undreamt of in any existing juncture would come into being. This would have the ironic effect of destroying the very social stability the Hand is so devoted to. When talented individuals have the power of entire platoons thanks to these new chi powers, they become impossible to control. Such individuals rise as new warlords during the 1850 juncture, plunging the world into super-powered civil war.

In the contemporary juncture, the Earth is ruled by the heirs of the winners of that war, who run a dictatorial world state in which the mightiest warriors compete in gladiatorial contests for rulership of various provinces and principalities.

In the 2056 juncture, rebels against the chi elite have, out of desperation, begun to explore hitherto neglected fields of technological development. They have developed rudimentary firearms, and have equipped the masses for a bloody worldwide uprising against the arrogant chi masters.

Note that this series of changes displaces almost all of the existing power groups. The innerwalkers of the Lotus, Architects, Jammers, and Four Monarchs would no doubt be camped out in the Inner Kingdom. From there they'd be launching attacks on the various junctures in an effort to get them back the way they want them. Meanwhile, the innerwalkers of the Ascended might be helping the chi masters, who need to keep the magic level low. The Hand would try to hold onto its sites in 69, while trying to seize back control of the others.

In other words, the background might be changed completely. (And whenever you want to throw your players for a loop, you can do the same!) But one thing that would not change is the need of secret warriors to clash, testing their courage—and butt-kicking capabilities—against one another.

ERASING THE BACKSTORY

One last important rule of time in *Feng Shui*: no matter what you do, you can't use the junctures to erase events that happen "onstage" in the course of a series. One trick that your PCs will likely try when they find out they're in a time travel story is the old "letter from the past" trick. They'll try to send letters or useful stuff to themselves from a past juncture so they can pick it up in a future juncture. Any plans of this sort that try to reverse events that have already happened are doomed to failure. However, if the plan doesn't aim to nullify events that have already happened, the trick might work. (Or it might not, depending on what happens to be entertaining at the time.)

Example One: Johnny Tso gets stomped on May 31st of 1995 in an ambush by a Lodge member of elephant heritage. This prevents him from executing an important mission. He heads to the year 1850 via the Netherworld. There he writes a letter and arranges for a law firm to deliver it to Johnny Tso in Hong Kong on May 30th of 1995. The letter warns him of the ambush.

Unfortunately, Johnny's wasting his time. We know the fight takes place, because it's already happened in the plot line. Somehow the letter goes astray: the courier fails to deliver it, it gets intercepted by the evil Lotus sorcerer Johnny tried to smoke in the last session, or the letter gets lost in the law firm's vaults decades before the delivery date.

Example Two: Jack Donovan and Mad Dog McCroun are in the 69 juncture, where they have stolen a jade ring of magical power from Lotus honcho Jueding Shelun. They know that, in order to get back to the nearest Netherworld portal, they have to pass a checkpoint where they will be searched by Imperial Troops looking for the ring. So they bury it under a large boulder in the middle of the wilderness. When they get to the contemporary world, they'll head over to the same spot and dig it up.

This doesn't reverse any events in the storyline, so it might well work. Of course, if you have a cool plot twist that depends on them being at least temporarily frustrated in their attempt to recover the ring, go to it. Lots of things could have happened to that spot in the intervening centuries: it could be in the middle of a river or under an apartment building. The ring might have been recovered by archaeologists, or even by magic-sniffing enemies of our stalwart heroes.

Neither PCs nor GMCs can be returned from the dead as the result of a time shift. Lateral reincarnation only works on the living.

Chapter 17

May 28

The Fire Pagoda I'd heard so much about was pretty weird all right, but I was getting used to weird. I was in a long corridor hiding behind a conveniently-placed tapestry. I say conveniently because I didn't exactly have permission from the King of the Fire Pagoda to be prowling around his scene. I had permission—well, orders is more like it—from his sister, the Queen of the Ice Pagoda. But the four monarchs of the Netherworld don't exactly see eye-to-eye on everything. The say-so from one don't mean the rest won't rip your head off.

I was starting to sweat. Not from nervousness—I get nervous but I don't sweat when I'm nervous. The sweat was purely a temperature thing. The Fire Pagoda is called that for a reason, the reason being that it's made of fire. The floors, the ceilings, the doors, the walls, the chairs, the kitchen utensils, the conveniently-placed tapestries: all made of flame. Now it's flame that's been magically screwed with, mind you. You can walk on its fiery floors without burning your feet or melting the soles of your Guccis. You can grab a door handle of fire without getting blisters. But it does feel hot to the touch. Air conditioning is not a factor at the Fire Pagoda. Ice-cold beer wasn't on the menu.

And of course, a solid floor made of dancing flames is the kind of contradiction in terms that magic is all about. I'm still trying to get used to that kind of stuff, to just keep my cool if you'll excuse the pun. Everything in the place is kind of mesmerizing, just like looking into a campfire when you were a kid. Always shimmering and leaping with reds and yellows and oranges and whites and hints of blue. The tapestry I was hiding behind was something to see. It was a design of the King of the Fire Pagoda, Li Ting himself, nailing an entire army of what looked like Moslem warriors with a hellacious blast of flame the size of a DC-10. The magically trapped flames animated the picture so you could see his enemies writhing and screaming as the flesh cooked itself from their bones. Unlike a tapestry made of threads, this one happened to be just as picturesque from the backside as from the front. You understand that it jacked up my anxiety level in a big way, considering that the Big Flamey Dude himself was just on the other side of said tapestry. I had Mr. Browning warming up in my left hand, but I didn't think that even a slug between the eyes would put Li Ting down. The Four Monarchs are not to be messed with in direct combat—or in any other way, if you want my take on the matter.

So add to that the fact that he was talking to his sister, the Queen of the Darkness Pagoda, making that two monarchs to one mere assassin trying to make good, and the source of my trepidation is clear to you, yes? This of course was why I was here—my popsicle of a patroness wanted to know just what kind of cozy alliance her unloved siblings were cooking up. I wasn't sure how this connected to the whole feng shui business, or healing Steve's condition like she promised. But she knew which of my buttons to push, so here I was, risking severe and unholy injury pulling an eavesdropper act.

The gist of what they were saying was that they wanted to work some kind of arrangement, but neither trusted the other. Something about blocking the entranceways from the Netherworld back to my home time. That would be a Bad Thing. The Inner Kingdom was a nice place to visit, but I had no intention of living here. Fortunately the two of them sounded like they were just a couple of inches from coming to blows. The negotiation was falling down over the guarantee issue. They'd agreed on hostages, but then each was attempting to screw the other over the details. It occurred to me that the Four Monarchs weren't so different from all the Triad Big Brothers I knew so well. Just weirder and tougher.

So I swallowed hard and did something potentially deeply stupid. I swept the tapestry aside and introduced myself—as an experienced mediator in such matters.

And just like gangsters, Netherworld monarchs turn out to be impressed by a display of cojones.

CHAPTER 17

Netherworld

THE INNER KINGDOM

The Netherworld, also called the Inner Kingdom, plays an important role in any *Feng Shui* series that uses the secret war plot device. It serves as a place for the PCs to gather information as well as a route between junctures. It is also a place for adventure and intrigue in its own right. Most of the factions in the secret war have installations in the Netherworld. Even those inhabitants of the Netherworld with little interest in other junctures often find themselves at violent odds with one another.

GEOGRAPHY

The Netherworld is a series of twisting underground passageways connecting a network of caverns, some of them quite massive. There is no real sky anywhere in the Netherworld, although some of its inhabitants have created something that *looks* like a sky over their homes. In its original state, a Netherworld passageway is gray and undefined. Undisturbed passageways are made of a gray material that looks vaguely like moist limestone—but when you reach out to feel it, it is warm to the touch and has a smoothness of texture that feels artificial. Passageways smell musty and damp, and the air is moist. Oddly, the place is extremely dusty most of the time. Temperatures in the Netherworld are uncomfortably hot and humid, at a steady temperature of 28° Celsius (82° Fahrenheit) and 80% humidity. Individuals highly capable at shaping the Netherworld environment can change these conditions with an exercise of will. Areas controlled by the Queen of the Ice Pagoda, for example, are a chilly -5° C (23° F) at all times.

A dim, diffuse light bathes much of the Netherworld. Unaltered passageways have no visible light sources, but it is nonetheless always possible to see in them. Light behaves strangely here. Sometimes you'll see stark, tightly-defined shadows but have no idea what is causing them. At other points blazing shafts of colored light come from nowhere to cast a spotlight on nothing.

It is possible for some Netherworlders to reshape the features of a passageway or cavern at will; see "Shaping," on the next page. While many of the countless small and winding passageways are still in their undisturbed state, just as many are not. Caverns, which are in much higher demand as living space, have invariably changed hands many times over the centuries. Currently uninhabited areas which have been shaped in the past offer a bizarre assortment of features to the viewer. When a shaper ceases to impose her will on an area, it very gradually returns to its former state. Passageways and caverns in this state of decay will provide vague and tantalizing hints of their old shapes. A tunnel wall might be embedded with half-visible human or animal skulls, faded architectural remnants in styles ranging from ancient Babylon to alien futures, or deteriorated decorations that recall anything from Neolithic cave paintings to animated Picasso etchings.

The Netherworld is finite, but its passageways stretch for kilometer upon kilometer and much of it is uninhabited. Its populace tends to congregate together in what is called **the Center** of the Inner Kingdom. This area makes up a rough circle with a radius of approximately 400 kilometers (about 640 miles). Not all of the Center is inhabited, but beyond its reach there are only the rough homes of a few deliberate outcasts, separated by long stretches of trackless passageways. All of the places described in this chapter fall within the Center or are not far from its boundaries.

Since it's made up of tunnels and caverns, fighting in the Netherworld is like fighting indoors. Although the Four Monarchs all maintain small armies, the terrain of the Inner Kingdom is not well suited to mass warfare. Small groups of guerrilla combatants are much more effective here than are platoons of troops. Thus, your PCs will find themselves and their preferred tactics in high demand in the Netherworld. There are few military tasks that are not best performed here by small bands of fighters with fu powers, magic spells, and/or itchy trigger fingers.

GATES

Dotted throughout the Netherworld are gates or portals. Each gate is the terminus of a passageway, and is obscured by blindingly bright light, like that of a gigantic magnesium flare. If you step into the light, you end up on Earth in one of its four open junctures or time periods: 69 AD, 1850, our time, or 2056. Gates are two-way affairs; it is possible to use them to get from one of the junctures to the Netherworld as well as the other way around. On Earth, gates are not so obvious in appearance as they are in the Inner Kingdom. They tend to blend in with the features, natural or otherwise, of the landscape. To name just a few examples, they can be doors, elevators, stairways, waterfalls, underwater cave mouths, or invisible holes in the air. On the Netherworld side, it is possible to shape the appearance of gates in your area so that they better match your decor and are less painful to the eyes. They may have been transmuted into mirrors, fog banks, grandfather clocks, stairways—you name it.

Gates are stable; it is very difficult to destroy them. There are dozens upon dozens of gates to each open juncture. Gates to the different junctures are distributed throughout the Center—and in the outer reaches of the Netherworld, for that matter. There is no one area that has a monopoly on portals to 1850, for example. When new junctures open up and fresh factions enter the secret war, the first thing these inexperienced groups often try to do is control all entrances to their time frame within the Netherworld. This is always a fruitless task; there are just too many gates to any given juncture to successfully defend against determined enemies. It is, however, much easier to defend a mere handful of gates from unwanted intruders. Gates that happen to lead somewhere inconvenient are the most heavily guarded. For example, there is one portal that leads from the Netherworld into the Chinese Emperor's palace in 69 AD. The Eaters of the Lotus have stationed a truly formidable force of demons and fu fighters on the Netherworld side of this gate, and so far no one has survived an attempt to get through it without a personal invitation from Gao Zhang.

SHAPING

Shaping is the art of changing the features of Netherworld tunnels and caverns to match your specifications. Anyone who has been attuned to a number of feng shui sites can become a shaper. Although related to Sorcery and the use of fu powers, it is a unique method of manipulating chi energy. The sages of the Ice Queen's court have speculated that the Netherworld itself is made up of pure chi energy, which supposedly explains the properties that allow it to interact with the human mind.

Shaping as a Skill

In game terms, Shaping is treated as a skill: characters have a rating in Shaping which is used for task checks. However, one's rating in Shaping is not based on an attribute. Shaping can't be taken during character creation; it can't be gained or increased with experience points in the course of play. A character's rating in shaping equals the maximum number of feng shui sites the character was ever attuned to at any one time.

Example: Li Zeng has been attuned to seven different feng shui sites in his long career as a secret warrior. However, the highest number of sites he was attuned to at one time was 5. This is his rating in the Shaping skill. Although he is no longer attuned to any sites, he retains this rating. The only way he can increase his rating in Shaping is to become attuned to 6 feng shui sites at the same time; this would increase his rating to 6. Needless to say, going from 0 to 6 feng shui sites is not an easy matter.

Difficulty numbers for Shaping depend on the size of the area being shaped, the speed with which the changes are to take place, and the complexity of the result. When a PC wants to engage in shaping, ask the player how long he wants his character to take trying to make the change, how big the area changed will be, and the exact nature of the change he wants to make. Then add together

Netherworld

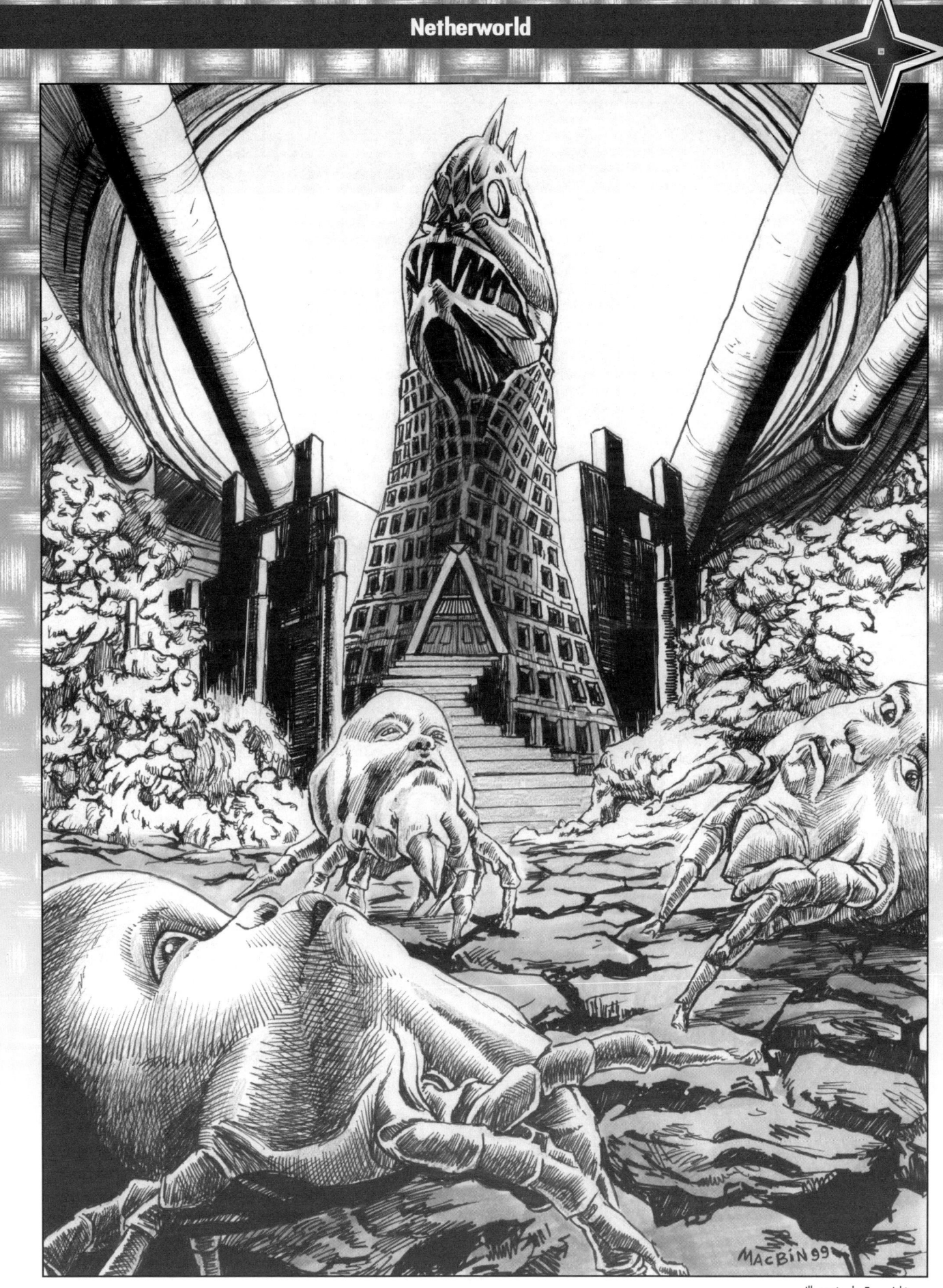

Illustration by Toren Atkinson

Chapter 17

Shaping Difficulty Chart

Diff. Mod.	Time	Size	Complexity
+1	1 week or more	small painting	color change
+2	3 days	mural	texture change
+3	1 day	large wall	decorative features
+4	8 hours	small dwelling	box-shaped building
+5	4 hours	medium building	intricate decorative features
+6	2 hours	temple or cathedral	unnatural lighting
+7	1 hour	pagoda or palace	complex architecture
+8	30 minutes	small community	mechanical devices w/ moving parts, temperature change
+9	15 minutes	town	electronic devices, odd weather effects
+10	1 sequence	city	physics-defying architecture

the Difficulty numbers associated with each factor, using the Shaping Difficulty Chart as a guide.

The character then spends the amount of time specified; at the end of the process, his player makes a Shaping task check against the Difficulty you have determined. If the task is successful, the character gets the desired result. If not, the character likely gets a partial result. The bigger the gulf between Action Result and Difficulty, the more pathetic the payoff. It is possible to spend a Fortune die to increase the chance of success on a Shaping check.

Example: Li Zeng is lost in the trackless outer reaches of the Netherworld, far beyond the center. He wants to construct a radio out of the undifferentiated material of the tunnel wall, so he can contact his friends at the Thunder Pagoda. The GM consults the Shaping Difficulty Chart to determine the Difficulty of Li Zeng's Shaping check.

His player is willing to spend an entire week at the task, so for the time factor the GM assigns the minimum Difficulty modifier of 1. The size is likewise minimal, another 1. But an electronic device like a radio is a 9 on the complexity scale. The Difficulty is the total of these three numbers: 1 + 1 + 9 = 11.

Li Zeng's Shaping rating is a measly 5, so his player figures he'd better spend a Fortune die to pump up his chances of building that radio. With the Fortune die factored in, he gets an Action Result of 12. That beats the Difficulty, so Li Zeng has his radio. He's in contact with his Thunder Knight cronies within minutes.

The GM may rule that your character must be familiar with the thing that he wants to shape, and must make a relevant skill check as well as the Shaping check.

Examples: To create a mechanical or electronic device, you need the Fix-It skill. To build a Gun, you need the Guns skill. To fabricate a magical item, you need to make a Sorcery check. If you want to build an ancient Greek temple with authentic features, you need Info / Archaeology or some other appropriate Info skill. And so on.

If you make the Shaping check but blow the check for the type of item, you get something, but it's not what you wanted.

Examples: Instead of a working radio, you get a hunk of plastic with knobs that doesn't send or receive radio signals. Instead of a gun, you get an inert replica. Your supposedly accurate Greek temple has Roman columns.

Staying Shaped

The natural inclination of the Netherworld is to return to its undifferentiated state. If you want to maintain the form of something you've shaped, you must periodically return and renew your chi connection to it. A shaped building or item normally lasts a number of days equal to your Shaping rating. If you want it to last longer than that, you must go to the item or place in question before this duration elapses and then make a Shaping task check with a Difficulty of 5 to keep it in its current form. Again, it stays in this form for a number of days equal to your Shaping rating; you must continue to keep it in shape in this manner until you no longer want the item or place to remain as is.

Shaped Items

As shown in the earlier example, it is possible to create objects from the material of the Netherworld. If you're frighteningly good at Shaping, you could even spend a sequence whipping up an M-16 from a tunnel wall, and then yank it loose to spray your adversaries with 5.56 mm rounds. (That's Difficulty 19, for those keeping track.) This might seem like the ideal manufacturing method, but it has two big drawbacks.

One, as mentioned above, you need to periodically concentrate on the object to prevent it from turning into goo and becoming one with the floor. Two, it's impossible to take objects made of Netherworld material through a gate.

Some of the secret war factions, the Architects being a prime example, have developed technologies based on items that can only be manufactured through Shaping. This is why they need the Netherworld and maintain bases here.

Shaping and Feng Shui

Unaltered Netherworld passageways and caverns are neutral as far as feng shui goes: they direct chi to their inhabitants in a way that is not notably positive or negative. Shapers familiar with the principles of geomancy can alter the features of sites so that they become positive feng shui sites. People maintaining such sites have an advantage in their struggles with others: Like characters attuned to any other feng shui site, they advance more rapidly in their abilities. However, possessing such sites in the Netherworld confers no ability to change the fundamental reality of the place, and no influence over the course of history. Currently, the most auspicious feng sites in the Netherworld are the pagodas of the Four Monarchs, but these do not give the Monarchs any influence over events on Earth. They just help the Monarchs maintain their power in the Netherworld.

INHABITANTS

The inhabitants of the Netherworld are almost invariably here because of the secret war. There are a few individuals whose ancestors accidentally stumbled through a portal and ended up stuck here. But most of its people are either exiles who have been displaced by the erasure of their native timelines, or are operatives of the current factions in the secret war who have good reason to keep tabs on events in the Inner Kingdom.

We're not going to put a number to the population of the Netherworld. This gives you wiggle room when creating plot lines. If you have an inquisitive player who wants to quantify things, remind him that no one's ever taken a census of the Inner Kingdom.

DIS-TIMED PERSONS

The majority of the people of the Netherworld are **DPs**, or **dis-timed persons**. Other names for his group include **exiles** (the term they prefer themselves) and **Netherworld Rabble** (a term they distinctly dislike, no matter how appropriate it might be). It is made up of individuals who have been cut off from their home times, or the descendants of same.

There are several ways to get exiled in time. One is to have a critical shift happen in your timeline, so that your old history is erased and you are laterally reincarnated—see p. 194. In order to notice this, you have to have visited the Netherworld already; this preserves your original memories when critical shifts occur. Some consider it a blessing, but exiles are likely to think of it as a curse: their friends and families now have different histories and memories, and are therefore slightly different people. You no longer share memories with these people, but are a stranger in your own skin. Secret warriors who find this too heartbreaking often exile themselves to the Netherworld. Many of them start out planning to reverse history to get their old lives back, but they soon learn that this is extraordinarily difficult. Some find new happy lives among the humble villages of the exiled. Most waste away in lives of grim desperation enlivened only by frequent drunken punch-ups.

The other way to get exiled in time is to be in the Netherworld when the gates to your home juncture unexpectedly close up. This is upsetting, but at least those who suffer this fate can tell themselves that their loved ones still exist somewhere. If only the connection between that juncture and the Inner Kingdom can somehow be reestablished, these exiles can return to them—or so they tell themselves.

Exiles live together in ramshackle villages, their buildings cobbled together with their inhabitants' limited Shaping abilities. Exiles can be identified by their distinctive mish-mash of clothing styles. They look like they've picked up their wardrobes at thrift stores stocked with the refuse from the entire history of fashion. An exile might wear a Roman breastplate over a Plains Indian buckskin shirt, with Elizabethan leggings topped off by Doc Martens boots.

Not all exiles are humans. There is a small contingent of escaped demons and abominations among them. These are generally peaceful souls who are out of tune with their monstrous origins. These types still have the full array of creature powers and/or arcanowave devices, though, so it's generally a bad idea to put their serenity to the test.

SUBJECTS

The second largest group of people in the Netherworld are the **subjects**, which is Netherworld slang for the servants and retainers of the Four Monarchs. They do not make a cohesive group,

Chapter 17

as the Monarchs themselves are perpetually plotting intrigues against one another, forming and discarding alliances with predictable regularity. They do all tend to look down upon the exiles. None of the subjects want to think that they too are exiles, no more likely to recover their magical version of the 20th century than the huddled masses in the DP shacks are likely to find their own timelines intact.

SECRET WARRIORS

All of the factions involved in the secret war have agents in the Netherworld. Some have power bases and major presences; others just hang around and run the occasional time-traveling errand.

The Four Monarchs, Dragons, and Jammers are all headquartered here. The Monarchs have been exiled here by the erasure of their history from the time stream. Still recovering from a shattering blow that dispersed their organization, the Dragons maintain a small outpost here as their leaders search desperately for more followers to represent the forces of liberty and fair play in the secret war. The Jammers are exiles by choice, since it's much easier for them to operate here than in the highly efficient Buro police state of their home juncture, 2056.

The Architects of the Flesh employ Shaping to create arcanowave tech devices not reproducible through normal means. They use the Netherworld as a route to 69 AD, where they find ogres and demons to convert into abominations.

The Ascended don't like the Netherworld. Lodge members risk being turned back into their animal forms here, and they avoid the place at all costs. Their inability to travel freely through the Netherworld is probably the Ascended's greatest liability in the secret war. They usually rely on Pledged followers to run operations in and through the Netherworld. The Pledged who operate here are among the most effective and senior humans in the organization.

The Guiding Hand come here because the Shaping ability allows them to build perfect meditation chambers which allow them to harmonize most effectively with the teachings of their founder, Quan Lo.

The Eaters of the Lotus have not yet taken full advantage of the unique properties of the Netherworld. They use it primarily as a way of getting to other junctures. But they have stationed a small force here with the dual mission of gathering facts about the place and thwarting the enemies of the Lotus whenever possible. They also maintain a formidable group of warriors and demons who guard a portal to the 69 AD juncture—which happens to lead into the heart of the Emperor's Palace.

PLACES OF NOTE

Here's a brief rundown of interesting places that the PCs can ~~visit~~ blow up.

TEMPLE OF BOUNDLESS MEDITATION

A monastery complex run and viciously guarded by the Guiding Hand. It is here that high-level Hand monks go to attempt to follow in Quan Lo's footsteps and achieve a state of perfect mastery. The secret heart of this complex is a series of seven meditation chambers, each of which has been Shaped to faultlessly manifest Quan Lo's Six Color Principles and its grand synthesis, the Principle of Principles. The Temple of Boundless Meditation also serves as a way station for Hand agents traveling between junctures, and as a base of operations for intrigue within the Inner Kingdom.

BIOMASS REPROCESSING CENTER

This mirror and steel fortress of gleaming black is the Netherworld research station for the Architects of the Flesh. Here they perfect cutting edge techniques for fusing magic and technology, using Shaped equipment which can't be reproduced even in the arcanowave-receptive 2056 juncture. The complex is constantly creating new variations on the abomination theme, which it periodically looses on unsuspecting DPs in a grisly spirit of experimentation. An installation this unpopular needs to be heavily guarded, and this one certainly is.

Note that while items Shaped from Netherworld material cannot be taken back to the real world, the Architects are using Shaped tools to manufacture items out of real-world materials. As a result, the

Netherworld

products of this center are fully operable in the real world as well as in the Netherworld.

THE HUB

This ultramodern military installation is the Ascended's headquarters in the Netherworld. Its commander, Pledged mastermind Rebecca Dupree, has arranged for the Hub to be Shaped to bend light around it. Only those who know where to find it can do so; to anyone else, it is invisible. Apparently the place is laid out like the wheel symbol of the Ascended: As a series of spokes radiating out from a central hub—hence the name. Dupree is given considerable latitude to make decisions for the Ascended in regards to actions in the Netherworld because her Lodge superiors dare not set foot here. She is rumored to have agents planted in all of the Inner Kingdom installations of all of the other secret war factions. Whether this rumor is true or is just demoralizing disinformation remains to be seen. It is certainly the case that she maintains a crack force of guerrilla warriors for those moments when the secret war gets hot.

IKTV

Inner Kingdom Television is a peculiar institution run by twin sisters Columbia and Laurel Towson. They are voluntary exiles from our contemporary juncture who stumbled across the Netherworld without being a part of the secret war, and fell in love with the place. Unable to get broadcasting jobs on Earth, they set up permanent shop in the Inner Kingdom and created a homegrown TV station. Broadcasting eight hours a day, IKTV can be received only by those who have access to television sets. These are rather hard to come by in the Netherworld; most of those that do exist have been Shaped by their users and aren't exactly reliable. Neither is the IKTV service, which operates according to the unpredictable whims of its twin managers. One day might be entirely made up of *My Mother the Car* reruns and the next devoted to a libelous monologue delivered against one of the Four Monarchs. The station's irregular news show must be taken with a large chunk of rock salt, but it's the closest the Netherworld has to a mass communications system. The current IKTV headquarters has been Shaped so that it itself has a twelve-story television screen on one face. A number of Netherworld operators are currently scheming to smash its tube; the previous four IKTV station buildings have already been blown to bits. The station is now guarded day and night by a fanatical band of Netherworld Rabbles called Ickies; they love their television and would rather die than give it up.

LUSIGNAN'S TOWER

Lusignan the Fool is a curious fixture on the Netherworld scene. The former court jester of Thunder King Huan Ken, he is now an independent operator whose allegiances seem to swing back and forth in the Inner Kingdom's nonexistent wind. The true purpose of his bizarre tower is just as mysterious as the motivations of its builder. A teetering structure composed of clown masks and grinning skulls, it has a curious habit of becoming the location of crucial battles in the Inner Kingdom's ongoing power struggles. Through mockery and subversion, Lusignan is both making a point and advancing an agenda. But so far no one has quite figured out what either of these are. Only the grinning, grotesque Fool himself knows, and he's not saying.

GENOCIDE LOUNGE

This charmingly-named night club is the public gathering place of the Jammers and their many fans and hangers-on in the Netherworld. The Jammers have more influence in the Inner Kingdom than in any juncture on Earth, in large part due to their knack for rallying the Rabble to their cause. The Lounge has been attacked on numerous occasions, usually by Architect agents. Therefore, you won't find the Battlechimp Potemkin or his top brass openly rubbing elbows with the Genocide's scruffy clientele. But if you want to get word to the Jammers, this is the place to pass a note to the bartender. It is also one of the few places where modern entertainment can be found in the Netherworld: it is a frequent touring stop for the edgiest hardcore bands from the contemporary world who have Jammer buddies.

GUIYU ZUI

This demonic parody of the Chinese Emperor's palace is situated on the sole direct connection between the Netherworld and the Underworld. The Underworld is the otherworldly realm of demons and evil spirits. A gaping, living demonic mouth occupies the basement level of the Guiyu Zui. To get to the Underworld, one walks into the mouth of the giant demon, is swallowed, and is eventually excreted in the Underworld. It's extremely unpleasant, but then again, so is the rest of the Underworld. So are you, probably, if you want to go there.

Apart from guarding an entrance to a place no one else really wants to venture, the Lotus use the complex to run Inner Kingdom operations and as accommodations for operatives roving between the junctures.

THE JUNKYARD

This place is just what the name says: a massive junkyard full of the detritus of centuries of history, both current and erased. Under the junkyard is a small but secure complex where the Prof, a techie mastermind who is among the last of the Dragons' leaders, currently hides out. The Prof is unable to leave the Netherworld, due to a magical curse cast upon her by Lusignan the Fool (see the previous page). Strangely enough, the Prof doesn't seem too concerned about this curse; nor does she appear to be pursuing any sort of vengeance against the Fool. She does want to assemble a new band of heroes to fight the fights left unfought by her old comrades, though—and maybe the PCs are likely candidates.

THE PAGODAS

The four fabulous palaces of the Ice Queen, Thunder King, Darkness Queen, and Fire King are the most famous structures in the Netherworld, Shaped or otherwise. The Ice Pagoda is a breathtaking beautiful series of fortresses composed of pure and gleaming ice. The Thunder Pagoda mixes Chinese and medieval European features and is made of solid clouds. Solid fire comprises the Fire Pagoda, which combines Chinese and medieval Arabic features. And the Darkness Pagoda mixes Aztec and Chinese features in a pyramidal complex of pure and malign darkness.

In each complex live the servants of each of the Four Monarchs, including humans, quasi-humans, spirits, and (in the case of the Fire King and Darkness Queen) demons.

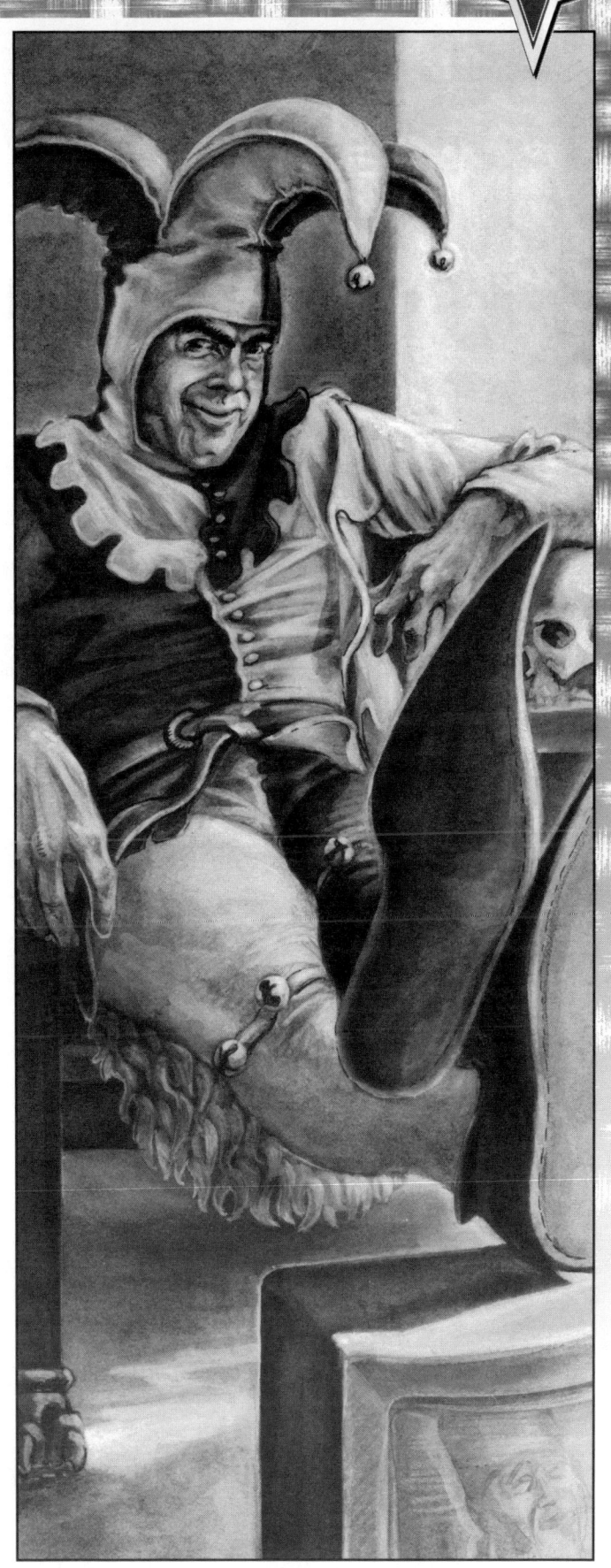

CHAPTER 18

Hong Kong

THE BATTLE GROUND

We recommend that you start your *Feng Shui* series in Hong Kong, in our contemporary juncture. (That's 1996, for those of you who weren't paying attention in chapter 16.) Because it's part of the modern world, it will be familiar enough for players to know the basics of the setting without a lot of explanation beforehand. Yet it's unfamiliar enough, at least to most Westerners, to seem cool and exotic.

We'll cover Hong Kong in more depth in the supplement *Blowing Up Hong Kong*. But in the meantime, here's some introductory material on Hong Kong, and the secret warriors stationed there.

HONG KONG AND THE NEW TERRITORIES

The 75 sq. km island of Hong Kong is just part of a colony that has been controlled by the British for a little over a hundred years. When people refer to "Hong Kong" they may be referring to the entire colony—which is properly known as **Hong Kong and the New Territories**—or they may be referring to just the island itself. The island is colloquially known as, well, the island. The island was taken over by the British in 1841.

The New Territories is a big chunk of land jutting out from the southeastern tip of the mainland; it was leased by Britain from China in 1898. The southern tip of this land mass, across the harbor from the island itself, is **Kowloon**. (The English had settled in Kowloon many years before the lease arrangement.)

Both the island and Kowloon are highly urbanized, with gleaming and not-so-gleaming skyscrapers jostling one another for limited real estate space. Modern glass and steel towers exist side-by-side with traditional temples to Taoist deities. If you can emphasize just one thing to your players about this setting, it's how crowded the place is. One neighborhood of Kowloon grabs the world record for population density: a mind-numbing 165,000 people per square kilometer!

Go north of Kowloon and you find an agricultural area with plenty of fertile land. Lately this has been turning into a polluted factory zone.

Lantau is a large island just west of Hong Kong; it is still a largely unspoiled, primarily rural area. The colony also includes another 234 small, outlying islands.

On June 30, 1997, all of this will revert to the control of the People's Republic of China. It will become a "special administrative region." China has promised to maintain existing freedoms in Hong Kong for 50 years after the takeover, but, in 1996, no one is quite sure whether they'll keep this promise. To cover their bets, many wealthy Hong Kong residents have arranged to emigrate to Canada, Australia, or the United States.

URBAN LOCATIONS

The action in most *Feng Shui* episodes set in Hong Kong will be set against an urban backdrop. This means rain-slick streets, garish nightclubs, sleazy

210

Hong Kong

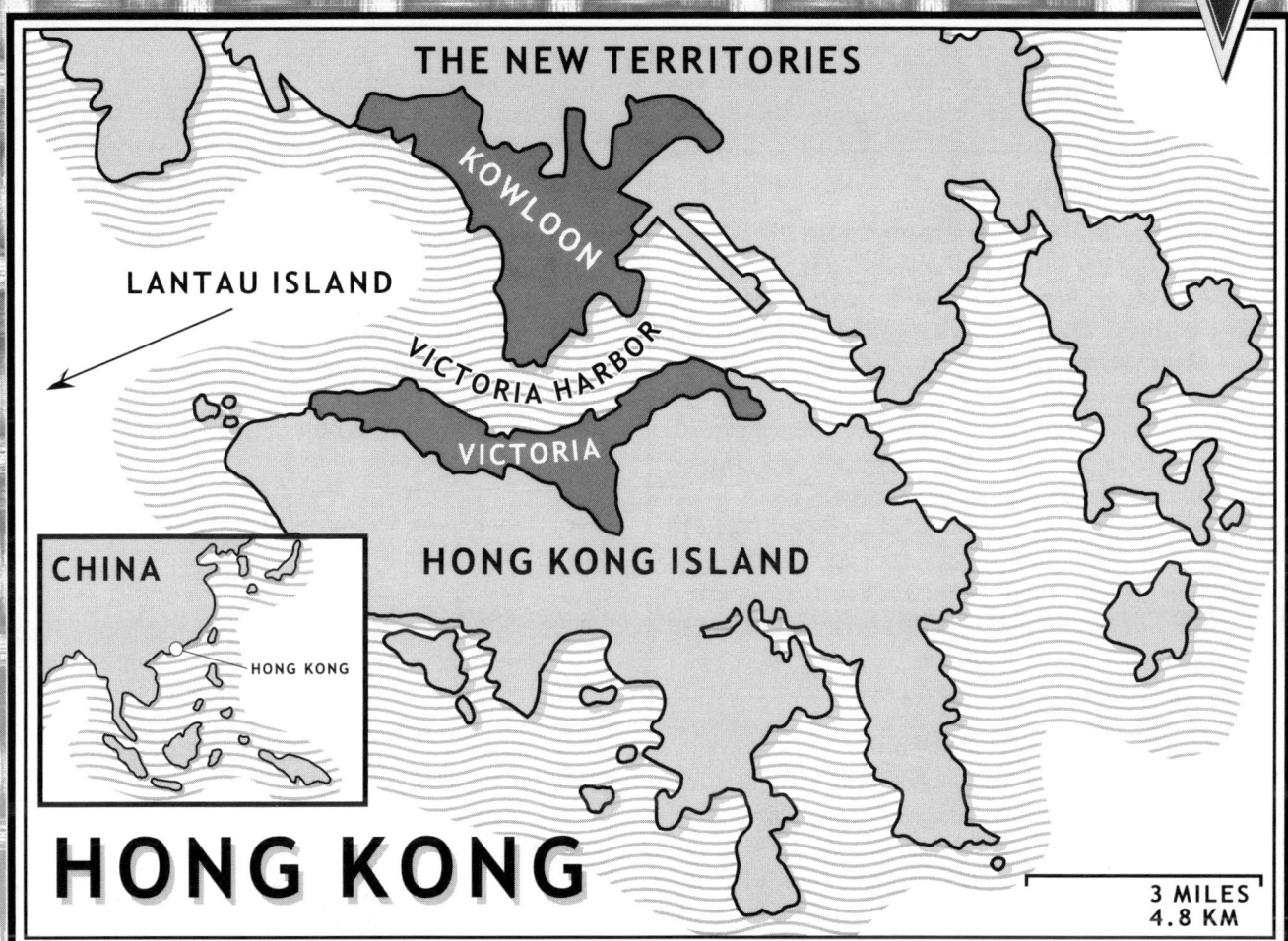

bars, run-down police precincts, and all the other staples of the genre. Think of every gritty crime flick you've ever seen, or even television shows like *Hill Street Blues* or *Homicide*. It's the kind of backdrop that's usually only seen by cops, crooks, and other street-level types. If the GM is the Director of our *Feng Shui* 'film,' think of the following as the report from the location scouts: Here's a bunch of great places to blow things up.

The major parts of Hong Kong—Hong Kong island, Victoria, and Kowloon—are outlined in the following text. The neighborhoods of each area have their own flavor; as you and the players get to know HK better, these areas will come to serve as a kind of shorthand. A violent murder in the Central District is going to mean something very different to the PCs than a similar murder in Wanchai. Mysterious goings-on in Little Hong Kong probably means smugglers and/or Triads; mysterious goings-on in Happy Valley could be *anything*.

Hong Kong Island

The sprawling reach of Hong Kong Island is home to a sizable industrial district as well as large stretches of coastline.

Victoria Peak

Although an island, Hong Kong is home to a number of modest mountains. The least modest of these is Victoria Peak, the tip of which is about 550 meters above sea level. This is accessible by tram, and, as we all know, trams are great places to set fight scenes (*Where Eagles Dare* has a cool tram fight). The top of the peak itself is a haven for bird-watchers and other nature lovers. The area around "the Peak," as it is called, is home to business tycoons and well-connected civil servants, many of whom might be open to kidnap by the bad guys. Hong Kong's zoological gardens are also in the area. Don't let your PCs leave the island without being thrown in a lion habitat at least once! The zoo is also a good place to have tense meetings with Ascended members, who will naturally gravitate to the part of the zoo containing the animal they used to be. That way, the Ascended guy can make veiled threats by referring to the animal nearby. ("Ah, I see it's feeding time... ")

> ### Details, Details
> A few important facts for GMs running episodes set in Hong Kong:
> **Climate:** Hong Kong is semi-tropical. Good weather comes in the fall. From September to November there are cool nights, dry days, and little humidity. December to February is what passes for cold in Hong Kong. The PCs will want to have sweaters or even heavy jackets on hand. March heralds the rainy season, with overcast skies and happy vegetation: a good time to hide concealed weapons inside umbrellas and raincoats. From May to September it's the unpredictable typhoon season. That means HK is hot, that the humidity hardly ever drops below 90 percent, and that a disastrous cloudburst can sneak up on you at any time.
> Typhoons make North America's hurricanes look like amateurs. They can kill you real dead-like if you don't retreat to your home and stay there. Of course, you as GM should arrange for some fights to happen in the midst of raging typhoons.
> **Currency:** The HK unit of exchange is the dollar. Exchange rates fluctuate, but for our purposes treat the ratio as $8 HK = $1 US.

Eastern Hong Kong

The area east of Victoria Peak is HK's industrial zone. Factories are a popular place for movie fights, and your series should be no exception. This is a great place for late-night rendezvous/shootouts between opposing gangs, or as a locale for a Netherworld portal. The climax of *Terminator 2* is a great example of a cinematic fight in an industrial zone.

Little Hong Kong

Little Hong Kong, on the western end of the island's southern shore, is a refuge for thousands of Hong Kong's boat people, who live on junks and *sampans*. Known by Westerners as Aberdeen, the area is popular with boat people because it is a good typhoon shelter. It's also a haven for smugglers, so there should be plenty of triad goons hanging around itching to be wasted.

This is also where you get to Hong Kong's famous floating restaurants: brightly lit ships converted into dining establishments. You should arrange for at least one fight to be held on one of these, undoubtedly with some kitchen worker screaming "The boiler's gonna blow!" at a crucial moment. In *Feng Shui*, every big boat should have an explosion-prone boiler.

Southside

The south side of the island is a playground for the rich. There are beaches, golf courses, a cricket ground, markets, Ocean Park, an aquarium with dolphin shows and amusement park rides, and other locales of relaxed entertainment that would make great places for shoot-outs. Included with admission is entry to a living history exhibit called the Middle Kingdom; it recreates Chinese history in a way that will make refugees from the 69 juncture feel right at home.

Southside is also host to Stanley Prison. Depending on how circumspect your PCs are as they blow up Hong Kong, they may end up here at some point. Or they may come here to foil a riot, or even go undercover inside in order to get crucial clues from imprisoned wrongdoers.

An Ascended-controlled military base, Stanley Fort, is located on a peninsula here—details appear later in this chapter.

Victoria

Straddling the Northern coast of Hong Kong Island, Victoria is the heart of commerce in Hong Kong—much as Manhattan is for New York City. Victoria tends to be stylish and upscale, though Wanchai has its share of sleaze.

Central District

This is the financial district, where the business wheelings and dealings that are the colony's reason for existence are conducted. It is centered around Hong Kong Harbor, a port that sees thousands of ships every year. The island was originally selected by the British because of the shelter offered by the island's harbor, which is located on a channel between Hong Kong and present-day Kowloon. It provides excellent protection from the typhoons that rock the area every year.

The Central District is home to bold office towers, government buildings (and other monuments of colonial rule), a large park, the ferry terminal, a fashion district, and tourist-oriented shopping areas. Action scenes you can stage here include robberies, hostage-takings, kidnap attempts, and car chases. As the daily hub of power and money, plots involving shady business deals or corporate espionage will often unfold in this neighborhood.

Happy Valley

Insipidly optimistic place-naming didn't start with 20th century subdivisions. The Brits settled in this area of the island in the 1840s, after discovering that their first choice was a fount of malaria. Now it's primarily known for its well-attended race track,

Hong Kong

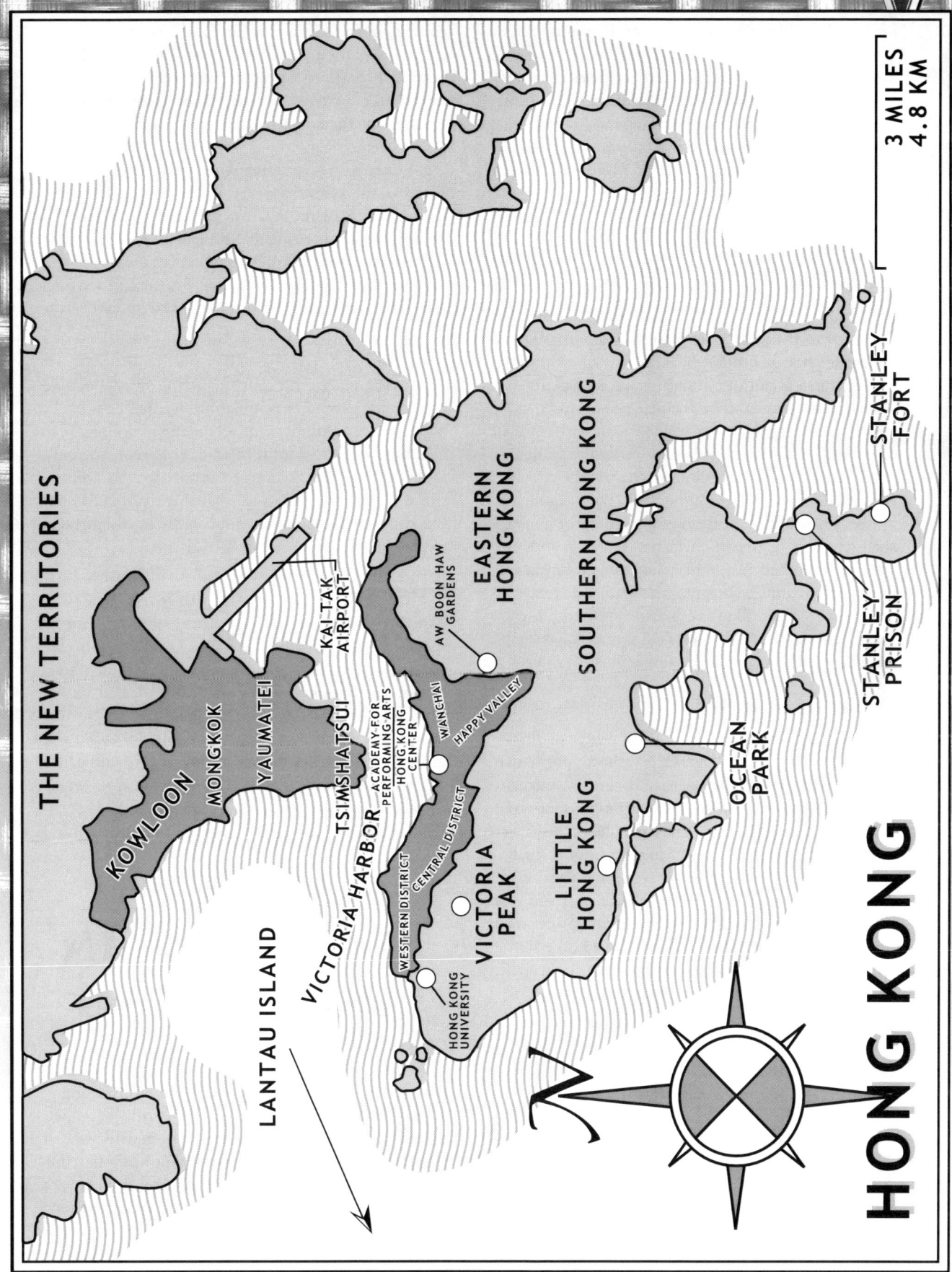

a bunch of historic cemeteries, and an amusement park: the Aw Boon Haw Gardens. This obvious gold mine for action set pieces is decorated with statues from Chinese mythology that the author of one travel guide describes as "psychedelic" and "zany." A bomb on the roller coaster is a natural, as is the obligatory assassination inside the Tunnel of Love.

Wanchai

Once a famous red-light district, Wanchai is a center of night life, especially for Westerners and tourists. Its topless clubs, streetwalkers, pubs, and gaudy nightclubs provide all of the seedy urban atmosphere you want to throw at your players. Many bars are open twenty-four hours.

The area is not one hundred per cent sleaze. Wanchai also seems to be the place to go for cheap custom tailoring, if any of your PCs are fashion plates on a budget. Tailors are often open until midnight, just in case one of the heroes needs to replace a bullet-ridden, bloodstained dinner jacket on a moment's notice. It's also the location of a number of good restaurants for gourmet characters to eat at and/or fight in, as well as two performing arts complexes: the Academy for Performing Arts and the Hong Kong Arts Center. Wanchai is also home to lots of Taoist temples and two sports stadiums. Anyone up for a Hong Kong remake of *Two Minute Warning?*

Western District

If the Central District is a stubborn refuge of British influence, the Western District is a thoroughly Asian urban landscape. It is home to an open-air market and countless retail outlets, from artisan's shops to great shopping complexes. Here the PCs can shop for calligraphic stamps, Chinese wine, traditional medicines, antiques, or cheap goods from mainland China. After shopping to their heart's content they can stop in for a bite at one of the famous Jervois Street snake restaurants. The Western District is also home to Hong Kong University, in case the PCs need to talk to an expert in the course of their clue-seeking.

Kowloon

Just across the harbor—reachable by ferry or tunnels (one for cars, one for a mass transit rail line)—is Kowloon, where many more mysterious clues and gut-crunching fights await your player characters. The districts of Kowloon are outlined here.

Tsimshatsui

This peninsula is where the various transit points from Hong Kong terminate. Shopping centers, hotels, a planetarium and space museum, an art gallery, and a performing arts center are all potential locations for set-piece battles. Entertainment choices range from classy (Peking opera, legit theater) to glitzy (hotel cabaret revues) to sleazy (topless bars).

Hong Kong's Kai Tak Airport is not far from Tsimshatsui. It terrifies passengers and pilots alike; the airport is in the heart of the city and planes descend at a grotesque angle through a thicket of high-rises. It's an insanely busy airport with very tight security. Not so tight that you couldn't set a gunfight there at rush hour, of course...

Mongkok

This is the place with that staggering 165,000 people per square kilometer population density. Lots of enormous and unpleasant tenement buildings. If the PCs have to hunt for an informant here, wish them luck; think of the Shangri-La towers in *Brazil* and you'll have a good idea of what these places are like. On the other hand, it's a good place to disappear for a while if you don't mind the vermin.

Yaumatei

Yaumatei is a neighborhood where ordinary citizens shouldn't venture alone at night. Of course, the PCs are not ordinary by any measure. The Night Market detailed in Baptism of Fire (p. 228) is located in Yaumatei. It provides another typhoon shelter, home to more of Hong Kong's boat people. PCs who want to buy or sell jade artifacts, or investigate said artifacts, should check out the big open-air Jade Market. Temple Street, the location of the Night Market, is also known for—what else?—several famous temples.

SECRET WARRIORS IN HONG KONG

Okay, now that we've covered the tourist stuff, here's what's really going on. This section describes the major GMCs who pull the strings in Hong Kong. This little corner of the world happens to be a locus not only of overt trade and financial activity, but of covert action in the secret war. Hong Kong has the highest concentration of powerful feng shui sites of any place in the modern world. Each of the factions has different theories to explain this curious fact. However, they all share the opinion

Hong Kong

Illustration by Roger Raupp

that it's more important to control these sites than to figure out exactly why there are so many of them.

It is important to the Ascended and Hand as a source of free-floating political power, somewhat separate (at least for the moment) from any one world government or alliance. It matters to the Lotus and Monarchs because it is the only place on Earth that is simultaneously highly modern and highly magical; as noted earlier, the normal juncture modifiers against Creature Powers and Sorcery don't apply in Hong Kong or the New Territories. The Architects like contemporary Hong Kong for similar reasons; it is the best place in this juncture to blend magic and technology. The Jammers think it's important, because its magical nature is exactly what they're trying to destroy; they want to figure it out in order to wreck it.

As for the Dragons, they are likely represented by the PCs. Why they're in Hong Kong is up to their players.

Your PCs shouldn't immediately be meeting up with the really-powerful GMCs described in this section. These are the heavy hitters who make things happen behind the curtain; some of them could toast beginning characters without batting an eyelash (or tree branch, as the case may be—see Kun Chau.) Instead, they should initially encounter lower-echelon agents, mooks, and lackeys. Only after many sessions should they be able to find the trail of clues that leads to the real powers of Hong Kong. Even then, it may be more interesting to dramatize non-combat encounters with these nefarious masterminds. If there is a fight later on down the road, it's more fun if the PCs already know and fear their opponents. That way *it's personal.*

ASCENDED INFLUENCE

For the Ascended, Hong Kong is both a success story and a headache. On one hand, it is vitally important for its rich concentration of feng shui sites, the greatest in the modern juncture. It is also significant for the role it plays in the mundane sphere. Hong Kong is a trade and financial center for all of East Asia, and wherever there is money and influence, the Ascended want—and usually get—a chunk of the action.

On the other hand, the very strength of Hong Kong's chi is a problem for the Lodge, the group of transformed animals who form the inner circle of the Ascended. They avoid Hong Kong like a balloon avoids needles. Despite their efforts over the centuries, and despite their possession of the majority of Hong Kong's feng shui sites, they have not been able to tame the area's innate magical resonance. Hong Kong is the only highly-urbanized, densely-populated area in the modern juncture where magic is easy to work. Lodge members hate sorcery: prolonged exposure to it threatens to awaken their dormant animal genes and turn them back into snakes, spiders, rats, and so on.

Therefore, the task of maintaining Ascended dominance in Hong Kong is left to high-ranking, unquestionably-loyal members of the Pledged. These are humans who have risen so far in the Order of the Wheel or Jade Wheel Society that they know the truth about their masters, and about the secret war. To qualify for this knowledge, they need to have enough ambition to get through the ranks of one of the secret societies, and enough humility to accept the fact that they're never going to get any closer to the inner circle than learning its big secret. This is an extremely rare combination of qualities.

The post of Hong Kong Operations Chief, or HKOC, is as high a post as any human member of the organization can hope for. Only the best candidates are even considered for the job. It offers autonomy, influence, and luxury. But it also brings temptation. The last HKOC, businesswoman Connie Bo, was found dead last year in her swank condo in the Victoria Peak area. She'd been shot seven times in the chest at close range with a 9mm pistol. Police officials made no arrests, hinting that a foreign government was involved. Those under her knew better: the hit could only have been ordered by the Lodge. Bo had been building her own empire, attuning cronies and family members to the feng shui sites controlled by the Ascended without Lodge permission. This incident left those under Bo's command all the more aware of the long reach of their masters.

An investigation of this officially-unsolved homicide by the PCs might make a good plot hook for an episode introducing the Ascended. Perhaps one of Bo's close friends wants out of the whole thing and offers evidence in exchange for protection.

Colonel Baynes Wilhelm

British military intelligence officer **Col. Baynes Wilhelm** is the current HKOC, but he knows that his is a temporary posting. When the Chinese take over in 1997, this long-term Order of the Wheel member will step aside in favor of a Jade Wheel Society counterpart from the Chinese military. Near retirement age, Baynes is loyal but not very ambitious. For most of his life, he thought of the Order of the Wheel as just a very special officer's club within the British military, never guessing that its branches could be found in similar power structures throughout the world. He obeyed the orders given him as a member of the Pledged with his usual quiet efficiency, never thinking that he served masters far beyond the British government. He had no idea that he was impressing the masters of the Lodge, and was so surprised when he was ushered into the top ranks of the Pledged and informed of the group's true nature that he nearly fainted. Since that day, he has been rather frightened by his new view of the world. Restrained to a fault, he managed to conceal his astonishment from the members of the Lodge. Baynes has continued to carry out their demands, fearing the dire consequences that would certainly result if they found out he was a loyal servant more out of reflex than respect.

Baynes is a cautious, conventional man who finds himself in the middle of a very unconventional situation. He follows the instructions of the Lodge to the letter; all he wants to do is last until the handover of power and his subsequent retirement from the military without making a mistake that will get him in trouble with his dangerous masters. He is married and has three children and two grandchildren. He knows that the Ascended are sufficiently ruthless to hurt his family if he ever revealed their secrets. So far he hasn't had to do anything truly terrible in order to please the Lodge, but he's sufficiently concerned about the safety of his family to do just about anything they require. Although at the age of 64 he is hardly a skilled combatant, he does have undeniable resources at his disposal, including the toughest unnamed characters in the New Territories. If the actions of the PCs were ever to make him fear for his position or family, he wouldn't hesitate in ordering the PCs' deaths. He'd feel bad about it afterwards, but that would be small consolation to the dead.

Stanley Fort

Baynes is commander of Stanley Fort, a top-secret military installation located on Stanley Halbinsel—the long, bulbous peninsula that forms the western shore of Tai Tam Bay on the south side of the island. It is primarily an intelligence-gathering installation which monitors satellite signals beamed at governments throughout the area. It is nominally a British intelligence operation, but is in fact a major Ascended base. British intelligence in HK is riddled with Order of the Wheel members who make sure that all positions of authority at the base are filled with Pledged officers. They also arrange for Pledged members of other Western intelligence agencies to be assigned to Stanley Fort on a regular basis.

The surveillance capabilities of the Fort are highly useful to the Ascended: They use it to spy on their enemies in the secret war. One highly-secret group of satellites is capable of monitoring levels of chi energy, whether regular or magical. The Ascended therefore know the location of every major feng shui site on the planet. They can detect the minute chi fluctuations that occur when sites are attuned to new users. Minor sites, such as the ones PCs are likely to be attuning to, can be detected with the equipment at Stanley Fort, but only with extreme difficulty. Unless the Ascended have a reason to be checking into a minor site, you can assume that it is not being monitored by the Stanley Fort installation.

This system is only possible because Stanley Halbinsel is itself a major feng shui site—the most powerful one in the entire colony. Ascended geomancers need to slightly tweak the laws of physics in order for the special chi-monitoring equipment to operate, and being positioned on Stanley Halbinsel allows them to do so.

Baynes discreetly crafts his duty rosters to make sure there's a Pledged officer on duty in the monitoring room at all times. The displays generated by the monitoring equipment are sufficiently subtle that an uninitiated intelligence officer will notice nothing unusual when a critical feng shui site is unexpectedly attuned to a new owner. However, the officer in the know will recognize the change in an instant. Within moments, the Pledged officer picks up the phone and alerts either the Colonel or **Rain Yuen**, the second-ranking Pledged member stationed at Stanley Fort. The officer contacted may decide to take immediate action, launching a lightning strike by one of the crack commando teams who are ready around the clock at the installation. Such dramatic steps are only taken in the direst of emergencies, since the appearance of a military assault team draws the kind of attention that the Pledged are taught to avoid. It is much more likely that Rain will be assigned to supervise more subtle and covert measures to regain possession of the site, assuming it was an Ascended site to begin with. If the site changing hands did not belong to the Ascended, it is unlikely that they'll do anything other than note the shift in their next report to the Lodge.

Rain Yuen

Rain, a native of Hong Kong, is a special liaison appointed by the Brits to manage the transition of the Stanley Fort installation to the Chinese. She is

> **Colonel Baynes Wilhelm**
> Attributes: Bod 5, Chi 0, Mnd 6, Ref 5
> Skills: Deceit 13, Guns 8, Info/Intelligence Analysis 12, Info/Military Procedures 15, Info/Secret War 10, Leadership 10, Martial Arts 7, Sabotage 7
> Weapons: Sig-Sauer P-220 (11/2/9 + 1)

> **Unnamed Pledged Commandos**
> Attributes: Bod 7, Chi 0, Mnd 5, Ref 7
> Skills: Driving 10, Guns 10, Intimidation 10, Martial Arts 8, Sabotage 10
> Weapons: fist (8), kick (9), Sig-Sauer P-220 (11/2/9 + 1), Ruger MP9 (11/3/32)

> **Rain Yuen**
> Attributes: Bod 7, Chi 4, Mnd 6, Ref 10
> Skills: Detective 10, Driving 13, Fix-It 8, Guns 13, Intrusion 12, Martial Arts 16, Sabotage 14
> Schticks: [Fu Powers] Signature Weapon (katana); [Guns] Signature Weapon: Colt Delta Elite MKIV, Both Guns Blazing
> Weapons: katana (11), Colt Delta Elite MKIV(12/2/8 + 1)

also Pledged, and has much more authority at the installation than her official position entitles her to. She acts as a *de facto* second-in-command to Col. Wilhelm. The Lodge has already arranged for her to stay on at the base in the same capacity when their Jade Wheel Society operatives take it over in 1997.

Her real job is to manage counterintelligence in the Hong Kong area against rival factions in the secret war. Although Baynes keeps urging her to take a more distant approach to operations, she will often take personal charge of violent field missions. Her lover, a Lodge member, was recently killed in an incident in Guatemala; although on the scene, she was unable to save him. Since that incident, she's been moody and withdrawn, except when hurting people. She doesn't know which enemy faction was responsible for the death of her lover. When she finds out who did it, she's going to go on a serious killing spree. Until that time comes, she'll settle for taking out her anger on anyone who crosses her path. The Lodge has assigned her to duties in busy Hong Kong in the hope that the activity will snap her back into emotional shape. She's one of their best human field agents and they don't want to lose her.

Rain is a very attractive woman in her mid-thirties. Once talkative and witty, she now speaks only when spoken to. When alone in her office or apartment, she cranks up her stereo and plays syrupy Hong Kong pop ballads at inhumanely high levels.

Rain commands a crack team of Pledged commandos. These gung-ho fighters have a sky-high sense of morale, despite the moodiness of their commander.

The game statistics for the Pledged commandos are higher than normal for unnamed characters. You may want to avoid using them in your series until the PCs have spent some experience points. If your story requirements demand that you use them right away, you should downgrade their attack Action Values.

ARCHITECT INFLUENCE

The Buro maintains a considerable number of research and development agents in contemporary Hong Kong, plus a smaller security and surveillance detachment both to protect them and to advance Buro interests in the secret war. The R&D team is in place because there is something unusual about contemporary Hong Kong. Its collective chi is unusually receptive to both magic and technology, making it the best place in the modern juncture to test and create arcanowave devices, and to conduct bioengineering experiments. This team has been personally assigned by the Buro's CDCA chief Curtis Boatman to study the chi of Hong Kong, and figure how to spread a similar chi pattern throughout the rest of the modern world. This would make it considerably easier to stage an invasion from the future, subjugating our world to Architect rule.

Dr. Felix Mei

Dr. Felix Mei was assigned to head the team because of his expertise in the study of chi energy and his Cantonese background. Although he speaks with a slight 2056 accent, he blends in well with Hong Kong society. He has even begun dating a chronologically-local woman named Diana Ching. Dr. Mei is a middle-aged balding Chinese man with a big frizz of unruly hair framing the hairless top of his head. His thick glasses make his eyes seem unnaturally large. If he fits a stereotype, it's more that of the absent-minded scientist than the progress-crazed madman. He is so apolitical as to be amoral, never having given any thought whatsoever to the actions of the repressive regime he contentedly

Hong Kong

serves. He's just interested in his little branch of arcanowave science, pursuing its secrets with the dogged devotion of a crossword puzzle expert or a British train-spotter. He understands that he has to keep a low profile and make sure that no one from the present day finds out who he is. But he thinks of this as merely a way of avoiding interruption of his research, rather than an essential element in his bosses' lust for conquest. He's continually sending his assistants through the Netherworld back to headquarters to lobby for more funding and equipment. Scoring more goodies from his masters is the one thing other than pure science that he's a genius at.

Although it is strictly against CDCA policy, Felix has followed in the footsteps of his scientific hero, Madame Curie, and has used himself as an experimental subject. He has turned himself into a cyborg. He knows that he'd get into serious trouble—maybe even lose his funding—if anyone at headquarters found out, so he'll only use his Arcanowave Device abilities in truly desperate circumstances.

Felix's goals are to expand the size of his operation and the number of scientists working under him, and to figure out how to expand the chi field of Hong Kong. The PCs are most likely to run into him as a result of one of his more blatantly amoral research projects: he's assigned the Buro security team to abduct slum kids, who then become guinea pigs for his experiments. He thinks the unique chi balance of Hong Kong is due to the radical mix of modern and ancient beliefs held by its inhabitants. By turning these kids into arcanowave cyborgs at an early age, Felix believes he can isolate the unique genetic component that allows HK residents to generate this unusual chi field. So far all he's done is turn a bunch of innocent kids into twisted freaks. If some of them were to escape and raise havoc, the PCs might eventually be led to Felix's doorstep.

Felix carries the Helix Ripper only when he expects serious trouble, which is not very often. He does know enough about the dangers of his situation to routinely carry his Buro-issue .22 pistol.

Denis Clech

Denis Clech is the head of the Buro security team assigned to watch over and protect the CDCA's Hong Kong operation. Technically, Felix is his superior. In reality, he has decided that Felix is a first-class idiot, a danger to Architect plans in the modern era and to anyone around him. There is a fierce institutional rivalry between the CDCA and Buro Security, one privately encouraged by Buropresident Bonengel himself. The CDCA's interest in advancing arcanowave science and the Buropresident's interest in crushing every civilization in the timestream are not always in perfect harmony. Buro security agents

Dr. Felix Mei
Attributes: Bod 5, Chi 7, Mnd 9 (Cha 5), Ref 6
Skills: Arcanowave Device 13, Fix-It 13, Guns 8, Info/Physics 13, Info/Genetics 13, Medicine 13
Schticks: Feedback Enhancer, Helix Ripper, Neural Stimulator, Spirit Shield Generator
Weapons: Helix Ripper (17), Buro Backup Arm (9)

Denis Clech
Attributes: Bod 8, Chi 0, Mnd 6, Ref 7
Skills: Arcanowave Device 15, Guns 10, Martial Arts 10, Sabotage 8
Schticks: Neural Stimulator, Helix Ripper, Robot Limb (Arm), Slap Patch, Reinforcer, Wave Scanner
Weapons: Helix Ripper (17), Katana (14)

Unnamed Buro Lackeys
Attributes: Bod 6, Chi 0, Mnd 5, Ref 6
Skills: Driving 8, Guns 8, Police 8
Weapons: Buro 9A (11/1/17 + 1), Buro Blue Flag (14/4/30)

assigned to these duties are always told that their job is as much to keep the scientists under surveillance as to further their requests. Denis takes this standard tension one step further. Although a decorated hero of numerous Buro covert actions and microwars, he secretly despises his new, bioengineered form. In his heart, he blames all scientists for his condition. If he could find any dirt on Felix and get him executed, he'd do so with rigidly-concealed glee. He'd do the same to any arcanowave researcher.

In the meantime, though, he's dominated by his need to prove himself worthy despite his tangled DNA structure. He wants to please his Buro superiors at all costs. This makes him a bit of a loose cannon. If he discovers someone who he sees as a threat to Architect interests, he'll go after them with all of the resources at his disposal—most likely without bothering to get authorization from the head office over in 2056. So if the PCs begin poking around into Architect affairs, he'll be less than subtle in trying to eliminate them.

The Chen Chien Building

The Architect headquarters in Hong Kong is the Chen Chien Building, a black steel monstrosi-

Chapter 18

ty of an office tower on the shores of Repulse Bay Beach on Hong Kong's southside. Even in Hong Kong, which sneers at the very idea of governmental interference in real estate development, the erection of the Chen Chien Building was greeted with howls of protest. When inhabitants of this posh area got a look at the models for the structure, they freaked. Its weird curves and sharp, upwards-thrusting edges made it look like some kind of demon rising from the sea. Of course, this is just what its designers—the CDCA's feng shui architectural experts—intended. The building is intended to further Architect domination of the area by driving a cruel spike into Hong Kong's chi, funneling it down into the basement of the building where it can be used in Felix Mei's experiments. So far the building hasn't had any measurable effect on the area's chi, but then again it has just recently opened. Felix figures he can use it as a broadcast site for Architect-friendly chi energy in the near future; whether he ever manages to get it working is up to you and your plotting needs. If he does succeed, he could crock the area's juncture modifiers to match those of 2056. How wide an area this covers is up to you. Certainly, if he were to send his nasty occult emissions too far into mainland China he'd arouse the unhappy attention of the Guiding Hand and Ascended. Neither group wants magical energy to spike upwards, and the PCs might find themselves in the middle of a two-way—or even three-way—war. Or they might find temporary allies in the Hand or Ascended camps in an effort to shut Felix's operation down—which means destroying the Chen Chien Building.

While inside the Chen Chien building, Arcanowave Device task checks and task checks made by abomination characters get a +2 bonus.

The guards in the Chen Chien building are statted out on page 219.

HAND INFLUENCE

The Guiding Hand hate Hong Kong. They didn't like it when the British imperialist swine claimed it as their own in 1841, and they don't like its bright lights, its greed, or its hedonistic lifestyle one whit more today. It's Guiding Hand infiltrators in the Chinese Communist Party who are agitating behind the scenes to clamp down on Hong Kong most thoroughly when 1997 rolls around. If they could just sink it into the South China Sea, they'd do that, but they realize they need a more sophisticated way of dealing with it. Their approach is two-pronged: spiritual and political.

Xiaowen Hu

Xiaowen Hu is a high-ranking official of the Chinese Communist Party. He has been assigned to oversee the transition of power from British rule to the People's Republic. He is also a member in long standing of the Golden Candle Society, the covert arm of the Guiding Hand.

His orders from his official masters are to make the changes as smooth as possible. The Politburo in Beijing has no interest in Tienanmen Square-style unrest in Hong Kong. Individual members of the Politburo are more interested in getting their cronies and relatives installed in lucrative business deals within Hong Kong than in forcing any ideology down the throats of HK residents. In modern China, the old party rhetoric is just a screen for a corrupt system of favors and bribes. Xiaowen has always been seen by his official masters as a gray and unthinking instrument of their greed: he performs his tasks efficiently and never asks questions. This makes him, in their view, the ideal man for the job. He'll make things work, keep feathers unruffled, and make sure that the favors flow to the right bosses.

Xiaowen Hu has behaved as an uncomplaining party functionary for years, but not because he likes it. He has come to despise the hypocrisy and materialism of his Politburo superiors. But he has contained his fury on the orders of his Golden Candle masters. He's just one of hundreds of moles that the Hand has carefully and patiently guided towards positions of influence within the Party. As noted, however, the Ascended have placed just as many if not more of the Pledged in the same hierarchy. The genuinely important struggle in Hong Kong is not between the forces of capitalism and the minions of communism, but between the Candle and Pledged factions within the Communist Party itself.

Ultimately, the Hand wants to control as many of Hong Kong's many feng shui sites as possible. The main obstacle to their doing so is the Ascended, who control the majority of Hong Kong's sites, just as they do in most other locations in the modern era. The Hand would like to use the 1997 shake-up to put Golden Candle officials in charge at these new sites. In order to do so, they must triumph over their Pledged counterparts in bureaucratic infighting. As far as Xiaowen Hu is concerned, the secret war is fought not with guns and fu powers, but with memos, staff meetings, and blackmail.

Sometimes, however, the surgical use of violence can aid in a battle fought with shuffled papers.

Xiaowen occasionally has reason to have rivals

Hong Kong

and their associates threatened, kidnapped, or even bumped off. On other occasions he needs to have his enemy's private files stolen, copied, or hacked into via computer. He needs to do so without tipping his Hand—er, I mean, showing his true allegiance. If he were to be revealed as a Golden Candle agent, the Pledged and Lodge members within the upper echelons of the Communist party could easily arrange for his reassignment to some rural backwater on the Mongolian border. The minute he's exposed, he's toast. If this happens, the Hand may or may not be able to get another Candle member appointed to his position. So he exercises extreme caution whenever he orders covert action of any kind.

This is where **Tortoise Shell Information Services** comes in. This company, run and staffed entirely by Westerners, cannot be connected to Xiaowen by any paper trail. Xiaowen uses an old-fashioned dead letter drop system to contact them when he needs his dirty work done for him. Although Xiaowen gives the orders, it's the staff of Tortoise Shell that carries them out.

Physically, Xiaowen Hu is a thin, almost emaciated man. He dresses badly even for a Communist official, wearing threadbare suits with terribly clashing ties. He has a high forehead, snowy white hair, and bad teeth. In conversation, he seems befuddled and inarticulate. Although he is not good at expressing his thoughts, he is a careful and clever man, one whose abilities should not be underestimated.

Tortoise Shell Information Services

This front for the Golden Candle Society is run by Westerners sympathetic to the cause of the Guiding Hand. It was founded in the 1930s by the Reverend Charles Birdsall, a British missionary who "went native" and came to believe in the cause of Chinese liberation more fervently than most Chinese. Aided by a disillusioned former member of the Soviet secret service, Birdsall quit the clergy and set up the ultimate private espionage organization, Tortoise Shell Imports. In the years since it has changed with the times, keeping up with sophisticated new methods of illicitly gathering information. In the 80s, the company changed its name to Tortoise Shell Information Services, which had the advantage of being at the same time less suspicious and more vague.

TSIS has a permanent staff of four highly-skilled covert operators; they often hire freelancers to perform particularly risky or specialized tasks. This makes it an expensive operation. Its funds

> **Xiaowen Hu**
> **Attributes:** Body 4, Chi 0 (For 8), Mnd 8 (Cha 6), Ref 5
> **Skills:** Deceit 15, Info/Communist Party Bureaucracy 15, Info/Geomancy 10, Info/Espionage Techniques 12, Intimidation 12, Leadership 12

come from squeeze money siphoned out of the Chinese government by Golden Candle infiltrators. The members of TSIS are all inductees into the Golden Candle Society. However, at the same time they indulge themselves in all of the luxuries and diversions that the "decadent" world of Hong Kong has to offer them. It might be said that the present staff of Tortoise Shell loves the gamesmanship of the secret war more than the purity of the Hand's cause. Although they might become rebels in the event of a successful Hand takeover of Hong Kong or the world, for the moment their loyalty is unquestioned.

The head of Tortoise Shell is **Emma Birdsall**, granddaughter of the firm's founder. She's a dazzlingly-attractive young woman whose specialty is her insight into human behavior. She spends most of her time behind her desk in her luxuriously-appointed office, listening to Bach cantatas on the stereo as she analyzes the intelligence reports brought to her by TSIS operatives. She constructs psychological profiles for every person who might become even peripherally involved in a TSIS operation, from allies to targets to neutral parties. A master of disguise, Emma sometimes assumes a cover identity and arranges to meet individuals she needs to know more about. Emma has a bad habit of falling in love with people that TSIS is supposed to be targeting. Fortunately for her—and unfortunately for the objects of her affections—she falls out of love just as abruptly, and finds it easy to betray her targets.

The firm's intrusion expert is **Penelope Gidlow**, an elegant and energetic 70-year-old who was once the lover of Charles Birdsall. She is not Emma's grandmother—there's a whole love triangle bit that's too involved to get into here—but has been her mentor since Emma was a child. Penelope is very effective at what she does because she looks eminently harmless. On those rare occasions when she is caught inside a restricted area, she pretends to be a befuddled old lady and gets off scot free. Penelope has salted away quite a bit of money over the years, and owns a fine estate in the Victoria Peak area. This gives her social access to the wealthiest strata of Hong Kong society. In her spare time, she plays tennis, is an avid cricket spectator, and uses society gossip to speculate successfully on the stock exchange.

TSIS' in-house assassin is **Judy Birdsall**, Emma's bubbly kid sister. Like her colleagues, Judy is successful because she doesn't look like a hardened secret warrior. Barely out of her teens, she looks more like a spoiled rich kid than a trained

> **Emma Birdsall**
> Attributes: Bod 6, Chi 0 (For 8), Mnd 7 (Per, Cha 9), Ref 7
> Skills: Deceit 15, Detective 12, Driving 12, Guns 12, Info/Psychology 12, Leadership 12, Martial Arts 10, Seduction 15
> Weapon: American Derringer Mini Cop (12/1/4; 4 shots to reload)

> **Penelope Gidlow**
> Attributes: Bod 4, Chi 10, Mnd 7, Ref 7
> Skills: Deceit 12, Detective 12, Driving 10, Gambling 12, Info/Cricket 15, Info/High Society 12, Intrusion 15, Martial Arts 15
> Schticks: [Fu Powers]: Bite of the Dragon, Breath of the Dragon, Claw of the Dragon, Fire Strike, Fire Stance, King on the Water, Willow Step, Walk of a Thousand Steps

> **Judy Birdsall**
> Attributes: Body 7, Chi 0, Mnd 6 (Will 8), Ref 9
> Skills: Deceit 12, Driving 13, Guns 16, Intrusion 10
> Weapons: Browning BDM (11/2/15 + 1), Walther P-5 Compact (11/1/8 + 1), S&W Combat Magnum (12/2/6), H&K MP5 (11/3/30), Franchi SPAS-12 (14/5/7)

> **Denholm Nuttall**
> Attributes: Bod 5, Chi 0 (For 5), Mnd 7, Ref 5
> Skills: Deceit 10, Driving 8, Journalism 15, Info/Secret War 15, Martial Arts 8

assassin. Her favorite outfit to wear on a hit includes a baseball cap and jacket, T-shirt, jeans, and sneakers. She tops this innocent look off with a cute ponytail. This perky little outfit is very effective for making her seem harmless to unthinking victims. Judy is the ideal assassin because she thinks very little about the consequences of her actions. She likes guns, she likes challenges, and she likes danger. The fact that she's mowing down other living, breathing human beings doesn't mean much to her. Even her sister finds this chilling at times; Emma periodically thinks of checking Judy in for psychological treatment. But that would reduce her usefulness to the cause, and, anyway, she's extremely cheerful and personable for an utter psychopath.

Denholm Nuttall is the firm's legwork expert. He's not much use in a fight, but he has contacts throughout Hong Kong, and if he doesn't know something today, he knows how to find out by tomorrow. He routinely funnels high-quality intelligence on the secret war to Xiaowen Hu in the form of highly encrypted, anonymous e-mail messages. A former journalist, Denholm was in the last stages of drinking himself to death when he was kidnapped by Emma's father, who forced him to go on the wagon and gave him a reason to go on living. After nearly two decades of sobriety, Nuttall is still pays homage to Emma's father by carrying on his work on behalf of the Guiding Hand. Of all of the TSIS permanent staff, it is Denholm who is most sincere in his dedication to the cause. He is also the one who has his fingers on the pulse of the secret war. He knows the identities of all of the operatives described in this section, with the exception of Lotus demon-agent Kun Chau. A frequent visitor to the Netherworld, he conducts an on-again off-again love affair with Dou Sheng, an attendant to the Queen of the Ice Pagoda. He has a kindly disposition, but believes that sometimes brutal things must be done to a few for the good of the many. Because he has a very modest demeanor, not even the other TSIS staffers realize just how important Denholm is to the Hand's cause in Hong Kong.

Now in his late fifties, Denholm has a face that shows his many years of hard living. Deep creases cross his forehead and bisect the tip of his nose. He may be wrinkled, but his clothing is always sharply turned out, even in the wiltingly-humid summer months. Emma and company suspect that he has had his sometime-lover cast a spell that keeps his clothes looking perfect even under the worst of conditions.

Shih Ho Kuai

The third and final element comprising the trigram of Hand influence in Hong Kong is **Shih Ho Kuai**, a martial arts master and priest. Shih Ho Kuai's official job is as a humble assistant at Hong Kong's largest and oldest temple, the Man Mo Temple on Hollywood Road in the Western District. The Man Mo Temple is dedicated to two gods: Man, the god of literature, and Mo (more commonly called Kuan Ti), the god of war. This god is the patron of police officers, gangsters, and martial artists. Shih Ho Kuai is an old master who has dedicated himself to the service of Kuan Ti—and the Guiding Hand.

While Xiaowen Hu and the TSIS dedicate themselves to thwarting the Ascended, it is Shih Ho Kuai's job to monitor the agents of the other secret war factions in Hong Kong. He keeps an especially sharp eye out for Lotus and Architect activity.

Shih Ho Kuai has created a small secret society

of his own to aid him in his struggle. It is called **Tomorrow's Immortals**, and is composed of an unlikely mix of cops, triad members, and martial artists of all stripes. The members of the group are all worshippers at the temple and kung fu students of Shih Ho Kuai's. They don't know about the Guiding Hand; the philosophy Shih Ho Kuai teaches them is only coincidentally related to Quan Lo's neo-Confucianism. He knows the types of people who are attracted to the worship of Kuan Ti: they're risk-takers, independent folk who are sometimes a little rough around the edges. Shih Ho Kuai knows that these types aren't going to go for a doctrine of obedience and self-sacrifice.

Actually, Shih Ho Kuai himself has a little too much pride and fire in his belly to get along with the Hand leadership. This is why he was given the assignment to watch over the much-despised Hong Kong area: like the colony, he is brash, impulsive, and even a little boastful. Tomorrow's Immortals are dedicated completely to him; they adore him as their *sifu* (master) and willingly risk their necks in order to please him. Most of them would happily die for him, as long as that death was a glorious one earned in the heat of combat. Shih Ho Kuai doesn't expect them to forget their other obligations of loyalty—like those to their bosses or families—in order to serve him. A triad member who is also a Tomorrow's Immortal won't betray his mob superiors in order to fulfill a duty to Shih Ho Kuai. Cops won't break the law for him, although they may bend it considerably. This can lead to some odd situations: a triad gunman and a virtuous cop might be fighting alongside each other for Shih Ho Kuai in their spare time, and fighting against each other during their work days. There could well be novice members of the Dragons who are also members of Tomorrow's Immortals, and don't yet realize what they've gotten themselves into. The two groups could also work as allies in certain circumstances.

As mentioned above, Shih Ho Kuai is a fiery individual with a quick temper. In combat, his normally easy-going persona melts away. He becomes extraordinarily fearsome, both in appearance and deed. Aware of this failing, he now avoids getting into fights. Several times in the past he has been swept away in the passion of battle and slain opponents he was supposed to merely capture. He is especially prone to losing control when he activates his fu powers. Quan Lo has diagnosed him as having a too-powerful connection between his anger and his chi flow. He has been ordered to keep out of fights except in the direst of emergencies.

Although Shih Ho Kuai gets angry easily, he's no fool. He knows that he has wily enemies and limited resources. Most of the time he confines his operations against his foes to petty harassment. Only if it becomes apparent that the foes of the Hand are

Shih Ho Kuai
Attributes: Bod 5, Chi 11, Mnd 7 (Cha 9), Ref 10
Skills: Info/Buddhism 10, Info/Secret War in Hong Kong 10, Leadership 15, Martial Arts 18, Medicine 7
Schticks: [Fu Powers]: Abundant Leap, Claw of the Tiger, Flying Sword, Fortress of Righteousness, King on the Water, Natural Order, Tiger Stance, Prodigious Leap, Unyielding Tiger Stance, Vengeance of the Tiger, Vertical Charge, Walk of a Thousand Steps, Willow Step
Weapons: fist (6), spear (8), saber (9)

Unnamed Tomorrow's Immortal: Cop
Attributes: Bod 5, Chi 0, Mnd 5, Ref 6
Skills: Driving 8, Guns 8, Intimidation 8, Martial Arts 6, Police 10
Weapons: Colt Detective Special (10/1/6), fist (7), kick (8)

Unnamed Tomorrow's Immortal: Gangster
Attributes: Bod 5, Chi 0, Mnd 5, Ref 6
Skills: Driving 8, Guns 8, Intimidation 8, Martial Arts 6, Sabotage 8
Weapons: Glock 17 (11/1/17 + 1), fist (7), kick (8)

Unnamed Tomorrow's Immortal: Martial Artist
Attributes: Bod 6, Chi 0, Mnd 5, Ref 6
Skills: Info/Buddhism 8, Martial Arts 8, Medicine 6
Weapons: Colt Detective Special (10/1/6), fist (7), kick (8)

going to make some kind of significant advance does he pull out the stops and send out large numbers of Tomorrow's Immortals with guns blazing and fists flying. He sees the Architects and Lotus as the worst threats, and keeps a special eye on them. The other groups become a concern only when they do something really nasty.

Unlike his superiors, Shih Ho Kuai rather likes Hong Kong; sometimes he thinks of himself as more of a defender of the people of the colony than a servant of the Hand. Although this is not a question he has given any thought to, he might even rebel against the Hand if he thought that they were going to do something terrible to Hong Kong.

Chapter 18

Sabrina Ferran

Sabrina Ferran is a refugee from the future, the daughter of a top Architect scientist. She herself is a precociously-talented arcanowave researcher, having learned the principles of this strange branch of science at her mother's knee. Sabrina wants to get back at her cruel and distant mother by any means possible. This is why she ran away at the age of seventeen and joined the Jammers, the Architects' nemesis organization.

Naturally, she also wants to be a rock star. In order to further this second aim, she convinced Battlechimp Potemkin to assign her to a mission in the contemporary juncture. She has a small band of Netherworld outcasts with her to aid her in her research. Not so coincidentally, they also happen to be okay rock musicians. They work steadily on their assignment, but their top priority is their band, the **Dump Warriors**. They'd like to move somewhere more punk-friendly than pop-saturated Hong Kong, but they know that Battlechimp would recall them if they pulled a stunt like that.

When a Jammer operation is launched in Hong Kong, Sabrina plays host to the agents assigned to complete it. Otherwise, she stays as far away from covert activities as possible. So far the Architects in Hong Kong don't know about her or the other Dump Warriors, and that's the way she'd like to keep things.

Note that Sabrina doesn't employ Arcanowave Devices; her rating in that skill reflects her knowledge of the theoretical science behind their use.

LOTUS INFLUENCE

The Eaters of the Lotus, as relative newcomers to the secret war, have the smallest presence in Hong Kong of the five major factions. They are still learning about the contemporary world. Gao Zhang has sent many agents through the Inner Kingdom into the modern era to find out what's going on and report back. He plans to establish power bases in our juncture, but has not yet marshaled the knowledge and resources to do so. His reach into Hong Kong is largely limited to the activities of agents sent from 69 to accomplish particular missions. The sorcerer Ta Yu, who is one of the major villains of the Baptism of Fire adventure (it starts on p. 228) is a typical example of such an agent. He's been sent to set up an organization by allying with the Poison Thorns, and to grab a vulnerable feng shui site or two—such as the Eating Counter restaurant that is the center of that adventure.

JAMMER INFLUENCE

The Jammers are a minor faction in the secret war, and there is only a small cell of them in Hong Kong. They are studying the high chi level of the area, hoping that it will provide them a clue that will further their ultimate goal of destroying the world's chi.

Kun Chau

The most powerful permanent agent of the Lotus in the Hong Kong area is **Kun Chau**, a powerful demon. Kun Chau is a tiny island off the north coast of Lantau. That's right—she's not stationed on the island, she *is* the island. Kun Chau was created by a powerful sorcerous ritual enacted by Gao Zhang and his inner circle of eunuch sorcerers in 69 AD. It was a normal, nonsentient island before the ritual; Gao summoned a powerful and willing spirit from the Underworld and bound it into the very soil of the island. In the current version of the timeline, Kun Chau outlasted the Eaters of the Lotus by centuries, continuing to exercise its baleful presence throughout the South China Sea. Kun Chau was active as late as the eleventh century, when the Ascended, in the guise of the Jade Wheel Society, took effective control of the area's feng shui sites and reoriented its chi energy to dampen magical power. She then became dormant, remaining in this state until mere months before the opening of your series. At this time, Ta Yu and other Lotus sorcerers traveled through the Netherworld to the island and performed a ritual of awakening on the sleeping demon within.

Since that time, Kun Chau has been slowly growing in power. A small number of peasant fishermen, perhaps two dozen families in all, live on the island. She has been exercising her Influence abilities to turn these unfortunates into mental slaves. She can at any time impose her will on these people, as long as they remain within 16 kilometers of her; effectively this means she can control them as long as they remain within the New Territories. When they are under her influence, they will do anything she commands, no matter how suicidal. But since the number of fishermen she can command is small, she doesn't consider any of them expendable.

Kun Chau is a being of subtle and malign intelligence. She may be a land mass, but she's no fool when it comes to the politics of the secret war. She's been fully briefed on the war, its factions, and the goals of the Lotus. Islands are very patient, with an innate bias towards long-term planning. Kun Chau wants to assemble a permanent, stable power base for the Lotus in the Hong Kong area. To this end, she has influenced the headman of the fishermen to open negotiations to lease a big chunk of the island to wealthy developers who wish to build a luxury resort on Kun Chau. She figures that this will enable her to invade the minds of wealthy and influential people from all over the world, and thus spread the authority of the Lotus across the globe.

In the meantime, she's been sending her mental thralls to make frequent trips to Hong Kong, gathering news and gossip. Using this information, she has become an expert on local politics, and on

Sabrina Ferran
Attributes: Bod 6, Chi 0 (For 6), Mnd 5, Ref 6
Skills: Arcanowave Device 15, Guns 9, Info/Hardcore (Punk Music) 11, Leadership 10, Martial Arts 10, Sabotage 12
Weapons: punch (7), kick (8), Buro 9 (11/1/7 + 1)

Unnamed Dump Warriors
Attributes: Bod 6, Chi 0, Mnd 5, Ref 6
Skills: Guns 8, Info/Hardcore (Punk Music) 8, Martial Arts 8
Weapons: punch (7), kick (8), Buro 9 (11/1/7 + 1)

Kun Chau
Attributes: Body: see text, Chi 0 (For, Mag 30), Mnd 12, Ref 7
Skills: Creature Powers 40, Deceit 13, Info/Ancient History 20, Info/Modern Life 13, Info/Secret War 13, Intimidation 20, Leadership 23, Sorcery 40.
Schticks: [Creature Powers]: Blood Drain (Fortune drain, Memory drain), Brain Shredder (Damage 19), Corruption, Inevitable Comeback (x 5), Rancid Breath (Damage 19), Regeneration, Tentacles (8); [Sorcery]: Blast (Acid, Chi, Disease, Disintegration), Divination, Fertility, Influence, Weather.

Unnamed Mental Thrall
Attributes: Bod 5, Chi 0, Mnd 5, Ref 5
Skills: Martial Arts 8
Weapons: machete (8)

the technology and society of the 20th century in general. This is the main aid she can provide to Lotus agents newly-arrived from 69. She can quickly inform them of modern ways, and give them advice that will help them to fulfill their missions. She is unwilling to risk her own resources to further the plans of other Lotus operatives. This sometimes leads to conflicts with Gao's agents, who expect more concrete assistance from her. But whether they like it or not, there's little they can do to force her to comply with their demands. Having existed for centuries, she is a much more powerful sorcerer than any field agent Gao has ever sent to our juncture.

Kun Chau's greatest fear is exposure, especially to the Ascended. She knew about the Jade Wheel Society's original efforts to suppress magic before she went under, and doesn't want to go dormant again. Having recently learned about the power of the Jade Wheel Society in the modern world, she has no doubt that they could readily acquire these new creations called atomic bombs if they were to uncover the existence of a demonic island. She has no idea whether she could survive a nuclear strike, but has no great desire to find out. She'd rather move slowly towards her goal than risk arousing the notice of hostile secret warriors. On the other hand, were someone—like the PCs—to find out of her existence, she would spare no effort to snuff them out before they spread the word.

Kun Chau is herself a feng shui site. As long as she is alive and sentient, only those she wishes to attune to her may do so. She has attuned all of her fishermen.

As an island, Kun Chau's game statistics need a little explaining:

She has no Body rating per se; it is not possible to damage her physically with the sorts of weapons at the PCs' normal disposal. She *might* be damaged by something as powerful as a nuclear strike, but no one's tried it yet, so who knows? She can be damaged by Arcanowave Device, Creature Power, and Sorcery attacks.

Kun Chau combines her Divination and Influence schticks to allow her to see through the eyes of those she dominates. This allows her to aid her mental slaves even when they are far from her shores (but still within 16 km). She can spend Fortune dice on their behalf. Her thrall's senses count as a "remote viewing aid" for the purposes of Sorcery schticks that allow their use; she can, for example, use the Steal Chi schtick of Fertility against opponents seen through the eyes of her fisherfolk.

If secret warriors set foot on Kun Chau, she will attempt to make them her mental slaves as well. In order to achieve this unusual degree of Enchantment over any PC or GMC, she must get an Outcome of 35 or more on her Sorcery task check, which is made against the higher of the character's Magic or Will attributes. Characters so enchanted are under her control until active measures are taken to break her magical hold on them. The Restore Chi schtick of Fertility can cancel Kun Chau's domination; the Difficulty is 40 (her Sorcery rating) when the character is on Kun Chau. It is the character's Will rating when the subject is not on the island. Of course, Kun Chau will do her best to prevent the PCs from removing any of her thralls from her clutches.

As to her creature powers, Kun Chau can cause her tentacles to materialize anywhere on the island. Likewise, she can subject anyone on her to Rancid Breath. But she prefers to do so using camouflage to disguise herself. Unless desperate, she'll use her Rancid Breath ability only when her victims are near one of the several miniature bogs on the island. Normally she'll manifest her tentacles as the branches of the many twisted, stunted trees that dot her surface. She exercises her Blood Drain schtick through these sharpened branches as well.

At the moment all of Kun Chau's thralls happen to be peasant fishermen and their families. But she could at any time gain more thralls as new people step onto her shores. At some point, you should further the plot idea about the resort being built on her; this would provide her with a steady supply of thralls and a global reach.

Kun Chau is by far the most powerful of the GMCs presented in this chapter. Handle her inclusion in your storylines with care! She can easily smoke the average gaggle of PCs foolish enough to step on her soil. But that doesn't mean she will automatically try to destroy or enthrall them. Remember, she wants to keep her existence a secret. That means she's going to be cautious about who she tries to enslave, and even more careful about revealing her true nature. She may well be *tempted* to whip out those tentacles, but she's smart enough to restrain herself in service of her long-range goals.

MONARCHS INFLUENCE

The Four Monarchs are peripheral players in the Hong Kong theater of the secret war. Since their version of history was erased, their power has been dramatically reduced. Right now, they are preoccupied with fighting amongst themselves in the Netherworld. If they did try to reconquer the modern world, they might well do so from Hong Kong. But as the action begins, they are laying low and taking potshots at one another instead of acting with any sort of unity.

A couple of the Monarchs do have contacts in Hong Kong. These are more allies than underlings. One such ally is Leslie Lau.

Leslie Lau

Leslie Lau, playboy inventor and entrepreneur, is a frequent visitor to the Netherworld who has become a carousing buddy of Huan Ken, the King of the Thunder Pagoda. Leslie discovered the Inner Kingdom while working on one of his high-tech gadgets, a device that was supposed to eat pollution. It didn't destroy any pollutants in the atmosphere, but it did open a portal to the Netherworld. Curious to a fault, Leslie stepped through the portal without hesitation, and soon found himself in a fantastic world. After escaping several unfortunate run-ins with the more dangerous denizens of the Netherworld, he came upon the Thunder Pagoda. He charmed his way into the place, and soon hit it off with Huan Ken, who is always on the lookout for someone new to party with.

Since that time Leslie has attuned himself to several minor feng shui sites in the Hong Kong area. This has allowed him to use the mutable properties of the Netherworld to set up an ideal laboratory within the Thunder Pagoda. He can create devices in the lab that he could never build in the real world. Although there is no way so far for him to manufacture these devices in quantity, he has made a more-than-comfortable living for himself selling his one-of-a-kind devices to wealthy clients. Some of these clients are secret warriors. Although Leslie's moral sense is not exactly finely-tuned, he does have the sense not to sell anything to the Architects or Lotus.

In exchange for his hospitality in the Netherworld, Leslie keeps an eye out for the Hong Kong activities of Huan Ken's rivals, the Darkness Queen and Fire King. He also hosts Huan Ken's occasional pleasure trips to Hong Kong. Lau, the King, and the King's entourage trawl the sleazy dives of Wanchai a couple of times a year, drinking themselves silly and risking a wide variety of social diseases. The King and his Thunder Knights dress like GQ fashion plates for these evenings of debauchery, but their peculiar manners and speech patterns are a tip-off to anyone familiar with the secret war. On a couple of occasions the Thunder Knights have touched off epic brawls with the locals or other secret war factions.

Leslie is a very attractive man in his mid-thirties. He favors full Armani regalia during the hot months and a leather jacket and jeans when it's cool. He likes fun, money, and inventing things, in that order. Although capable of handling himself in a fight, he doesn't enjoy violence and avoids it whenever possible. If he does get wind of a threat, he's more likely to travel to the Netherworld and borrow a bunch of Thunder Knights than to go off to fight it alone.

If Leslie has Thunder Knights with him, they'll be dressed and equipped for Hong Kong. Instead of magical armor and great whacking swords, they'll have cool suits and great whacking guns.

Leslie's Inventions

Here are some examples of Leslie's weird gadgets. These are prototypes that he has kept around for his personal use. You are encouraged to come up with more: Leslie should use at least one new gadget for each session he appears in. It should be very difficult for PCs to acquire these and use them permanently. If a PC takes one of Leslie's doodads, it will shortly thereafter get wrecked or just stop working. If Leslie wants a PC to own one of these items,

Leslie Lau
Attributes: Bod 6, Chi 5, Mnd 8, Ref 6
Skills: Driving 11, Fix-It 15, Gambling 9, Guns 12, Martial Arts 9, Sabotage 14, Seduction 13
Weapons: fist (7), kick (8), Emerging Technologies Laseraim (12/3/8 +1)

Unnamed Thunder Knights
Attributes: Bod 7, Chi 3, Mnd 5, Ref 6
Skills: Gambling 8, Guns 7, Info/Beer 10, Intimidation 8, Martial Arts 8, Seduction 8
Weapons: fist (8), kick (9), Colt King Cobra (12/3/6)

and the PC pays 8 experience points for it, the item will continue to work except when it totally messes up your plots.

Dusk-O-Matic. A hand-held device that looks like a calculator. It temporarily draws light waves towards it, capturing them within a field of chi energy. The result is that an area with a five meter radius becomes almost pitch black, reducing visibility within the area to about ten per cent. To activate it, the user must spend a Fortune or Magic point. Roll one die; this is the number of sequences the Dusk-O-Matic works for.

Speedball. A rubber ball with an electronic guidance system inside it. If you bounce it against a hard surface while making a Martial Arts check, it will ricochet off various available surfaces for a number of shots equal to the Action Result. It will then strike a target you specified when you made the check, using the original check value to determine the success or failure of the attack. The Speedball has a base damage rating of 3 and requires just 1 shot to activate.

Ultraviolet Penetrator. A modified laser sight which Leslie can install on any gun; he has one on his Laseraim. Make a Guns check; if successful, you bathe your chosen target in an aura of light that causes all metallic, ARB, and magically-charged items on her body to fluoresce. This effect can be seen even through heavy clothing. Using the Ultraviolet Penetrator takes 1 shot.

APPENDIX A

Baptism of Fire

YOUR FIRST FENG SHUI EPISODE

This is the introductory adventure that gets a disparate group of PCs together and forges them into a team. They get the first glimmers of the secret war plotline as their players familiarize themselves with the combat rules for *Feng Shui*.

Premise: The PCs protect a family restaurant from vicious gangsters.
The Twist: The restaurant is a minor feng shui site, and the gangsters are pawns of the Eaters of the Lotus.
The Climax: Heroes and bad guys battle it out in a burning tenement complex.

BACKSTORY

This section tells you what's gone on before the action starts. It gives you advice on getting your PCs into the storyline. It also gives you the basic scoop on the supporting cast, both bad guys and bit players. The PCs will learn about these characters as they go along, but you'll find this adventure easier to understand if you start with this information in mind. This section concludes with a few brief notes on the neighborhood in which much of the action takes place.

GETTING STARTED

When your players create characters, tell them that they should all have a reason to be eating at a restaurant called the **Eating Counter** on a Wednesday night in February. The Eating Counter is located in the heart of Temple Street in the Yaumatei district of Kowloon; see "On Location," p. 231. The Eating Counter is known to food fans as one of the best places to eat in the entire colony.

Here are some reasons why a PC might be found at the Eating Counter:

They've heard the food is good.

They have an appointment to meet someone, perhaps someone connected to their melodramatic hooks. (These people never show up.)

If they're gamblers, they are on their way to an illegal high-stakes gambling den but have stopped for good food first. The food served at the casino is putrid.

Cops, masked avengers and/or private detectives might be working on an unrelated case in Temple Street, where petty crime of all sorts abounds. You can employ an interesting twist later on if you establish that a PC is trying to get the goods on Fast Eddie Lo. He is the local mob boss, described later on in this adventure. If you establish ahead of time that a PC has a grudge against Fast Eddie, there's a chance for some interesting irony, because the PCs end up doing a favor for Fast Eddie by taking on the main villains.

Magic cops might be tracing a dead-end lead about supernatural activity in the area. If so, tell the player that the character has already decided that the case is a wild goose chase, so he doesn't send his character off in pursuit of a red herring. Alternatively, if the magic cop's player is already familiar with the surprises of the setting, you can tell him that he received a tip that a new gang in the Temple Street area has occult connections of some sort, and that he's come here to check out those rumors.

A humble martial artist type might be working at the restaurant to earn a living while he trains. He might even be a distant relative of the owner (see "Bit Players," p. 231.)

A ninja might have just had an inconclusive meeting with a local crime boss, who wanted to meet her in one of his Kowloon social clubs. The crime boss wanted to check her out in case he needs to hire someone with intrusion skills for a job. If the player goes for this, the crime boss is **Fast Eddie Lo**, described later on in this adventure.

A techie might have been combing junk shops for parts and stopped off for chow.

Characters from other junctures have just exited a portal from the Netherworld and have ended up on Temple Street. Since going through a portal from the Inner Kingdom always makes you hungry, they've come here for a bite to eat. They may still be wondering just how they're going to pay for the bill, lacking as they are in HK dollars.

There's a problem integrating characters of obviously nonhuman appearance into this storyline; you should strongly advise players designing abomination and supernatural creature characters to take the Transformation schtick. This will allow them to be properly slurping soup in the restaurant along with everyone else when the action begins. If the players decline to follow your advice, tell them that their characters have just arrived from the Netherworld and have managed to conceal themselves from the throng of sin-seekers and sin-purveyors on Temple Street. Becoming hungry, they ducked into an alley and are now munching away on spoiled food in the trash bins outside the Eating Counter. If there is more than one such character making your life as GM inconvenient, they meet while cruising the garbage for edibles.

THE BAD GUYS

The main bad guys here are the **Poison Thorns**, a newly formed street gang headed by **Furong "Sneezy" Teng**. Sneezy and most of his cronies have been in Hong Kong for about a year; they're from the mainland and have connections to well-connected mobsters there. Sneezy isn't content with his lot as a mere street-corner ruffian, and wants to be a big-time mobster. That means muscling in on the territory of triad middleman Fast Eddie Lo. If Sneezy does enough damage to Lo's operation without getting snuffed, he can then petition Fast Eddie's big brother to take over his territory with the blessings of the higher-ups. (A big brother is a mentor and superior in the triad gangs.)

Sneezy's right-hand man is **Kaibong "Happy" Cheung**. Sneezy relies on Happy to do his dirty work, whether it be disciplining an insubordinate gang member or shaking down a mark. He's the first of the three named bad guys that the PCs will encounter.

Sneezy and the Poison Thorns haven't had much success at muscling in on Lo until recently. Lo's men are too professional and well-equipped for Sneezy's amateurish crew; even drunk, few of Sneezy's boys have the courage to take on Lo's smooth operators. Looking for some backup, Sneezy contacted one of his mainland connections, who put him in touch with a man named **Ta Yu**. Ta Yu started giving advice to Sneezy and pep talks to Sneezy's boys. Then suddenly everything started going right. The Poison Thorns recently won a couple of minor rumbles with Lo's enforcers, and are now feeling confident enough to make a major move.

The secret here is that Ta Yu is an ancient eunuch sorcerer, an operative of the Eaters of the Lotus. He has been dispatched here by Lotus leader Gao Zhang himself, to investigate opportunities to start capturing feng shui sites in the contemporary era. In order to find instruments for his plan, Cheng has immersed himself in the Chinese underworld, setting himself up as an advisor to several mainland bosses. He knows that the Eating Counter is a place with good feng shui. He wants the Poison Thorns to intimidate its owner into signing the place over to him. He will then attune himself to the site and magnify his sorcerous power.

GMC Notes

This section provides notes that will help you portray the antagonists of this story.

Sneezy Teng

Sneezy Teng is a man with little going for him but ambition. He grew up dirt poor, and sure as heck doesn't want to die that way. He's willing to do anything it takes to get ahead. If that means becoming a crook and allying himself with ancient evil sorcerers, that's fine by him. Although he hasn't done so yet, he'd murder without a second's hesitation if he thought it would get him closer to his goal of luxury and wealth. Unusually for a gangster, Sneezy wants money and success more than respect. He knows he needs to make people fear and respect him

Appendix A

to get that money, but the approval of others means nothing to him. He always has his long-range goals in mind, and can coolly shrug off any slight or setback that doesn't move him towards them. He

---

Sneezy Teng
Sample Dialogue: "Listen to me and listen well. Times are—achoo!—changing. Fast Eddie is on his way out. Achoo! The Night Market belongs to Sneezy Teng now!"
Attributes: Body 7, Chi 0, Mind 5, Reflexes 9
Skills: Guns 14, Info/Gangland 8, Leadership 8, Martial Arts 14
Weapons: punch (8), kick (9), Intratec Tec-9 (10/3/32 +1), Tokarev (10/2/8 +1)

Happy Cheung
Sample Dialogue: "No one beats me!"
Attributes: Body 10, Chi 0, Mind 5, Reflexes 8
Skills: Guns 10, Martial Arts 12
Weapons: punch (11), kick (12) club (13), Tokarev (10/2/8 + 1)

Ta Yu
Sample Dialogue: "Ignorant devourers of dung! You have no conception of the enormity of the situation you have blindly stumbled into!"
Attributes: Body 5, Chi 2 (Magic 10), Mind 7, Reflexes 6
Skills: Deceit 12, Info/Gangland 11, Intimidation 10, Leadership 12, Sorcery 17
Magic Schticks: Blast (base damage 14 with ring), Divination, Heal, Movement, Summoning.
Magic Items Ring (Adds +2 to Blast damage)

Unnamed Poison Thorns
Sample Dialogue: "Get them!"
Attributes: Body 6, Chi 0, Mind 4, Reflexes 6
Skills: Guns 7, Martial Arts 7
Weapons: punch (7), kick (8), machete (9), revolver (9/2/6)

---

hasn't yet met a person he cares a fig for other than himself. He sees Happy Cheung and Ta Yu as mere tools to move him along his path. Sneezy knows that Happy is a pliant and easily manipulated tool, and that Ta Yu is too clever and dangerous to fully trust.

Sneezy gets his nickname due to persistent allergies that plague him all year long. He speaks quickly in strong, staccato sentences, but the threatening effect of these is lessened by his constant sneezing. When you play him, keep a Kleenex on hand as a prop; keep dabbing your nose with it as you speak Sneezy's dialogue.

Ta Yu

Ta Yu is a trusted confidant of Eaters of the Lotus leader Gao Zhang. Originally a corrupt civil servant, he allowed himself to be rendered a eunuch in order to get closer to the seat of power in the Emperor's palace. Once there, his seething lust for power was observed by Gao Zhang, who quickly introduced him to the arcane secrets of the Lotus.

Ta Yu is your basic off-the-rack evil sorcerer. He is prone to gloating when ahead of the game. Used to getting his way, he flies off the handle when challenged. He thinks of Sneezy Teng as nothing more than a useful idiot, underestimating him somewhat. In fact, he has a habit of underestimating anyone other than his superiors in the Lotus organization, and will write off the PCs as morons also. He places no value whatsoever on human life and will kill anyone to further the inexorably corrupt plans of the Lotus.

Like any eunuch in a Hong Kong flick, Ta Yu speaks in an annoyingly high and squeaky voice. He uses florid, blustering sentences. His knowledge of big words, particularly insults, is vast.

Happy Cheung

Happy Cheung is anything but happy. He's a Big Bruiser with a disposition that "nasty" doesn't even begin to describe. He likes breaking things and hurting people. He follows Sneezy Teng because Sneezy gives him all sorts of opportunities to do just that. Although the two of them have been cronies for years, Happy bears no special affection for Sneezy, or anyone else. He just likes to hurt people. The other Poison Thorns are afraid of his temper and will do anything he says. They saw him kill a guy with his bare hands once, just for bumping into Happy in a bar.

In any encounter, Happy's main priority is to prove himself the biggest, baddest human being on the planet. He becomes enraged when anyone stands up to him. If a PC insults him—or, even worse, bests him in combat—Happy will thereafter think of nothing else but exacting painful and bloody vengeance upon the PC. This will distract him from all other goals, including following Sneezy's orders.

Happy speaks in simple sentences, avoiding words of more than one syllable whenever he can. He's not actually dumb, just brutally single-minded.

The Poison Thorns

These guys are your basic stupid, fearful, reflexively-violent mooks. If you're giving them any more personality than that, you're thinking too hard. They're just breathing sacks of cement with guns, itching to be thrown through windows, crushed under collapsing ceilings, and otherwise dispatched like the bottom-feeding no-name scum they are.

THE BIT PLAYERS

The owner of the Eating Counter is **Shen Kar-Wai**. He's getting on in years and is hoping to turn the day-to-day operations of the place over to his pretty young niece **Carina Shen**. He's raised Carina from the age of five, after his brother and sister-in-law were killed in a boating accident. Kar-Wai is extremely protective of Carina; he's been a bachelor all his life and she's the only family he has. In case you were wondering, Shen is the family name; Kar-Wai puts it first in his name in the traditional manner, while Carina puts it second in the Western manner.

If any of the PCs work in the restaurant, they already know these two bit players. They know that:

Kar-Wai is a grouchy, irascible man with a heart of gold. He's always yelling at his employees, but when they're in trouble, he'll slip them extra money under the table. He loves Carina more than anything in the whole world. He has a serious heart condition. The doctors have told him to take it easy. But when he's at the restaurant he's incapable of taking it easy—he's an obsessive perfectionist. This trait is good for business but bad for his health.

Carina is a painfully shy young woman, even around the other restaurant employees. She could have gone to college this year, but stayed home to look after Uncle. (Carina always refers to Kar-Wai as "Uncle.") She doesn't think she's up to the challenge of running a successful restaurant in one of the toughest neighborhoods in the world, but feels duty-bound to try. She wants to convince Kar-Wai to retire; she's afraid that he'll keel over from a heart attack at any moment.

What employed PCs don't know is this: The Thorns have been by twice recently, demanding protection money. They came by after hours, after the other employees had left. Kar-Wai angrily refused, protesting that they already pay the legitimate gangsters of the neighborhood: Fast Eddie's men. Sneezy Teng ended their last argument by threatening to send some of his boys around next time. Kar-Wai has kept this a secret from all but his most trusted of employees, not wanting to alarm his staff. His motivation is not entirely unselfish; he doesn't want people to quit for fear of being harmed by the gangsters.

ON LOCATION

The Eating Counter is in the Yaumatei District of Kowloon, across the channel from the island of Hong Kong itself. The entrance is at street level, but stairs lead immediately up to the second floor where the dining room, kitchen, and restrooms are. It is situated on Temple Street, so named because of its Temples to various Taoist gods. It is now better known for its Night Market, a brightly-lit, bustling row of shops and clubs. Temple Street is also home to the lowest, grittiest rung of the prostitution business. Numerous squalid second-floor brothels cater to customers with less money to throw around than the patrons of Hong Kong's tourist-oriented topless bars and hostess joints. There's always something going on in Temple Street: when the PCs hit the scene, describe a crush of people, a wild din, strobing neon, and the competing smells of street-level food stalls.

Every businessman who owns a business in the Night Market pays protection to Fast Eddie Lo, the local Triad bagman. That includes Kar-Wai. Fast Eddie, despite his name, is a smart and cautious gangster. He knows the limits on extortion, and is careful not to bleed off so much money that he drives people out of business. After all, unhealthy businesses mean fewer dollars to pass along to his demanding superiors. For their part, the business owners look on the protection money as just another level of taxation. In fact, you could argue that the triads give better service than the government. When people on Temple Street get into trouble, they go to Fast Eddie, not to the cops. Not that the distinction is that clear-cut: Most of the local cops are on Fast Eddie's payroll anyway.

OPENING SCENE

The PCs are dining at the Eating Counter when a bunch of Poison Thorns barge in, rudely shoving aside diners waiting in line for tables. Describe the Poison Thorns as a large number of toughs in their late teens and early twenties. Many of them have noticeable facial scars; they all wear leather jackets with the symbol of a thorn piercing a hand painted on the back. The jackets are all big and bulky, and there could be all manner of weaponry concealed under them. Like all of the patrons of the Eating Counter—with the possible exception of some PCs—the Poison Thorns are Chinese. A character with an appropriate Info skill can identify their accents as Fukienese: these guys are originally from

Appendix A

the mainland. There are three times as many Poison Thorns as PCs, plus one. The one in the lead is about a head taller than the rest of them. He has a permanent sneer carved into his face; the left side of his upper lip has been sliced away and replaced by a white ring of scar tissue. This is Happy Cheung; see earlier for his game statistics and character profile.

Carina notices the hubbub, and comes up to the front to see what's going on. Describe Carina to the PCs who don't already know her. Tell the players she seems obviously frightened, looking anxiously back to the kitchen area at the back. (She's worried that Uncle, who is in the kitchen, will hear the commotion, come out, and get into a fight with these dangerous hoodlums.)

Carina pulls a small wad of HK dollars out of her own purse and hands it out to Happy; trembling. Happy slaps it out of her hand.

The PCs can join the scene whenever they want. If they're already into the action hero mode, one of them will stand up right about now and tell them to stop bullying the girl. If not, Happy and company commit a series of further provocations, giving the PCs more reason to kick their butts:

Happy motions to the others, who start to swarm into the restaurant. Carina throws herself in their way. One of them pushes her over.

Uncle runs out from the back. Describe him to the PCs if they don't already know him. He's short, in his early sixties, wears a chef's hat, and has a hearing aid. He looks pretty frail. He starts angrily swearing at the Poison Thorns. Happy picks him up by the shirt and throws him roughly to the floor.

If the PCs haven't joined the fight by now, the Thorns start viciously kicking Kar-Wai. That oughtta do it.

If one of the PCs challenges Happy to single combat, Happy will oblige. This can go on, with Thorns and bystanders looking on, until somebody decides to escalate the confrontation into a general brawl. Your PCs may well elect to do this themselves, unable to restrain themselves from taking on the mooks. The mooks will get edgy if looks like the PC who is going *mano a mano* with Happy is winning. They'll start a general brawl by diving on the character fighting Happy.

Illustration by Grey Thornberry

RUMBLE IN THE RESTAURANT

Once the fight is joined, the Thorns will start beating on the nearest customers. If PCs directly attack them in hand-to-hand combat, the Thorns will leave the bystanders alone and concentrate on the PCs instead. They stick to punches and kicks until someone else (i.e. a PC) introduces deadly force into the fight. Then they'll pull out their revolvers and start blasting away. Once they run out of ammo (these losers don't have the Lightning Reload gun schtick!) they'll switch to machetes instead of reloading, and stick with them for the duration of the rumble.

Happy, on the other hand, will start with punches and haul out his club after he takes a solid hit. He will also attempt stunt actions. His favorite is picking up one of the large (1.5 m radius) tables round tables and hurling it like a frisbee at PCs across the room. He's smart enough to realize that the PCs are more than a match for his mooks. He doesn't care if he bowls over a few of his own men in taking out a PC, and so will hurl tables even at PCs in close combat with other Thorns. His Action Value when attempting this is 10; the damage rating of the attack is 8. If two PCs are close together, he will try to hit them both at an Action Value of 9. If this fails more than twice, he'll stop doing it. In the meantime, he will be flipping and rolling through the restaurant from one table to another, hurling each in turn.

Here are some things that can happen during the fight:

- Someone should get his face shoved into a sizzling hot plate on the countertop.
- Thrown plates, bowls, and wine bottles make excellent weapons.
- There's a lobster tank beside the cash register. It should get smashed. Maybe somebody's head should be plunged into it. If there's a mage throwing blast spells around, a stray blast can hit the tank and flash-fry all of the lobsters; supernatural creature PCs might enjoy a quick snack.
- The cash register can be lifted up and smashed down on someone's head with a distinct "ding!" sound effect.
- The Eating Counter's dining room is on the second floor. There are great big plate glass windows facing the street. People could get tossed through these windows, suffering 15 points of Damage; the one-story fall to the street inflicts another nine points of damage. Subtract the character's Toughness from each source of damage separately before inflicting Wound Points.

END OF THE FIGHT

The Poison Thorns think they're tough, but they're still cowards at heart. If the PCs can put down half of them (recall there are three times as many Thorns as there are PCs, plus Happy) then the rest will make a beeline for the stairs. Players usually hate to let combatants get away when they're winning, and will likely try to stop them from splitting. In this case, one of the Thorns grabs a grandmotherly diner and puts his machete to her throat. He threatens to kill her if the Thorns aren't allowed to leave in peace. He's holding the blade really tightly to her throat, and any attempt to get the machete out of his hand without seriously cutting the hostage should have a Difficulty of 18.

If the Poison Thorns are allowed to leave, they take the hostage with them; they're dumb, but not dumb enough to let the PCs pick up the pursuit the minute they step outside the restaurant. Before they go, they pick up their unconscious or incapacitated fellows, who they then drag away. Any dead Thorns are left behind.

Assuming they make their getaway with the hostage, they run *en masse* down Temple Street, pulling the frightened woman along with them. They then vanish into an alleyway; at the end of the alley they've parked their motorbikes. Unless they know the PCs are following them, the Thorns then rudely dump the woman in the alley garbage and roar off into the night.

LOOKING FOR CLUES

The next fight happens at a construction site where the Thorns hang out. To get themselves to that fight, the PCs must find out that this is one of their hideouts. You should also try to establish the following plot points before the construction site fight happens:

The local triad boss, Fast Eddie Lo, wants the Thorns smoked for horning in on his territory and assaulting one of his protection "customers."

The Thorns are mixed up in sorcery as well as ordinary racketeering.

Appendix A

The PCs can gather useful info by talking to the Shens, talking to area merchants, having a meet with Fast Eddie, interrogating the captured Thorns (if any), and by getting in a fight with walking corpses from beyond the grave. They don't have to do these in any particular order. Each option is covered in a separate section.

TALKING TO THE SHENS

Kar-Wai Shen can tell the PCs the following, in true grouchy-old-man style:

- The Poison Thorns are stinking rat bastards.
- They've been around twice before, asking for money. The last time, they threatened to chop off Kar-Wai's hands and feed them to his customers.
- The Poison Thorns are scum.
- The guy with the cutaway lip is named Happy Cheung.
- The Poison Thorns should be publicly whipped and beaten.
- The leader of the Thorns is Sneezy Teng.
- The Poison Thorns stink of sewage.
- Cheung, Teng, and most of the other Thorns are mainlanders.
- Kar-Wai already pays protection to Fast Eddie Lo. He doesn't want help from the PCs, or the cops. The cops are corrupt and cowardly. Lo will take care of these upstarts.
- If the Poison Thorns all died immediately, they'd be doing the world a big favor.

Carina can shyly confirm everything her uncle says. If taken aside from him, she will add the following:

- Uncle has a heart condition; she's terrified that the stress of the confrontation with the Thorns will kill him.
- She'd rather deal with the police than Fast Eddie; mobsters don't do favors out of the goodness of their hearts.
- She's trying to convince her uncle to sell the place, but he won't if the Thorns are sniffing around. She says he's the most stubborn man on Earth; although he does want to retire, he won't do so if it would look like the Thorns drove him to do it.

TALKING TO AREA MERCHANTS

If the PCs talk to other Temple Street business owners, they learn the following. You should dramatize this clue-gathering by playing out at least one scene in the voice of a suspicious, temperamental business owner.

- Like Kar-Wai, the other merchants in the area are more distrustful of the police than of Fast Eddie, who they trust to straighten out the matter.
- About half of the other merchants in the area have had visits from the Poison Thorns demanding protection money.
- The attack on the Eating Counter is the first actual strong-arming the Thorns have done. Until tonight, they've been issuing threats but not really doing anything.
- It's a little surprising that they went for the Eating Counter first. It's a big place full of people, much harder to shake down than some of the emptier shops in the area. And several of the merchants have been much more outspoken in cursing out Sneezy Teng than Kar-Wai was.

If pressed on this last point, a merchant might guess that maybe the Thorns wanted to be as splashy and violent as possible, so that terror would spread down the rest of Temple Street and they'd meet lots of opposition. As the PCs will later learn, this isn't the real reason.

INTERROGATING THE THORNS

The PCs may or may not have live Thorns on hand to interrogate. If they do, they will find the Thorns highly reluctant to talk. They've all been hypnotized by the sorcerer Ta Yu, who has convinced these back-country rubes that their heads will explode if they ever say anything to betray him or Sneezy. No matter how rough the PCs get, the Thorns simply won't talk. When playing an interrogated Thorn, be sure to make the fear obvious. The players should be able to realize from your portrayal that these guys are *way* more frightened of their superiors than any garden variety Kowloon street punk reasonably ought to be. ("No! No! I *can't* tell you! You don't understand!

Ahh!") That in itself is an important indication that there's more to the Thorns than meets the eye.

The only way that the PCs can get a captured Thorn to even start to talk is employ sorcery of their own. If a character with the Sorcery schtick Influence uses it to try to break through a Thorn's fear response, the Difficulty of the check is the punk's Will of 4. Interestingly enough, their heads really *will* explode if they squeal. Ta Yu has planted a combined Blast and Influence spell to kill them if they should even think of uttering his name, or giving away his or Sneezy's whereabouts. (See? You really *can* do cool stuff with magic!)

Play this out in the role of a frightened and dull-witted thug. Rub imaginary sweat off your forehead. Stutter a lot. When asked a question that sorcery compels you to answer, start to shake furiously, your face an eruption of facial tics. Then make a big *ka-boom* sound and tell them that the mook's head has blown up. Whether you go into the specifics of where the chunks land is up to you.

The exploding head is actually a better clue than anything the punks could have told the PCs anyway; if this happens, they'll know that the Thorns are mixed up in something much weirder than everyday extortion.

WALKING CORPSES

Another way for the PCs to discover this plays out if they kill any members of the Thorns. (The following will also happen if a Thorn's head blows up.)

If one of the PCs is a local cop and arranges for bodies to be sent to the police morgue, this bit is especially easy to pull off. When things get dull and the PCs are in need of shaking-up, the cop is informed by morgue attendants that someone has stolen the bodies! Upon rushing to the morgue, the PCs can ask enough questions of the staff to realize that no one should logically have been able to get past security to scoop up the corpses. It's almost as if they got up and walked off on their own!

You know where we're headed with this one. The corpses *have* gotten up and walked off on their own, courtesy of Ta Yu. He used his Summoning schtick via long distance to reanimate the dead Thorns. (He has a personal object for each gang member, enabling him to establish the necessary mystic link without knowing exactly where they are.) Ta Yu wants to interrogate the corpses to find out what happened to them; he's been involved in the secret war long enough to suspect the involvement of one of the rival power groups, such as the Ascended or the Architects, whenever something goes wrong.

Ideally, the PCs will catch up with the walking corpses and end up fighting them. Being undead doesn't change their game statistics.

If the PCs are inconveniently clever, they might follow the walking corpses to see where they're going. It's now the dead of night, and they're headed to a deserted city square where Ta Yu awaits them. Ta Yu is using his Divination schtick to warn him of the approach of anyone other than the corpses. He'll fly away (using Movement) long before any PCs get close enough to prematurely end the storyline by taking him on when they outnumber him.

If the PCs don't have a cop among them and therefore would not be contacted when the corpses vanish from the morgue, Ta Yu's reason for reanimating the corpses changes: He wants them to find the people who killed them and return the favor. The corpses have a mystic link to their killers and are able to track them wherever they go. They therefore show up at an inconvenient moment—possibly when the PCs have gone their separate ways—to ambush one or more of their killers.

Either way, once killed a second time the corpses stay dead. There is no further trace of occult energies around them. A coroner examining them will be able to find only a set of wounds administered after death—i.e., the ones used to put down the Thorns the second time. Under no circumstance will an authority figure believe any wild stories the PCs might try to tell about the dead coming back to life.

MAGICAL INVESTIGATION

If the PCs have a sorcerer of their own on hand, and she has the Divination schtick, she can consult the *I Ching* to get a clue. If she does this, read the following to the sorcerers' player, or paraphrase it in your own words:

You separate the yarrowstalks in the prescribed ritual fashion and get hexagram 46: Sheng, or Pushing Upwards. The lower trigram represents either wood or wind, and pushes upwards into the upper trigram, which represents the earth. The traditional interpretation is that success can come, but only through an effort of the will, just as a sapling must exercise great will to push through the earth into the sky.

Moreover, one of the lines of the hexagram, the sixth line, is what is known as a moving line. This gives you an additional image: the pushing upwards is into darkness. This traditionally means that victory will come, but only after great perseverance and struggle.

This reading refers to the set of the next fight, a construction site. The earth is being disturbed to dig the big foundation of a skyscraper; the pile of earth beside the hole is like Earth over Wind. The moving line warns not only that the PCs are getting into danger by pursuing this matter (surprise, surprise), but that they should do so under cover of darkness.

Pretty obscure, huh? That's because we don't want the PCs to get exactly the right clue just by having one of them make a task check. We want them to have to interact with the reigning kingpin of Temple Street, Fast Eddie Lo.

FAST EDDIE

Fast Eddie Lo is a bad guy who can help the PCs in defeating a greater evil. He is a member of the Pledged, the group of humans who serve the Ascended. He is not a high-ranking member of the organization; Fast Eddie wouldn't recognize the word "Ascended" as meaning anything significant. He has no idea that the Lodge members are the descendants of transformed animals, and thinks that feng shui is just superstitious nonsense.

He does know that his membership in the group has helped him professionally. He joined the Jade Wheel Society (see p. 176) back in 1965, when he was just a young punk slashing tires for a petty loan shark. His initiation into the society introduced him to ranking triad members. Soon he ditched his low-rent employer and began to work for the triad. Rising through the ranks with the help of his Jade Wheel patrons, he was eventually given the franchise for racketeering activities in the lucrative Night Market area. He operates rather openly; crooks and cops alike all know who he is. Occasionally a maverick cop goes after him and tries to take down his operation, but there are as many Jade Wheel members in the upper echelons of the Hong Kong police as there are in the triad organizations. Whenever an investigation gets too close to him, the officers on the case find themselves mysteriously re-assigned to "higher-priority" cases.

Fast Eddie is not so-named because he is physically quick; he weighs in at just under 150 kilograms. Fast Eddie gets his name from his well-publicized lifestyle. He is known to have at least six official mistresses; the famous feuds among them are fodder for the Hong Kong gossip rags. Fast Eddie is a prodigious eater and a connoisseur of fine wines and brandies. He has smoked enough expensive Cuban cigars in his lifetime to give cancer to the entire nation of Singapore. Whenever the PCs encounter him, he will be wreathed in a blue cloud of cigar smoke. (You might want to have an unlit cigar on hand to use as a prop when playing him.) The only excess he won't indulge in is drug use; he's happy to sell hard drugs but not stupid enough to take them. Fast Eddie is so well-known that many poor kids growing up in Kowloon look up to him as a role model; they want to grow up to be just like him. His seemingly-charmed life plays a big part in this: So far he's escaped four attempts on his life. It is said that none of the operators who put contracts out on him were so lucky when Fast Eddie's boys took their vengeance.

Fast Eddie is a wily character who has succeeded not only because of his Wheel connections—they only go so far—but because he is a student of Sun Tzu's *Art of War* who believes in always looking three steps ahead. He rewards loyalty and swiftly punishes betrayal. He is also known for his patience.

Any PC familiar with modern Hong Kong who makes a Police, Detective, or relevant Info check knows all of the information given in the above two paragraphs; Difficulty of the check is 5.

If Sneezy Teng didn't have sorcery on his side, he wouldn't have a chance against Fast Eddie. But for the moment he does have an edge. Fast Eddie has checked him out and written him off as scarcely a minor threat. He doesn't even know that Ta Yu exists. In fact, he doesn't even know enough about the secret war to believe that sorcery is real.

The Bun Festival

The PCs can look up Fast Eddie at The Bun Festival, a nasty topless joint on Temple Street, two blocks south of the Eating Counter. Anyone who works in the Night Market can tell the PCs that this is Eddie's standard hangout; he's not the owner on paper but everyone knows he runs the place.

The Bun Festival looks cheap and sleazy, but it's loaded with top-of-the-line security gear, including a complete set of hidden cameras. No one can pull anything in the place without Fast Eddie's boys in the back room knowing about it instantly. They're no dummies, and are continually on the alert for hit attempt number five. If the PCs try to barge in like bulls in a china shop, they'll soon be confronted with a wall of combat-ready goons.

Fast Eddie's boys don't want to start a fight, especially in the boss' place. But they will retaliate if they think Fast Eddie is being threatened. However, they'd much sooner cool a situation out than resort to violence. Fast Eddie has taught them all that talking is almost always more profitable than shooting.

It makes much more sense for the PCs to try the subtle approach in applying for an audience with the big man. They can come in as customers; if they take a seat they'll soon be waited on by rather unpleasant topless waitresses. The waitresses know it's not their place to arrange interviews with the boss, and will evade any questions about Fast Eddie.

The key to getting in to talk to the man is the bartender, an Australian named Bri Davis. ("Bri" is short for "Brian.")

Bri Davis is also Pledged. He, like his father before him, is a member of the western branch of the organization, the Order of the Wheel. He keeps a low profile, but is in reality Fast Eddie's chief fixer, adviser, and all-around troubleshooter. As far as anyone on Temple Street knows, he's just a tough, no-nonsense bartender. Bri actually has a higher rank in the Wheel than Fast Eddie, but doesn't know the truth behind the Lodge. He does know that Fast Eddie is just one link in a big chain of power that stretches worldwide. If his Wheel superiors told him to snuff Eddie tomorrow, he'd do it without a second thought. But he doesn't expect that to happen. Bri rather likes Eddie, even though he himself rarely indulges in any of the vices his boss is so famous for. Obsessive kung fu training is his addiction. He keeps his incredible martial arts skill to himself; he does not have a rep in accordance with his abilities.

Bri is a blunt, humorless fellow who doesn't take guff from anyone. If you want to use a prop while playing him, polish a shot glass with a piece of cloth.

The way to get to Fast Eddie is to discreetly approach Bri and respectfully ask for an audience. Bri will inquire as to the nature of the PCs' business without admitting that he's even heard of Fast Eddie. If it relates in any way to the Poison Thorns, or if the answer otherwise seems like a credible reason to visit a mob boss, Bri escorts them to the door of Fast Eddie's complex of back rooms. If the PCs are evasive, Bri gives them the brush-off. If they are less than polite, he will give them a lecture on face: "If you're moving in the kind of circles where you have to meet with Fast Eddie Lo, you could stand to learn a little about showing respect." Eventually the PCs should take a hint and realize that Bri is more than just a menial employee.

Once he decides that the PCs should be allowed an audience with Eddie, Bri presses a button beneath the bar to summon two of Eddie's boys. Bri chooses at most two of the PCs to talk to Fast Eddie. He will choose the two who did most of the talking. The boys will pat them down, and pass their weapons to any remaining PCs. If there are no additional PCs in the Bun Festival, Bri keeps any

Fast Eddie Lo
Sample Dialogue: "I believe we can work out an arrangement that will be mutually profitable. Care for some more tea?"
Attributes: Bod 5, Chi 4, Mnd 7, Ref 6
Skills: Gambling 8, Guns 12, Info/Triads 10, Leadership 12, Martial Arts 9
Weapons: Colt King Cobra (11/3/6), Benelli 90 shotgun (13/5/7)

Bri Davis
Sample Dialogue: "You're going to have to learn some manners if you want to survive on Temple Street, lad."
Attributes: Bod 8, Chi 0, Mnd 5, Ref 8
Skills: Detective 7, Driving 12, Martial Arts 16, Sabotage 7
Weapons: punch (9), katana (12)

Fast Eddie's Boys
Sample Dialogue: "You don't want to screw with the boss."
Attributes: Bod 7, Chi 0, Mnd 4, Ref 7
Skills: Guns 8, Martial Arts 8
Weapons: machete (5), Norinco M1911 (6/3/7 + 1), Mini UZI (6/3/25)

weaponry behind the bar. If the PCs seem nervous about leaving their firepower behind, this just makes Bri think of them as amateurs. Any real operator would know that they can't expect to walk into somebody's home turf loaded down with weaponry.

The boys then escort the PC(s) meeting Fast Eddie to an inconspicuous steel door in the wall of the bar. They unlock the heavy door and wave the PCs down a musty corridor to a meeting room. The room is lavishly appointed, with antique mahogany furniture. The PCs can't help but notice a security cam staring at them.

The Meet

A few minutes later, Eddie enters the room, flanked by four new and different goons at his side. He settles himself down into an oversized chair while his boys stand behind him. He offers the PCs cigars, lights up one of his own, and then asks what he can do for them.

The PCs should learn the following when talking to Fast Eddie:

- Fast Eddie would like to see the Poison Thorns "taken care of." He would feel a great sense of indebtedness to anyone who arranged for their departure from the scene.
- One of the problems with being an "honest businessman" in Hong Kong is that you're always having to deal with upstart mainlanders who want to take you down. The Thorns are just the latest in a long line of such punks.
- Sneezy Teng has some connections to mainland gangs, but he's not protected by any Hong Kong figures. There will be no reprisals from the triads if he's taken out.
- Fast Eddie hasn't met Sneezy and doesn't think much of him.
- He has heard that Sneezy's right-hand man, Happy Cheung, is a tough opponent. Apparently Happy has killed some errant Thorns with his bare hands. He's the big challenge for anyone raiding the Thorns.
- If anyone should decide to raid the Thorns, they might do well to make their way to a certain construction site on Canton Street in the Mongkok District. (Eddie supplies the exact address should this be required.) The place is a new high-rise being built by mainland business interests; obviously Sneezy has a connection to them. In exchange for "guarding" the premises, he gets to put up his men in the construction shacks at night. They're not there during the day. Only some of them are there at night. But if someone were to break a few heads there, that someone could find out where Sneezy and Happy are holed up.

If asked about weird stuff or sorcery, Eddie has no useful information to supply. He waves his hand at such suggestions: It's all hogwash for the tourists.

If Heads Roll

The PCs shouldn't get into a fight at Fast Eddie's, but PCs have been known to get into extra trouble they don't really need. If this happens, there are four of Eddie's boys for each PC. Bri grabs a katana hidden under the bar and joins the fight. He will select another fu character to challenge, if available. Fast Eddie will not join the fight; he'll be scooted out the back and ushered into his bulletproof Rolls Royce.

Fast Eddie's boys have no compunction about using heavy firepower; they'll go straight for their Mini UZIs and start blasting away.

- There are pool tables for characters to be slammed into or hide under.
- Bottles and pool cues can be used as impromptu weapons.
- The bar has a tacky western motif, including huge wagon-wheel light fixtures. These are great for swinging on.
- Bad guys will dive behind the bar, allowing them to open up on the PCs with 90% cover.
- There are lots of bar patrons and waitresses to get mowed down in the crossfire. Try to make the players feel guilty for causing unnecessary carnage.

If the PCs do shoot up Fast Eddie's joint, they've made an enemy for life. He'll not only send unnamed goons after them to engage in gratuitous violence whenever the plot slows down in future sessions, but will later hire top assassins to bump them off. These assassins are named characters of your creation; they should have game statistics roughly equal to those of the PCs. In other words, they're a real threat to the PCs' continued good health that could have been avoided if they'd only been sensible.

Even if things escalate to this point, Fast Eddie is not beyond accepting an abject apology and large cash settlement for the insult the PCs have done to him. The abject apology must involve public kowtowing—that is, bowing and scraping while goons and bar customers look on and snicker.

OTHER SOURCES OF INFORMATION

The Thorns are street thugs; people on the street talk a lot. Any PC who has access to street contacts—cops, crooks, bums, or what have you—can start asking questions about the Thorns. For that matter, nearly any PC can just hand out cash to seedy-looking folks around Kowloon and sooner or later they'll get results. Efforts along these lines will get them the info that the Thorns' mooks doss at the construction site described in the next section.

If the players go straight to the street without exploring other options, though, they shouldn't get this info right away. Let them pass out some bucks and wait a day or two; in the meanwhile, they should keep looking into other leads, hopefully including Fast Eddie. If they just sit around waiting for their money to do their work for them, set them up: they bribed a Thorn by accident, and the Thorns feed the PCs some bogus info that leads them into a

Baptism of Fire

nasty ambush. This is still productive, though: once the PCs have gotten kicked around by the Thorns (or vice versa), surviving mooks high-tail it for the construction site and can be followed.

CONSTRUCTION SITE FIGHT

On the other hand, there should definitely be a fight at the construction site Fast Eddie names. It's a future skyscraper; right now it's just a big hole in the ground with four or five stories of steel girders put up. Beside the hole are two big shacks, each of them containing a number of Thorns equal to the number of PCs who make the assault. Try to work the fight so that the Thorns come charging out of the shacks with guns blazing; an outdoor battle is much more interesting than a battle in the little buildings.

Fight choreography ideas:

- The shacks are made of wood. An enterprising PC might set them ablaze, magically or otherwise.
- Some bad guys should plunge into the hole, which is several stories deep.
- A crane still holds a big girder above the site; a gun character could make a stunt shot and hit the cable holding the girder, sending it crashing down on some Thorns.
- There are rows of porta-potties which could provide cover to PCs.
- Someone has left rows of highly flammable liquids lying about in big rusty metal drums. (The crooks behind this development must also be using it to illegally store dangerous chemicals. Yeah, that explains it.) Anyway, they're highly likely to blow up in spectacular fashion.
- There are various heavy pieces of construction equipment around: a steamshovel, a front-end loader, and a cement mixer. Conveniently enough, the construction crew left the keys in all of these vehicles—they've got Thorn guards,

Illustration by Grey Thornberry

after all. Either PCs or Thorns could climb in them and try to run over their enemies.

THE BARRISTER

There is one character in the fray who is not a member of the Poison Thorns. He is Paul Chang, a cheap lawyer who came here to meet Sneezy. Unfortunately for him, he arrived early—which means he ends up in the middle of the battle between the Thorns and PCs.

Paul Chang is a short, dumpy man in his mid-thirties. He is balding at the front, and has wild, frizzy hair at the back. His suits are permanently rumpled. He is not a particularly talented or reputable lawyer, but he's the best Sneezy could find. His main goal in any encounter with the PCs will be to avoid being hurt.

In the middle of the fight, he runs from the shack, trying to reach his rusting compact car. He will not fight back if attacked; instead he will drop to his knees and beg for mercy.

> **Paul Chang**
> Sample Dialogue: "I don't gotta gun! I don't gotta gun! Don't hurt me!"
> Attributes: Bod 5, Chi 0 (For 3), Mnd 6, Ref 5
> Skills: Deceit 10, Info/Law 8
> Weapon: punch (1)

If captured, he is the only one willing to talk. Like the previous Thorns, the mooks at the site know that their heads will blow up if they spill the beans. Lacking this compulsion, Paul will reveal everything he knows in exchange for not being hurt.

- He was hired by Sneezy Teng to draw up a contract between Kar-Wai Sheng and one Ta Yu to transfer title of the Eating Counter restaurant from the latter to the former. (This should be the first the PCs have heard of Ta Yu.)
- The contract is a little odd; the payment for the restaurant is ridiculously below market price for such a thriving business.
- Paul has never met either party to the contract; all of his dealings have been with Sneezy.
- He was supposed to come here to meet Sneezy tonight, but when he got here, the Thorns told him that he'd been called away unexpectedly. He asked where Sneezy was but was told to mind his own business and hang tight for a little while.
- Sneezy found Paul by looking him up in the phone book.
- Sneezy already has a draft copy of the contract. It only has a few minor clauses that need fixing. If the draft copy were signed it would still hold up in court.

If the PCs happen to have accidentally killed Paul in the course of the fight, they can still find his briefcase and read the contract within, getting the most important of the clues he's supposed to provide them.

THE MAPS

A little talk with Paul should hip the PCs to the fact that the Eating Counter means more to the Thorns than just another mark to squeeze for extortion money. They can further confirm this by subjecting the shacks to a casual search. Even if the shacks have been burned to the ground, the PCs find a metal strongbox containing several maps of Temple Street, with the location encircled in red marker on each of them. There is also a hand-drawn detail map of the restaurant's floor plan with extensive marginal notes in Ta Yu's hand. Among these scribbles are various trigrams and other mystic signs. A PC making a Sorcery or Info/Geomancy (or other relevant Info skill) check with a Difficulty of 6 will realize that whoever drew up this map thinks that the Eating Counter is a place with powerful feng shui.

Between Paul's contract and this map, the bad guy's fiendish plot should now be obvious: They want to take over the Eating Counter for its mystic properties.

BACK TO THE EATING COUNTER

When the PCs next visit the Eating Counter, they find it closed—but the lights are on inside. If they knock on the door, Kar-Wai comes down the stairs and shakes his meat cleaver at them, thinking them at first to be the Poison Thorns. After some initial confusion, allow the PCs to identify themselves to Kar-Wai as the good citizens who kicked Thorn butt earlier on.

He lets them in, tears streaming down his cheeks. Carina has been kidnapped! He shows them a message, made of Chinese characters cut from newspapers and glued to rice paper. The note tells him to come alone to a particular apartment number in a tenement building in Kowloon. It concludes: "If you bring Fast Eddie's men, the cops, or anyone else, she's dead." An arrow in red marker leads from this sentence; it points to a lock of black hair taped to the piece of paper. Carina's hair. As if there were any doubt as to who was responsible for this, the red marker on the note matches that on the maps the PCs have recovered from the construction shack.

Kar-Wai has no idea that the Thorns want his restaurant; he thinks they're just going to put the squeeze on him. He is, however, willing to do whatever they ask to save Carina. If the PCs tell him what the Thorns are really after, he says he'll gladly sign the restaurant over.

If the PCs have no misgivings about this, tell the players of any characters familiar with magic or feng shui that the Thorns will undoubtedly prosper if they gain legal title of the Eating Counter. That's bad news for anyone who has crossed them, as well as for the people of Temple Street in general.

TERROR IN THE TENEMENT

Sneezy, Happy, and Ta Yu are waiting for Kar-Wai's arrival in an apartment in a crowded Kowloon highrise. The apartment belongs to one of the Thorns who has already been killed or injured.

Sneezy personally followed Carina home after work; he waited until she was alone outside her apartment before pulling his gun on her. He then drugged her and brought her here. They have handcuffed her to the bed. There is a member of the Thorns watching her at all times.

There are six Thorns crammed into the apartment along with the three main bad guys. There are another eight Thorns loitering in the hallway outside the apartment. The last of the Thorns are down in the apartment's lobby, waiting to see that Kar-Wai comes in alone. They have a cell phone with a speed dialer and will immediately alert Sneezy if anyone comes with Kar-Wai, or if anyone who looks like a cop or obvious combatant enters separately from Kar-Wai.

Exactly how the final fight plays out depends on the tack the players decide to take, so you'll have to react to what they do to describe an exciting fight scene.

- The apartment itself is extremely cramped, making wild fu moves extra difficult if not impossible.
- Dodging is also extra hard. Subtract 3 from each character's Dodge ratings when fighting inside the apartment itself. Fu powers that provide Dodge bonuses may be impossible.
- Martial arts attacks employing clubs, swords or other long weapons are also penalized; reduce Action Values by 3 for any such attempts.
- Happy sticks to punches for this very reason.
- Sneezy leaps behind a couch, gaining 90% cover until he and the couch are somehow separated. He then blazes away with his high-capacity Tec-9.
- Ta Yu still wants, at least at first, to avoid being identified as a sorcerer. He has a small device which is supposed to look like a flamethrower; he has a tank full of air strapped to his back. He uses this as a disguise for his Blast spell, shooting out fire bolts as if they're coming from the device. The device itself is useless.
- These are truly bad people. Unless the PCs somehow burst in and immediately get between Carina and the Thorns watching her, they'll shoot and kill her immediately. Just like a Hong Kong movie, there's no guaranteed happy ending here.
- As soon as Ta Yu realizes what awesome opponents he's facing, he decides to make a break for it. But first he does something truly nasty: he directs a flame Blast at the apartment's oven, igniting its gas outlet. The entire building is heated by natural gas. An explosion ensues as Ta Yu uses his Movement schtick to make his escape, zooming out a (previously closed) window. Another sorcerer or flying character can pursue him to conduct an aerial battle. Note that arcanowave characters with Aerial Mobility Units aren't able to take off in the enclosed confines of the apartment.

FIERY FINISH

Once Ta Yu ignites the gas lines, the final scene goes from action flick to disaster movie. Did I forget to mention that the apartment is on the twenty-first floor? That safety regulations aren't exactly up to snuff? That there are dozens of kids and helpless elderly people who happen to be alone in the building without able-bodied people to help them?

If the PCs are intent on finishing off their enemies instead of getting out of the building or helping innocent citizens, let them know that they hear the cries of terrified children as they pummel away at the Thorns.

- Some players, particularly those with supernatural abilities, will want to put out the blaze. Sorry; it's already in the gas lines, and it's just too big a conflagration to put out.
- The fire really gets going two sequences after Ta Yu ignites the gas lines. At that point, roll a single die. This is the number of shots that will elapse before a piece of flaming debris falls from the ceiling and lands on a randomly-determined character. When the debris falls, roll again to get the number of shots until another piece falls. Repeat until all PCs are out of the burning building.
- Debris should fall on good guys and bad guys alike; it is possible that Happy and/or Sneezy will be killed by the fire instead of by the PCs.
- To get the Damage value for falling debris, make an open roll and add 6; victims subtract their Toughness from this number to get the Wound Points suffered.
- It is possible to avoid falling debris by making an active Dodge with a shot cost of 1. The Dodging character makes a task check using the relevant skill; if the task check exceeds the Damage value of the debris, the character suffers singed clothing instead of Wound Points.
- Carina has been drugged; assuming she hasn't been executed by the Thorns, someone should remember to carry her unconscious body out of the building.
- If the PCs' plan involved bringing Kar-Wai with them, he collapses from smoke inhalation when the fire starts. He needs to be dragged out too.

WRAPPING UP

The escape from the fiery tenement is the end of the adventure, so make sure it feels appropriately dramatic. Be sure to throw in details that emphasize the scale of the action: lots of fire trucks, ambulances, a throng of frightened onlookers, and so forth. If Carina, Kar-Wai, or any of the PCs die, make plenty of room for a big final death scene.

This adventure should lead to other action-packed episodes in the Hong Kong area. First, there's the matter of the Eating Counter, a powerful feng shui site. If Ta Yu is still alive, he'll come back for it.

If the adventurers have learned about the significance of feng shui sites, they may want to arrange to attune themselves to it. They can do so by acquiring a small stake in the restaurant:

- If Kar-Wai and Carina survive, Kar-Wai will be happy to sell small shares in the restaurant to the PCs for saving their lives.
- If Carina is killed, Kar-Wai will sadly abandon the restaurant; he'll sell the place to them if they can make the payments.
- If Kar-Wai is killed, Carina doesn't want to stay in the restaurant business. She'll also be willing to sell to the PCs.

We've described Fast Eddie Lo in detail so that you'll have a GMC to bring into future adventures. Maybe Fast Eddie finds another threat for the PCs to take on. Or maybe he becomes the threat himself: perhaps his Jade Wheel Society superiors find out that the Eating Counter is a feng shui site and want it taken so that none of the enemies of the Ascended can claim it. If the PCs take over the restaurant, he'll at least want his usual share of protection money. If they're as stubborn as the average PC group, they may start a gang war simply because they're unwilling to pay their unofficial taxes.

APPENDIX B

Hong Kong Action Movies

YOUR GUIDE TO THE GREATS

Hong Kong action movies are slowly but surely percolating into the awareness of Western movie fans. From trendy film festivals to cult-oriented video stores and mail order outlets, these pop culture treasures are becoming more accessible every day. Every time I go to a gaming convention, I find more and more people who are hip to HK cinema. If you've been into these movies for a while, you've probably seen great films that I haven't. But if all of this is new to you, here's a brief introductory guide to a world of eye-popping stunts and pulse-pounding action.

If you've recently left your local movie theater shaking your head at the latest piece of atrocious junk Hollywood has foisted on you, you may have said something to the effect of: "They sure don't make 'em like they used to." Well, not here they don't. But in Hong Kong, there's a film factory that's turning out pure entertainment films just like Hollywood did in its heyday. Like the classic studio system, they have a roster of genuine movie stars who work regularly, many of them appearing in what seems like a film every couple of months. These movies are set up as star vehicles, and revolve around the charisma and persona of their lead actors. And Hong Kong still knows how to do genre movies, from melodramas to the various subgroups of action flicks that concern us here. There's an enthusiasm for movie making—a sense of flying by the seat of the pants—that has long since been squished out of focus-group, demographics-driven Hollywood product. They may not be subtle, and they may throw Western notions of good taste out the window, but they're fun. Sure, there's lots of forgettable junk, just as there was during the glory days of MGM and Warner Brothers and Paramount. But there are a lot more gems, and just plain entertaining fare, coming out of Hong Kong than appear at the multiplex at your local mall. Here's a guide to get you started.

JOHN WOO

The first and most obvious place to start is with the films of John Woo, the director whose films have led the wave of interest in Hong Kong action movies. He's melded the visions of Sergio Leone, Sam Peckinpah, and Akira Kurosawa into an unmistakable style all his own. Happily, the best starting point for HK flicks happens to be the most readily-available to Westerners: *The Killer* (1989). This was released in theaters in North America and is available here on videocassette in video stores nationwide. There's both a dubbed and a subtitled version; insist on the latter. This is a brilliant showcase for Woo's super-kinetic action choreography, as well as his unique sense of melodrama, which manages to be over-the-top and ironic at the same time. It's also a superb introduction to one of Hong Kong's greatest stars, the inimitable Chow Yun-Fat. Chow is a combination of Clint Eastwood and Spencer Tracy with screen presence to spare. Chow plays a mob assassin who accidentally blinds a lounge singer (Sally Yeh) while executing a hit in a restaurant. Torn by remorse, he decides to do one last job in order to raise the money for her eye operation. He's pursued by a determined maverick cop (Danny Lee) who ends up as his only ally in a stunning final showdown with his double-crossing boss. The clever tag line for the North American promo material says it all: "One Vicious Hitman. One Fierce Cop. Ten Thousand Bullets." You must see this movie.

Woo has had a long career in the Hong Kong studio system, but his first breakthrough hit was the gangland melodrama *A Better Tomorrow* (1986). Chow Yun-Fat stars as another angelic mobster in another story of torn loyalties. He's the best buddy of a fellow gangster (Ti Lung) whose kid brother (Leslie Cheung) just happens to be a rookie cop. Lots of blood is spilled in glamorous fashion as this triangle of intrigue plays out.

Bullet in the Head (1990) is Woo's grimmest and most emotionally-grounded film. Once again the theme is loyalty and betrayal as we follow a trio of ambitious young would-be gangsters in HK who decide to go to Vietnam to strike it rich in the black market—in the late 1960s. Since the war is in full bore at this point, things go horribly wrong and the second act of the picture switches from gangster action to war picture mode. When a member of the trio goes bad and puts the title round of ammo in the skull of one of his buddies, the stage is set for an apocalyptic waterfront showdown back in Hong Kong between him and the third buddy. This is my personal favorite of all the Woo films—scratch that, of all the films mentioned here. But I was lucky enough to see the director's cut of the film at a festival; the usual commercial cut is missing half an hour of footage. Since I can't imagine one frame being taken out of the version I saw, that's a serious drag. Watch for the unedited version in mail-order catalogs.

His next film, *Once A Thief* (1991), is a light-hearted contrast with the psychic devastation of *Bullet in the Head*. It's a tribute to the Hollywood caper flicks of the sixties, with Chow Yun-Fat as a devil-may-care master cat burglar. This time the emotional triangle—consisting of Chow and his young accomplices (Leslie Cheung and Cherie Chung)—actually includes a woman! Sure, there's melodrama and lots of shooting and killing, but the accent here is on fun. Definitely wins the award for most audacious end-sequence plot twist.

Some people prefer Woo's last Hong Kong movie to date, *Hardboiled* (1992), for its straight-ahead action. This time Chow plays a police inspector fighting triad gangsters. Tony Leung is an undercover cop on the inside of the gangs. The blistering final action sequence in a hospital, complete with babies in jeopardy, makes this worth checking out even if the usual emotional weight isn't there. The poster has a great shot of Chow with a baby in one hand and a combat shotgun in the other.

Woo has since gone Hollywood, starting with the Jean-Claude Van Damme vehicle *Hard Target* (1993). He didn't write the screenplay—yet another rehash of *The Most Dangerous Game*—in which a man becomes the quarry of jaded big game hunters. Jean-Claude has less screen presence than Chow Yun-Fat's discarded toenail clippings, but it's worth checking out for the action sequences. If you happen to be in a part of the world where HK films are hard to come by, this heavily-compromised John Woo is better than no Woo at all.

Since *Feng Shui* was first published, Woo has directed *Broken Arrow* (1996), starring John Travolta and Christian Slater in a tale of a U.S. military warhead gone missing, and *Face/Off* (1997), which features Travolta and Nicolas Cage, where Travolta plays an F.B.I agent whose mission is to bring in one of the world's deadliest terrorists.

JACKIE CHAN

Jackie Chan is Asia's biggest superstar, an actor/director/producer who combines a lovable, everyman charm with jaw-dropping acrobatic ability and a staggering willingness to risk his life to get that money shot. (Jackie does his own stunts, and given the action-packed style of his movies, that's saying something.) His films may be formulaic, but they're also pure popcorn-crunching joy. His best films deftly mix comedy and action; if Buster Keaton had occasion to launch kung fu kicks or now and again pick up an AK-47, he might have made movies a lot like Jackie Chan's. Except that Jackie's screen persona is way warmer than the deadpan master of the silents.

One of the jarring things about Jackie movies is their credit sequences: he ends with a blooper reel, except that the bloopers inevitably include failed stunt attempts. We see Jackie being tended after falling thirty feet to a concrete floor, being fitted for a walking cast, walking off staggeringly painful-looking accidents, and—in one blood-curdling instance—being taken away in an ambulance for brain surgery! One often does a double-take during a Jackie Chan action sequence. At first, you're just enjoying the stunt, as you would any similar Hollywood shot. Then you realize, *holy @#$%!, he's really doing this!* You can tell the really dangerous shots because they're repeated several times in quick succession to enable you to see them from multiple angles.

My favorite Jackie movie is 1982's *Mr. Canton and Lady Rose*, also known as *Miracles: The Chinese Godfather*. It's his best combo of comedy and action, set in 1930s Shanghai. The acrobatic finale in a rope factory is an amazing display of coordinated fight choreography.

The *Police Story* series are the closest to standard Hollywood action flicks. Particularly entertaining is the most recent installment, *Police Story III: Supercop* (1992). Jackie teams up with a combat-ready female officer from Communist China (the splendid Michelle Yeoh) to put an opium lord out of business. If you like vehicle chases and explosions, this flick has all the interactions of trains, motorcycles, cars, and helicopters you could hope for.

Armor of God (1986), and especially its sequel, *Armor of God II: Operation Condor* (1991), are also well worth a look. Jackie plays a composite of James Bond and Indiana Jones as a modern day adventurer in search of fabled artifacts: magical armor in the first one and Nazi gold in the second. International intrigue, gadgets galore, and love triangles are all part of the fun.

For pure fu action, seek out *Drunken Master II* (1994), in which Jackie reprises the role that initially made him famous: 19th century bumpkin Wong Fei Hong, who, in Popeye-like fashion, becomes an unbeatable kung fu master whenever he gets sloshed. Fei Hong battles evil factory bosses in collusion with the nasty Imperialists. The concluding steel plant battle includes Jackie skidding across a bed of hot coals and spitting flaming industrial alcohol at his foes. Remember, he's really doing all of this stuff!

Rumble in the Bronx (1995) takes Jackie's usual formula to New York City, which is played (not entirely convincingly) by Vancouver. The melodrama is gentle and realistic, and the stunts are something to behold. I never considered the possibility of a hovercraft/bus crash before seeing this film. As of this writing, it was announced that New Line Cinema had acquired North American rights for this and future Jackie films: let's hope this really happens, so that these way-cool movies can become common in video stores.

TSUI HARK

A veritable one-man cinema factory, director/producer Tsui Hark is probably as responsible as anyone for the current high-flying, physics-defying style of Hong Kong action. If John Woo is the baseline for the way *Feng Shui* presents contemporary action, Tsui Hark films are the basis for our ancient masters, seductive ghosts, and acrobatic fu powers of old China. The HK term for this genre is *wuxia*, which roughly translates as "flying people." These movies portray magic and fantasy elements in a much more RPG-like way than Western movies ever have. Magic-using characters frequently yell out the names of the spells as they cast them, for example. And kung fu is treated in just as fantastic a manner as magic: this is not your basic black belt workout tape, Toto.

Start with the *Chinese Ghost Story* series. All of them combine magic, swordsmanship and monsters: the thrills escalate through the three movies (1987, 1990, 1991) along with the special effects budget. Tree demons! Walking corpses! A 100 foot tongue! And, best of all, the gorgeous Joey Wang, who specializes in playing seductive ghosts. What more could you ask?

Hark's first ground-breaking *wuxia* film is called *Zu: Warriors of the Magic Mountain* (1982); it's fun but not as spectacular as the later flicks. It's worth seeing for reference if you're playing a *Feng Shui* series with lots of action in the 69 AD setting.

Another great inspirational source for swords 'n' fu action is the *Swordsman* series, also in 3 parts: 1990, 1991, 1992. Just don't expect it to make a lot of sense; these puppies move too fast to bother with exposition. The heavy in the first movie is your classic evil eunuch sorcerer. It also contains a quintessential HK movie moment, in which a character slashes one opponent in two and then steps through the halves to nail another. Part II features *wuxia* stalwart Brigitte Lin as a magically transsexual villain. (Gender bending is a standard feature of *wuxia*; don't ask me why.) Also appearing in II is Jet Li, who has become one of HK's hottest action stars.

Li is the star of the first three installments of another Hark series, the *Once Upon A Time In China* films. He stars as legendary doctor and hero Wong Fei Hong. This series puts a completely different spin on this historical figure than the Jackie Chan *Drunken Master* films, mentioned above. This series places Hong in the 19th century, and pits him against a variety of bad guys from evil sects to collaborators with the cruel Western powers. It uses a much more realistic style of fu than the *wuxia* flicks, although many of the fights still defy gravity with the aid of wires.

Dragon Inn (1991) tells the story of a band of revolutionaries fighting the ambitions of yet another evil eunuch bad guy. Good guys and bad guys end up staying at the Inn of the title, an establishment with definite Sweeney Todd overtones.

Appendix B

Beware of the meat buns! Yet another movie with a jaw-dropping final fight sequence.

Burning Paradise (1994) pits an evil cult against Shaolin monks who make a pretty good visual starting point for the Guiding Hand. This is one of the darkest and most doom-laden swordplay flicks I've ever seen. The good monks, including legendary hero Fong Sai Yuk, spend most of their time imprisoned in the grim temple of the cultists.

Hark is more than just a maker of *wuxia* and kung fu flicks. *Better Tomorrow III* (1989), his prequel to Woo's gangster epic, is a rousing guns-blazing picture set in wartime Saigon. *Peking Opera Blues* (1986) and *The Raid* (1991) take place in 1911 and 1934, respectively. They're both rollicking, light-hearted action movies which take their conflicts from a very troubled period in Chinese history and gloss over the unpleasant stuff with fast-moving stunts and high spirits. *The Wicked City* (1992) depicts modern magic cops fighting off supernatural creatures known as rapters; it ends with a magical battle fought with a 747 as a weapon. It stars Tatsuya Nakadai, who appears in many of Japanese director Akira Kurosawa's classic films.

(Not all of the films mentioned here were directed by Hark, but even when he serves as producer his distinctive high-speed style is usually in place.)

JET LI

The aforementioned actor Jet Li can also be seen in *Kung Fu Cult Master* (1993), a wild *wuxia* that really cranks up the fantasy element. There's one point where the Jet Li character guesses how many experience points his tough opponent must have!

After breaking with Tsui Hark, Li made two movies similar to *Once Upon A Time In China: Fong Sai Yuk* and its sequel, *Fong Sai Yuk II* (1992 & 1993). Once again Li plays a legendary figure in 19th century action. Like many HK movies, its sudden shifts from comedy schtick to melodramatic emoting may be a little jarring to the new viewer. But the action is great, and Josephine Siao is way cool as Fong Sai Yuk's butt-kicking mom.

If you want to see Jet firing a Colt .45 as well as engaging in serious fu, look for *Bodyguard From Beijing* (1994), a take-off on the Hollywood hit. Many more people get blown away in this one than in the Whitney Houston version. Li plays an earnest karate cop from mainland China assigned to protect a beautiful client in Hong Kong. My favorite gun stunt from this film occurs when Li knows there are assassins hiding in his client's darkened house; he grabs a flashlight and sends it spinning end over end through the room, taking advantage of the moment when the mooks are briefly illuminated to plug them with his pistol. The furious fu battle with the thoroughly psycho main villain in a gas-filled house is primo action. Because of the gas, you see, they can't use guns and have to fight it out hand to hand; this is a trick any GM should use at least once.

Fist of Legend (1994) is a remake of the Bruce Lee flick *Chinese Connection,* set in Japanese-occupied Manchuria in the thirties. Li plays a nationalistic hero dedicated to getting rid of the invaders; the twist is that he's in love with a Japanese woman. Lots of intense kung fu battles, on a much more realistic scale than the *wuxia* films.

As of this writing, there is talk of a Jackie Chan-Jet Li team-up movie. Like the long talked-about John Woo/Quentin Tarantino project, this may never happen but my fingers are certainly crossed.

MORE SWORDPLAY

For an art movie take on the *wuxia* genre, check out *Ashes of Time* (1994), a dream-like and hypnotic film with an all-star cast playing legendary warriors. If you like your action straightforward, this may not be your cup of green tea. But as a major Sergio Leone and Akira Kurosawa fan, I ate this one up with a spoon.

MORE GANGLAND ACTION

One of my fave HK flicks of 1994 was the simultaneously disturbing and romantic *A Taste of Killing and Romance,* in which attractive and alienated assassins fall in love and have to defend themselves from their vindictive former employer.

City on Fire (1987) reteams the stars of *The Killer* in a naturalistic crime drama. Chow Yun-Fat plays an undercover cop infiltrating a ring of armed robbers; he develops an uncomfortable bond of loyalty with one of the crooks. Avowed HK film fan Quentin Tarantino obviously used the premise and one memorable sequence (the three-way standoff) as inspiration for *Reservoir Dogs.*

Full Contact (1992) features Chow Yun-Fat as a motorcycle-riding bouncer who gets sucked into an arms hijacking scheme by his weasely best friend. It's a mean and gritty vengeance flick, and has the added attraction of Bullet-Vision: in key fight scenes, the camera follows each bullet as it zooms across the room!

To Be Number One (1991) is HK's answer to either version of *Scarface:* a realistic take on Hong Kong's triad scene, with a meandering narrative punctuated by shocking episodes of violence. Although not as satisfying a film as some of the other films mentioned here, it's definitely worth checking out as source material on Asia's gangland.

MODERN ADVENTURE

The *Feng Shui* roleplaying game uses the fight for feng shui sites as its central plot conceit. *Bury Me High* (1990) is a modern adventure that sends its heroes on a quest to deprive an evil third-world dictator of the prime feng shui site that's responsible for keeping him in power. Our young hero is aided by a rich heiress and a geomancer; on the other side is an entire army.

There are a number of movies in which ancient warriors travel through time to our modern era to swing swords and raise havoc. A good example is *Time Warriors* (1989), with frequent Jackie Chan co-star Yuen Biao as a Ming Dynasty warrior who gets sent into suspended animation along with a demented outlaw. He falls in love with a bad girl while he tracks down the villain, who takes to modern crime, UZIs, and steam cookers like a duck to water. Yuen Wah plays perhaps the most over-the-top villain in HK movies, which is really saying something. A somewhat cheesy film, but at least it's exuberant in is cheesiness.

However, in the Gouda and Cheddar sweepstakes, it comes nowhere near the level of fromage found in the horror/adventure *The Seventh Curse* (1986). The hero is a doctor and amateur anthropologist who begins suffering spontaneous wounds as the result of a curse meted out to him by an evil high priest in the jungles of Thailand. He returns to Thailand with a meddling but cute reporter and his pipe-smoking mentor (Chow Yun-Fat again, absurdly miscast as an expert in the occult.) Throw in buckets of gore, some goofy monsters, and the infamous baby-grinder, and you've got a seriously wacked-out film that's worth seeing just to boggle at its excesses. Plus, it can serve as inspiration for modern-day confrontations with the Eaters of the Lotus and other sorcerous *Feng Shui* baddies.

A much better film based on the same series of novels is *The Legend of Wisely* (1987), in which our pulp author hero gets conned into stealing an ancient magical pearl artifact from Nepalese monks. His efforts to make good and return the pearl get him mixed up with a no-nonsense crime boss and a homicidally homesick UFO alien.

FUTURISTIC FUN

Dazzling production design distinguishes *Savior of the Soul* (1991), which places the *wuxia* style in a science-fiction setting. Anita Mui and Andy Lau are City Guards, futuristic cops who end up in a bloody grudge match with deadly mercenary "the Silver Fox." Interlocking love triangles and great costumes are all part of the fun. The sets and lighting are just gorgeous. This is what we imagine the Netherworld looks like.

For HK's take on superheroes, check out *The Heroic Trio* (1993), which features three of HK's biggest female stars (Michelle Yeoh, Anita Mui, and Maggie Cheung) as costumed avengers (Anita wears a mask, even) facing down an evil sorcerer and his minions in a modern metropolis. Its sequel, *The Executioners* (1993), takes the setting into Mad Max territory as the villain tries to corner the water supply after the collapse of civilization.

THAT'S NOT ALL

Although they fall outside the purview of this piece, it's worth briefly noting that Hong Kong turns out more than just action movies. Along with a flood of low comedies that would make Mel Brooks blush, the HK studios have produced many fine films that stand on their own among the best of world cinema. If you're a film fan and not just an action fan, the following titles are just the tip of the iceberg: *Reincarnation of Golden Lotus, Actress, Red Dust, People's Hero, Song of the Exile, ChungKing Express, Queen of Temple Street, Autumn Moon, Three Summers,* and *King of Chess.*

Appendix B

Illustration by Heather Hudson

HOW TO FIND 'EM

Hong Kong movies are usually subtitled in English, even for screenings in Hong Kong itself. Oddly enough, laserdiscs may or may not have sub-titles; for example, Golden Harvest, Jackie Chan's home studio, doesn't put titles on its LDs. If you live in a big city with a Chinese community, hunt around for a video store catering to that community. If you're really lucky like I am here in Toronto, there are actual cinemas where you can look at the posters and try to guess if the movie is any good. This gets easier once you come to recognize your favorite actors. There are also various mail order houses that sell HK videos.

You can find out about these and other sources of HK movies if you have access to Usenet newsgroups on the Internet; subscribe to alt.asian-movies. This group also serves as a starting point for finding WWW sites on the net, and paper zines devoted to Asian cinema.

Feng Shui Task Check Briefing

Whenever you tell the group that your character is trying to do something, your GM has to decide whether he is successful. If he is successful, your GM will need to decide just how successful he is. If he fails, the GM needs to know what the consequences of the failure might be. This process is called a **task check**.

The Dice

Whenever you are called upon to roll dice in a *Feng Shui* game, you will be rolling **two standard six-sided dice**. Each should be a **different color**. One die represents a **positive** value; the other, a **negative**. At the beginning of each session, tell your GM which color is which and stick to this choice. No fair deciding which is positive after you've seen the roll results!

Whenever you roll the dice, subtract the negative die roll from the positive. The result may be a negative number.

Example: Mary designates her green die as positive and her red die as negative. She rolls and gets a 3 on the green die and a 1 on the red. She subtracts the result for the red die from the green die: 3 - 1 = 2. Her die result is 2.

Closed and Open Rolls

Sometimes your GM will ask you to make a **Closed Roll**. This is a normal roll of the two dice, as given above.

Most of the time, you will be asked to make **Open Rolls**. In an open roll, you reroll any die that comes up 6, adding to that die's total. This gives a wider range of results, which simulates the wild and chancy actions typically undertaken by *Feng Shui* characters.

Example: Mary makes an open roll, and gets a 6 on her green die and a 5 on her red die. She rerolls the green die, getting a result of 4. She adds the results of the two green die rolls: 6 + 4 = 10. She then subtracts the negative result, 5: 10 - 5 = 5. Her final result is 5.

If, on an Open Roll, both dice come up sixes (**boxcars**), the GM should decide that something unusual happens. You re-roll both dice, ignoring each instance of boxcars (but not a single 6) in your final total. The unusual happening may be good or bad, depending on the overall result of the roll.

Determining Success or Failure

Usually when you make a roll, you will then add the result to another number—that number is usually one representing one of your character's abilities, and is called an **Action Value** (abbreviated as **AV**). When you choose your character type, you will want to make sure that she has high Action Values in the abilities you want her to be especially good at. There's a chart in the rulebook (p. 10) that gives you an idea of the level of ability that various Action Values correspond to.

When you add the final roll to an Action Value, you get a number we call the **Action Result**. When your character tries to do something, that Action Result is compared to a number decided upon by the GM which represents the difficulty of the task your character is attempting. This number is called—surprise, surprise—the **Difficulty**. If the Action Result equals or exceeds the Difficulty, your character succeeds at the task. How well she does depends on the difference between the Difficulty and the Action Result. The difference is called the **Outcome**. If the Action Result is lower than the Difficulty, the attempt fails. Again, the difference between the two numbers can determine the degree of the failure if necessary.

Example: Chin's character, Jimmy Kwan, is attempting to break a board with his head at a kung fu tournament. His Action Value for Martial Arts is 6. The GM decides that the Difficulty of breaking the board without injury is 6. Chin rolls 2 on his positive die and 4 on his negative die, for a total of -2. He adds this to his Action Value: -2 + 6 = 4. This is below the Difficulty, so Jimmy Kwan fails. The GM decides how to describe the failure. Since the difference between the Action Result and the Difficulty is only 2, the GM decides that Jimmy half-succeeds—he breaks the board but stuns himself in the process, embarrassing himself in front of the large audience. Had the difference been 4 or more, the GM might rule that not only did Jimmy fail to break the board, but he also injured himself.

Way-Awful Failure

Even outrageously skillful heroes have their off moments. Bad luck can strike at any time, bringing with it humiliation, agony, humiliation, slapstick embarrassment, or humiliation. A task check that results in this sort of way-awful failure is called a **fumble**. Fumbles occur in one of two ways:

- You get a negative Action Result.
- You roll double sixes (boxcars) and then fail to meet the Difficulty of the check when you re-roll.

Most of the time, your GM will think up excruciatingly appropriate fates for your character to meet when you fumble. Standard fumble results are provided for some common task checks. Gun-wielding characters who suffer fumbles usually have their guns malfunction on them. Sorcerers suffer something nasty called **backlash**. But that's detail, and you can find the details in the rulebook.

Feng Shui Character Creation Briefing

Characters in action movies generally conform to a number of basic types: the maverick cop, the stalwart young kung fu student, the crusty old kung fu master, and on and on. So do characters in a *Feng Shui* game. Each of these is presented as a **type**, which provides you with a numerical starting point for your character as well as ideas that will help you portray your character in play. Available types are described on pp. 20-45. Pick the one you think is coolest.

Once you've picked a type, then you should think of all of the things that makes your character unique. Pick a name for her. Figure out what her past history is. Decide on her basic personality traits—is she humble, boastful, obnoxious, witty, bitter? Pick a couple of catch phrases she uses in conversation.

Each *Feng Shui* character must have a **melodramatic hook**. This is a fact about your character that the GM can use to create storylines. It should be a classic staple of adventure fiction, one that motivates or haunts the character. Whenever this hook comes up in the story, your character should have a strong emotional reaction to it.

Attributes

Attributes are numbers that measure the character's innate physical, mental and spiritual abilities. These are all natural talents or aptitudes rather than learned capabilities. There are four **primary attributes**; each of these can, if you want, be broken down into three or four **secondary attributes**. This allows you to refine your notion of what your character is talented at. A character's score in all secondary attributes is the same as the relevant primary attribute unless otherwise specified.

Skills

Skills are things that your character has learned to do. They are measured by **Skill Bonuses**, which reflect the level of training that your character has invested in a skill. The Action Value for each skill is based on a secondary attribute (such as Fortune or Perception), which is called the **Base Attribute** for that skill. To get your Action Value for a given skill, you add the Skill Bonus to the Base Attribute.

Don't Forget This

If an attribute or skill appears after an '=' sign on your type, you can't increase that number at all during character creation.

Changing Attributes

After the type's starting attributes, you are given some changes you can make to attributes that don't appear after an '=' sign. Some attributes also give you a **Maximum Action Value**, abbreviated as **Max**. You may not increase an attribute beyond its max during character creation.

Example: The Big Bruiser type's starting attributes are: Bod =11 (Tgh =12), Chi 0, Mnd 5, Ref 5. This type allows you to "Add 2 to one primary attribute." You could therefore increase Chi to 2, Mnd to 7, or Ref to 7. (Bod can't be changed here.)

Changing Skills

For each skill, you are given a Skill Bonus and an Action Value.

Changes you make in your character's attributes affect the character's skills, also. Before you start changing your skills around, note which skills have increased because the secondary attribute on which they are based has increased.

Below the skill listing for each type, you are given a number of skill bonuses you can use to customize your character. You can add these to the existing skills, or use them to start new skills. Adding a new skill doesn't cost you any extra. You just spend one of the skill bonuses you have available, and you get that skill at +1.

Skills may also have Maximum Action Values, in which case you can't raise them above that number. If you add a skill that does not appear on your type, it automatically has a Max of 12.

Pick Your Shticks

Most characters come with **shticks**—particular nifty things associated with their character types. For example, many martial artist types can perform a number of fu shticks, which are described in detail in Chapter 5 (p. 75).

Some characters are given Unique Shticks that apply only to their types. You can decide not to take a Unique Shtick if it doesn't fit your character conception, but you can't trade it for something else.

In game terms, shticks operate differently from type to type. Some shticks use skills as a base number, while other shticks use an attribute, such as Kung Fu or Chi. Still other shticks don't have a base skill or attribute. Look over the descriptions of each ability, and you'll be able to tell soon just how that shtick works.

For each type, we provide a number of **quick shtick picks**. These are good choices if you're in a hurry to create a character and want to get started right away. You're not obligated to take them, though, so if you have the time, feel free to look over the relevant chapters and pick the shticks you like best. If you don't have time and the GM wants to get started quickly, take the shticks given for your first session. Like attributes and skills, you can always choose different ones before the next session if you don't like the ones you've chosen.

Feng Shui Sequence and Shots Briefing

Combat is handled in **sequences**. Each sequence represents roughly three seconds of time. In turn, each sequence is divided into a variable number of **shots**. Shots are a game abstraction; they are a way of determining who gets to do something in what order within a single sequence.

Initiative

At the beginning of each sequence, each participant in the fight makes an **Initiative Check**. This is a roll of one die, to which the character's Speed is added. Sixes are not re-rolled. The resulting number is the shot at which the character first gets to act. A sequence starts with the highest Initiative Check Result of any character participating in the fight.

Once the highest shot has been determined, the character with the highest shot gets to act. Then the GM counts down shots from highest to lowest to see who gets to act next. Actions that take place during the same shot occur in the order of the GM's preference. When a character's shot comes up, he can act. The complexity of the action he chooses to make determines how many shots elapse before he can act again. Even the slowest characters generally get to act several times during a sequence.

Shot Cost of Actions

Most complex actions cost three shots. In three shots a character can (for example) attack in hand-to-hand combat, aim and fire a weapon, reload a revolver, draw and nock an arrow, pick up an object, or throw an object. At the same time, he can also travel a distance up to his Move rating in meters. If just running, he can travel twice his Move rating in meters (this can't be a snapshot). In a sequence in which he rolled initiative, he can move a total of three times his Move. (If not in combat, he could go four times his Move.)

Some simple actions take only one shot. In one shot a character can, for example: parry or block an attack, resist a wrestling maneuver, draw a weapon from a scabbard or holster, reload a clip-fed gun, duck or dive flat, or catch a thrown object.

Once the GM has counted down through the shots, and resolved all actions that take place on shot 1, a new sequence starts with a new round of Initiative Checks. There is no shot 0.

Running out of Shots

At shots 2 and 1, characters may take actions that cost up to 3 shots even though there aren't enough shots left. There's no penalty for this, and the unaccounted-for shot cost is not carried over to the next sequence.

Actions with a shot cost higher than 3, however, do carry over. See "Extra-Long Actions" for more information.

Defensive Actions

It is possible to take defensive actions even when it is not your shot, as long as your next shot is greater than 0. Defensive actions include dodging or parrying incoming blows and dodging incoming missiles such as bullets or arrows. Reduce your next shot number by 1 unless otherwise specified.

If your opponent is significantly faster than you, it is possible to spend all of your shots on defensive actions and not ever get to take an offensive action. Hint: You're in big trouble.

When attacked, often the best thing to do is to execute a stunt to not only prevent your opponent from attacking you, but to give yourself an advantage of some sort over that opponent. See the discussion of stunts that begins on p. 127.

Snapshots

It is possible to decrease the shot cost of an action by doing it recklessly. An action performed in this manner is called a **snapshot**. To reduce the shot cost by 1, subtract 2 from your action value for the task check. To reduce the cost by 2, subtract 5 from the action value. You can't reduce your action value any further with a snapshot.

For those of you who really like putting things into categories, a snapshot can be considered a type of stunt. It is possible to combine a snapshot with other stunt elements for an even greater Action Value penalty but a cooler result.

Continuous Actions

Sometimes your character will be doing one thing throughout a sequence while also trying to perform other actions. These are called **continuous actions**. Examples of continuous actions include driving, attempting to remain balanced on a precarious or slippery perch, or using certain fu powers. These do not have a shot cost, but increase the shot costs of all other attempted actions by 1.

Extra-Long Actions

Some actions in a sequence take more than 3 shots. Certain fu powers require more time than it takes to make a standard attack. Or your character might also be engaging in a non-combat action, such as defusing a bomb or frantically trying to repair an out-of-control vehicle, while her pals and enemies are furiously hammering on one another.

Characters who wish to take actions that take 4 or more shots when there aren't that many shots left in the sequence subtract the remaining number of shots from their first shot of the next sequence. This result gives them the shot on which their current action is completed and a new one may begin.

Feng Shui Combat Briefing

When you want your character to hit another character in combat, you make a task check using the appropriate combat skill. If you are hitting in hand-to-hand combat, the relevant skill is Martial Arts. If you are hitting an opponent from a distance with a missile weapon, the relevant skill is Guns. If you are attempting to hit an opponent with a spell, use Sorcery. Some attacks can be made with the Arcanowave Device or Creature Powers skills; if you have a schtick that requires that these skills be used, this will be indicated in the schtick descriptions.

If your opponent is stationary and does not defend against you, the Difficulty of the task check is 0. If the opponent is dodging or parrying, the Difficulty equals the Action Value of the opponent's dodge or parry attempt (this is covered in the next section). Your opponent might also successfully execute a reactive stunt that prevents you from attacking him at all.

Other factors such as range, cover, and impairment from wounds can alter Action Values and Difficulties during combat.

How Not To Get Hit

Few characters who know that they're in the middle of a fight are going to stand stock still waiting to be creamed. Any character engaged in combat is assumed to be moving about; this is considered to be a *passive dodge* and has no shot cost. If a character is making a passive dodge, the Difficulty of any attempt to hit her equals her Dodge Action Value.

A character's Dodge Action Value equals her highest Action Value from the following list: Arcanowave Device, Creature Power, Guns, Martial Arts, Sorcery (if they have Blast), or the Agility secondary attribute. You should always have the Dodge Action Value for characters you are running available for easy reference.

Characters may also choose to make an *active dodge* against any attack. This means that the character is, for the moment, concentrating entirely on not getting hit. An active dodge has a shot cost of 1. Making an active dodge increases your Dodge Action Value by 3.

An active dodge counts as a defensive action, as does a parry (explained next).

In especially close quarters, dodges—whether passive or active—may be especially tricky: your GM will reduce your Dodge Action Value accordingly.

A *parry* is a kind of active dodge, in which you are placing a hard object such as a shield or sword between you and the incoming blow. Or maybe you're grabbing the guy's sword arm or otherwise forcefully preventing him from going upside your head. Your Parry Action Value is always equal to your Martial Arts Action Value (though Sorcerers can use Blast or Movement schticks instead if they have them). There is no other rules difference between active dodging and parrying, but the result is described differently by GM and players. It is merely a matter of style. GMs may rule that parrying is inappropriate in certain circumstances, and insist that characters dodge instead.

Unnamed Characters

Many of the opponents you will be facing are of low skill; their only advantage is numbers. Heroes in action flicks mow through cheap henchmen with little trouble. In *Feng Shui*, we call these opponents *unnamed characters*. If the GM hasn't bothered to give them a name, they're not really important to the plot. They're set dressing, basically, but more fun to beat up. (Don't get too overconfident, though—they can still do damage to you when the GM rolls high.) Unnamed characters follow a different set of rules than named characters, as explained below.

When Unnamed Characters Get Hit

If an unnamed character is hit and the Outcome of the attack was 5 or more, he is out of the fight. If the Outcome is between 1 and 4, the GM may elect to describe various ill effects of the fight that the unnamed character might be suffering, but this is simply a style thing: the character suffers no impairment or other game consequence.

Named Characters

Named characters are harder to take out in a fight, because they are sufficiently important to the story for the GM to have given them names. PCs are all named characters, as are the main bad guys your characters will be fighting.

When Named Characters Get Hit

Here's the basic formula for determining the result of a successful hit on a named character: **Attack Outcome + Damage - Victim's Toughness = Wound Points suffered**.

Here's how this works: when a character hits an opponent, take the Outcome of the attack check; this is the difference between the attacker's higher attack Action Result and the defender's lower Dodge or Parry Action result.

Add this figure to the *damage* value of the attack form. Each type of attack does a different amount of damage: see the Damage Values Charts on page 139. Then subtract the victim's Toughness value.

The result of the equation is the number of Wound Points that the character suffers. If the result is 0 or less, the character suffers no Wound Points.

Master Guns List

Archaic Weapons

Bow and Arrow	7/5/1
Black Powder Pistol	7/3/1
Crossbow	7/4/1
Musket	8/5/1

Autoloader Handguns

American Derringer Mini Cop	11/1/4
AMT Automag IV	11/3/7 +1
AMT Automag V	12/3/5 +1
Auto-Ordnance Pit Bull	10/1/7 +1
Beretta 92 Centurion	10/2/15 +1
Beretta Model 21 Bobcat	8/1/8 +1
Beretta Model 950BS Jet Fire	8/1/8 +1
Browning BDM	10/2/15 +1
Browning Hi-Power	10/2/13 +1
Colt Delta Elite MKIV Series 80	11/2/8 +1
Colt 380 Gov't Pocketlite	8/1/7 +1
Colt 1911A	10/2/7 +1
Desert Eagle .357 Magnum	11/3/10 +1
Desert Eagle .50 Magnum	12/3/9 +1
E.T. "Series One Laseraim"	10/3/8 +1
Glock 17	10/1/17 +1
Glock 18	10/1/17 +1; 10/2/33 +1
Grendel P-12	9/1/12 +1
Grendel P-30	8/1/30 +1
Heckler & Koch P7	10/2/8 +1
Kahr K9	10/1/7 +1
Intratec Tec-9	10/3/32 +1
Intratec Tec-22	8/2/30 +1
Llama Large Frame	10/2/7 +1
Makarov	10/2/8 +1
Norinco Type M1911	10/3/7 +1
Norinco Tokarev	10/2/8 +1
Ruger K89	10/2/15 +1
Sig-Sauer P-220	10/2/9 +1
Smith & Wesson 2213	8/1/8 +1
Smith & Wesson 3566	11/3/15 +1
Smith & Wesson Sigma	10/1/14 +1
Walther P-5 Compact	10/1/8 +1
Walther PPK	9/1/6 +1

Revolvers

Colt Detective Special	9/1/6
Colt King Cobra	11/3/6
Rossi Model 515	8/2/9
Rossi Model 851	9/2/6
Smith & Wesson Model 19	11/2/6

Sub Machine Guns

Colt M6351	10/5/32
Heckler & Koch MP510	11/5/30
Hechler &Koch MP5	10/5/30
Heckler & Koch MP5 K	10/3/30
Heckler & Koch MP5 Police	11/3/30
MP40	10/5/32
M3	10/5/30
Mini UZI	10/3/25
Ruger MP9	10/3/32
Thompson M1A1	10/5/30
UZI	10/4/40

Shotguns

Benelli 121	13/5/7
Benelli 90 M3	13/5/7
Beretta 1201 Riot	13/5/6
Bernadelli	13/5/10
Franchi SPAS-12	13/5/7
Mossberg Special Purpose	13/5/9
Remington 870 Police	13/5/7
Ruger Red Label	10/5/2
Winchester Model 1300 Marine	13/5/8

Rifles

AK-47	13**/5/30
AK-74	13*/5/30
K2	13*/4/30
M16	13*/5/30
M14	13**/5/20

Buro Weapons

Buro Backup Arm	8/1/5 +1
Buro Beat Patroller	9/1/7 +1
Buro 9	10/1/17 +1
Buro Avenger	11/2/6
Buro Godhammer	12/4/5
Buro Crimestopper	13/5/7
Buro Blade of Truth	10/3/30
Buro Blue Flag	13*/4/30
Buro 16	13*/5/32
Buro Blue Spear	13**/6/30
Buro Hellharrower	14**/8/20

Statistics are Damage/Concealment/Capacity. An asterisk after Damage (*) indicates unnamed characters go down on an Outcome of 4 or more. Two asterisks (**) indicates they go down on an Outcome of 3 or more.

Index

abomination (type) 20
absorption (schtick) 102
abysmal spines (schtick) 102
Action Result 10
Action Value (AV) 9, 50
actions *(see also shot cost)*
   continuous 130
   extra-long 130
active dodge 132-133
aerial mobility unit (schtick) 120
Agility (Agl) 15
agony grenade (schtick) 120-121
aiming 137
amphibian (schtick) 102
ancillary effects and sorcery 91
arcanowave
   device (skill) 16, 53
   desperate efforts 119
   gear 116-125
   history 173-175
   input/output port (AI/O) 117-118
   juncture modifiers 120
   malfunctions 119-120
   mutation 118-119, 124
   new schticks 119
   resonating biopolymer (ARB) 117
   schticks 120-125
Architects of the Flesh *(see also arcanowave)* 9, 173-175, 218-220
armor 138
armor (schtick) 102
Ascended, The *(see also transformed animal)* 8, 175-178, 216-218
attributes 19, 50
   base 15, 50
   primary 14
   secondary 14
attuning 165-167
backlash 10, 91
backstory 154-155, 199
"Baptism of Fire" 228-242
Battlechimp Potemkin 189
bear (package) 110-111
big bruiser (type) 21
Biomass Reprocessing Center 206-208
blast (schtick) 92-93, 102
blood drain (schtick) 102
Bobos (Architects of the Flesh) 189
Body (Bod) 14
   Move (Mov) 14
   Strength (Str) 14
   Toughness (Tgh) 14
Both Guns Blazing (schtick) 62
brain shredder (schtick) 102-103
bulletproof vests (see also armor) 138-139
called shots 137-138
   and sorcery 91
Carnival of Carnage (schtick) 62
Central District 212
Chan, Jackie 244-245
character
   advancement 160-161
   generation 12-45

   named 129
   sheet 256
   types 13, 20-45
   unnamed 129
Charisma (Cha) 15
Chi 14-15
   Cost 76
   Fortune (For) 14-15
   Kung Fu (Fu) 14-15
   Magic (Mag) 14-15
chi 5
Closed Rolls 9
clue paths 158
combat *(see also fights)* 126-142
conditional escalation (schtick) 103
contacts 48-50
continuous actions 130
corruption (schtick) 102
cover 138
crab (package) 111
creature
   abilities 100-107
   healing 101
   juncture modifiers 101
   powers (skill) 16, 53
   qualities 100
   schticks 101-107
   schtick acquisition 101
critical shifts 195, 197-198
cyborg (type) 22
damage 133-134, 138, 139
damage immunity (schtick) 103-105
de-attuning 167
death 135
   and medical attention 137
   and recovery 136-137
death resistance (schtick) 105
deceit (skill) 16, 53
deceptive speed (quality) 100
defense 130
desperate efforts 119
   and sorcery 91
detective (skill) 16, 53-54
difficulties 10, 11, 52, 90, 128, 135, 138, 141, 142, 204
dis-timed persons (DPs or Netherworld Rabble or exiles) 205
divination (schtick) 93-94
dodge
   active 132-133
   passive 132
   and sorcery 91
domination (schtick) 105
dragon (package) 111
Dragons, The 9, 178
driving (skill) 16, 54
drunkenness 142
Dusk-O-Matic 227
Eagle Eye (schtick) 62
Eastern Hong Kong 212
Eaters of the Lotus 8, 179-182
elephant (package) 111
enforcers *(see also Ascended, the)* 178
everyman hero (type) 23
ex-special forces (type) 24

exiles (DPs or Netherworld Rabble) 196
experience points (see also character advancement) 160-161
explosions 140
extra-long actions 130
Fast Draw (schtick) 62
feedback enhancer (schtick) 121
feng shui
   explanation of 5
feng shui sites
   attunement to 5, 165-167
   burning 168
   de-attunement to 167
   defending 167
   harming 164-165
   improving 164
   special sites 168
fertility (schtick) 94-95
fights *(see also combat)* 126-142
   active dodge 132-133
   aiming 137
   armor 138
   called shots 137-138
   continuous actions 130
   cover 138
   damage 133-134, 138, 139
   death 135
   defense 130
   difficulties 141, 142
   drunkenness 142
   explosions 140
   extra-long actions 130
   fortune dice 133
   hand-to-hand maneuvers 140
   hitting 132
   impairment 135
   inanimate targets 140
   initiative 129
   lifting 142
   medical attention 137
   moving targets 140-141
   named characters 129
   parry 133
   passive dodge 132
   range 141
   recovery from death 136-137
   recovery from wounds 136
   shot cost 130
   signature weapons 141
   snapshots 130
   throwing 142
   unnamed characters 129
   wounds 134-135
fix-it (skill) 16, 54-55
flight (schtick) 105
Fortune (For) 14-15
fortune dice 133
foul spew (schtick) 105
Four Monarchs, The 9, 182-186, 226-227
fox (package) 111-112
fu powers *(see also paths)* 75-87
   Chi Cost 76
   learning 77
fumble 10

gambler (type) 25
gambling (skill) 16, 55
Game Moderator (GM) 6
   Characters (GMCs) 6
   tips 143-159
Genocide Lounge 208
geomancy *(see also feng shui)* 5, 163-164
ghost (type) 26
gnarled marauder 169
groups, influential *(see also individual names)* 172-189
   in Hong Kong 214-227
Guiding Hand, The 8-9, 186-188, 220-221
Guiyou Zui 208-209
guns *(see also weapons)* 60-74
   69 AD juncture 66
   1850 AD juncture 66
   2056 AD juncture 73-74
   ammo 65
   concealment 63-64
   damage 64
   malfunctions 64-65
   modern 66-73
   reloading 65
   schticks 61-62
guns (skill) 16, 55-56
Hair-Trigger Neck Hairs (schtick) 62
Hand *(see Guiding Hand, The)*
hand-to-hand maneuvers 140
Happy Valley 212-213
Hark, Tsui 245-246
heal (schtick) 95
helix rethreader (schtick) 121
helix ripper (schtick) 121
history
   changing 192-193
   elastic 193-194
   erasing 199
   shifts 195-196
hitting 132
Hong Kong 210-227
   action movies 243-248
   Architect influence 218-220
   Ascended influence 216-218
   geography 210-214
   Hand influence 220-221
   Jammer influence 224
   Lotus influence 224-226
   Monarchs' influence 226-227
   secret warriors in 214-216
   Tomorrow's Immortals 223
   Tortoise Shell Info Services 221-222
hopping vampires (jiangshi) 170
horrific appearance (quality) 100
Hub, the 208
IKTV 208
impairment 135
inanimate targets 140
inevitable comeback (schtick) 105-106
influence (schtick) 96
info (skill) 17, 56
initiative 129
Inner Kingdom *(see Netherworld)*
Innerwalkers *(see Secret Warriors)* 5

Index

insubstantial (schtick) 106
Intelligence (Int) 15
intimidation (skill) 17, 56
intrusion (skill) 17, 56-57
Jade Wheel Society *(see also Ascended, The)* 176
Jammers, The 9, 188-189, 224
jiangshi (hopping vampires) 170
journalism (skill) 17, 57
journalist (type) 27
juicer (schtick) 121
junctures 19, 50, 52, 90, 101, 120, 144-145, 190-199
Junkyard, the 209
karate cop (type) 28
killer (type) 29
King of the Fire Pagoda *(see Four Monarchs, The)*
King of the Thunder Pagoda *(see Four Monarchs, The)*
knowledge 47-48
Kowloon 210, 214
Kung Fu (Fu) 14-15
Lantau 210
lateral reincarnation 194-195
leadership (skill) 17, 57
Li, Jet 246
lifting 142
Lightning Reload (schtick) 62
Little Hong Kong 212
Lodge, the *(see also Ascended, The)* 176-178
Lotus *(see Order of the Lotus, The)*
Lusignan's Tower 208
Magic (Mag) 14-15
magic *(see also sorcery)* 88-99
magic cop (type) 30
Manual Dexterity (Dex) 15
martial artist (type) 31
martial arts (skill) 17, 57-58
masked avenger (type) 33
maverick cop (type) 34
medic (type) 32
medicine (skill) 17, 58
melodramatic hook 13-14
Mind (Mnd) 15
   Charisma (Cha) 15
   Intelligence (Int) 15
   Perception (Per) 15
   Will (Wil) 15
Mongkok 214
monkey (package) 112
monster hunter (type) 35
monsters 169-171
   gnarled marauder 169
   hopping vampires (jiangshi) 170
   reconstructed, the 170
   snake men 171
Move (Mov) 14
movement (schtick) 96-97
movies, Hong Kong action 243-248
moving targets 140-141
multiple targets and sorcery 90
named characters 129
Netherworld (Inner Kingdom) 5, 8, 174, 196-197, 200-209

geography of 201-202
inhabitants of 205-206
places of note 206-209
shaping of 202-205
Netherworld Rabble (DPs or exiles) 205
neural stimulator (schtick) 121-122
New Territories, the 210
ninja (type) 36
old master (type) 37
Open Rolls 9
Operation Killdeer 178
Order of the Lotus, The 224-226
Order of the Wheel *(see also Ascended, The)* 176
Outcome 10
Pagodas, the *(see also Four Monarchs, The)* 209
parrying 133
   and sorcery 91
passive dodge 132
paths (power) 76
   of the Brilliant Flame 80-81
   of the Clever Eye 79-80
   of the Empty Bottle 83
   of the Hands of Light 79
   of the Healthy Tiger 84-85
   of the Immutable Clay 81-83
   of the Leaping Storm 86-87
   of the Passive Wings 79
   of the Selective Master 81
   of the Shadow's Companion 78
   of the Sharpened Scales 78-79
   of the Storm Turtle 85-86
   of the Tightening Coils 80
   prerequisites 76
   Shot Cost 76
Perception (Per) 15
physical ability 47
Player Characters (PCs) 6
Pledged, the *(see also Ascended, The)* 176-178
poison (schtick) 106
police (skill) 17, 58
polymer shell uniforms *(see also armor)* 138-139
poor 18
prerequisites 76
primary attributes 14
private investigator (type) 38
pulser (schtick) 122
Queen of the Darkness Pagoda *(see Four Monarchs, The)*
Queen of the Ice Pagoda *(see Four Monarchs, The)*
rancid breath (schtick) 106
range 141
rat (package) 112-113
reconstructed, the 170
reference section 249-255
Reflexes (Ref) 15
   Agility (Agl) 15
   Manual Dexterity (Dex) 15
   Speed (Spd) 15
regeneration (schtick) 106

reincarnation
   lateral 194-195
   soul memories 194
reinforcer (schtick) 122
rich 18
robot limb (schtick) 122
Rolls
   Closed 9
   Open 9
rooster (package) 113
sabotage (skill) 17, 58-59
scenario 158-159
schticks 17, 19
   arcanowave 120-125
   creature 101-107
   fu (powers) 75-87
   gun 61-62
   quick picks 18, 19
   sorcery 92-99
   transformed animal (packages) 109, 110-115
scorpion (package) 114
scrappy kid (type) 39
secondary attributes 14
Secret Warriors (Innerwalkers) 5, 206
   in Hong Kong 214-216
seduction (skill) 17, 59
set pieces 152-153
Shadowfist 7
shaping 202-205
Shot Cost 76, 130
Signature Weapon (schtick) 62, 141
skills 14, 19, 46-59
   bonuses 15, 50
slap patch (schtick) 122-123
snake (package) 113-114
snake men 171
snapshots 130
sorcerer (type) 40
sorcery *(see also magic)* 88-99
   ancillary effects 91
   backlash 91
   called shots 91
   desperate efforts 91
   dodging 91
   learning new schticks & skills 92
   multiple targets 90
   parrying 91
   schticks 92-99
sorcery (skill) 17, 59
soul memories 194
soul twist (schtick) 106
Southside 212
special effects 89
Speed (Spd) 15
Speedball 227
spider (package) 114
spirit shield generator (schtick) 123
spy (type) 41
Strength (Str) 14
stunts 127-128
   and sorcery 90-91
subjects 205-206
subskills 50
sucker rounds (schtick) 123
summoning (schtick) 97-99

superficial shifts 195
supernatural creature (type) 42
tangrams 164
targets
   inanimate 140
   moving 140-141
Task Checks 8-11
techie (type) 43
Temple of Boundless Mediation 206
tentacles (schtick) 106-107
thief (type) 44
threat evaluator (schtick) 124
throwing 142
tiger (package) 114-115
time shifts
   superficial 195
   critical 195, 197-198
time war *(see also juncture)* 190-199
Tomorrow's Immortals 223
Tortoise Shell Info Services 221-222
tortoise (package) 115
Toughness (Tgh) 14
tracer resin projector (schtick) 124
training montage 51
transformation (schtick) 107
transformed animal (type) 45
transformed animals 108-115
   chi cost 109-110
   gaining new schticks 110
   packages 109, 110-115
   reversion 110
   shot cost 110
Tsimshatsui 214
turtling 167
types 20-43
Ultraviolet Penetrator 227
unnamed characters 129
Unspoken Name, the *(see also Ascended, The)* 177
Victoria 212
Victoria Peak 211-212
Wanchai 214
wave scanner (schtick) 124
wave suppresser (schtick) 124
wealth level 18, 19
   rich 18
   working stiff 18
   poor 18-19
Weapons 19, 60-74
   Dusk-O-Matic 227
   signature 62, 141
   Speedball 227
   Ultraviolet Penetrator 227
weather (schtick) 99
Western District 214
Will (Wil) 15
Woo, John 243-244
working stiff 18
wounds 134-135
   recovering from 136
wuxia 243-248
Yaumatei 214

Character Sheet

Name:
Wealth:

Type:
Juncture:

Body (Bod) _____
Move (Mov) _____
Strength (Str) _____
Constitution (Con) _____
Toughness (Tgh) _____

Melodramatic Hook:

Description:

Chi (Chi) _____
Fortune (For) _____
Kung Fu (Fu) _____
Magic (Mag) _____

Story:

Mind (Mnd) _____
Charisma (Cha) _____
Intelligence (Int) _____
Perception (Per) _____
Willpower (Wil) _____

Fortune Dice Remaining:
Wound Points Sustained:
Unspent Experience Points:

Skills

Skill	Base	Bonus	AV
_____	____	____	____
_____	____	____	____
_____	____	____	____
_____	____	____	____
_____	____	____	____
_____	____	____	____
_____	____	____	____
_____	____	____	____
_____	____	____	____
_____	____	____	____
_____	____	____	____
_____	____	____	____

Reflexes (Ref) _____
Agility (Agl) _____
Dexterity (Dex) _____
Speed (Spd) _____

Schticks

_____
_____
_____
_____
_____
_____
_____
_____
_____
_____

Weaponry

Weapon	Stats
_____	_____
_____	_____
_____	_____
_____	_____
_____	_____
_____	_____
_____	_____

Notes

_____
_____
_____
_____
_____
_____
_____